JOHN & PAULA SANDFORD

HEALING THE WOUNDED SPIRIT

VICTORY HOUSE, INC.
Tulsa, OK

All Scripture quotations are from the New American Standard Version of the Bible unless otherwise identified. Italics in the Scripture quotations were added by the Sandfords.

Healing the Wounded Spirit
© 1985 John and Paula Sandford
All rights reserved
Printed in the United States of America
ISBN: 0-932081-14-2
Library of Congress Catalog Number: 85-071640
Victory House, Inc.
6506 S. Lewis, Suite 112
Tulsa, OK 74136

Dedication

In loving memory
of Agnes Sanford,
our first mentor and friend
in the ministry of
inner healing.

Table of Contents

Acknowledgments

We are indebted to the entire Body of Christ for this book. Whatever wisdom manifests itself in it has evolved from counsel and friendship, conflict and forgiveness through thirty years in the Lord's school of hard knocks within the Body of Christ. We are especially grateful for the prayers and financial contributions of the many who enabled us to reserve this sabbatical year of 1984 for research and writing. It is most of all to our Elijah House board members and friends, whose counsel and support kept us encouraged and straitened to the task, that our deepest thanks belong. Without them, we could not have begun, much less finished.

Our thanks to Bonnie Millar and Bonnie Crouch to whom the Lord gave especial dispensation to decipher hieroglyphics, transferring longhand scribblings hour by patient hour onto typewritten paper ready for editing and transformation to final copy. Again to Bonnie Crouch who rushed in response to our SOS to help us type final copy before the deadline. To Katie Cranford who took over the flood of correspondence to set us free to write. To Llewellyn Fletcher who handled all the phone calls and letters necessary to set up our 1985 teaching schedule, thus freeing not only our time but our minds and spirits to cogitate and commit to paper. Our thanks to our son Mark, and to

Janet Wilcox and Jim Tiffany, who took over the counseling chores, and with them to our new daughter-in-law, Mark's wife Maureen, our daughter Andrea and our friend Donna Campbell, all of whom ran to the phone a thousand and one times so that we wouldn't have to. To our son Loren and his wife Beth, and all our Elijah House team, especially Martha Brookhart and Ruth Hughes, who conducted all our seminars this year without us. To Maryanne Ruff, our treasurer and shipping clerk, who labored beyond the call of duty in order not to burden us with the details of shipping and supplies. To Larry Ruff, who served as President of Elijah House.

Appended is a bibliography, the listing of which in no way begins to express our gratitude for all the accumulated experience and knowledge of mankind which has been our bank to draw upon.

Again, as in our previous books, there are many whose stories are told (in disguised form), most of whom have granted permission to include their names, though in many cases we thought it wiser not to.

In 1982, as we were preparing final copies of *The Transformation of the Inner Man*, Leanne Payne's fine book, *The Broken Image*, came off the presses. In our acknowledgments, we recommended that our readers use that book as an aid to our Chapter Sixteen, "Archetypes and Homosexuality." Again, as we were editing final copies of this book, Leanne Payne's new book, *Crisis in Masculinity*, came off the presses. It is excellent! We highly recommend that all who would understand our fifth chapter, "The Slumbering Spirit," study her book. Her "Introduction" alone is worth whatever trouble it may be to find the book.

The book is dedicated to Agnes Sanford; many stories of our experiences with her adorn the book. We hope that she approves from her side of eternity, having ascended there on Ascension Sunday, 1983, and that her remaining family approves of our recollections.

Our highest and best gratitude is of course to God our Father, to His Son our Lord Jesus Christ, and to the Holy

Spirit, whose patient tutelage deserves all honor and credit for whatever true revelations can be found here. We regard our task, as prophets, to be as pathfinders who find long-long tracks of truth needed for the Body to walk into the ministry of healing the wounded spirit. We are of course responsible for whatever error is taught as truth. We trust succeeding generations to filter and keep the gold. We are all pioneers in rediscovering ancient paths to walk in (Isa. 58:12). Our prayer is that our revelations may become a quantum leap to safe harbors for all. A wounded world needs our help.

Preface

In 1959 I met Agnes Sanford, and Paula and I embarked upon the career of counseling and teaching which has occupied us since. As we delved further into the heart, discovering the labyrinthine paths of the flesh and teaching the Body how people can be freed from their grasp, we moved step by step into revelation deeper than conscious memory could recall. More and more often we found ourselves led to see traumatic events and resultant behavioral patterns far beyond what we had thought ought to be within the recall of memory. We found ourselves dealing with events which occurred the first months of life, like being dropped, or not nursed, or shouted at in the crib, then with birth traumas, and finally with vast numbers of in utero experiences.

We were stunned. How could anyone have understood and reacted so early in life? Or is there a primal understanding in our spirit before the conscious mind is formed? We could not understand what was happening. But the results could not be denied. "You will know them by their fruits" (Matt. 7:16). People were being permanently healed. Counselees who previously had been caught in a pattern of seeming recovery followed by continual relapse responded and remained whole when we delved at last into prenatal formative experiences. We began to think the Lord had finally lead us to the taproots of human formation. (We have since discovered there are many other kinds of roots, more to Adamic sin than we had thought, generational sin inherited and transmitted, societal and cultural influences such as archetypal formation, etc.)

We soon discovered that if the Body of Christ already found it difficult to accept that our Lord intended to minister beyond conversion to the deep things hidden in our heart which can be consciously recalled, it was in no way ready or capable of hearing about such deep revelations, below the level of conscious recall. We touched on it here and there, like seeding possibilities into the minds of men. Only in the last four or five years have we opened up and begun to present entire teachings directly on the subject of pre-natal experience.

Many have been as astounded as we were, and some have reacted adversely. We understand how they feel. On the whole, however, both Christians and non-Christians have received, retained and used with great beneficial results the keys we gave. To date we have yet to hear of damage resulting from such inquiry and therapeutic practice.

In 1973 the Lord set us in Coeur d'Alene under orders to write seven books. The fourth, *Healing the Wounded Spirit*, was to encompass all the areas that could not be contained in *The Transformation of the Inner Man*. We have been reluctant to write it, and have stalled until this sabbatical year of 1984, until we could be sure of the Lord's timing and of the Body's and our maturity to handle such knowledge.

We feared what people might do if set loose in areas discoverable sometimes only by revelation, through gifts of perception and knowledge. We worried about rash, impetuous blundering into fields in which sometimes there are no living parents or relatives with whom to check and counterbalance revelation knowledge. We wanted to live with it long enough to discover the pitfalls and limits before going to print.

Now the time seems ripe. Good fruits have come from oral teachings. Response to the little pamphlet, *New Life for*

Your Adopted Child, written by Paula in response to the request of adoption agencies, but viewed by us as a feeler, a test of the ability of the Body to receive these teachings, has surpassed our expectations. The Body seems ready.

We ask all who read to have a "both and" response. On the one hand, to take hold and act with holy boldness to set people free. No one can know, until he enters such a field of healing, how great is the cry in the heart of God for the Church to act to set men free (read Psalm 82 with this in mind!). And on the other, to minister with holy caution, to check with relatives and friends whenever possible, to act with sensitivity and grace, and not lay heavy trips on people. In areas in which we didn't see accurately, God can use our prayer to apply and heal what is really there. When ministering in counseling, our perceptions about possible incidents in the lives of people may or may not be accurate, so we need always to lay them into hearts tenderly, as possibilities for them to consider, and pray accordingly. What a joy it is to stand and see as God heals and sets people free. Let's conduct our ministry so it *is He*, and not the flesh of *we*. He will do a good and gracious work. Let's rejoice in Him, and let Him do it.

John Sandford

Introduction

As John indicated in his preface, for twenty-five years we have been growing in the ministry of the transformation of the inner man as the Lord has given us grace and insight to meet the depths of people's needs. We have discovered increasingly that the Lord's desire and power to set us free far surpasses our abilities to diagnose and our sensitivity to apply insights appropriately. Whenever we have tuned into His purposes and have laid the groundwork of repentance and forgiveness in the one to whom we are ministering, we have invariably experienced the healing power of the Lord flowing through the door of prayer more powerfully than we could ask or think.

Again and again we have been led by the Holy Spirit to pray obediently in ways that we did not understand. Experiencing the undeniable and lasting fruit of those prayers, we have then delved into the Scriptures for understanding concerning what we have seen the Lord accomplish. Our first three books were results of that long-term experiencing and studying with the Lord. Recognizable and often predictable patterns of cause and consequence have appeared so frequently that we have been tempted to develop techniques of prayer guaranteed, when properly applied, to work in every situation. In the process, the Lord has made it abundantly clear that He insists on being in charge. Ministry to another must always be fresh meeting in the presence and power of the Lord and by His leading. Our participation in that encounter is primarily to connect the person with Jesus, and to participate with Him in enabling the person to recognize and eliminate the blocks (at whatever level) to the life the Lord would lavish upon him in love. Patterns to look for in people's lives and ways to deal with them must always be submitted to the present moving of the Spirit or we will unwittingly attempt to "use" God to accomplish what we mistakenly perceive to be "our" ministry, and manipulate the other person by a technique we have developed.

Why the need to minister to the depths of already born-again Christians? In the first seven chapters of *The Transformation of the Inner Man* we explain more completely the biblical and theological base for this work. We tell it more simply here.

> . . . you were formerly darkness, but now you are light in the Lord; walk as children of light (for the fruit of the light consists in all goodness and righteousness and truth), trying to learn what is pleasing to the Lord (Eph. 5:8).

Many Christians are trying their best to walk as children of light. As they fail to produce the fruit of that light, they too often fall into striving, disillusionment and condemnation because they are blind-sided and driven from deep within by that of which they have been unaware.

They have rightly celebrated salvation as a free gift (Eph. 2:4, 5, Eph. 2:8, Rom. 6:23) but have not understood that they are to grow up in it (1 Pet. 2:2, Eph. 3:14-19) nor that they are to work it out in fear and trembling (Phil. 2:12). They have celebrated with Paul that "by one offering He has perfected for all time those who are [being] sanctified" (Heb. 10:14) without understanding santification as a process and without acknowledging with Paul, "Not that I have already . . . become perfect, but I press on in order that I may lay hold of that for which also I was laid hold of by Christ Jesus" (Phil. 3:12). They tend to press on in terms of managing behavior rather than by the renewing of the mind (Rom. 12:2) and the receiving of a new heart and spirit within (Ps. 51, Ezek. 36:26) which would naturally result in changed behavior. They have not in reality done away with childish things (1 Cor. 13:11) but have controlled them while allowing them to remain as a part of the treasure in the storehouse of the heart (Luke 6:43-45). When out of the heart and mouth come eruptive expressions of what has been accumulating for years, they have striven all the more to control the expression or rebuke the devil (who had to have raw material to work with even if he did trigger the outburst) rather than follow Jesus' command (in Luke 6:46-49) to "dig deep" to the foundations of their life (what was trained and practiced into the fibre of character and personality in the first six years of experiencing and reacting to life and forming attitudes, judgments and expectations by which to interpret each succeeding experience). Their "eye" is bad, and therefore their body is full of darkness (Matt. 6:22, 23). Matthew 5:29 prescribes a drastic solution for this way of seeing that causes one to stumble: "tear it out, and throw it from you. . . ." Jesus is able to transcend time and space to deal with the deep cracks in our foundations and to establish every hidden part of us securely on the rock which He is. But we must give Him access through prayer.

Many Christians have tried to forget "what lies behind" (Phil. 3:13) by ignoring the past rather than by letting the Holy Spirit search the innermost parts of the heart (Ps. 139:23, 24) to allow Jesus to deal specifically with the deeply ingrained attitudes and ways of their childhood. They have attempted to put aside the old self with its practices (anger, wrath, malice, slander, etc.) (Col. 3:8-10, Eph. 4:22ff.) as if those were present external expressions only, whereas Jesus called the Pharisees (and us) to clean the *inside* of the cup (Luke 11:39-41). Jesus knew that our speech may be smooth as butter while at the same time our heart is at war (Ps. 55:21). God has always desired "truth in the innermost *being" (Ps. 51:6). For this reason John the Baptist said that the "axe is already laid at the root of the trees"* (Matt. 3:10).

To born-again Christians it was said,

> And do not participate in the unfruitful deeds of darkness, but instead even expose them; for it is disgraceful even to speak of the things which are done by them in secret. But all things become visible when they are exposed by the light. For this reason it says,
> "Awake, sleeper
> And arise from the dead,
> And Christ will shine on you.
> —Eph. 5:11-14

We, the Body of Christ, the Church, are that sleeper. Our old self has been crucified with Him. We have attempted to "die daily" (1 Cor. 15:31) by willful efforts to conform to Christian standards. But we have not yet experienced the fullness of that process of inner sanctification and laying down of our life by which we can come into the fullness of resurrection power now.

This book, which deals with wounds and sins of the spirit, is another step in the direction of that deep revealing and inner transformation which can help make possible experiential living in the fullness of our inheritance in the Lord which has been positionally ours from the moment we accepted Jesus Christ as Lord.

We offer to you what the Lord has given to us, for

> . . . no one after lighting a lamp covers it over with a container, or puts it under a bed; but he puts it on a lampstand, in order that those who come in may see the light. For nothing is hidden that shall not become evident, nor anything secret that shall not be known and come to light (Luke 8:16, 17).

We risk with you, the readers, as we share with you insights concerning our personal spirit from the time of conception that seem not to be so clearly laid out in the Word of God as were our earlier teachings. We have in these areas often depended first upon the Holy Spirit's gifts of knowledge and perception for discovery, and the tests of time and effectiveness for validation. Many times we have had to take an Emmaus walk with the Lord to have revealed to us what was always in the Scriptures but hidden to our understanding. We continue to expect to do so. We invite you to do the same with all that seems unfamiliar and perhaps threatening to you. Ponder new concepts in your heart, lift them to Him, and

> . . . take care how you listen; for whoever has, to him shall more be given; and whoever does not have, even what he thinks he has shall be taken away from him (Luke 8:18).

To him who has *what*, shall more be given? We believe that to mean "trust" in a God who is able to lead us out of the confines of what we thought we knew into knowing the love of Christ which "surpasses knowledge" (Eph. 3:19). Like Paul, we are

> . . . confident of this very thing, that He who began a good work in you will perfect it until the day of Christ Jesus (Phil. 1:6).

Paula Sandford

SECTION I
Incarnational Wounds and Sins

Chapter One

The Forgotten Functions of Our Spirit

The purpose of this book is to reveal the wounds and sins of the personal spirit in each of us, for healing. Healing means in this context not only forgiveness through the blood of Christ, not only death on the cross to practices built in childhood in the hidden inner nature, not only resurrection to new life. It also means simple comfort and balm which repairs and restores.

Sometimes we preach and teach forgiveness and crucifixion so ardently we lose sight of the other aspects for which Jesus came:

> Surely our griefs He Himself bore,
> And *our sorrows He carried;*
> Yet we ourselves esteemed Him stricken,
> Smitten of God, and afflicted.
> But He was pierced through for our transgressions,
> He was crushed for our iniquities;
> The chastening for our well-being fell upon Him,
> *And by His scourging we are healed.*
> All of us like sheep have gone astray,
> Each of us has turned to his own way;
> But the Lord has caused the iniquity of us all
> To fall on Him.
>
> Isa. 53:4-6

One might ask, "Isn't resurrection healing in itself?" Our answer is yes, but it doesn't cover all the ground. Perhaps a simple analogy will help. If as a boy I leave my hoe in the garden and leap the back fence to play basketball (which in fact I did, more than once), I have committed a sin of disobedience. It would have been all right to play basketball if I had finished hoeing the corn as I was commanded. But I disobeyed and stole that time, and of course lied about it to my parents. That not only left me with guilt and fear of discovery, it hurt my heart and darkened my ability to be at ease with my dad and mom.

Enter a counselor, either then or later. He may elicit a confession and pronounce forgiveness. He may have me confess to my parents and be forgiven. He may also have the wisdom to ferret out whatever resentments I may harbor at having to work when I wanted to play basketball with my friends instead, and whatever sibling jealousies or other factors also lay behind my disobedience. He may follow through to take to the cross whatever practices of deceit, or malingering, or fears of discovery may have been built in me. He may even cause the boy then, or the grown one whose inner child is being discovered years later, to be reconciled in full with the parents, beyond forgiveness to full acceptance and reinstatement in the family life.

All that is good. But that may not yet be enough. What is full healing? What more is needed in that example? It is that my inner spirit and heart were bruised by guilt, estrangement, fear of rejection, perhaps fear of further punishment, and loneliness. Listen to Isaiah's description:

> Where will you be stricken again,
> As you continue in your rebellion?
> The whole head is sick,
> And the whole heart is faint.
> From the sole of the foot even to the head
> There is nothing sound in it.
> Only bruises, welts, and raw wounds,
> Not pressed out or bandaged,
> Nor softened with oil.
>
> Isa. 1:5, 6

4

That is not mere poetic expression. There are indeed "bruises, welts, and raw wounds" if we but had eyes to see our heart and spirit.

"There is a Balm in Gilead to heal the sin-sick soul." How truly that old hymn sings. That balm is the oil of the Spirit. The blood washes away guilt. The cross crucifies sin structures. His resurrection life restores our life. But there are still wounds and bruises that need His gentle touch. The "oil of the Spirit" is the comfort of His healing presence.

At night shepherds felt the faces and ears of sheep for ticks. Finding some, they did not pluck them for fear of leaving a portion which could cause disease. Instead, they poured on oil until suffocating ticks were forced to back out. But the oil accomplished more than that. It soothed dry sun-parched skin. It entered the wound and acted as an antiseptic balm. But most importantly it simply comforted and healed.

How awful it would have been to call Lazarus forth and leave him bound (John 11:44)! Not only did Lazarus need to be unbound, but if we think practically for a moment, how dreadful it would have been to bring him back to life only to leave him still ravaged by whatever disease or condition brought him to death in the first place! He needed more than resurrection. He needed physical healing, and comfort for whatever wounding his spirit suffered in death and loss of fellowship with his loved ones whom he had been forced to leave behind.

We rejoice, as we ought, when a lost soul finds salvation, or a sin is discovered and forgiven, or some ancient practice in the self is hauled to the cross. But have we perhaps rejoiced and resigned the task too soon? There may be wounds not yet ". . . pressed out or bandaged, nor softened with oil." And we wonder why that fellow falls to the same sin again. There may be many reasons a man falls, of course, but we need to take responsibility to comprehend and administer in *fullness* our commission from the Lord to do His works of healing.

I thank God that our Lord gave my father (John's) the wisdom to know the need to heal our wounded spirits—or whether he ever consciously knew—and the grace to do it. My brother and I could guess how many minutes—usually about a half hour—would lapse after a spanking before we would hear dad's feet coming up the steps to take us in his arms, Hal on one knee and me on the other. "You know that hurt me more than it did you, don't you?" And we would think, "Did not, y' mean ol' thing!" And then he would hug us against himself and sometimes wet our brow with a tear. And despite our stubborn hearts, the balm of his presence would soothe us through and through. We had not only been hauled to account, forgiven and restored, we had been healed in heart.

Had dad not so healed our spirits, we would have known forgiveness and discipline, but something of the heart's ability to expand and relate in embrace would have remained crippled. We would still have retained sores and reticences blocking openness between us and dad and mom. We could have functioned again in the family, but with holes in us like Swiss cheese, areas in which a heart not fully healed would have engaged in role play to cover inability to embrace honestly and uninhibitedly. But who could resist that warm heart and those big gentle hands? So we were disciplined and forgiven, restored—and healed.

Our purpose is to call the Body to heal in that sense, to make it aware of what needs His healing touch, and to teach how to reach and heal in simple ways the inner spirit of each person to whom we minister.

The first difficulty we encounter is that the Body of Christ, and mankind generally, have nearly lost awareness that we do each have a personal spirit and that it has particular functions and needs of its own, distinct from our heart and mind and soul. In addition to that, there is much confusion and controversy about whether soul and spirit are indeed two different things and, if so, what is the correct theological or biblical interpretation or distinction between them?

Paula and I are neither particularly interested in or concerned about settling biblical or theological debates, and hope not to become entangled in them. We will use the words "soul" and "spirit" in a descriptive way, to help people understand how to minister. If a scholar of Greek or Hebrew or doctrine or theology objects, let him transfer whatever words fit his theology into our meanings. We know we are solid in Christ and are concerned for fruits, and though we try to be as accurate and true as we can be theologically and doctrinally, we know we can't fit everyone's theological traditions. We define soul and spirit only to make clear our understanding in order to focus this discussion on how to comfort and heal people.

Paula and I have learned to use and love the New American Standard Version of the Bible, understanding that it is among the most scholarly and accurate. We are aware that some think the King James Version misses it, but we like the way the KJV translates Genesis 2:7: "And the Lord God formed man of the dust of the ground, and *breathed* into his nostrils the breath of *life;* and man *became a living soul."*

That describes the process as we see it. First God breathes our spirit into us, and then we *become* a soul. The word for "breath" in Hebrew is "ruach," which we take to mean that breath of God's life which is our own personal spirit. What we see is that as our spirit experiences the events of life in our body, and reacts, our soul is formed. We see the soul as the structure of heart and mind, character and personality through which our spirit continues to encounter life and expresses responsively according to the way it has interpreted experience. We see "self" as an aspect of our soul. As we develop the structure of our character, in which the mind and heart interplay, that entire soul becomes in some areas a temple through which our spirit gloriously worships God and meets others, or in other areas a captivity, or worse yet, an armored tank by which our spirit rushes out to attack others.

7

We do not see soul and spirit as separate in space, for our spirit permeates every part of us. But we do see separate functions. The soul is more like clothing, and the spirit lives in and through it. Throughout the Bible, from fig leaves and coats of skin in Genesis 3 to fine linen as the righteous deeds of the saints in Revelation 19:8, especially in Colossians 3 in the metaphor of putting off unrighteousness and putting on righteousness as in putting garments off and on, the Lord uses the metaphor of clothing to describe aspects of our soul. Others may call that nexus of practices our "old man" or "carnal nature" or our "unregenerate self." Those terms are biblically correct. We simply see that "old man" as a part of our soul, the total structure of us through which our spirit expresses who we are in all of life. Every part of us—body, soul and spirit—needs redemption. In the end we who are in Christ will fulfill the clothing metaphor, as St. Paul predicted:

> For this perishable must *put on* the imperishable, and this mortal must *put on* immortality. But when this perishable will have *put on* the imperishable, and this mortal will have *put on* immortality, then will come about the saying that is written, "Death is swallowed up in victory" (1 Cor. 15:53, 54).

We shall then have become, fully and forever, the perfected soul we only wear and express imperfectly now. Our spirit, soul and body will then be as St. Paul prayed, "preserved complete, without blame at the coming of our Lord Jesus Christ" (1 Thess. 5:23).

Until and in preparation for that time we are to be involved in the process of cleansing and healing the heart and spirit. We need to see what are the functions and needs of our spirit, that He may make us whole.

It is the first function of our spirit to worship God. We shall see, especially in Chapter Five, "The Slumbering Spirit," what enables the spirit to worship *in truth*, and what prevents it from doing so.

The fact is that our spirit has many distinct functions. As the body must be fed to be healthy, so our personal spirit must be nurtured and disciplined, else it cannot sustain and perform as God intended. The horrifying fact is that almost no one now in the Body of Christ, far less of course in the world, comprehends the stark reality that our spirit requires nurture!

A painful paradox is that parents who mean to be dutiful knowledgeably feed their children's bodies three balanced meals a day, see to it that their minds are well fed by means of schools and books and in many forms of training and discipline, and provide so that their souls are trained in the Word of God and Sunday school. Yet these same conscientious parents may have almost no awareness that the primary immortal aspect of man, his spirit, needs even more careful nurture and training!

Understand that though we speak of distinct functions of our spirit, we are not speaking in a Docetic way, that is, as though our spirit were apart from and separate from our body. What touches the body touches the spirit. We are incarnate beings. That means that we are not spirits *in* a body, as water fills a can. We are spiritual bodies. "And the Word *became* flesh, and dwelt among us . . ." (John 1:14a). It is not that our Lord came down from Heaven, donned a body, like putting on a suit of clothes, and then returned to Heaven to be a spirit. That way of thinking is Docetic, from the Greek word, "docein," "to appear," as though He appeared to be a body but was in reality a discarnate Being.

The Word *became* flesh, it did not merely visit in a body. He arose in His body, nevermore to be without the human body. Our spirit *becomes* flesh; we *are* that body, spirit and body having become one, though remaining distinct. *Death is the divorce of the union of spirit and body.* When our spirit can no longer retain its union with the body to keep it alive as a functioning reality united to itself, it returns to God. Death then means that "the dust will return to the earth as it was, and the spirit will return to God who gave it" (Eccles. 12:7).

We were not designed for death. God so built us that body and spirit were to sustain one another, the spirit so healing and rejuvenating the body that the union need never have been broken. Sin fractured the ability of the personal spirit to sustain the body. Ezekiel 18:4 says, ". . . The soul who sins will die." The Lord is very careful in His use of the words "soul" and "spirit." When He says "soul," we believe He speaks concerning our entire inner being, heart and mind and soul, and within all that, our spirit. But sometimes He distinctly refers to our spirit, as in John 4:23 above or in St. Paul's 1 Thessalonians 5:23 ". . . and may your *spirit* and *soul* and *body* be preserved *complete*, without blame at the coming of our Lord Jesus Christ."

At times the Bible speaks of how our Lord felt in His soul. At the Last Supper, "Now My *soul* has become troubled; . . ." (John 12:27). In the garden of Gethsemane, "My *soul* is deeply grieved, to the point of death . . ." (Matt. 26:38). At other times the Word speaks distinctly of what He felt in His spirit. Before the tomb of Lazarus, "When Jesus therefore saw her weeping . . . He was deeply moved in *spirit*, and was troubled . . ." (John 11:33). At the Last Supper He declared one would betray Him: ". . . He became troubled in *spirit* . . ." (John 13:21). On the cross, ". . . into Thy hands I commit My *spirit* . . ." (Luke 23:46). After His resurrection, ". . . a *spirit* does not have flesh and bones as you see that I have . . ." (Luke 24:39). The Word is as careful when speaking of others, such as St. Paul, "Now while Paul was waiting for them at Athens, his *spirit* was being provoked within him as he was beholding the city full of idols" (Acts 17:16). Or Mary, "My *soul* exalts the Lord, and my *spirit* has rejoiced in God my Savior" (Luke 1:46, 47). This would imply that because her spirit *has* rejoiced, her soul is now able to exalt the Lord. In each case the Holy Spirit is incisive in the choice of words. Our Lord means to speak of the personal spirit as distinct from heart and mind and soul.

Therefore when He says that the soul which sins shall die, we understand that to mean that our spirit loses its capacity to seek and embrace God and others and therefore the structures and desires of our soul and heart no longer are enabled. They consequently tend to block. Therefore we die to the ability to relate as we were intended to God, man, nature and ourselves. If sinful structures in the mind and heart, and waning strength of spirit continue, the body is afflicted.

> When I kept silent about my sin, my body wasted away
> Through my groaning all day long.
> For day and night Thy hand was heavy upon me;
> My vitality was drained as with the fever-heat of summer.
> I acknowledged my sin to Thee,
> And my iniquity I did not hide;
> I said, "I will confess my transgressions to the Lord";
> And Thou didst forgive the guilt of my sin.
>
> (Ps. 32:3-5)

Physical death may become the final result. When all mankind's redemption is finally consummated and sin is no more, "then will come about the saying that is written, *'Death is swallowed up in victory'* " (1 Cor. 15:54).

Some are tempted to think that if any Christian were able to live purely in Christ, he would not have to die. But we are not capable of such perfection; more importantly, we are corporate creatures afflicted by the sins of others. Therefore none shall live eternally without death until the consummation of Christ's purpose for all His own; "The *last* enemy that will be abolished is death" (1 Cor. 15:26).

In this discussion lie several further functions of our spirit. If the first is worship, the second is to keep our bodies alive and functioning. Whatever medical definitions may be acceptable for death, Christians know that death occurs when the spirit can no longer abide in the body, and leaves it (Eccles. 12:7). Hundreds of testimonies are recorded in many life-after-death books which universally speak of the spirit leaving and returning to the body. Apparently our spirit requires a body which is capable of functioning in certain necessary ways, though it can suffer breakage and loss in others, or the unity of spirit and body is broken and the spirit must "return to God who gave it." How the spirit sustains and energizes the body and how the body houses and protects the spirit, no one knows. But the psychosomatic interrelation of the two is well documented both in the Scriptures and in psychosomatic medicine (though some medical researchers might not call that life force or "psyche" within us the "spirit," as Christians would). The fact that the body instantly begins to decay beyond natural repair the moment the spirit leaves ought to prove to us that it is our spirit which sustains the body and keeps it from death as long as it is able.

The third basic function of our spirit is to interrelate, to reach out across space beyond the body and sometimes beyond the five senses to meet and interreact with others. There is nothing weird, strange or mystic about this. When a father holds his infant child in his arms, their spirits flow past their skins and through each other. That is what makes such moments so tender. That is what makes love a real and practical interchange of energies rather than an isolated feeling or attitude within the father or the baby alone. When St. Paul said, ". . . do you not know that the one who joins himself to a harlot *is one body with her?*" (1 Cor. 6:16), it is that meeting and uniting of personal spirits in and through human touch, beyond each one's skin into union with the other, which is the basis of his statement that a man becomes "one body with her."

All of us have at times felt the presence of another in a room, perhaps a moment before we turned to look to the exact place where our inner spiritual sense told us the other would be; or we may have felt the energy of peering eyes and looked to find someone staring at us. While we were in college, Paula and I returned from a weekend visit to my home and stepped into a gloom so heavy about the campus, though no one was in sight, that the dullest, least mystically sensitive person could not have missed it. We learned then that earlier in the day four popular students had been killed in a car crash. The sadness in the spirits of all on the campus was an overwhelmingly real energy permeating the air everywhere. In an age accustomed to radio and TV waves invisibly filling the air, it should cause no wonderment at all that our spirits have "vibes" or energies or some kind of rays (whatever that radiation may be called) which reaches beyond our bodies.

It is because our spirits can reach out and feel within another person that we can empathize and share deeply with each other. We meet across space, commune with each other and communicate silently. We look for corroborative signs in the eyes, facial expressions, inflections and words of the other. Sometimes we are puzzled or hurt when a friend is obviously grieved in spirit, but so good an actor that his eyes, face and voice mimic happiness. Once, while making rounds calling on parishioners in the hospital, I turned as was my custom to pray for a lady in the next bed, whom I did not know. When I began to pray, however, I found myself unaccountably checked by the Holy Spirit. I could not utter a word, and found myself merely standing and praying silently for a long time, letting the Spirit flow through me to her. Having said "Amen" a little embarrassedly, I was surprised to see her face radiant with pleasure and to hear her exclaim, "Oh, thank you! Thank you!"

"For what?" I replied.

"For giving me communion. I'm a Quaker, and you just gave me communion in the spirit. How did you know?!"

Of course I hadn't known, though the Holy Spirit had. Quakers only consciously tune into what we all feel in every kind of meeting and union of spirits, sometimes light and joyous, sometimes sad or filled with tension, or bristling with dagger thrusts of animosity, sometimes refreshing or sometimes filled with weariness. As one cannot step into the same river twice, so meeting any person is different each time because what emanates from the spirit moment by moment is different. Sensitivity through our spirit is what actually guides conversations in ways and subjects we seem merely to have tumbled into. It is a primary basic function of our spirit to enable us to meet and commune with others and with God.

In Chapter Five we will discuss more fully nine functions

of our spirit. It is these three—worship, communing with others, and sustaining life in the body—which we regard as primal and basic. The first refers to our ability to meet, cherish and adore God; the second to our ability to commune and communicate with God, others, and nature; the third to our ability to relate to ourselves.

If we understand that our spirit acts within these basic functions, and that we are incarnational, that is, that our spirit acts in and through all that our bodies are, we are ready to attempt to answer the crucial question of this book: "What nurture does the personal spirit require, and how does it receive it?"

Our spirit finds nurture from its source, from God. It is personal devotion and corporate worship which are the first basis of nurture of our spirit. The Holy Spirit is by design the power of our life. "It is the Spirit who gives life; . . ." (John 6:63a). But what can keep Him from nurturing us? Lack of devotion. What allows Him to do so? Devotional prayer. Children too young or who do not yet know how to pray are filled with His presence by the devotional life of their parents. Intercession fills us all with His life, when friends or strangers pray for us. Prayer is thus the key to life.

How often have we heard prayerful saints testify that if they go one day without prayer, they know it; if two days, their mate knows it; if three, the world knows it! We can tank up on Sunday or by the intercession of others, but all experienced Christians know that sooner or later they will have to return to His presence in their own devotions, or run out of spiritual capacity to function as they ought. I know of no sound spiritual leader who does not know that his spirit absolutely requires daily, momentary nurture in the presence of our loving Lord. The least Christian a few days old in the Lord is already learning that he can only walk His life if his own spirit is continually, regularly charged in private devotion and worship.

We all know that simple truth. The strange thing is two-fold. First, we forget it so easily and so often.

But stranger is the second; somehow we seldom apply the same common sense to the needs of children! Did we think their spirits can run forever on a single initial charge from God's inexhaustible bank? Perhaps their natural vitality and ebullience beguile us. We are writing this book to reveal wounds and sins, and here lies the most common and grievous! When parents fail to pray regularly with and for their children, their children's spirits literally starve and wither! How often did Jesus try to tell us that He himself is food and drink to our spirits?

> Jesus answered and said to her, "Everyone who drinks of this water shall thirst again; but whoever drinks of the water that I shall give him shall never thirst; but the water that I shall give him shall become in him a well of water springing up to eternal life" (John 4:13, 14).

> I am the living bread that came down out of heaven; if anyone eats of this bread, he shall live forever; and the bread also which I shall give for the life of the world is My flesh (John 6:51).

> Jesus therefore said to them, "Truly, truly, I say to you, unless you eat of the flesh of the Son of Man and drink His blood, you have no life in yourselves. He who eats My flesh and drinks My blood has eternal life; and I will raise him up on the last day. For My flesh is true food, and My blood is true drink. He who eats My flesh and drinks My blood abides in Me, and I in him" (John 6:53-56).

> Abide in Me, and I in you. As the branch cannot bear fruit of itself, unless it abides in the vine, so neither can you, unless you abide in Me. I am the vine, you are the branches; he who abides in Me, and I in him, he bears much fruit; for apart from Me you can do nothing. If anyone does not abide in Me, he is thrown away as a branch, and dries up; and they gather them, and cast them into the fire, and they are burned (John 15:4, 6).

Oh, that the Body of Christ might come to think as practically and truly about the spirit as it does of the body!

No conscientious mother would fail to feed her children three balanced meals a day. Famine or poverty devastate her when she knows she cannot feed her loved ones. Pictures of starving children grieve our hearts. If only there were some way parents could see the spirits of their children in the same way, as they see those photos! Can we not come to realize that our spirit needs feeding perhaps even more desperately than the body?

Once we see it, the remedy is so simple. Bedtime prayers. Mealtime thanksgiving. A short blessing before the children catch the bus to school. Flash prayers for the children during the day. Knowing our Lord as someone with whom we live and walk, not something we grab hold of in frantic times when all else fails. Sunday school. Regular worship service. Christ in all our life in the Church (and out of it) as a loving Presence who meets us, teaches, empowers, holds us accountable, forgives, disciplines, heals, restores. Never form, law, or religion without relationship.

So often when counseling parents of errant teenagers, we hear, "I can't understand it. We gave them everything! A good home. Three squares a day. They never lacked for a thing." A few moments' questioning reveals that the most important form of nurture had been almost totally lacking. They had never given their children's spirits a thought. Some even took the kids to Sunday school and church, thus feeding their souls somewhat, and their spirits one quick meal a week. What parent would think his child could eat one physical meal a week and have the strength to be a normal child? But let the reader check his memory to see whether he knows of even a few parents who think and act in these terms, consciously and dutifully *nurturing* and *feeding* their children's *spirits* daily in the presence and power of the Holy Spirit? Do we see that we have not even thought in these terms, much less acted on them? Herein lies the first grievous wounding of most children to whom we will minister as adults.

The rule is (given that almost no one now thinks in terms of daily feeding the personal spirit), in those families where much prayer and tactile affection regularly occur, children are less starved or wounded. In those families where there is little of this, or none at all, children's spirits grieve and starve. Their inner spirit is angry and hurt, whether the mind and heart are aware of it or not. The mind may know something of loss, but our spirit intuitively hungers. "As the deer pants for the water brooks, So my soul [and the spirit within us] pants for Thee, O God. My soul thirsts for God, for the living God" (Ps. 42:1, 2a). Imagine a sunflower in a darkened room sadly and slowly turning its face to find tiny glimmers of light, gradually withering, slumping and dying. That is a profoundly accurate picture of children's spirits in such homes. We will see later (in Chapter Five) why that condition is directly the cause of rising crime rates and all manner of sexual perversion.

When we discover that the adult to whom we are ministering was raised in such a home, we ask the Lord to find that starving inner child and take him into His own loving arms. We ask Him to restore to him as many years as the canker worm has eaten and the locust destroyed (Joel 2:25). This prayer has full scriptural warrant, "For my father and my mother have forsaken me, But the Lord will take me up" (Ps. 27:10). We ask the Lord to come to him day after day, loving and wooing him to life. We tell the person after the prayer to become part of a prayer group and to plop himself into "the mercy seat" (where people gather around and pray with laying on of hands) every week for a while. A child needs many many touches.

When a child is old enough, the greatest feeding place, from seven to seventy and all the way to the grave, is at the Lord's table. Did the reader ever wonder why the Lord commanded us as He did:

> For I received from the Lord that which I also delivered to you, that the Lord Jesus in the night in which He was betrayed took bread; and when He had given thanks, He broke it, and said, "This is My body, which is for you; do this in remembrance of Me." In the

17

same way the cup also, after supper, saying, "This cup is the new covenant in My blood; do this, as often as you drink it, in remembrance of Me" (1 Cor. 11:23-25).

There are many reasons, of course, among them forgiveness, remembrance, the unity of eating together in worship, healing, etc. But is it possible the Lord was also responding to what He knew is the primal need for all of us? He knew our souls, specifically our spirits, needed to feed on Him through a simple act. From this vantage point can we see that it may be that Roman Catholic and other liturgical churches can be very wise to encourage daily attendance at Mass? What a treasure you have, my Roman Catholic friends! We Protestants feed the soul grandly on the Word of God, and rightly. But sometimes I think we overlook the greatest feeding place for our spirit. All segments of the Church would do well to learn from one another, that the banquet we enjoy in the presence of the Lord might be more full and rich to nurture both soul and spirit. This is not to say that Catholics and Protestants alike are not fed in spirit by all other aspects of worship, only that I personally treasure and know that the Lord's table feeds my spirit more fully and directly than anything else I know. I believe that is so for every one of us.

Other things feed the spirit. God's laughter is in the chuckle of a friend. His Spirit touches us in the flit of a monarch butterfly on the wing. God is in all and through all, touching us. But the key is this: only as we commune with Him directly do we retain the capacity to let His Spirit touch ours meaningfully through the creation. I have wept in spirit as I watched my dead-in-spirit friends crush a lily without a thought or a spark of awareness. Haven't we all, who can still be profoundly moved by beauty, grieved in similar situations?

Beauty seems all but lost to so many in this calloused generation. God created beauty to feed our weary hearts and souls and spirits. There was a time when artists and musicians thought that their highest aim was to create

18

beauty. Theirs are still the great works on which our souls and spirits feed. Today, strident nonsense struts itself across canvases and musical scores, witnessing to the world of the death of starving spirits who can no longer sing beauty's refreshing song of creation. How this generation needs its new John Talbots to create songs for the rejuvenation of the spirits of God's children! Few people know how much most rock concerts and weird forms on canvas jangle spirits. How many parents today take their children to something like Tchaikovsky's beautiful *Nutcracker* ballet? I used to spend my Sunday afternoons as a child flat on my back with my head below the sounding board of the grand piano while my mother played music by Chopin, Debussy and others, and my spirit soared. It seemed the notes played themselves up and down my body in glory. Where does spiritual stamina come from but in such moments? Even as I write in my office, Beethoven's Fourteenth and Eighteenth Piano Sonatas have been bathing my spirit with inspiration.

I have scriptural precedent for how I feel. King Jehoram of Israel enlisted King Jehoshaphat of Judah in his war against Moab. For three days they sought water, and finding none, searched for a prophet. When someone recommended Elisha, he responded that he would act for the sake of Jehoshaphat and said, " 'But now bring me a minstrel.' And it came about, when the minstrel played, that the hand of the Lord came upon him." Elisha told them water would come without rain, to dig trenches and be ready, and it did (2 Kings 3:4-20).

Devotional music is the soaring vehicle of the spirit, and the place of power. At the dedication of Solomon's temple, the musicians and the singers were designated and trained to make music unto the Lord, and such glory fell that none could stand:

> And when the priests came forth from the holy place (for all the priests who were present had sanctified themselves, without regard to divisions), and all the Levitical singers . . . and their sons and kinsmen,

clothed in fine linen, with cymbals, harps, and lyres, standing east of the altar, and with them one hundred and twenty priests blowing trumpets, in unison when the trumpeters and the singers were to make themselves heard with one voice to praise and to glorify the Lord, and when they lifted up their voice accompanied by trumpets and cymbals and instruments of music, and when they praised the Lord saying, "He indeed is good for His lovingkindness is everlasting," then the house, the house of the Lord, was filled with a cloud, so that the priests could not stand to minister because of the cloud, for the glory of the Lord filled the house of God (2 Chron. 5:11-14).

Music fuels our spirit; it is itself power. When the "evil spirit from God" was upon Saul, he called for David, and when he played and sang, that evil spirit would leave him for a while (1 Sam. 16:14-23). When Jehoshaphat went forth to battle:

And they rose early in the morning and went out to the wilderness of Tekoa; and when they went out, Jehoshaphat stood and said, "Listen to me, O Judah and inhabitants of Jerusalem, put your trust in the Lord your God, and you will be established. Put your trust in His prophets and succeed." And when he had consulted with the people, he appointed those who sang to the Lord and those who praised Him in holy attire, as they went out before the army and said, "Give thanks to the Lord, for His lovingkindness is everlasting." And when they began singing and praising, the Lord set ambushes against the sons of Ammon, Moab, and Mount Seir, who had come against Judah; so they were routed. For the sons of Ammon and Moab rose up against the inhabitants of Mount Seir destroying them completely, and when they had finished with the inhabitants of Seir, they helped to destroy one another (2 Chron. 20:20-23).

How often do we parents consciously feed our children's spirits on devotional music? Paula's mother played the piano as her children gathered around and sang the grand old hymns of faith. My mother and I spent hours together as she played and I sang the hymns of God. Our grown family now gathers at holidays to sit around to sing choruses or the familiar old Christmas carols.

Reading feeds both heart and soul and spirit, depending on what we read. The Word of God is a complete diet; it does feed our heart and soul *and spirit*. In Ephesians 3:16 St. Paul prayed that the Ephesians might be ". . . strengthened with power through His Spirit in the inner man." It is strength in our spirit we need to stand for Christ in the world. We have found that if counselees find every other kind of nurture for their spirits so that they should be strong in Him but fail to feed daily on God's Word, their spirits do not long retain whatever strength has been gained elsewhere. Reading God's Word is like building strong banks for the flow of God's Spirit in our spirit, without which our life's strength ebbs away as a river is lost in desert sands.

Who among us did not find his spirit soaring in dreams of glory when as children we read the grand stories of heroes and heroines? I am sure that the stories of knightly chivalry and of the sacrificial lives of the saints fed my spirit with determination to serve God beyond the call of duty. My mother read Wordsworth, Tennyson, Keats and Shelley to me and taught me to love and understand poetry, which still feeds my spirit today. My parents provided several sets of children's books, among which was *Journeys Through Bookland,* which took me from simplest nursery rhymes into Greek mythology and the great fables and legends of all the world's peoples. That training and provision has nurtured my spirit well throughout my life. I still find refreshment by the habit of good reading.

Mealtimes. My English father demanded that we all be washed and dressed nicely for supper, *together,* around the dining room table. We joked and teased and bantered and sometimes laughed so hard we wound up rolling on the floor. Far more than our bodies were fed. Our spirits drank family fun and fellowship. Our own children's friends' eyes sometimes have widened in surprise when they have sat at supper with us. "You people actually eat together, and have fun," they say. "My family never eats together. We just all grab a bite here or there." Their spirits lagged from lack of nurture in the family.

So far we have been speaking mainly of how God feeds our spirit through worship and beauty and music. But since we have begun to speak of the family, let us turn to how He would feed us through others, most especially the family.

In child raising one thing is more important than all others. Parents can succeed in feeding their children's bodies nourishing food, their minds good schooling, and their souls sound teaching in the Word, and yet still fail miserably. If they do not give copious amounts of simple affection, their children starve. Affection is the without-which-nothing in child raising. Every child needs to be held in loving arms many times daily. Because we are incarnational beings, spirit touches spirit in every hug, and His Spirit touches each in the embrace. Jesus said, ". . . to the extent that you did it to one of these brothers of Mine, even the least of them, you did it to Me" (Matt. 25:40). He was speaking of every person. He resides in each and every person. His influence is made weak in the lives of many by their neglect or denial. He expresses himself in power in others. But He is there in all. His life is love. When we act in love, His life flows in ours and nourishes each in every embrace.

Think of the nature of Jesus in each person. Can He pour who He is through us when we are yelling abuse? Will He love through us when we are kissing our neighbor's mate? Will His strength energize us when we want to beat up on someone in jealousy? Of course not. He is there, in us, but can only grieve and pray.

But suppose we want to nuzzle a baby against us? The sluice gates open and His own person flows in what we do, and both the baby and we are refreshed. If a father reads a bedtime Bible story, the Holy Spirit joins the father's and penetrates to the child's spirit in the sound of his voice.

When a mother sets a lovely table and bows her head to take her children's hands in her own as papa prays, whose love pours through her hands and his voice but that of the Lord? God's Spirit pours forth healing power when a mother's hand touches a fevered brow. Even the hands of discipline bear the stamp of God. In all that is right and true, the love of God refreshes.

Dogs will nose and push against hands to ask for petting and stroking. I have often wondered why they become so insistent. What did it mean to them, or do for them, that made them press us for more and more? Then the Lord revealed to me that He had given them a spirit which can feel our spirit cascading in heaping waves of glory through their bodies when our hands stroke them.

Perhaps the simile is inept, but infants and young children still retain that same sensitivity. Their little spirits are still open and vulnerable, present and able to melt into us or drink our presence through our touch. Every nursing mother knows that her baby drinks far more than milk from her.

Unfortunately, most people, especially fathers, do not know their worth to children. In a world of materialistic science and hard objects, the world of the personal spirit has seemed abstruse and far remote from reality. In a secular world which demands practicality identified and measured by the five senses, too many fathers have lost track of the *most* practical and real, the power of the spirit through human touch.

The remedy is so simple as to seem inconsequential in a world of technology and computers. A little conscious effort to remember is enough. Merely to hug each night upon arrival home. To take a child on the lap while watching TV. To put a hand on a shoulder or give a pat on the back. A light kiss at bedtime. A romp on the floor occasionally. Holding hands at prayer times. Sitting with a child nestled under the crook of an arm in the car or at the movies or even in church.

Hear a simple maxim: when affection is given in normal

healthy ways, people's spirits stay whole and seek normal healthy ways of expression. When affection is not given, drives and urges express themselves in wrong ways, and the spirit sickens, seeking out wrong answers for right needs. True affection does not lead to improper sexual touch and embrace, but away from it. It is the rare touches of inadequate affection which turn into lust. In wholesomely affectionate homes all the forms of child abuse almost never manifest themselves. We do not need to fear touch, only the absence of it.

When children have not received enough affectionate touch, it is the task of counselors and the Body of Christ to heal. Affection given to fifty-year-olds can warm the hearts of five-year-olds within. When questions in counseling reveal starvation diets of affection, counselors need to pray with the person, enabling their inner child to forgive. Never mind that the person's mind may never have consciously identified resentment or anger. Our personal spirit has a mind of its own; it has desires which, when they are thwarted, turn to anger. It is to that inner spirit we minister when we ask the grown one to say, "I forgive you, dad and mom, for not holding me enough." When the counselee says the words of forgiveness, we should then pronounce that his inner child is forgiven that sin of dishonoring his parents. Never mind that in all his outward attitude he may have honored to the best of his ability. It is for the sins of the heart our Lord holds us accountable. ". . . God sees not as man sees, for man looks at the outward appearance, but the Lord looks at the heart" (1 Sam. 16:7b). "For out of the heart come evil thoughts, murders, adulteries, fornications, thefts, false witness, slanders" (Matt. 15:19). Angers in the heart toward parents may be so well controlled, suppressed, forgotten, overlaid with love and loyalty that they are thought not to be there; but those same angers may fuel perplexing explosions in other areas of our lives, toward mate, children, friends, employers, pastors, etc. Having forgiven, we need to pray that the bruised and starved spirit be healed and nurtured by our Lord.

Finally, nurture comes to us by our own cherishing of our own person. In this, we are not advocating narcissism. Rather, here is another true maxim: When we disobey the great commandment to love our neighbor *as ourselves* and cannot truly love being who we are, our spirit becomes so drained and empty, we develop ways to puff ourselves up in pride, braggadocio and in false love, to fill the vacuum. Whoever loves himself as he ought need not fear pride or selfishness. True love of oneself will overflow to others as naturally as a creek may begin to form a pond but, overfilling its banks, spill out to bless the earth beyond. We only love ourselves wrongly when we fail to love ourselves rightly.

True love of self manifests itself most directly in the way we think of our bodies. We need to stop cursing and blaming our bodies. "What a fat slob I am!" "What a klutz! I can stumble over the linoleum!" "I'd forget my own brain if it weren't attached!" "I detest the way I look!" Our spirit manifests itself in and through every part of the body and takes every railing as hurt and rejection. Being grateful for our body, and expressing that gratitude, blesses and invigorates our spirit.

Devotion to God, Bible reading, loving relationships and services to others, all the ways which emulate our Lord, bless the body and spirit, for we flow in His Spirit as He intended. Imagine a man dragging burning feet across sun-fired sands mile after mile, thirsting after water which he cannot find, while in fact green grasses stretch in lanes beside rivers not ten feet away, parallel to him. That is an accurate description of the condition of our spirit when we walk apart from Christ and His way. Our spirit was not made to walk apart from our Lord. We force it to starve in alien, darkened alleyways when we walk any other path than that for which He created us.

Enough. It is enough if we see that our spirits are not amorphous foggy things somewhere inside of us. Our spirits suffuse and reach beyond every cell of our being. They require nurture of their own. The main import of this chapter is to awaken us all to the simple fact that not only do our spirits have specific functions of their own, they need to be fed daily, in as practical and disciplined a manner as we feed our bodies.

Chapter Two

In Utero Encounters

A joyful heart makes a cheerful face, But when the heart is sad, the spirit is broken (Prov. 15:13).

A soothing tongue is a tree of life, But perversion in it crushes the spirit (Prov. 15:4).

A joyful heart is good medicine, But a broken spirit dries up the bones (Prov. 17:22).

The spirit of man is the lamp of the Lord, Searching all the innermost parts of his being (Prov. 20:27).

Yet Thou art He who didst bring me forth from the womb; Thou didst make me trust when upon my mother's breasts. Upon Thee I was cast from birth; Thou hast been my God from my mother's womb (Ps. 22:9).

Thou hast been the helper of the orphan (Ps. 10:14).

A father of the fatherless . . . Is God in His holy habitation. God makes a home for the lonely (Ps. 68:5, 6).

For my father and my mother have forsaken me, But the Lord will take me up (Ps. 27:10).

In Luke 4:18 Jesus said, "He hath sent me to *heal* the brokenhearted . . ." (KJV). Many new adoptive parents, while well prepared and eager to love and nurture their long-awaited child and to provide bountifully for him or her, have not at all comprehended how deep and intense the brokenheartedness in that little one can be. And though they may have good solid faith in the power of the Lord to bless and heal, they can fall short of communicating that love to the spirit of a child and thus fail to effect real healing.

Many parents, natural and adoptive, have come to us saying, "I know that my baby needs affection and I *want* to hold him, rock him, but he won't let me. He stiffens in my arms," or, "My toddler seems to want comfort and love, and will come crying to me, but when I pick her up, she pushes me away." Some others may report, "This child is insatiable. He has to be held *all* the time, he can never get enough." We hear of older children putting their parents through endless rounds of testing, as if to say, "If I do this, will you still love me?" They will reject before they can be rejected, attempt to punish their parents by failure to achieve, or go to the other extreme and strive to please. When they do please, they are never able to come to rest in the sincere affirmation of family and teachers. They may refuse affection and then project onto parents, who have given consistent unconditional love, the accusation, "You don't love me." Such children may steal items they have no need of simply to get attention, or to express some unidentified sense of having been robbed themselves and their need to retaliate or fill the emptiness. They may lie for no explicable reason and to effect no practical purpose. Facing such actions parents cry out in desperation, "Where did we go wrong? Maybe we weren't cut out to be parents!"

They need to know that all such attitudes and behavior, especially in adopted children, can be summed up as the message in Psalm 109:22: "I am afflicted and needy, And my heart is wounded within me." Adoptive parents need to realize that their child came to them deeply wounded and that they should not regard manifestations of that woundedness as conclusive evidence of their failure as parents. As natural parents become aware, they should willingly and without self-condemnation accept responsibility for those wounding circumstances, attitudes and actions which were present in their lives to afflict their children from the time of their conception. This does not mean endless painful bearing of guilt. Forgiveness follows repentance. Neither does it mean that parents have to resign themselves to hopelessness. The brokenhearted can be healed and the depth of their woundedness can become the strength of their compassion and sensitivity for others.

First there is a need for parents to understand something of the origin, nature and functions of a person's personal spirit.

> But there is [a vital force] a spirit [of intelligence] in man, and the breath of the Almighty gives men understanding (Job 32:8, Amplified Bible).

As we mature we interpret experiences with our mind; but before we have a developed intellect with which to reason, we have a spirit within us. As soon as we begin to form within the womb, that breath from God which is the core of our essence is breathed into us, or we would not have life at all:

> . . . the body without the spirit is dead. (James 2:26).
> . . . the spirit will return unto God who gave it (Eccles. 12:7).

Our spirit, according to the Word of God, is capable of experiencing and expressing many things: troubledness (John 13:21); distress (Acts 17:16); fear (Rom. 8:16, 17); longing (Isa. 26:9). Our spirit testifies (Rom. 8:16, 17); prays (1 Cor. 14:14); sings (1 Cor. 14:15); praises (1 Cor. 14:16); tends toward envy (James 4:5); expresses faithfulness or unfaithfulness (Ps. 78:8); worships (John 4:23). In

Luke 1:41-44 as soon as the sound of Elizabeth's greeting reached Mary's ears, the baby (John the Baptist) leaped in her womb for *joy!*

Scripture tells us that we sin in our spirit:

> ... And in whose spirit there is no deceit! (Ps. 32:2b).

> Create in me a clean heart, O God, And renew a steadfast spirit within me (Ps. 51:10).

> I will give you a new heart and put a new spirit within you; and I will remove the heart of stone from your flesh and give you a heart of flesh. And I will put My Spirit within you ... (Ezek. 36:26, 27).

> ... let us cleanse ourselves from all defilement of flesh and spirit ... (2 Cor. 7:1).

That sinning in our spirit begins at our very beginnings:

> The wicked are estranged from the womb; These who speak lies go astray from birth (Ps. 58:3).

> ... I knew that you would deal very treacherously; And you have been called a rebel from birth (Isa. 48:8).

In the womb, every adopted child has in his spirit experienced rejection from his natural parents. He has absorbed all the elements of his environment: the fear, tension, uncertainty, anxiety, guilt, shame, confusion, hatred, anger and pain of his mother. He lacks the security of being invited, nurtured, supported in love and welcomed into the world. Before he sees the light of this earth he may be confused already about his identity, his right to live, his belonging. He may already have a sense that "something must be wrong with me or my parents would not feel the way they do." He may be bound with lies: "I'm ugly, unlovable." "I'm a burden, a threat, a mistake." "I'm crud." "No one will receive me." While in the womb he may have been reacting in his spirit with resentment, tightening up in defensiveness, punishing with aggressive anger, or withdrawing in fear or rebellion against life. Certainly rest and trust are neither born nor formed in him. The same wounding experiences and reactions to them may be registered in the heart of a child whose natural parents decide to keep him.

John and I discovered these insights into the awareness and capacity of the child to react in utero simply by the inspiration of the Holy Spirit over twenty years of counseling (and in the process of raising our own six children). We ministered as the Lord directed and were gratified to find our perceptions and prayers confirmed by changes in our counselees' behavior. Recently we have been delighted to see our findings and experiences confirmed by medical research.

Thomas Verny, M.D., has written a book, *The Secret Life of the Unborn Child* (Summit Books, New York, N.Y., 1981) in which he reports the findings of clinical studies conducted all over the world concerning experiences of the child in utero and and their effects on personality.

These many studies concur that the baby in the womb hears, tastes, feels and learns, and that *what* he thus experiences begins to shape his attitudes and expectations about himself. He can sense and react not only to large undifferentiated emotions in the mother like love and hate, but also to shaded emotions such as ambivalence and ambiguity. Studies reveal that the child in utero manifests a taste in music, responding calmly to composers such as Vivaldi and Mozart, but reacting with violent motion to performances of Beethoven and to all kinds of rock music. While still in the womb the baby learns to recognize his father's voice and to be comforted by quiet soothing tones that reassure. Within an hour and a half of delivery the baby can pick out his father's voice and respond to it emotionally. Quarreling of parents while the child is in the womb tends to produce fearful, jumpy, undersized, timid and inordinately emotionally dependent children. A chronic state of uncertainty, fear and deep-seated anxiety is built into a child in utero whose mother smokes, and he will react when his mother even *thinks* of having a cigarette! (Michael Lieberman, "Smoking and the Fetus," *American Journal of Obstetrics*, August 5, 1970). Dr. Verny related numerous fascinating stories of pre-natal memory and many case histories in which the doctors concluded that in some way the child made decisions to react, such as refusal to bond with the mother after birth because of her refusal to bond with the child before delivery. He reported the formation of attitudes and personality traits as a result of prenatal or birth trauma. The book says nothing of spirit, documenting only that which can be observed and evaluated clinically from a secular point of view, and offering many hypotheses for which there is growing evidence. The author suggested love as a powerful force for healing.

A friend of ours who has been a pediatric nurse for many years told us that she has learned to see a direct correlation between newborn babies' refusal to nurse and the attitude of one or both of the parents. Searching out answers, she has discovered that in such cases some sort of rejection of the baby was present during pregnancy. "Often," she said, "the baby will turn away from the embrace of the parent who was not wholeheartedly welcoming him while he was in the womb, even though he may be now." She described extreme anger in many newborns, and told us that, in talking with the mothers, she has discovered that the baby's father has left, or that the mother experienced sex with many partners and had no husband, or that the baby was the product of an affair, or that the mother simply hated being pregnant.

In our ministry we have observed that as a child grows he will—unless the transforming power of the Lord intervenes—tend to interpret each succeeding experience in the light of what he has already perceived life to be, and according to the way he feels about himself. His woundedness has clouded and colored his spiritual eyes. Dr. Verny's report says that a friendly or hostile womb creates personality and character predispositions and anticipation of the outside world. The Bible says, in Matthew 6:22, 23, "The lamp of the body is the eye; if therefore your eye is clear, your whole body will be full of light. But if your eye is bad, your whole body will be full of darkness. If therefore the light that is in you is darkness, how great is the darkness!" Parents may give lavish affection to their child, and if it is received it may be that their love may cover "a multitude of sins" (1 Pet. 4:8). But to reach the root level of a person's innermost being requires *light* in the person of Jesus Christ to penetrate the darkness in the heart of the one who is deeply wounded and confused, *truth* in the person of Jesus to counteract the lies the child has accepted about himself, the *forgiveness* of Jesus to cleanse, to heal, and enable forgiveness in the heart of the child, and the *power* of Jesus to completely transform and make new.

Our mandate to invite Jesus to minister specifically to the deep levels of the heart so that truly the "inside of the cup" is cleansed is found in the following:

> . . . why do you look at the speck that is in your brother's eye, but do not notice the log that is in your own eye? . . . first take the log out of your own eye, and then you will see clearly to take out the speck that is in your brother's eye (Luke 6:41, 42).

It may be that what we think we see as reality is not objective reality at all, but only a projection of the way we have learned to view life from our very beginning. We can have no new perspective until we have been set free from the first binding influences of our early perception which set the mold which shapes everything that pours into us. How often we read in the Scriptures, "Having eyes do you not see . . ." Daily we fail to see and understand one another and suffer hurt and pain and inflict the same. For instance:

A man works long hours because he loves his family and wants to provide well for them. His wife, because her father gave her no emotional support by his presence either before or after her birth, perceives her husband's absence as a sure indication that he does not care, that he does not love her, and that he is not a giving person. He, on the other hand, is bewildered by her hurt and anger and feels that he is in a "can't-win" situation with her. After a time, he fulfills the image she has projected of him by succumbing to an extra-marital relationship in which he feels more appreciated.

A young man suffered the devastation of being given away soon after his birth by his mother who had conceived him illegitimately. A part of his response was to form a judgment deep inside his heart that women will inevitably seek extra-marital relationships and are not to be trusted. Therefore he "sees" every friendly gesture his wife makes as a flirtation and projects his fear of being rejected again as false accusation upon his wife. She loves him dearly, and it is strongly built into her to be faithful to him, yet she has to fight to keep from being driven by his insecurity into a position of vulnerability.

I (Paula) struggled for many years with the reaction of people I loved to what they described as my defensiveness. From my own point of view I felt that I was not being defensive. I was only explaining myself, responding righteously to what seemed to be misunderstanding or unfair criticism and demand. It was difficult for me to receive helpful suggestions because to me they appeared not helpful but threatening. They seemed to intimate that I had not tried hard enough, or that I had failed to perform and was therefore not acceptable. Since I had already striven to do my best, my immediate compulsive response would often be to point that fact out to whatever primary person seemed not to be aware of it. My response was in effect a counter-attack, and hurtful to others. As the Holy Spirit (and loved ones in the family) made me aware (with some difficulty) that I was often defensive entirely without cause, and that their love and acceptance of me was truly unconditional, I accepted the new "glasses" on faith and began to discipline myself to catch my reactions. But my eyes did not "see" with new vision until specific insight and prayer enabled me to do so.

It was difficult to recognize my problem as having originated in my family, for I was raised in a Christian environment where love was expressed genuinely and consistently, if not perfectly. Loyalty to and appreciation of my family hampered the search. Recognition of my negative reactions to criticisms and legalisms that were indeed present in my upbringing, and prayers to forgive and be forgiven, alleviated the intensity of my defensiveness, but did not change the base of my reactions. One day as John and I were returning from a speaking engagement (the theme had been "Unity"), our unity was severely fractured when it appeared that John was not at all able to understand or accept an important point that I was attempting to make in conversation. (At the time, he *had* to understand in the way I wanted him to, and I can't even remember now what it was that we were talking about!) I pressed hard to break through what seemed to be a stubborn and obtuse stance. I recognized the impasse as he sank into a deep cave and icicles covered the entrance. "All right, I give it to you, Lord," I said nobly, to myself. In the next moment I was overwhelmed by feelings I could not understand—the urge to throw open the car door and jump out! I was appalled. I had counseled people who had done that sort of thing for one reason or another. But that was not the sort of thing that I would do! I sat on it, and we continued home. The Lord hears and answers the desires of our hearts.

A short time later my mother came to visit. In the midst of conversation about many other unrelated things she suddenly began to share with me about the experience of my birth. Soon after she and my father were married her appendix burst. Peritonitis set in. With no modern miracle drugs to treat the infection, she nearly died. In those days (I am into the second half-century of my life) surgery was not accomplished through neat buttonhole incisions; she was opened from one side to the other. After quite a long stay in the hospital, she was released with the admonition not to become pregnant for at least one, preferably two, years. Within a few months, however, I was on the way. The doctor wrapped her abdomen in tight binders, and she wore those wrappings for support throughout her pregnancy, apparently with some fear that the growing pressure of me inside was a threat to her newly healed incision. There was certainly a threat to her health, and in addition the constant fear of losing the baby. I came into the world crying, and only my father's presence (he was a traveling salesman) could console me.

As my mother related this story, the perplexing memory of my experience in the car came flooding with clarity into my mind. There was a meaningful parallel. In my mother's womb I was in a tight place and there was a real possibility of a spontaneous abortion. Under the circumstances, my parents' response to my mother's pregnancy had to be ambivalent at best. In the car I was in a tight place and felt I was not being wholly received. I had the urge to abort the situation. We prayed about my birth experience as soon as I could share it with John, and I felt a tremendous release and peace.

Some bonus benefits resulted: for the first time in my life I could begin to feel comfortable swimming. When on an airplane I no longer felt compelled to balance it by leaning to the opposite side should it bank steeply. And I did not fight feelings of suffocation anymore when a blanket was pulled over my head or when I was kissed for a long time. All of these had related to feelings I had experienced in the pre-natal state.

Later, prayers for my pre-natal trauma revealed that I had felt guilty for being in the womb. This resulted in my trying to perform to earn a right to be, and taking responsibility emotionally for endangering my mother. Consequently, I developed an overgrown sense of need to control, to keep situations in manageable order. The sort of shyness with which I had struggled all of my life was identified by the one who prayed with me as being rooted in feelings deep inside me that if I grew, I would take up space that would threaten another. And so I would hang back in fear and with hidden (to me) anger. This hampered John's and my working together. Whether the diagnosis was totally correct or not, the prayers had a profound effect upon my life. My base of emotion has been drastically changed, and my perceptions have been significantly corrected.

Matthew 5:29 says, "And if your right eye makes you stumble, tear it out, and throw it from you; for it is better for you that one of the parts of your body perish, than for your whole body to be thrown into hell." We do not need to live in the hell of confused relationships. Jesus is available to do away with our old sight through forgiveness and healing, to give us new sight by His Holy Spirit.

Luke 6 follows the call to take the log out of our eye with another figure which indicates how we shall know if we have something in us which needs changing. Verse 43 says, "For there is no good tree which produces bad fruit; nor, on the other hand, a bad tree which produces good fruit." Common sense tells us that industrious taking away of bad fruit does not produce a healthy tree. We must deal with the roots of our tree.

Luke 6:45 follows in the same line, telling us to look deep for the source of our problems: "The good man out of the good treasure of his heart brings forth what is good; and the evil man out of the evil treasure brings forth what is evil; for his mouth speaks from that which fills his heart." We begin to store treasure in our heart from the moment we become a living being; our treasure is made up of every experience we have ever had, the responses we have made to them, and the attitudes and judgments and expectations we hold. Some, when evil comes out of the mouth, would like to say the devil made them do it. Be assured that if he did, he had to have raw material to work with. We cannot escape responsibility for what we do with our own treasure.

Jesus, in this Luke 6 sermon, is building to the punch line. Notice particularly that he is speaking to Christians, those who already call Him "Lord."

> And why do you call Me, "Lord, Lord," and do not do what I say? Everyone who comes to Me, and hears My words, and acts upon them, I will show you whom he is like: he is like a man building a house, who dug deep

and laid a foundation upon the rock; and when a flood arose, the torrent burst against that house and could not shake it, because it had been well built. But the one who has heard, and has not acted accordingly, is like a man who built a house . . . without any foundation; and the torrent burst against it and immediately it collapsed, and the ruin of that house was great (Luke 6:46-49).

The first six years of our life are our foundational years. By the time we are six the structure of our character is formed. By the time we are ten that structure is set in concrete. That is why there is the necessity for death and resurrection when we come to Jesus. That is why we must be born again.

There is not one of us whose life was formed wholly on solid rock foundations of perfect parenting. Most of us made some sinful reactions to the good parenting we did receive. Fractures in our early foundations, caused either by wounding inflicted upon us, or by our sinful responses to events in our lives (or how we perceived those events), weakened our ability to stand in time of trial or in the face of crisis. When the rains of daily pressures beat heavily upon us, and the flood waters of our anxieties rise, our stability crumbles. When we are born anew in Jesus, we are in the position to begin again, to have our foundations built again upon the Rock who is Jesus. As His Holy Spirit searches the innermost parts of our heart, we can repent of the treasured garbage which has been stuffed into our fractures, and receive His foundation stones of a renewed mind and spirit. When we are born anew, we are born into the family of God, where we can receive human warmth and love, to nurture our growth in a way our natural parents were not able to do. If we follow our Lord's mandate to dig deep and lay a foundation upon the rock, we will have no cause to fear anything that comes into our lives. Unfortunately, much of the church has thought it to be some sort of suddenly-arrived-at magic to accept Jesus as Savior. They have failed to recognize that being born again means that one is a babe, just ready to begin the process of growing up. They have failed to press on to take hold of that inheritance for which Christ Jesus has taken hold of them. (Phil. 3:12).

Often, responsibilities which can be handled only by the mature in Christ are given to the newly born and they are thrust into positions of leadership before their fractured foundations have been discovered and repaired. Vulnerable, they fall, and in that fallen state suffer the condemnation of fellow Christians who do not understand. The call of Luke 6 cannot be avoided. Neither can Colossians 3 nor Ephesians 4. The laying aside of the habits and practices of the old self (which were developments on the foundations of our early years), and the putting on of the new (which is made possible because of what Christ has accomplished for us) is clearly a process following the fact of "for you have died and your life is hidden with Christ in God" (Col. 3:3). *Warning:* People who set out to "dig deep" in the power of their own flesh, rather than by the guidance of the Holy Spirit accompanied by the balancing nurture of the Body of Christ, can very easily become merely navel-starers, reinforcers of self-centeredness. In the process of serving, laying down our life for others, we will discover in us those areas of persistent problems for which we need some deep searching and healing. We can then confess our faults to one another and pray for one another that we may be healed (James 5:16). We do not have to be stuck with the mess we are. No matter what our stage of life, Jesus is able to reach to the little child within to enable forgiveness, administer healing to our deepest wounds, and effect change.

Clues for Idenfication of In Utero Wounds

The Condition In Utero	Commonly Observed Patterns of Attitude and Behavior after Birth
A child is not wanted.	Striving, performance orientation, trying to earn the right to be, inordinate desire to please (or the opposite, rejecting before he can be rejected), tension, apologizing, anger, wishing death, frequent illness, problems with bonding, refusing affection (or having insatiable desire for same).
A child is conceived out of wedlock.	Having deep sense of shame, lack of belonging.
The parents face a bad time financially.	Believing "I'm a burden."
The parents are too young, not ready.	Believing "I'm an intrusion."
The mother has poor health.	Guilt for being; child may take emotional responsibility for mother.
A child being formed is what one or both parents consider to be the wrong sex.	Sexual identification problems, sometimes one of the causes of homosexuality, striving to please to be what the parents want, futility, having a defeatist attitude, "I was wrong from the beginning."
This child follows other conceptions that were lost.	Being over-serious, over-achieving, striving, trying to make up for the loss, anger at being a "replacement," not getting to be "me."
Mother has inordinate fear of delivery.	Fear, insecurity, fear of childbirth.
Fighting in the home.	Nervousness, uptightness, fear, jumpiness, jumping in to control a discussion when differences of opinion emerge, feeling guilty: "I'm the reason for the quarrel," parental inversion: taking emotional responsibility for the parents.

Father dies or leaves.	Guilt, self-blame, anger, bitter-root expectation to be abandoned, inordinate hunger to find that one, having a death wish, depression.
Mother loses a loved one and is consumed by grief.	Deep sadness, depression, having a death wish, fear of death, loneliness, imagining "no support for me; I will have to depend on myself."
Unwholesome sexual relations, father's approaches to mother are insensitive or violent— or more than one sexual partner.	Aversion to sex, fear of male organ, general unhealthy attitude.
Mother is afraid of gaining too much weight, does not eat properly.	Insatiable hunger, anger.

These observations are those we have discovered during many years of counseling. Many are very much the same as reported in Dr. Verny's research. He added several more, among which are:

Mother a heavy smoker.	Predisposition to severe anxiety.
Mother consumes much caffeine.	Baby likely to have poor muscle tone and low activity level.
Mother consumes alcohol.	More than the chemical effect, the baby absorbs the negative feelings which caused the mother to drink.
Breech delivery.	Higher risk of having learning problems.
Unusually painful delivery.	Anger, lacking acceptable outlet, having ulcers, depression.
Relatively normal delivery.	Fury if pain, mother's or child's, seems to confirm rejection or ambivalence in utero.

Induced labor.	Can affect mother-child bonding, can result in masochistic personality or sexual perversion.
C-section.	Intense craving for all kinds of physical contact, trouble with concept of space, clumsiness.
Cord around neck.	Throat-related problems, swallowing, speech impediments, anti-social or criminal behavior.

For those who would like to delve further into the treasure of research that has been done on this subject, Dr. Verny included an extensive resource list in the back of *The Secret Life of the Unborn Child.*

But let us share more of our own personal experiences. These cannot be observed under a microscope, weighed or measured, but they happened to us, the Lord gave us insight, we prayed accordingly, and the prayers bore good fruit.

John and I were sharing concerning the healing of the wounded spirit at a seminar for Christian counselors. Loren, our oldest son, was also one of the speakers. As we taught about pre-natal and birth trauma, Loren was hit with the answer to a question he had been puzzling about during all of his adult years. Why had he always, against common sense and training, so fervently resisted going to bed at a decent hour? Why, when his wife retired at ten, did he feel a compulsion to busy himself with one thing after another until the wee hours of the morning when finally he was so tired he *had* to go to sleep?

He and Beth have a very good relationship. He loves to snuggle. He wanted for health's sake as well as for effective ministry to obtain sufficient rest. He recognized the pattern as one he had expressed all of his life. As a baby he would keep some part of his anatomy moving as long as he possibly could in order to stay awake, no matter how exhausted he became. As a toddler he would persistently drop again and again over the side of his bed the moment the lights were out, despite all that we could do to persuade him otherwise. And so on. As I finished speaking, Loren shared the new insight the Lord had given him, "I have to stay awake because if I go to sleep I might die."

How had he come to think this way? This is what we discovered. John and I were married while we were still students at Drury College in Springfield, Missouri. Loren came on the scene immediately and John still had three years of graduate school ahead of him. We spent the summer after graduation in St. Louis with my family before we went on to Chicago Theological Seminary a few weeks after Loren was born. I was nineteen, John twenty-one. We had no money with which to pay medical bills and seminary tuition except what we could earn day by day, but we were determined. Idealistic determination does not produce the same sort of peace and rest that real faith and trust provide, and at that point in our lives I'm sure we had more of the former.

I was at a church picnic playing baseball when I went into labor, and it was not until the next morning that I knew what was happening. No one was allowed in the labor room with me; I remember fighting fear and loneliness and praying, "God, don't let me die!" then feeling foolish that I should even think such thoughts. "I am a strong person." The doctor, without consulting me or my family, gave me a strong dose of ether, unaware that warnings had been given years before that I should never be given it. When I first saw Loren, he was pale blue, and extremely sleepy, and he remained that way long enough to cause everyone some concern. We had to work hard to keep him awake sufficiently to eat. Research has now revealed that alcohol, drugs, and anesthetics given to mothers are immediately experienced by the fetus. No wonder his little spirit was afraid to sleep. He had received the message, "I have to stay awake because if I go to sleep I might die."

When Loren finished sharing this, and more about how it related to his compulsive workaholic nature, everyone at the seminar gathered around him and prayed for him to be set free. And he was.

Our daughter Ami demonstrated the truth of the observation of some medical researchers that ambivalence in the parents can result in lethargy in their child. Ami began life as a tubal pregnancy. I spent ten days in South Chicago Community Hospital with my feet elevated. Prayer, a small miracle of moving by the Lord, and good medical care worked together to save that precious life. But Ami was so sleepy she would hardly eat. Throughout her early youth she seemed to be sleepily dreaming through life, unable to take hold. Further prayer for healing of the wounded spirit called her forth to blossom and take hold of her life dynamically. Prayer also set her free from fear of tight places.

Mark was the next to be conceived while we were still in seminary, and we had to fight to prevent the repeated threat of miscarriage. He also had to be called forth by prayer to take hold of his life. And the Lord showed us that the dyslexia he struggled with in his early years was a physical manifestation of his spiritual fleeing from life. Feeling unwanted—a third child when two were a financial strain—he did not want to be born. His feelings of expecting to be rejected caused subsequent scramblings of other parts of his being. The healing of his spirit and the disciplines he himself exercised to walk in his healing have now become part of the strength of his ministry as a gifted counselor.

Many references have been made by researchers to images they believe have registered in the memory streams of children in utero which then float to consciousness sometime later, usually in response to similar experiences which trigger recall. It is difficult to prove the validity of such information, but the testimonies are so common that they must be given serious consideration. One such story was told to us by our son John, and we still chuckle when we think of it. The triggering mechanism (at least that which caused him to share), was, as I remember, the difficulty we were having with this very strong son's struggle during his teenage years to become an individual. He related to us what was sometimes his dream, sometimes his daydream. He was in a dark, cozy place, and someone wanted him to leave, but he liked it there, and didn't want to go. He was happily occupied, playing with a long rope which he would handle, stretch it as far as it would go, wrap it around himself, bat it and shake it. The game gave him great pleasure. He was angry to think that he had to leave this place.

John was rather embarrassed to share this, but was serious in wanting to identify some meaning in the persistent picture. I was excited as I then shared with him that I had carried him nearly six weeks past the due date as we had figured it, that when he was born it was by induced labor, and that the immediate response of the nurse in the delivery room was one of intense concern. John's umbilical cord was extremely long. It was wrapped several times around his neck, and the little fellow was all tangled up in the rest of it! We laughed together through my apology. We prayed. We wonder what would have happened had we allowed that little person (who has always responded, "I want to do it myself") to do it himself by sending the message, "I'm ready to be born," which we now know every fetus normally sends to trigger the birth process.

John was one of our planned babies. He did not exhibit the list of behaviors which Dr. Verny associated with induced labors, but perhaps some of his virulent angers originated there. We hate to think we might have wounded him by our impatience to get him here. On the other hand, thank God for His redemptive power, and for His healing which not only creates glory from the death of our mistakes, but enables us to laugh at ourselves as well.

My husband John and I have sometimes joked about the fact of our call to minister to the Christian family and how that necessitated our raising six children because we are such slow learners. We don't really believe that; each of our six was a special gift from God. But it is true that wisdom accumulated as we all loved one another and matured together as a family. Tim and Andrea, coming last, did not have to suffer as much of our ignorance as did the older children. But God has provided the same for all, healing of the wounded spirit, and wholeness as His redemption reaches every depth and area of our lives. We knew that we had to pray for healing for Tim and Andrea as soon as they were born. They probably have been the most secure and relaxed of our half-dozen. But God has provided for them also the spiritual exercise they need to make them strong, and He will continue to do so through their and all our lives. The fact that we have been wounded so as to need healing is not necessarily a negative. Our Lord would build joyful, grateful, victorious hearts, tenderness, compassion, sensitivity and wisdom out of our healed hurts.

Whether you are praying for a baby or an adult, the reality of Jesus' affecting the spirit of a person is made possible through prayer for the innermost being of the tiny child inside the one for whom you pray. Jesus Christ is not confined to the dimensions of time and space. He can identify with and heal the spirit of a person at any time, past, present, or future. Our entire life is an open book to Him. Therefore it is a simple matter for Him, when we pray asking, to identify with a wounded spirit all the way back to the time of conception. When we have asked Jesus to make this identification, we speak the comfort, reassurance, and affirmation of the Lord directly to the inner spirit of the child. We pray something like this:

> We say to you in the name of the Lord Jesus Christ that your life is not a mistake. God made you out of the love that He is. He called you into being at the right time and the right place. He prepared a way for you and gave His life for you. You are a privilege, not a burden; a joy and a delight, not a disappointment; you are not an intrusion, you belong. You are a treasure just because you are, not merely for what you can do. You are one of Father God's own children, and He delights in you, and we delight in you.

We go on to ask the Lord to destroy whatever lies the child may have accepted, and to bring to the cross every resultant destructive attitude, expectation, and personality structure or habit pattern. We pray with vivid imagery, seeing the Lord pouring His love all about the child, breathing a fresh breath of life into his spirit, wrapping strong welcoming arms about the child, and inviting him to grow into the fullness of his own life, restfully, as God planned for him from the beginning. We pray that the inner child be enabled to forgive those who wounded him; we also pray that the child himself be forgiven his negative responses. We pour the healing love of Jesus into the wounded spirit like healing balm. We ask the Lord to give the person a sovereign gift of trust and rest and peace, and to cause his entire being to be integrated with wholeness and harmony as he is reconciled to being who he is where he is.

Then we place the cross of Christ (the stopping place for all sin) between the child and his parents and his parents' parents all the way back through his generations, declaring that all of his inheritance be filtered through that cross. This is not magic. It is simply a way of putting the Lord in charge, and of claiming His blessing and protection. (Every person must make that claim for himself at some time during his life, as he is ready.) All descendants of evil and every curse coming to the child through his family must stop on that cross. (See Chapter Thirteen, "Generational Sin".) We ask the Lord to hide the child in His own heart and to cast light into the eyes of any powers of darkness who might attempt to oppress, afflict or prevent his life. We stand in the Lord's authority against such powers.

Finally we place a blessing in the name of Jesus on the child's life. We ask the Lord to melt any hardness of heart, to strengthen with might in the inner man (which means his spirit), to enlighten the eyes of the heart, to open doors for him, to draw him to his destiny, and to place a mantle of protection on him for all his future life.

Concerning Prayers Using Imagery

We do not ask the person for whom we pray to form a picture in his mind which is in any way contrary to the way he remembers an experience. We do not ask the inner man to accept a lie. Lies never effect healing nor lead to freedoms which can last. We do ask the person to forgive everyone who was involved in the hurtful experience as he remembers it. We encourage him to ask forgiveness for his own responses. We assure him of that forgiveness, and we break the power of the habit patterns which resulted from his cherished and practiced responses.

For us, praying with vivid images means that we describe clearly and colorfully *the picture the Lord gives us* to convey new life to the inner child once the old has been done away with by repentance and forgiveness. We do not make up a picture by our own flesh, nor ask the person to take some kind of soulish trip in his imagination. All such things are neither necessary nor very helpful. We ask the Lord to give us a word picture, or a visual picture or symbol which will minister appropriately to the need of the individual, and we then describe it as accurately as we can. The counselee himself may be the one who receives the picture from the Lord, or he may receive a portion to add to that which the counselor is describing.

Concerning Emotional Response to Prayer

We do not press anyone to get in touch with an emotion. Emotion is often deceptive. People are capable of creating emotion to please the counselor, to dramatically attract sympathy, to satisfy expectations that valid experiences are always accompanied by tears, or simply to express something which is more of a religious cultural habit than it is an individual's specific expression of repentance or release. Such ways of creating emotions may be totally unconscious. Tears may even be a diversionary tactic to cover up what is really going on inside. They may also come as a real outpouring, to which wrong labels can then be attached. We say that if emotions come up naturally and easily as a result of the prayers, let them flow freely. But let us not strive to make them happen. It may be good if we do experience some emotional release at the time, but we should not judge the efficacy of prayers by the presence or absence of emotions. It may be that months later real emotions will come to the surface as the Lord brings something to ripeness. When that happens, the healthy response is to let oneself feel, then hand those feelings gratefully to the Lord as the One who has drawn them up from the depths of the heart. It is well to remember that much healing is realized without any emotions simply as the fruit called "changed behavior."

It is easy to pray for spiritual healing for a tiny baby newly arrived in your family. As you hold the baby to feed him or rock him, feed him with love and prayer, again and again. Close friends of ours made it their ministry for years to take foster babies into their home. Most of these little ones were rigid, fearful, restless and colicky when they first arrived. But after much hugging, rocking, sweet talk and prayer of the sort that we have described, such babies would relax and respond beautifully, with alertness in joy, and go into adoptive homes ready to melt into the new parents. Our friend, as the temporary foster mother, would talk to each tiniest baby about the joy prepared for him in his new home and how Jesus would be going with him. Our friends adopted one such child themselves whom the doctors had feared would be mentally retarded because of neglect, abuse and malnutrition. The love and prayer combination effected a miracle in that little boy and today he is bright and healthy and secure in love as a teenager.

Children under ten or so may be tucked into bed at night with prayers of thanksgiving for them and for the blessing that they are. Such prayers should be repeated over and over, until they learn from the depths of their spirit that they are cherished. Very young children may be prayed for aloud as they sleep, and their spirits will hear the prayer and be gradually secured in love. Older children who manifest a wounded spirit can be sensitively drawn into conversaion about their fears and animosities, and the source of these can be explained to them in simple terms. They can then be invited to participate in prayer either actively or by consent and asked to voice their forgiveness and to choose life.

Beyond prayer, persist with affection. Give them the material things they need, but far more importantly, give them *you.* Play games. Do things together as a family. Laugh. Joke, but do not tease; little children do not understand teasing at all. Don't be threatened by their questions concerning natural parents (if they have been adopted). Do not conceal the fact of adoption. In their spirit they already know, and if you do not make that known consciously, they will feel betrayed or lied to. Guide them to compassionate understanding of why they were given away, and to express forgiveness. If you are talking with your own natural child about early woundings for which you feel responsible, do not be afraid to ask his forgiveness. Do not be overly anxious to straighten out your own child merely to appease your own conscience. He will naturally be healed to a large extent as you allow the Lord to deal with your own inner man. Address the child's problems by conversation and prayer only when they persistently harm his attitudes and actions. Let your discipline be firm, loving, consistent, and appropriate to the trespass and the child's maturity level. Compliment. Affirm. Let your love be unconditional. Give your child opportunity to express his feelings. Give him room to fail, and let him have the assurance that he will never lose your love. Know that you are in resurrection business, to bring him to fullness of life, but don't wear that responsibility too heavily. God is in charge. You *will* make mistakes, but God is bigger than your propensity to fail. You may have to repeat prayers and verbal affirmations many times. This does not indicate lack of faith or mean that the first prayers were ineffective. It simply demonstrates the fact that when a little child hears the good news that he is loved, he says, if not with his mouth, certainly with his heart, *"Tell me again!"* until that message permeates the very fibre of his being.

When we pray for the wounded spirit of an adult, we do not pray without his consent for specific changes in his spirit. It is an invasion of privacy to mess around with the insides of another who must stand presently in relation to the Lord and be held accountable for the condition of his spiritual life. (There is one exception. Where husband and wife are concerned, they may pray more specifically for one another because they are in a one-flesh relationship. However, the Lord neither smiles upon nor honors manipulation, and each partner is held accountable for insensitivity to the other.) We believe that general prayer for the Lord's love and light to shine on another is always in order, for that creates an environment in which the person is enabled to come to freedom to make good choices. In Ephesians 1:18, 19 we are given a good prayer example which is appropriate to anyone: "I pray that the eyes of your heart may be enlightened, so that you may know what is the hope of His calling, what are the riches of the glory of His inheritance in the saints, and what is the surpassing greatness of His power toward us who believe." In Ephesians 3:16ff we find another: ". . . that He would grant you, according to the riches of His glory, to be strengthened with power through His Spirit in the *inner man; . . .*"

The goal of healing the wounded spirit is that all might be able to say to God, as we read in Psalm 139:13-16, 23, 24:

> For Thou didst form my inward parts; Thou didst weave me in my mother's womb. I will give thanks to Thee, for I am fearfully and wonderfully made; Wonderful are Thy works, And my soul knows it very well. My frame was not hidden from Thee, When I was made in secret, And skillfully wrought in the depths of the earth. Thine eyes have seen my unformed substance; And in Thy book they were all written, The days that were ordained for me, When as yet there was not one of them.

Search me, O God, and know my heart; Try me and know my anxious thoughts; And see if there be any hurtful way in me, And lead me in the everlasting way.

Chapter Three

Wounds From Feeling Rejected

Behold, children are a gift of the Lord;
The fruit of the womb is a reward.
Like arrows in the hand of a warrior,
So are the children of one's youth.
How blessed is the man whose quiver is full of them; . . .
(Ps. 127:3-5)

Our son Loren, who is also our pastor, asked in church one Sunday how many knew that they were unwanted children when they were first conceived. More than half answered in the affirmative. He then asked how many just a few months or even weeks later were very much loved and wanted. Almost all of that same group raised their hands. Then he made a statement in rebuttal to the cry "every child a wanted child" by those who support abortion on demand, "I hardly think that parental rejection early in pregnancy is an indication that the poor infant will lead a miserable life after birth." I thought of my own inopportune birth and of the fact that four of our six children were uninvited blessings. Memories of wonderfully warm and happy childhood experiences flooded into my mind: laughter at family gatherings, weekend excursions in the car, wild scooter rides down our alley, romps in piles of crispy autumn leaves, delightfully ooey-gooey mud puddles, trips to the St. Louis Zoo, my brothers imitating the monkeys for a week afterwards, the smell of clean sheets, carefully prepared meals we shared together, the Sunday morning hassle of getting us all to church, roller skating on the black satin of our asphalt street. . . . Through it all ran the assurance of our belonging, even while we were being spanked for our transgressions. "This hurts me more than it hurts you" may have brought forth an "Oh, yeah?" response from our heads, but our hearts knew it was the truth. Love was real. Our children can describe the same as their inheritance. Most of the woundings we received in our spirits early in life have been, and continue to be, healed in the laying down of life for one another, and by the presence of the Lord in the process of that sharing. Specific woundings, set into the patterns of our lives by our sinful responses, have been and are being dealt with as the Holy Spirit reveals them to us. *"Surely* our griefs He Himself bore, And our sorrows He carried; . . ." (Isa. 53:4). For that reason we are more and more enabled to appreciate and celebrate the joys of being who we are. As I witnessed those raised hands in the church service, I was also aware of the great number in the Cornerstone Fellowship who had received prayer for the healing and transformation of their inner man, from us, from the pastor and elders, and from the people in their home fellowship groups.

The way God intends is that all of His children be received as blessing and reward. A "full quiver" does not mean doing without the good things of life, but realization of the fullness of life, if priorities and perspectives are in line with the mind and heart of God. What society in general has not yet discovered is that there is a God who will comfort all our waste places, make our wilderness like Eden, and our deserts like the garden of the Lord (Isa. 51:3). Unfortunately the churches have not fully discovered that in real terms either.

In our church there is a family with seventeen children. Thirteen of them are adopted. Most of those thirteen are from handicapped minorities, some physically disabled and some mentally. The world says that it would have been better if none of these children had been allowed to live. Yet each one of these children is being healed, blessed, and set free by consistent lavish physical affection and heartfelt spirit-penetrating prayer. Everyone in Cornerstone would feel sadly diminished had we not the opportunity to minister to them, and they to us. We are painfully aware that each of those precious children was by the circumstances of conception a prime candidate for abortion, according to the view of a large portion of our society!

The following quote is from a book called *The Zero People* (essays on life edited by Jeff Hensley, Servant Books, Ann Arbor, Michigan, 1983) and is a reprint of an article from *California Medicine*, 113:67-68, Sept. 1970.

> The traditional Western ethic has always placed great emphasis on the intrinsic worth and equal value of every human life regardless of its stages or condition. This ethic has had the blessing of the Judeo-Christian heritage and has been the basis for most of our laws and much of our social policy. The reverence for each and every human life has also been a keystone of Western medicine. . . . The process of eroding the old ethic and substituting the new has already begun. It may be seen most clearly in changing attitudes toward human abortion. In defiance of the long held Western ethic of intrinsic and equal value for every human life regardless of its stage, condition, or status, abortion is becoming accepted by society as moral, right, and even necessary. *It is worth noting that this shift in public attitude has affected the churches, the laws, and public policy rather than the reverse.* Since the old ethic has not yet been fully displaced it has been necessary to separate the idea of abortion from the idea of killing, which continues to be socially abhorrent. The result has been a curious avoidance of scientific fact, which everyone really knows, that human life

begins at conception and is continuous whether intra- or extra-uterine until death. The very considerable semantic gymnastics which are required to rationalize abortion as anything but taking a human life would be ludicrous if they were not often put forth under socially impeccable auspices. It is suggested that this schizophrenic sort of subterfuge is necessary because while a new ethic is being accepted the old one has not yet been rejected.

I share the following story in the hope that it might make the churches more fully aware of healing power through our Lord Jesus Christ to redeem, transform, and bring to glory the "impossible" lives the new ethic would eliminate.

Bill and his twin were born by Caesarean section on June twenty-third, three months prematurely. Weighing in at two pounds three ounces, he was the smallest of the two boys, but the hardiest. His brother died soon after birth, and Bill went home to the dresser drawer that served as his crib. His parents already had two pre-school children and were not at all prepared to accept the responsibility of a growing family.

The neighbors were accustoned to hearing the baby cry, but one Saturday night they called the police when the crying went on till after midnight. Bill's parents had left him in the care of the two pre-schoolers while they went to the bar to drink. Bill, who had been clad only in a very soggy and smelly diaper, was wrapped in a blanket and taken to a shelter home. It was quickly apparent that there was something seriously wrong with him, and medical examination discovered double pneumonia, double hernia, and malnutrition. He was hospitalized for two weeks and released into the custody of foster parents, our close friends, as soon as his weight reached the five-pound mark in the latter part of August.

Bill had not been secure in the womb of his natural mother nor welcome in her arms. But he certainly found warmth and love in the embrace of his foster mother,

Donna, who with her husband and three children began a rebirthing process in him the moment he arrived in their home. For one and a half years she literally carried him night and day. His little body had become stiff, as happens to many babies delivered by C-section. He could be balanced like a board on the palm of a hand. He was listless and glassy-eyed at two months, unresponsive, at first, to anything around him. The doctor feared that he would be brain-damaged because of poor nutrition.

Donna spent hours massaging his little body. She rocked and cuddled him, carried him on one arm as she did her housework, sang to him, talked to him, nearly wore out his neck kissing him, and daily poured the Lord's healing into him by prayer. Prayers were not only for the strengthening of his physical body, but much more for the healing of his wounded spirit and for calling him forth to life (as we described in Chapter Two). At night he slept on Donna's chest. He was not allowed to cry because of the exaggerated protrusion of the hernia, and he was too little and too weak to undergo surgery.

God honored the prayers from the beginning by overcoming one outstanding error. Donna had nursed her own babies and so was not familiar with formula feeding. During Bill's first week with his new family he was fed undiluted formula, and his little body assimilated the rich mixture and he gained two pounds in one week!

It was not long before the baby began to respond with alertness to his nurturing environment. His new family was delighted with him as was his church family. Every Sunday after worship admiring friends gathered around him at coffee hour to celebrate his progress. It became more and more clear that he was so integral a part of the family that they couldn't let him go. He became officially, legally, a part of them the Christmas before he was two. Neither his natural parents nor his grandparents contested his adoption.

When Bill was eighteen months old he had his hernia repaired surgically. Donna held him and rocked him at the hospital. Not long after that a flu epidemic hit the area and Bill was hospitalized again. Donna held him and rocked him in a private room at the far end of a hospital corridor. The prayers continued. A month later Bill was circumcised. All seemed to be well, but the next day when Donna was changing the baby's diaper, she discovered broken stitches and profuse bleeding. During his first four years it seemed that he was continually sick with respiratory infections. Because of his tiny posterior we had nicknamed him "Bean Butt," and frequent penicillin shots made a pin cushion of that portion of his anatomy. It was determined that Bill was a bleeder, and so he had to be built up with vitamin K before he had his tonsils removed at the age of four. Again all seemed to go well at first. But he hemorrhaged and had to be taken back to the hospital. More holding. More prayer.

Bill seemed to be confused about whether he was right- or left-handed. He was intrigued with little matchbox cars, but he would switch them frequently from one hand to the other. When he entered kindergarten, tests revealed that his hands were cramping because of residual weakness due to the early malnutrition. Therapy corrected that, and he became right-handed. By the time Bill was nine he was of normal size, and his development certainly indicated no brain damage. Today he is a vigorous and healthy teenager with normal teenage interests and problems. He is more able to give and receive affection than most of his peers, and has a better than average willingness to explore in counseling the hidden depths of his heart which have held some self-destructive attitudes and anger. The inner healing continues.

The miracle of love is that Bill is a survivor of circumstances that would have killed many another child. The wonder of his rebirth is that he has the capacity to trust, to hold his heart open and to press on. The areas of conflict he has encountered as a teenager with authority figures have not broken the bonding he has with his adoptive parents, particularly with his mother, as so often happens even with non-adoptive parents and teenagers. Watching so closely the process of healing in Bill's life confirmed to us once again the truth that love does indeed overcome a multitude of sins (1 Pet. 4:8). "He heals the broken-hearted, And binds up their wounds" (Ps. 147:3).

Bill can say today what we read in Psalm 71:6: "By Thee I have been sustained from my birth; Thou art He who took me from my mother's womb; My praise is continually of Thee."

In Bill's case the past which needed healing and transforming concerned little more than the pre-natal and birth traumas. That being the most powerfully influential period of anyone's life because it is the seed out of which the rest of life grows, persistence in ministry was necessary to overcome the fruits of intense rejection and neglect. But that persistence was exercised step by step *during* the laying of each building block of his foundational years. That foundation, which was in itself healing despite imperfections, will continue to be made new as the Lord works in his life. "I am confident of this very thing, that He who began a good work in you will perfect it until the day of Christ Jesus" (Phil. 1:6).

We have stated that Jesus is able to transcend time and identify with us at *any* stage of our development to set us free from those dated emotions and expectations which shape the basic structure of our being and hold us in bondage. Let us now consider another case, one which began with much less wounding initially, but compounded day by day for thirty-five years before Jesus was given access to heal.

Joel came to us in a state of emotional and physical exhaustion. He was functioning in his job by sheer determination, but was suffering from chest pains, anxiety attacks, nausea, sleepiness so overpowering that, while driving, he would frequently have to pull off the road to nap. He was plagued with persistent feelings that he would die young and fears that his wife would die. No matter how much he slept, there was never any rest for him.

In the past ten years he had held ten jobs. He had been subject to frequent illness all of his life; he was still a prime target for every cold germ or flu virus that came along, and an ulcer gave him considerable discomfort. Finances were in poor condition, his present boss was always pressuring him, and his father was dying. No matter how diligently he applied his skill at work, projects seemed to collapse. At night he put off going to bed, not wanting to let go of the day; in the morning it was overwhelming for him to face the day. Sometimes he would become so stressed he would throw up. He existed in loneliness, even in the middle of a crowd, bemoaning the lack of permanent relationships. "In my whole life everything has gone queer." "Why can't I make anything work?" "What is missing in me?" "Why do I always turn out to be the victim of other people's decisions?"

As we explored Joel's history and observed him closely in his relationships we discovered that because he had never developed the power to be his own person he was overly subject to the decisions and actions of others. The message "Tell me what to do" came from him unceasingly. His sense of worth and belonging was dependent on how well he succeeded in pleasing others. He worked so hard to please that others felt as too heavy a burden his striving and desperate need for appreciation. His unconscious demand was a drain upon friendship.

We observed that his need to succeed, though it was often for the sake of others' welfare, was so intense that he would over-promote and over-organize, causing people to feel pushed and crowded or helplessly swept along with him. They would resist his efforts and eventually withdraw from him personally. He began to look upon money as his only real security and mark of worth.

Joel had not been an unwanted child. He was conceived soon after his mother's two miscarriages. She exercised every possible care to protect her pregnancy, but she lived nine months in an attitude of tension and fear of losing another child, and could not let her heart go in joy of anticipation. This was confusing to her and she was often depressed. Those emotions and that reserve registered in the spirit of her unborn child.

> Recent research indicates that abortion results in depression during a subsequent pregnancy and immediately post partum. This depression from abortion *or loss of a previous child* appears to delay a mother's preparation for her newborn by diminishing her anticipation. It has long been recognized that a significant personal loss without completed grieving will interfere with subsequent attachments . . . seems to truncate the mother-infant bonding mechanism so that it does not develop as well in subsequent pregnancies (*The Zero People*, Jeff Lane Hensley, p. 128).

Joel's mother had not completed the process of mourning the loss of her babies, and was unable to bond well with him as a result. Neither was she ready to risk giving herself unreservedly. Her heart was still self-protectively insulated. Her new baby experienced that withdrawal as abandonment. Neither parent was demonstrably affectionate, though they provided well for him materially. A small child understands and accepts love in terms of touch, not intellectual reasoning, so this circumstance continued to affect him adversely.

When Joel was two years old, his six-year-old brother fell ill and died. Since Joel had never felt completely accepted, and had entertained some jealousies in relation to his sibling, he assumed guilt for that death. As his parents sank into grieving for the lost boy, Joel's guilt was confirmed to him. He responded by becoming convinced that he had to strive to accomplish enough to make up for the others. Somehow he had always felt like a replacement from the beginning, and now he had to live for the brother whom the parents had so dearly loved. Of course that was not what the parents wanted. But in Joel's perception he was in a no-win position. He had to fill the vacancy in order to earn a place for himself. But by doing so, he could never *be himself.* He could never even admit his anger, because anger did not elicit pleasant responses from those he tried so hard to please.

> Behold, Thou dost desire truth in the innermost being, And in the hidden part Thou wilt make me know wisdom (Ps. 51:6).

Joel's healing was accomplished over a long period of time. First, in conversation we drew him out as much as we could to intellectually understand the dynamics working in his life as we have just described them. He declared that he wanted to be whole. We asked him to consciously reject the lies he had accepted from the beginning about his own lack of worth and belonging. In prayer we asked the Lord to minister to the spirit of the little child still living deep inside. Until then, the grown man remained trapped in the emotions he had experienced at the beginning of his life. We called both these lies and the power of those emotions to death in the name of Jesus, and we spoke directly to his inner being (as in the prayer we described in Chapter One) to direct and enable him to take hold of a new identity: "I am a child of God. I am chosen. I am precious. The Lord loves me because I am." We said to him, "If you do everything right, you won't be loved any more. If you do everything wrong, you won't be loved any less. You *are* loved; you didn't earn it and you can't lose it. It is God's gift to you. Before your parents knew you were on the way, God had created pathways for you to walk in. No one can live your life in the same way that you can. God has preserved your life for you, and wants you to walk restfully in it. You were not created to be a replacement for anyone else."

> Before I formed you in the womb I knew you . . . (Jer. 1:5a).

> For we are His workmanship, created in Christ Jesus for good works, which God prepared beforehand, that we should walk in them (Eph. 2:10).

We poured the balm of the Lord's healing into him and asked the Father to hold him until he was enabled to come to rest in the heart of the Father. We asked the Lord to write the truth of his belonging on his heart. Then we asked him to forgive his parents. We did not get involved in trying to determine their actual guilt. We were dealing with Joel's perceptions, his subjective reality. Forgiving others does not in such instances as this say that they are actually guilty. It says that we were guilty of unforgiveness. This kind of forgiveness is a matter of recognizing that we have made a sinful judgment against others for what we believe they have done, and now we are releasing them from our condemnation and are choosing to bless them instead. Then we went on to the more important aspect, Joel's need to be forgiven himself, for all the responses he had made to whatever his parents were, and for his responsibility for the life he had built on that base by his conscious and unconscious choices. We "saw" the Lord coming with His sword of truth to cut Joel free from the past, real or imagined, and to lead him forth into the fullness of his own destiny and purpose. We loosed him to be himself, to grow up inside himself in the power of the risen Lord. We prayed that the Lord would continually strengthen him in his spirit as he walked in the new way.

Joel needed specific absolution for the guilt he felt for his brother's death. We did not try to reason with him about false guilt; we knew that he needed more than comfort. He was guilty of jealousy and of wishing he could have his brother's place. Therefore he needed forgiveness for the murder he knew was in his heart, even though he had never experienced it as a conscious fantasy. He felt guilty. Saying something reasonable, like, "All little brothers are apt to feel jealousy and sometimes wish a brother would die or go away," only gives such guilt a place to retire for a time. Feelings of guilt are done away with only by assurance of forgiveness through the blood of the Lord Jesus Christ.

Prayers of affirmation and assurance were repeated each time Joel sank back into old familiar patterns. We prayed again and again that performance orientation would come to complete death. Beyond that, it had to be written on his heart that he was choosable and that others would take the initiative for him even when he didn't deserve it. We hugged him a lot. We visited. We ate together, laughed together in our small group of which he was a part. I remember one evening when he pulled one of his periodic pouts and retired to the bedroom to wallow in the self-pity of "nobody cares about the hopeless case that I am." We all followed him there to declare that we knew what he was doing, that there was no way he could cause us to be so frustrated with his repeated flopping and imperfectly disguised manipulating that we would drop him. "We are brothers and sisters. That is a forever relationship. You can't lose us." Finally after much perseverance he came to rest with us, with God, and himself. A number of years and many miles separate us now, but there is warmth in the memory of rebirthing one who will forever be a cherished part of us.

The important point to note here is that Joel's wounding started in the womb. He was, in a sense, a replacement. His mother's unhealed grief had left a void to be filled, rather than that he could come to fulfill a joyful expectation. If he had been fully received and nurtured with physical affection, as Bill was, much of his wounding would have been healed in the course of his growing up. But as it was, the lack of real nurture from mother and father compounded his woundedness. Joel's case is typical of many.

Far more wounded are those whose parents tried to abort them and failed. Their lives are usually plagued with frequent illness. They tend to struggle with periods of depression. Some attempt suicide. They have initially received the message, "You *should* die." Unconsciously they are keyed to respond to that. Some women try to abort their babies because someone tried to abort them. The golden rule works in their lives inside-out and upside-down. They *will* do to others what has been done to them, until the saving power of the Lord intervenes.

Observations we have made in counseling were confirmed by a statement in *The Zero People* (p. 125):

> Our clinical observations tend to confirm the reports of others; even young chidren know of their mother's early pregnancy, abortion, and miscarriage.

The book reports the case of a five-year-old who became severely disturbed by his knowledge that his mother had aborted a child when he was only two and a half. A seven-year-old reported a dream in which three siblings went to play with him in a sand bank. It collapsed and the three were buried. He didn't know them, but somehow he was sure they were brothers and sisters. His mother admitted to having had three miscarriages, but insisted there was no way he could have known.

Our purpose in this book is not to explain absolutely how such knowledge is possible, except to say that the spirit of a tiny child is extremely sensitive and his intellect as yet uncluttered. He seems to be able to tune in with keen receptors to things we adults might miss.

Studies show, and our experience confirms, that children who "know" in their spirits that brothers or sisters have been lost by abortion or miscarriage often experience a gnawing sense of guilt, as if it were somehow their fault. Such children may harbor an emotional distrust of parents for fear of what might be in store for them. Parents who have aborted a child because they were unable to provide financially, or because it was not convenient to have a child, or because of social pressures, will no doubt struggle to make sure they don't find themselves in that predicament again. The uptightness of these parents will reflect in the attitude and behavior of children already born into the family. Such children may interpret the fact of their survival in the family as a result of their being desirable only at that particular time. They may feel pushed to perform to maintain that desirability. Their sense of belonging becomes conditional. When disharmony rises in the family, they may express extreme anxiety and possibly assume guilt for the presence of the quarreling. A child whose sense of conditional belonging has been reinforced many times by family tensions may actually feel guilty for existing, helpless to do anything about it. He may react in his feelings of unworthiness by neglecting himself or trying to commit suicide. Or he may go to the other extreme and break out in anger which says in effect, "I didn't ask to be born. But here I am, I'm going to demand my place and I'll prove to everybody that I have the right to be a person!!!" We have counseled with some who unconsciously but vigorously styled their lives to punish their parents. "I'll show you! I'll throw away my glory, and you'll never feel any pride on account of me. You didn't want me and you deserve to be ashamed." In those cases, of course, the self-destruct message is operating as well as vengeful rebellion which desires to inflict pain for pain. Our prescription is always the same: healing of the wounded spirit by prayer, confession, repentance, forgiveness, and establishment of a new identification with the Lord Jesus Christ, followed by continuing human nurture through friendship and affection. Such a person may need to be carried a long time in the heart, which means that a rebirthing and re-parenting process must follow if healing is to be maintained. The re-parenting relationship is temporary, but must continue so long as the Lord indicates necessity. We must not pray and then drop such a person and run. That will likely only reinforce the problem; he always "knew" he was supposed to be aborted. Or, he "knew" it would happen to him as it had to his lost siblings who were not pleasing to his parents.

Thirty to fifty percent of conceptions in America today are aborted. Publicity for and against abortion is before us constantly. Every high school or junior high school girl knows that abortion is a legal option. It is common for people in our society to weigh the value of buying a new car and a bigger house against that of raising a child, and for the child to lose. Many abortions are performed because of the devaluation of children. It has been suggested by some that because of this general devaluation of children, coupled with the general breakdown of the stability of the nuclear family, children tend to devalue themselves. They have less and less confidence they will be cared for, and less and less hope for the future. Thus the increase of depression in our young people, and mounting statistics which already show suicide to be the third major cause of death in adolescents!

There are many other ways in which we inflict deep spiritual wounding to our children by devaluating them. Wounding can occur in families who have remained together, but are so concerned with providing a living which measures up to their desired material standard that they fail to nurture the ones for whose sake, they protest, they are working.

Recently I interviewed the principal of a day-care center. She was concerned for a pre-schooler who seemed listless, withdrawn, disinterested, and unable to participate with other children. The child was the only son of a corporate executive whose wife was also rising in a successful business career. The mother was called in for consultation. "Our child is the most important *thing* in our lives" actually meant that they were careful to give every *thing* they could think of to their offspring. But the only regular time spent with him was a forty-minute ride through heavy traffic on the way to school each morning, and thirty minutes spent religiously between the supper hour and bedtime, reading a story to the little fellow. He occupied an inviolate place in a busy schedule, just like all the other people who waited for their appointments. But the only real affection he received came from a nanny who brought him home in the late afternoon, fed him his supper, and came in to tuck him in and turn the lights out after the parents had retired to their guests or other pursuits.

Most working parents are not so blind as that, but scores of thousands of lonely children live in pockets of isolation from their parents, not really knowing what it is for which they yearn so sadly. Nor do they understand the sources of their sudden upsurges of anger, often when daddy has just run in to present them with a delightful new toy on his way to a golf game. "See you later," he says, and goes away. Or when mother, hurrying to put supper on the table, says, "Don't bother me now! We'll talk about that later." She has come home from work late, exhausted, and feels the pressure of an evening too short to accomplish her chores. But to her child who needs to share, "later" sounds like "never" and probably is. Even though children may accept with their minds that all of the busywork is for their well-being, and means that they are being cared for, they starve inside for loving attention and physical affection, and interpret the whole of life in an attitude of futility. The more material goods they are given, the more they demand, because *things* have become a substitute for love. Things are not love, they don't satisfy; thus the need for more and more. Disappointment builds anger. Anger at parents is then projected onto all authority figures and God. Respect for property disintegrates because material wealth has come out the winner in competition to be the parents' "dearest treasure." Vandalism is sometimes a means of trying to "kill the enemy." Some children steal because they have been stolen from.

Let us say clearly that it is not the fact that both parents work that causes a child to be wounded. Motivations, attitudes and priorities make all the difference. Sometimes both parents must work to pay rent and provide bare necessities. In one such family we see both parents sharing household chores and involving their children without laying too much responsibility on them. They all work together and they play together. Family TV, games, fishing, camping, and popcorn-making are corporate enjoyments. And they pray together. Money always seems to be scarce, but its presence or absence does not seem to affect the basic foundations of love.

Foundations of love may be fractured in children whose mothers returned to work too soon after they were born.

Baby sitters, be they sweet grandmothers or PhDs in child psychology, are still only substitutes for the real thing, and babies know it. God has designed babies to need their mothers and fathers to enfold them in physical embrace so that their spirits flow together to accomplish bonding between them. Breast-feeding is best (see Chapter Seven in *Restoring the Christian Family*). Holding and rocking are essential. The *active* presence of the father in the day-to-day care of babies is necessary to provide strength, and structure as a vehicle for tenderness. A baby comes to rest as he puts down spiritual, emotional and mental roots in the consistent, reliable nurture of parents who are always there when needed. Trust is built into his nature at root level. Most of the birth trauma can be healed in those early months. If a baby is left occasionally with a baby sitter, basic security need not be shaken. Rather, it could have the same effect the "peek-a-boo" game teaches: "Now you see me, now I'm gone, here I am again, and it's all right." But when a small baby is left all day, day after day, with a sitter, he feels abandoned by the parents no matter how physically well cared for he is. Seeds of confusion about identity and belonging and worth are planted. Full bonding does not develop between the child and his parents. In fact, if a child learns to accept and look for nurture from a very loving baby sitter who cares for him all day, and if the child spends only a short time each day with parents, he may at first be torn between the two, and then choose to bond with the one who has invested more vitally in his care. Being taken from that environment can cause as grievous a wound as the death of a parent.

We have counseled with countless numbers of people who in their adult years felt an unusually deep warmth and gratitude for grandparents who essentially raised them. "I was close to them, but I could never really talk to my parents." There is always in such cases a need to heal the wounded spirit. Such people live with unanswered, nagging questions, "Why did my parents not put me first?" "Why wasn't I loved more than what they were doing?"

"Was there something wrong with me that they didn't want to be with me?" Rational understanding of circumstances does not yet accomplish healing in the heart. Only the Lord Jesus can enable forgiveness and reach deeply enough through time to set an individual free from foundational insecurities so that he can restfully, trustfully expect to be chosen, cherished, loved and nurtured today by those who are primary to him.

How do we know whether ministry for early registration of rejection is still required, or if love from someone has already overcome a multitude of sins? Simply by evidence of fruit in the person's life (Luke 6:43). Consider these questions:

Are the person's feelings easily hurt?

Does he see hurt where none was intended? Does he nurse hurt feelings?

Does he take personally, as insult or slight, remarks that others would ignore, laugh at or enjoy?

Is he habitually defensive of himself and others?

Does he have to have a special invitation or encouragement to participate in activities others would simply volunteer to join?

Does he demand attention rather than invite it?

Does he withdraw into himself and find it difficult to share?

Does he talk a lot without revealing what he really thinks?

Does he need compliments but fail to hear them?

Does he expect to be overlooked?

Does he neglect his appearance, or anxiously spend too much energy on it?

Is he prone to jealousy in relationships?

Does he put himself down (or brag too much)?

Does he have trouble following through with projects he starts?

Does he always seem to be a spectator, on the outside looking in?

Unhealed rejection is often projected onto others. David's father left before his son was born. His mother hated this man, who had first abused and then abandoned her. Since David was very much like his father in appearance and temperament, she unconsciously projected her feelings toward her husband onto her son. As he matured, the relationship became more and more hurtful.

David was of course deeply wounded, and in no way was it built into him to expect anything but rejection. He would draw it to himself from friends, from his wife, and even from his own children. He managed to get himself fired from job after job. Often he would anticipate being fired and quit his job before the boss could move to dismiss him. As David began to receive counsel and prayer for inner healing, he was compelled to test again and again the sincerity of those who ministered to him.

Bringing the negative to death on the cross is a relatively easy task. Common-sense psychology and the Holy Spirit's gift of discernment discover problem areas and root causes. Applied prayer is effective because of what Jesus Christ has already accomplished on the cross. His resurrection power is also available. But learning to walk in that power is a process.

> As you therefore have received Christ Jesus the Lord, *so walk in Him,* having been firmly rooted and *now being built up in Him and established in your faith,* just as you were instructed, and overflowing with gratitude (Col. 2:6, 7).

> . . . He has now reconciled you in His fleshly body through death, in order to present you before Him holy and blameless and beyond reproach—*if indeed you continue in the faith firmly established and steadfast,* and not moved away from the hope of the gospel that you have heard . . . (Col. 1:22, 23).

Those who minister to the Bills and the Joels and the Davids who must now be built up and established in their faith so that they may walk in Him, rather than in what all their previous life has trained into them, may often find themselves saying, as Paul did in Galatians 4:19, "My children, with whom I am *again in labor until Christ is formed in you . . .*"

It may seem like a never-ending pregnancy till Christ be formed in some with whom we are in labor. Daniel was abandoned by his mother and father when he was five. His grandmother chose to care for his sisters, but wanted nothing to do with the difficult job of raising a boy; he was placed in a foster home. As wounds of rejection erupted into displays of anger and rebellious behavior, Daniel was moved to another home, and another, until he arrived at the eighth. There the foster parents said, "Look, we know what you're doing. You are testing to see if we'll kick you out. We won't, so you may as well settle down and decide to be a part of our family." When Daniel was eleven he was adopted by his foster family, and continued to respond positively in many areas to their love. But some patterns persisted for a long time: difficulty in applying himself consistently in school, choosing friends who were ne'er-do-wells, skipping school with them so frequently that he lost his credits. His choice to wear ragged jeans and tattered tee-shirts communicated his lack of self-esteem much more than it reflected a teen-age fad. And in his later teens what we called "the foster child syndrome" persisted. He would disappear for a week at a time, spending a day or two at one friend's house till he had worn out his welcome, then going to another friend to do the same thing. When friends or his own energies were exhausted, he would return home to shower and sleep long hours, only to repeat the behavior. His response to frustrated job hunting was, "Nobody wants me." His choices did not begin to change till people who loved him persisted in expressing that love unconditionally along with discipline which delivered the message, "God, and we, love you just as you are, but too much to leave you that way." Continuing prayer began to give him the strength to see where he was trapped and to make some positive choices to break out of built-in patterns and take hold of his life. Continued healing of his wounded spirit will empower those new choices.

John and I often teach concerning what we call "see-through faith," which those who minister effectively must have. This is the kind of faith that looks beyond the present circumstance to celebrate what the Lord is accomplishing by the struggle we are presently totally and perhaps frustratedly involved in. "See-through faith" is ". . . the assurance of things hoped for, the conviction of things not seen" (Heb. 11:1). It is made of the kind of love that "bears all things, believes all things, hopes all things, endures all things" (1 Cor. 13:7) for the sake of the one who cannot yet do that for himself. While we are yet "in labor" till Christ be formed in those whom we carry in our hearts, we will hurt with them and for them, even as Christ does. But in that identification is joy, as we read in John 16:21:

> Whenever a woman is in travail she has sorrows, because her hour has come; but when she gives birth to the child, she remembers the anguish no more, for *joy* that a child has been born into the world.

Chapter Four

Anorexia, Dyslexia, Schizophrenia, Child Abuse

Behold, Thou dost desire truth in the *innermost* being, And in the hidden part Thou wilt make me know wisdom (Ps. 51:6).

For nothing is *hidden* that shall not become evident, nor anything secret that shall not be known and come to light. Therefore take care how you listen; for whoever has, to him shall more be given; and whoever does not have, even what he thinks he has shall be taken from him (Luke 8:17, 18).

But all things become visible when they are exposed by the light, for everything that becomes visible is light. For this reason it says, "Awake, sleeper, And arise from the dead, And Christ will shine on you" (Eph. 5:13, 14).

Every plant which My heavenly Father did not plant shall be rooted up (Matt. 15:13).

Several years ago, at a seminar John and I were teaching, we met a medical doctor who for years had been engaged in research concerning one of the elusive questionable-cause-no-cure terminal diseases. She was excited because at long last she had found some answers, had sufficiently validated them, and submitted them to authorities for further scrutiny. As she talked about her work, it was revealed that she is a scientist who not only calls herself Christian, she knows God well enough to listen to Him, and, as in Luke 8, she takes care how she listens. We were intrigued as this brilliant doctor shared in a childlike manner how she has learned to submit her hunches to the Lord, and has practiced hearing and weighing the guidance He has given her. Sometimes He would speak to her through the Scriptures, sometimes directly, until she knew which alternatives to choose, what frontiers to press beyond, and what dark alleys to explore. There was an infectious joy bubbling from her in gratitude for the goodness of God, that He had blessed her so faithfully with insight to discover what had been hidden and also that He had protected her from the scorn of some colleagues who might have ridiculed her "unscientific" method had they known. As she talked, I found myself remembering George Washington Carver, who discovered a multitude of uses for the peanut by the same sort of listening process. I wondered how many of life's mysteries and blessings remain hidden to us because we fail to listen when God is quite willing to speak. "You do not have because you do not ask. You ask and do not receive, because you ask with wrong motives . . ." (James 4:2b, 3a). I am sure that many of the currently incurable diseases of mind, body and spirit which plague mankind would be rendered curable were more of us to come to the point of having what Luke 8:18 suggests some of us have: ". . . for whoever has, to him shall more be given; . . ." Whoever has what? I believe the answer to that question is "trust." If we had trust in a God who treads down all our adversaries (Ps. 108:13), who heals "all" our diseases (Ps. 103:3), who not only desires truth in the innermost being, but will "make me know wisdom" in the "hidden part" (Ps. 51:6), we would not have to continue to be defeated by the unknowns which now cause us to be afraid. "All things become visible when they are exposed by the light" (Eph. 5:13). Jesus is that light. He speaks to us by His Holy Spirit, and empowers us with the gifts of His Spirit. Inspiration comes to many as a gift from the Lord without their knowing the Giver. How much more to them who seek Him and obediently serve Him! It is time for the church to awaken from spiritual sleep and allow the light of Christ to shine in all our hidden parts to discover those things which block, and to shine on all our natural talents that they may break forth to bring healing and wholeness to the body of mankind.

As we pray for insight and wisdom to minister, and the Lord gives us a little, we are often too timid and fearful to use that little. We say, "I don't know enough to pray." "I don't want to go around messing with somebody's insides and hurt them more than they are already."

There is truth to be heeded in both of those statements. Humility, sensitivity, and caution are always prerequisites for effective ministry. But what often underlies is, "I don't know enough to be in control, and I'm afraid to risk. What if it doesn't work? What if I am not received? What if the flak hits the fan?" We need to understand that when we sit down to minister to one another we are not the healers. God is. We do not have to make anything happen. He will. We do not need the security of guaranteed success. He *is* the guarantee. "And He said, 'My presence shall go with you, and I will give you rest' " (Exod. 33:14). Romans 8:28 says, "And we know that God causes all things to work together for good to those who love God, to those who are called according to His purpose." To those of us who know we are called according to His purpose, but can't quite grasp the details, the Scripture is reassuring when it says, in Ephesians 3:20, that He is able to do "exceeding abundantly beyond all that we ask or think, according to the power that works within us." Thousands of times when John and I have prayed according to the glimmer of light the Lord has given, we have been overwhelmed with surprise and gratitude for the quality of the fruit that resulted.

Our responsibility is to listen to the Lord, respond to Him

as best we can, and offer whatever He gives us as a door-opener to more. Our faltering prayer may be just that which will enable a faint aroma of the Lord to flow in so that the one for whom we pray will "taste and see" (Ps. 34:8) and eventually fling wide the gates "that the King of Glory may come in" (Ps. 24:9)! When we have been faithful over a little, He will set us over much, and not before. And it is a comfort to know that God is bigger than our mistakes.

In the light of what has been said, I offer the following, which are simple clues too small to describe the whole of what we have seen the Lord accomplish. But they are clues which have become keys to unlock doors through which the Lord has given some miracles in our ministry and in the ministry of others.

Anorexia

In August, 1983, an article written by a young reporter for the Arizona Republic in Phoenix, Arizona, was sent to us. It read in part,

> Death is my constant companion. Slowly, day by day, I am killing myself, and though overwhelmed by fear, I seem powerless. . . . I have anorexia and bulimia. . . . At times I starve myself. Other times I gorge myself with food, then purge my body of its life-giving nutrients. I am being treated for these disorders, but so far with little success. God, how I hate myself for what I have become. I want to live, to let life fulfill its many promises, but this problem I have—these illnesses I know can be fatal—have taken over. They seem to be more powerful than my fear, stronger than my desire for life. . . . I am ashamed . . . my family is unaware . . . I have avoided developing friendships with my co-workers for fear they would discover my embarrassing secret. . . . I can't stand to be alone . . . I'm also afraid of being with other people.

She went on to describe the guilt, self-loathing, emptiness and periods of deep depression she suffered. Therapy had not had a lasting effect. She concluded with the heart-rending, "I am so lonely and afraid. How long will I continue with this?"

Many remember with great sorrow the death of Karen Carpenter, an anorectic. We remember being at the Beverly Hills Hotel not so long ago, watching the arrival of her wedding guests; we have enjoyed the revival of her music in recent months, and have lamented the loss of one who had so much to give.

It is not a hard thing to handle the heart tugs we feel for the pathos of strangers who seem unreal because they are far removed from us. It becomes more difficult to be detached when people call on the phone asking for help, even though it is nearly impossible to do much more than soothe problems long distance in short doses. But when the Lord places His hurting children on our doorsteps and places a burden in our hearts for them, we know we are involved, and we reach out then for answers only God can give.

Annette's case was typical of many we have heard of since. She manifested symptoms common to anorectics: significant weight loss, confusion about the seriousness of that symptom (she feared being fat), irregular and suppressed menstrual periods, insatiable appetite, vomiting and loss of hair. She suffered periodic depression which seemed to have less to do with concern over her physical condition than it did with a basic drive for perfection, and her feelings that she was incapable and worthless. Guilt was overwhelming, but unidentified except in terms of having gone through an extremely rebellious teenage period. She had accepted the Lord, and knew she was forgiven, but she did not feel forgiven.

We explored her hunger in order to find her emotional roots. Annette's parents, though they loved her, were unable to express their affection. There was no affection given to the children nor exchanged between the parents, who slept in separate bedrooms. In fact there seemed to be little or nothing experienced corporately in the family. As she described her scant childhood memories, we received an impression of a handful of nameless people dressed in gray, sitting around in insulated compartments, with no one to call them out. In response to questions concerning her birth, she replied emphatically that she was a disappointment. She was not invited, and she should have been a boy. Her father lived in his intellectual world. Occasionally he would attempt to draw her into conversation, but scorned her inability to keep up with him. She felt lost and ashamed in his world of interests, and he never entered hers. She felt that her mother was also looked down upon. Compliments were never given, even when deserved. Annette is a beautiful girl, but had never heard her father say, "You're pretty," or "I'm proud of you." She tried hard to please, but not feeling that she had made it, abandoned the effort for a while with a vengeance, going to the other extreme to do all the things she knew were not pleasing. When she was barely seventeen she had an abortion, and though she was pressured to do it, and chose to believe counsel that it was all right, she was devastated in her heart. As time went on, she became a Christian, and couldn't understand why the joy that other new Christians felt eluded her. She strove to perform as she felt a good girl should, to live up to every letter of the law. She even followed the strong urgings of a friend who said she should give her material possessions away. Rather than come to peace, she felt more than ever that she had failed miserably to be anything she was supposed to be. She brooded under a tyranny of feelings.

Ministry to Annette began with prayer for the healing of the wounded spirit of the inner child who had never felt wanted, never been nurtured, could never be what the people most important to her wanted even if she could perform perfectly, because she was the wrong sex in the first place. We called to death the lies that she had accepted about herself, affirmed her beauty and worth and belonging in the Father God, and called her forth in the name of Jesus to find her own place in the sun where she could thrive and grow. In our prayer we communicated that the Lord was now transplanting her, putting her into new soil. She was no longer in the darkness; now the light of the Lord was enfolding her. We asked the Father to hold her and let His delight be written upon her heart. Then we prayed that she be enabled to forgive, and that she be forgiven. We communicated the absolute forgiveness of the Lord Jesus in no uncertain terms, and spoke in the authority of the Lord Jesus to any voices that might tell her otherwise, "Be still, in the name of Jesus." Later we called her forth again in prayer, and again. Emotionally, she had never left the womb to venture into anything that was her own. She had been carried into destructive adventure by her hunger and her anger, and had allowed opportunists to use and abuse her. She needed repeated prayer and committed friendship from us to give her the strength and courage to walk in the new life the Lord offered her. In the process she began to gain a victory over anorexia. But the final victory came with the revelation that she had never really grieved for her aborted child. It was as if she could not really choose life until she had wept for the one she had taken.

It was clear to us that Annette had been punishing herself for failing to be what she thought people wanted, for failing to be what God called her to be, but far more importantly for the guilt that she had been unable to handle. The self-punishing focused in her body. She had wished herself dead.

The end of this tale and the beginning of a new is that a handsome prince came along, kissed her, married her, and they are now living happily ever after. This sounds like something out of a fairy tale. Yet it is true for the following reasons: Annette married a prince of a young man who because of his relationship to Jesus is able to give her the unconditional love and consistent compassionate affirmation she needs to support her decision to choose life. More importantly, Annette made a heartfelt personal commitment to the Prince of Peace himself. In her relationship to the Lord Jesus Christ she is choosing to exercise the kind of daily discipline necessary to hold fast the word of life (Phil. 2:16) and to walk as a child of light (Eph. 5:8).

With each temptation to fall back to former resentment, fear, guilt, anxiety, self-condemnation and striving, she is learning to obey Romans 6:11-14. That means to deny the tyranny of her feelings and offer herself to Jesus in each instance. Because the wounds, griefs and guilts of her heart have been seen, faced, and forgiven, and the habit patterns brought to death on the cross in prayer, she is set free to grow into the abundant life promises of the Lord. Her discipline is empowered by Him. When she begins to fail in the discipline of walking in her new life, those who love her bear her up in prayer and by gentle reminders.

Not long ago I (Paula) came across an article in *The Journal of Christian Healing*, Volume 5, Number 1, which confirmed almost point by point what we had experienced with Annette. There R. Kenneth McAll, M.D., quoted R. Gladstone (Mind Over Matter, Jr. AM. Acad. Child Psych. 1974) saying that

> . . . in fifty cases of anorexia nervosa the most common single factor was the anorectic's devotion to the idea of perfection. Gluttony, acquisitiveness and pleasure were cardinal sins. Guilt was to be expiated by punishing the body mass.

He then reported from a lecture given by a psychiatrist named Graham at Chichester Hospital, England, 1979, that

> . . . children who feel better off dead . . . are afraid of further loss of communication especially after the loss of a parent through death or divorce or when a parent becomes mentally disturbed.

"Divorce," said Mr. McAll, "creates more of a problem than death. . . . In line with this thinking, anorexia can be seen as a manifestation of morbid grief."

The article went on to report a study of eighteen anorexia cases over a five-year period. All had failed to respond to hospital treatment. In the family histories of seventeen cases there was a total of twenty-five deaths which were either by suicide or other violent causes. There were five terminations of pregnancy for non-medical reasons and eight miscarriages. There were deaths from accidents or suicide in ten families. Abortions and miscarriages that had not been mourned were found in seven families.

A ritual mourning process was prescribed for all these cases. By this we mean that a service was held at which the patient and/or his family could go through the mourning process, accept forgiveness for sins (attitude or deed), and commit the dead to God. "In this service," said Dr. McAll, "the whole purpose of the life and death of Jesus Christ is consciously shown forth for the benefit of the living and the dead." Later in his article he reported,

> In fifteen of the cases relief from anorexic symptoms followed a ritual mourning process. Three patients who followed the suggested course of action claimed to be cured within twelve months, one within a week, seven within six months and four over a period of fourteen months. None needed re-admission to a hospital. All were followed up over a period of at least one year.

Dr. McAll reported that by the time his article was completed for printing, he had treated sixty-four cases in this way (through 1981). Four families refused to cooperate; in ten cases the results were not complete, but in forty-nine cases relief was sustained. According to Dr. McAll there are at least two other doctors who have had successes with similar treatment: Dr. William Wilson, Professor of Neuro-Psychiatry at Duke University, North Carolina, and Dr. Raimbault at the Children's Hospital, Rue de Sevres, Paris.

We agree with Dr. McAll and others who say that much of the etiology of anorexia nervosa is still a mystery. But we, like them, have experienced many cases in which these factors are present: unresolved guilt in the patient or an immediate family member, or unmourned death or loss. Usually there has been great trauma which has not been adequately faced and therefore has not been healed. Often there is a history of aborted or miscarried babies which has not been recognized in terms of guilt or loss.

In our experience we have not prescribed a funeral service as a means of helping the patient to go through the mourning process. We have pursued this effect by prayer, and have shown forth "the whole purpose of the life and death of Jesus Christ . . . for the benefit of the living and the dead" in the process of counseling. However, we applaud the ritual mourning process as valid in any case and perhaps even necessary in many.

Dyslexia

It is not our purpose here, nor are we qualified, to present a scientific discussion concerning dyslexia. We do consider it valuable, however, to share with you the clues the Holy Spirit gave us which enabled us to pray very effectively for a number of dyslectics who came to us for help.

Those who suffer from dyslexia are often deeply wounded. First of all, their frustration level is high because of the difficulties they experience with language, especially with reading. It is hard for them to tell left from right; a "d" may look like a "b," or a "u" like an "n." They may confuse "p" and "q." Some dyslexic children write letters backwards. What they see on the printed page appears backwards to them and they must translate. Pronunciation of words may be twisted: "bakset" instead of "basket," for instance, and "aks" instead of "ask." They have difficulty with math for the same reason. The symbols do not appear to them as they do to others. Dyslectics are confused about time and space dimensions: up and down, yesterday and tomorrow. We have observed that they have difficulty sensing the passing of time. One six-year-old child had to be watched to insure that he arrived at school on time because he could lose himself in the game of kicking dry leaves, not realizing that literally hours were passing. We have seen a number of dyslexic children and teenagers who expressed sincere intention to follow a schedule, but responded to some disruptive stimulus which drew them off course, then to another, and another, which totally fractured intended plans and purposes. Later they could not account for loss of time.

The second wounding comes in terms of the expressed frustration of others who do not recognize or understand the problems of dyslectics. Parents and teachers often pressure such children to learn and perform as if it were simply a matter of choice. Ridicule is often piled on them by teachers and fellow students. Hurtful forms of discipline to make them pay attention are often applied. One third grader was continually thumped on the head by his teacher because his attention wandered; he would lose his place in reading and stumble in his efforts. The other children in the class found this punishment a source of merriment and laughed mercilessly. That same dyslexic child had difficulty in physical education because of his space disorientation, and the teacher belittled him day after day in the presence of the class, calling him "Suzie" and "Pansy."

It is not surprising that a dyslexic child often becomes withdrawn and hostile if his problem is not diagnosed and treated. Many become dropouts and juvenile offenders. Almost always they suffer tremendous feelings of loneliness because of the isolation effected by misunderstanding and emotional abuse. It might be comforting to some to know that there are many famous people who were dyslexic, among them Albert Einstein, Thomas Edison, Leonardo da Vinci, George Patton, Woodrow Wilson, Nelson Rockefeller, and Bruce Jenner. Obviously dyslexia has nothing to do with lack of intelligence or ability, as these lives testify. The child I described in the above paragraph went on to earn his master's degree, and is presently an extremely gifted artist by avocation, and counselor by vocation. The Lord has healed his dyslexia, and is not only *healing* his wounded spirit, but is *transforming* that to be part of the very essence of his sensitivity to others in his ability to counsel excellently.

How do we pray for a dyslectic? We first sought the Lord about this some fifteen years ago when we were speaking at a church in Ohio. A despairing mother brought her ten-year-old son to us. We questioned as we usually do concerning family history. I don't remember the details, only that there were elements of his not being wholly welcomed in the family. The Lord clearly spoke to our hearts a message which startled and puzzled us: "He didn't want to be born. His spirit is in his body backwards!" We didn't know if that was a literal or symbolic description. To think of being in the body backwards even violates our understanding of the relation of spirit and body. We still do not know. But we prayed obediently as the Lord led, first that he be forgiven his rebellion against the life that God had created for him to live. We asked if he would forgive those who had wounded him by rejection at his conception and by ridicule and impatience as he grew up. He consented. The Lord directed, "I want you to see me by vision reaching in and turning his spirit around to face forward in life, and then to heal his coordination." We prayed obediently, and then asked the Lord to integrate every part of his being into a harmony. We instructed the boy to make a daily discipline of saying, "I choose life."

The next day we received an excited call from his mother who informed us that his teacher had called to say that somehow suddenly the boy could read, and that the school was advancing him two grade levels.

Healing is not always that quick. More often improvements manifest themselves steadily over a period of time. But consistently we have observed the same general conditions in those suffering from forms of dyslexia:

1. woundedness in the spirit dating back to conception and/or infancy;
2. fear, anger, fleeing back from and rejecting life;
3. resultant breaking of inner harmony and a physical manifestation of the scrambling of the inner being.

We have prayed, using the same basic ingredients, for:

1. healing for the wounded spirit;
2. forgiveness for the rebellious fleeing back;
3. prayer for ability to forgive those past and present who wounded;
4. prayer describing the Lord reaching in and turning the spirit around to face forward and to be integrated and coordinated with every other part of the person;
5. prayer to empower the person to choose life.

One young man in his late teens, who had experienced extreme trouble with dyslexia all of his life, said he actually felt a spinning sensation inside himself as we prayed. The next day the first change he noticed was that he easily knew the difference between left and right. He entered college (something the "experts" had said earlier he would never be able to do) and succeeded very well in making better than average grades. For him the process of healing continues in terms of

1. healing of relationships which were strained during the years of his struggles with learning;
2. acquiring written-language skills he was unable to develop earlier;
3. breaking old habits and building in new disciplines.

As he now joyfully puts it, "The cloud has lifted."

Paranoid Schizophrenia

For such psychotic disorders, we strongly urge that those who minister in the Body of Christ not do so unless in cooperation with a doctor of psychiatry. General prayers may be said that healing might come, that the light and love of the Lord might enfold the patient, and that God might clearly direct those who are in charge of treatment. But it is dangerous to become involved in such cases more specifically than that without the balancing and protective judgments of those who have gained adequate professional training and experience. For the purpose of suggesting the direction of your prayers, should you establish that relationship with the patient and his medical doctor, we offer the following:

The devastating mental disorder of paranoid schizophrenia seems to have *roots in the womb*, when normally well-ordered *cells* deep within the brain of an unborn child *are thrown into disarray*, UCLA researchers report. Microscopic examination of brain tissue from 10 deceased schizophrenics ages 25 to 67 revealed a striking *disorganization among cells* within the hippocampus, a portion of the brain believed to be *associated with the expression of emotion*, said Dr. Arnold Scheibel and Joyce Kovelman of UCLA's Brain Research Institute. . . . The researchers conceded their study involved few subjects and only those with paranoia, one of several versions of the disease. "But," Kovelman said, "this is the first of many studies that will help us understand the full meaning of this." . . . Kovelman said the new study "is the first quantified study made under very rigid and controlled conditions" to find structural changes [italics ours]. —Associated Press, *Lewiston Tribune*, 6/7/83).

The questions this discovery raises to counselors such as we, are, "What caused normally well-ordered cells to be thrown into disarray? Could pre-natal trauma have effected the scattering? What was happening in the family at the time? If the disorganization could be caused by a virus or a genetic defect, then why the vulnerability to the virus? Why the genetic defects?" If information concerning pre-natal trauma and family history is available from family members, and the Lord leads you to pray concerning early wounding, by all means do so, but it would be advisable to pursue that both with the knowledge of the psychiatrist who has charge of the case and his advice concerning whether this would be best effected in the presence of the patient or apart from him.

John and I have sometimes grieved to hear that some enthusiastic but ill-advised Christian has rushed forward to cast demons out of a person suffering from such a disorder. *If* a demon is present, and that is *not* often the case, there is a time to deal with it and a time to leave it alone. Untold damage can be done by indiscriminate attempts at exorcism. On a few occasions John and I have been asked by a psychiatrist to exorcise, but without professional medical consultation to confirm and balance discernment we would not do so in the case of a schizophrenic.

Spiritual Wounding Caused by Child Abuse

Time magazine, September 5, 1983, page 20, featured a report on various kinds of violence in America. The report stated:

> One thing is certain: The number of reported cases of child abuse in the U.S. is rising sharply. In 1976 the American Humane Association found that 413,000 cases of child abuse had been reported to state and local authorities that year. By 1981 the count had doubled to 851,000. Last year (1982) it climbed by 12%.

The same report said that bona fide experts "extrapolating and guessing" cited figures as high as six million in their attempts to determine the number of actual abuse cases, reported and unreported, there might be.

Some say the increase of reported cases might be largely due both to the increased alertness of authorities to cases of violence and the willingness of more people to talk about abuse. We personally believe it is not only the number of reported cases that is on the increase, but also the actual number of abusers, though we cannot provide statistics to support our opinion.

It is our observation that stress factors in our society are becoming more powerfully oppressive. Among these factors are:

—economic anxiety, due often to inadequate household income;

—single parents attempting to raise children without the presence of supportive adults to share responsibilities;

—breakdown of real corporate relationship even in families who remain under the same roof;

—disintegration of understanding concerning:
> sanctity of marriage
> holiness of sex
> nurturing quality of affection
> blessings of self-sacrifice
> art of forgiveness.

—ignorance of the operation of the laws of God as principles which govern the running of the universe. Energies spent in opposition to the flow of life spelling inevitable exhaustion, to say nothing of the reaping of seeds sown;

—absence of relationship with God as loving Father as source and sustainer of life through Christ Jesus and the Holy Spirit.

Pressures to succeed, to "have it all together," have increased simultaneously with the rejection and loss of those gifts the Lord designed for our strength, refreshment, protection and balance. As strain becomes unbearable and frustration levels uncontrollable, anger, guilt and perverted cries for help are projected as abuse onto children who are close at hand and defenseless.

Studies show that battered children grow up predisposed to batter their own offspring. (See the chapter on bitter roots in our book *The Transformation of the Inner Man*). Sexually abused boys often become pedophiles and rapists, while sexually victimized girls are likely to become battered wives. *Time* magazine's report says it is typical that the physical and emotional humiliation inflicted by an out-of-control parent is then recycled as abuse on the children's children. Studies of prison populations show that ninety percent of all inmates claim to have been abused as children. Most violent criminals were raised in violent homes.

Our own experience in counseling, confirmed by friends who have been foster parents to many abused children over the years, is that girls who have been sexually abused by fathers, stepfathers, other male relatives or friends they trusted, respond usually in two extremes: they either become very promiscuous, or they shut down their sexuality totally. Some of the reasons they behave promiscuously are:

— a sense that much of their glory, dignity, and worth is gone, so why not blow it?!
— a desire to punish, to turn the men on and then leave them;
— a desire to prove that men are nasty and no good;
— sex has become identified with love and attention; they will endure the sex to receive the affection they hunger for.

The latter reason manifests itself the most frequently. In fact, the lack of a father's wholesome nurturing affection is often that which sets the stage for sexual abuse. A girl's need for love sends out signals which are misread. A man, confused about his own masculinity and unaware of his God-given role as protector, "turns on" when he catches the "I need to be loved" signals, and then "shorts out" to set a fire of abuse that burns and destroys.

Sexual abuse, we believe, is the most damaging of all abuse. That is because the body was built to be a temple of the Holy Spirit (1 Cor. 6:18-20), to be shared with a mate in sanctification and honor, not in lust (1 Thess. 4:3-6). As we are joined to one another in sexual embrace, it is never a physical union only; it involves our whole person. It is impossible to touch body only, because it is the spirit living in every cell which gives life to the body (James 2:26). In the marriage relationship, we are designed to become one flesh in blessedness as God ordained (Gen. 2:24). To come together in any other way is defilement (Heb. 13:4). Woman is described as a deep well of refreshment for her man in Proverbs 5:15-19. A man who drinks from a well which is not his not only violates and uses the woman, he defrauds the brother who is to become her future husband (1 Thess. 4:3-6). Wholesome sexual relationship in the sanctity of marriage strengthens personal identification in the sense of being chosen and cherished, belonging and resting where God has called us to be. Sexual abuse confuses identity, plants fear of being chosen, offers no promise of being cherished, and makes a girl wonder how God could allow such a horrible thing to happen.

Time magazine reported:

> The majority of parents who batter their helpless children or molest them sexually or simply deprive them of sustenance do not know—or are not able to admit—that they need help. If somehow accused of maltreatment, they deny it. The few who do want aid frequently do not know where to find it. Far too often those who are asked to help do not know how to provide it. Even the experts disagree on how best to treat the offenders. Less is known, and less is done, about helping the victims. (op. cit., page 20)

God is revealing to the Church the way of healing. He is purging our hearts and calling us to be a shelter and a refuge and protection from the storm and rain (Isa. 4).

> The Spirit Himself bears witness with our spirit that we are children of God (Rom. 8:16).
>
> ... it is not the will of your Father who is in heaven that one of these little ones perish (Matt. 18:14).
>
> ... whoever causes one of these little ones who believe in Me to stumble, it is better for him that a heavy millstone be hung around his neck, and that he be drowned in the depth of the sea (Matt. 18:6).
>
> See that you do not despise one of these little ones, for I say to you, that their angels in heaven continually behold the face of My Father who is in heaven (Matt. 18:10).

> Like a shepherd He will tend His flock, In His arm
> He will gather the lambs, And carry them in His
> bosom; He will gently lead the nursing ewes (Isa.
> 40:11).

> Whoever receives one chid like this in My name
> receives Me; and whoever receives Me does not receive
> Me, but Him who sent Me (Mark 9:37).

It is clear that the Lord is intensely concerned for the sake of His children. How then do we minister to the lost and abused and wounded lambs in the Name of Jesus?

By Repentance on Behalf of Those Who Are Abusers

We may never have thrown a child against a wall to stop his crying, nor held his hand over the burner on a hot stove to teach him a lesson, nor have violated anyone sexually. But we have all participated to some degree in feelings of anger, impatience, resentment, jealousy, envy and lust. We have the same capacity to sin as anyone else, and the old adage applies, "There, but for the grace of God, go I."

Non-Christians are not the only ones guilty of child abuse. Many children who have to be placed in foster homes come from Christian families where parents have been caught in a performance-oriented religious spirit, interpreting the faith legalistically, and trying too hard. When the children rebelled, their parents' image of themselves as good parents was threatened. In a frantic attempt to control a situation that seemed to be getting out of hand, they turned from discipline to abusive punishment. In some cases behavior of children triggered into hidden areas in the parents they could not stand to have revealed, attributes they hated in themselves as children, for instance, but never forgave. They then projected their angers and frustrations toward self onto their children, punishing their own sin there. Many times we have been called to counsel fathers who call themselves born-again Christians who nevertheless have regularly sexually abused their daughters.

In 1 Corinthians 12:26, 27 we read, "You are Christ's body, and individually members of it. . . . If one member suffers, all the members suffer with it. . . ." We pray then, not only that "they" be forgiven, but that "we" be forgiven, because "we" are a part of "them." We also need to repent of our sins of omission in not being sensitive soon enough to the stressful condition of others which continued and compounded to the point of violence.

Repenting as one with other members in the body does not do away with any individual's need to repent of his own sins. But it certainly removes the "pointing of the finger, and speaking wickedness" (Isa. 58:9) from our own hearts so we may be more free to minister in power to be a "repairer of the breach" (Isa. 58:12).

When the Lord indicates that it is appropriate, we find it effective to express our repentance verbally in the presence of the one who is wounded. If *the* parents of an abused child have been unable to ask forgiveness, it is some comfort for the child to hear those words expressed sincerely by *a* parent. Abusive parents may experience intense guilt, pain and horror for what they have inflicted, so much so that they may enter into delusion, feeling that someone else has done what they have actually done. But they will not be able to come to real repentance, meaning change, until their own woundedness has been healed. Until parents have dealt with their problem of abuse and demonstrated that healing has been accomplished, separation from their children is necessary, however hurtful.

By Calling Our Own Attitudes of Condemnation to Death

We are horrified when we encounter the effects of violence, especially when it has been done to children. Our natural response is to rise up in righteous anger to see to it that the guilty ones receive what they deserve! We need then to remember that those who abuse were once abused, or were in some other fashion seriously wounded. They must be held accountable to the laws of our land as surely as they will be by the law of God, "So then each one of us shall give account of himself to God" (Rom. 14:12). But the attitude of our calling one another to account must be tempered by compassion and mercy.

> And so, as those who have been chosen of God, holy and beloved, put on a heart of compassion, kindness, humility, gentleness and patience; bearing with one another, and forgiving each other, whoever has a complaint against any one; just as the Lord forgave you, so also should you (Col. 3:12, 13).

Forgiveness does not mean that we say to the guilty one, "What you did was all right." It does *not* mean that we should make excuses for the offender nor that we should deal softly with him. It does mean that insofar as it is possible we should have the mind of Christ. At the same time as we may be called morally and legally to be part of determining and executing judgment against an offender, we must also grieve for him in love even as our Lord does. What we do in relation to him must be for his good because we care about him. If our hearts are not free from hatred and condemnation, we will be unable to identify with the abuser, who needs healing ministry as desperately as the abused. And we will communicate a destructive attitude and compound the negative emotions in the one who has been abused, blocking his healing.

By Ministering to The Abuser

The causal roots of his behavior must be found and healed. He must sincerely and completely forgive those who wounded him. As he repents of the violence he himself has committed, he needs assurance of forgiveness, and the grace of the Lord to enable him to forgive himself. Beyond that he will need the supportive love of friends until he is restored in the eyes of the family and to those segments of society who know about his sin.

By Leading the Wounded Party to Forgiveness

The Bible states some clear principles concerning forgiveness:

> For if you forgive men for their transgressions, your heavenly Father will also forgive you. But if you do not forgive men, then your Father will not forgive your transgressions (Matt. 6:14, 15).

That is for the simple reason, as we read in Galatians 6:7, "Do not be deceived, God is not mocked; for whatever a man sows, this he will also reap." If we insist on sowing unforgiveness, we will inevitably reap unforgiveness.

While we want at some point to communicate to the one to whom we minister what the laws of God are, we must be careful not to use the Word as a weapon against one whose head and heart are already bloodied. It is very difficult for one who has been deeply wounded by abuse to understand that forgiveness *must* be given. It seems that the abuser deserves to be punished. In the victim's helplessness, his hate, anger and resentment may have seemed to be his only means of retaliation. An effective way to begin, then, is first to empathize, then to explain that anger, hate and resentment held in our hearts work inside us like a poisonous substance. If allowed to remain, they sicken not only our hearts, minds and spirits, but affect our physical health as well because of the tension they create. "When I kept silent about my sin, my body wasted away Through my groaning all day long" (Ps. 32:3). We thereby lose peace, joy, and the ability to expect and receive kindness from those who are prepared to give it, because hate is like a greedy cancer which destroys healthy body cells. If hate is allowed to remain and grow, it will someday be out of control, and we will find ourselves hurting someone else in the same way we were hurt. At this point it is often possible to begin to talk somewhat about how his abuser would not have done what he did had he not been wounded himself. If the counselee can make an identification with the woundedness of his abuser, some basis for compassion may be laid, which more eaisly allows forgiveness to occur.

God will deal with those who sin against us. "Never take your own revenge, beloved, but leave room for the wrath of God, for it is written, 'Vengeance is Mine, I will repay, says the Lord' " (Rom. 12:19). Our call is simply, "Be kind to one another, tender-hearted, forgiving each other, just as God in Christ also has forgiven you" (Eph. 4:32).

Forgiveness is not easy. It is not something we can accomplish by an act of our will. But we *can choose* by an act of our will to forgive. We can choose to be made willing. We probably will need to make that choice again and again; in the process the Lord himself will cause it to become real in our hearts because we are no longer willfully hanging on to the "right" to hate.

Children are often amazingly willing to forgive because their hearts yearn so powerfully for reconcilation with their parents. The wounded child in the heart of an adult finds it more difficult. He has practiced his feelings for so long a time. Or he has suppressed them, covering them over with a facade of forgiveness. The telling point may come when the counselor says, "Imagine, now, that you are a little child, and your parents who abused you are standing right here. Can you tell them you forgive them?" In our experience adults will often break into sobs as their real feelings come rushing to the surface. And sometimes they try to say, "I forgive," and choke on the words.

By Pronouncing Absolution (Assurance of Forgiveness) to the One Who Was Abused

Many people resist the idea that the wounded one needs forgiveness for anything. They see him/her as an innocent victim and want only to give comfort. But the victim, no matter how much comfort may be given, may still retain *feelings* of guilt until guilt, real and/or imagined has been addressed in prayer, "On the basis of the Word of God, you are forgiven . . . I forgive you in the Name of the Lord Jesus Christ." It is good to quote such passages as

In Him we have redemption through His blood, the forgiveness of our trespasses, according to the riches of His grace, which He lavished upon us (Eph. 1:7, 8a).

If we confess our sins, He is faithful and righteous to forgive us our sins and to cleanse us from all unrighteousness (1 John 1:9).

As far as the east is from the west, So far has He removed our transgressions from us (Ps. 103:12).

Why the feelings of guilt? First of all, there is real guilt in terms of anger, hate, loathing, wanting to kill, perhaps even wanting to die. Second, there is guilt which proceeds from confusion. A girl who has been sexually abused by a family member or friend knows she has done something to attract attention. But she was not looking for the kind of attention she received. She fears that there is something wrong with her that such a terrible thing was done by someone she admired and trusted.

Every girl needs to develop a sure and wholesome sense that she is beautiful, loveable, and a treasure. She learns to rest in the loveliness she was created to be as she sees the sparkle in her father's eye, as he compliments and affirms her, and as he expresses affection for her. The confidence she develops in relation to her father enables her to meet her husband and nurture him in warm relaxed freedom, knowing she is a blessing to him. This happens only if her father responds to her as admirer and *protector*, if he *shields* the beauty he sees developing and unfolding in her, if his affection is *clean*, and his attention *trustworthy*. But if a girl reaches out in a normal healthy way for appreciation and fatherly affection, and her father (or indeed any other male relative) violates the God-given trust he was assigned to protect her, she is horribly betrayed. She feels guilty for reaching out, for needing, for wanting to be thought pretty. She may unconsciously make an inner vow not to be pretty if beauty attracts nastiness. She may later neglect herself or develop a severe problem with obesity. She may make a deep inner vow never to allow herself to get into a situation of vulnerability where anything could possibly go out of control and become destructive and dirty. Later, when she marries, she may want desperately to embrace her husband fully, but then find built-in shut-off mechanisms operating the moment he begins to approach her.

We Need to Break the Power of Inner Vows by the Authority of the Lord Jesus Christ, and Loose Her to Be Fully Committed to Her Husband.

This breaking is accomplished by a simple word of prayer, but the one who was so bound by woundedness and fear will have to walk it out. By prayer for balm to heal the wounds, love to dissipate fear, and strength to fortify her spirit, she is equipped to exercise a discipline of choosing to risk, to open her heart, to trust, and to give herself.

Her spirit needs to be loosed from the one who violated her, since, as we have said, there is no physical touch without involvement of one's personal spirit which breathes in and through the physical body, giving it life. We simply picture the sword of truth in the hand of the Lord Jesus, cleaving between her and her abuser, and we direct her spirit to forget whatever degree of union was made. She may not forget the incident, but her memory of it will be without a hurtful shudder or a feeling of uncleanness.

If the sexual abuse was perpetrated by her father or stepfather, another feeling of guilt may have to come to the cross. Though the girl may clearly have been a victim, though she may have been terrorized by threats of what might happen to her should she tell anyone what was happening to her, she may still feel guilty that she had been in a position which rightfully belonged to her mother. Nothing short of expressed forgiveness will lift that cloud from her and reconcile her to her mother. If her mother was aware of the abuse, and did not act to stop it, the girl will almost certainly feel doubly betrayed and abandoned.

A number of other aspects of wounding need to be ministered to in prayer before the one who has been sexually violated is healed.

The Need for Cleansing

She feels unclean. We therefore pray with vivid imagery, seeing volumes of living water washing over, in and through her till she is "squeaky clean." Then we pray thanking the Lord that He has made her new. We may quote the Scripture, "What God has cleansed, no longer consider unholy" (Acts 11:9). We use the water image as a symbol of cleansing rather than the "blood of the Lamb" simply because it is difficult for a little child to think of being cleansed by being covered with blood. Later we might talk about what it means to be covered with the blood of Jesus, but little ones relate more easily to soap and water. Jesus is himself the water of life.

Prayer for the Sense of Isolation

Sexually abused children tend to feel that they are the only ones this terrible unspeakable thing has happened to, and if anyone knew, they wouldn't be accepted. The fact of your knowing, accepting them, and valuing them is the beginning of restoration, but it is good to pray also that the walls of isolation which they have built to hide their shame be melted down, and that they be set free to come forth in the light and glory of the Lord.

Though I have used as my example the girl who is abused, the same principles of healing may be applied to boys. Consider the case of a young man we shall call Phil. At the age of four he went to spend the afternoon at a farm belonging to some family friends. There were a number of older boys there that day, and they would not allow him to take part in their fun and games. He was angry. Late in the afternoon the boys ran off beyond a fence into a grove of trees after telling him he was absolutely not invited to go along. He followed them there nevertheless and was horrified to see them circled around two who were engaged in homosexual activity. Phil tried to hide, but the boys saw him and chased him, finally knocking him down. One grabbed him in the groin and violently squeezed, causing a great deal of pain, and promised to cut off his penis if he ever told what he had seen. Then they chased him home shouting taunts about what a cute little "girl" he was.

In the days that followed, he seemed withdrawn, and on two occasions strangely concerned with his male parts. But when his mother questioned him he stoutly denied that anything was wrong. The entire memory was then stuffed into forgetfulness.

As he grew up, he partially suppressed his masculinity. After struggling with some fear that he might have homosexual tendencies, though he never allowed himself to act them out, he fought his way clear of effeminate traits that had brought wounding ridicule during his teens, and embraced his own masculinity fully. At this point of choosing to be the man God created him to be, the Holy Spirit caused the memory of the four-year-old to come to consciousness so he could deal with several delusory burdens which had held him in bondage. The first demonstrates how small children can accept tremendous burdens of guilt and apply them wrongly; Phil felt guilt for following the older boys after they had forbidden him to do so. The guilt became twisted, convincing him that he had somehow caused the perverted act he had witnessed. The second demonstrates the power of fear over a child. He believed they really would cut off his masculinity. Therefore he would hide it so they couldn't find it. And third, he saw that suppression of his masculinity was mainly derived from his desire to reject masculinity, if being like them was what it was to be male.

How was the suppressed memory revealed? Two people who were ministering to Phil were given a mental picture of him standing by a white picket fence near a weeping willow, looking very perplexed. They shared that, and the door to memory was unlocked. As the memory returned, they were able to pray for the frightened, guilt-laden little boy, and the weight that had borne him down for years was lifted. Not only that, but a mystery which had been heavy on the family was made light. Phil's father had never been able to understand why his example and his love had not been enough to bring his son to life and balance. The agony of unanswered questions was ended by the operation of the "gift of knowledge," one of the nine gifts of the Holy Spirit.

> Pursue love, yet desire earnestly spiritual gifts . . . (1 Cor. 14:1a).

> But earnestly desire the greater gifts. And I show you a still more excellent way (1 Cor. 12:31).

SECTION II
Sicknesses and Sinful Conditions
of the Spirit

Chapter Five

The Slumbering Spirit

His watchmen are blind, All of them know nothing. All of them are dumb dogs unable to bark, Dreamers lying down, *who love to slumber* (Isa. 56:10).

... God gave them a spirit of *stupor*, Eyes to see not and ears to hear not, Down to this very day (Rom. 11:8).

And this do, knowing the time, that it is already the hour for you to awaken from *sleep;* for now salvation is nearer to us than when we believed (Rom. 13:11).

Awake, awake, Clothe yourself in your strength, O Zion; Clothe yourself in your beautiful garments (Isa. 52:1, 2).

Therefore, be on the alert—for you do not know when the master of the house is coming ... lest he come suddenly and find you *asleep* (Mark 13:35, 36).

You, brethren, are not in darkness, that the day should overtake you like a thief; for you are all sons of light and sons of day. We are not of night nor of darkness; so then let us *not sleep* as others do, but let us be alert and sober (1 Thess. 5:4-6).

Behold, I am coming like a thief. Blessed is the one who *stays awake* and keeps his garments, lest he walk about naked and men see his shame (Rev. 16:15).

About five years ago Paula and I were counseling a number of Spirit-filled people who, no matter how much help they received, remained incapable of walking straight in the Lord. One was a young man who loved the Lord, had been born anew and filled with the Spirit, attended church regularly, loved his wife and children, but seemed unable to discipline himself to pay his bills. When bill collectors sent overdue notices, he was furious at them for bothering him! At the same time he kept falling into adultery, with no apparent conscience about either the adulteries or the overdue bills. He seemed to spend life caught in the temptations and gratifications of the moment, unable to understand how his actions robbed and hurt others. He learned no lessons from past hard experiences and had no real awareness that there would come a day of reckoning.

We wore ourselves out discovering and praying about fractures and sinful practices in his nature, but he could not take hold of life and walk uprightly. We kept asking God, "What's missing? Why doesn't he have a functioning conscience?"

Another was a minister who seemed devoted to hurling hard words at his people. No matter how we prayed, he could not understand how his hearers could be hurt by what he said. He related to the plan of salvation, to letter and to law, but not to people's hearts. I would make him aware logically that his sermons were unloving, lacking both humanity and hope, and were genuinely harming his people. But next Sunday he would be at it again. Counseling sessions revealed that though he had gone through the ritual of inviting Jesus into his heart and of being filled with the Holy Spirit, he had never experienced His presence nor heard His voice, nor known Him in any other than an intellectual way. We finally came to the end of our rope with him, crying out to the Lord, "What is missing? Why can't he come to know you personally?"

At the same time, traveling as teachers and counselors across the country, we crossed the tracks of many other Christian leaders. People came to us for ministry, wounded and angry at more than a half a dozen itinerant Spirit-filled teachers of God's Word who had had sexual affairs with relatives and friends of theirs! One traveling miracle-working evangelist had caused a pregnancy, forced the girl to have an abortion, and subsequently denied ever having known her. We ministered to her parents, tried to explain how God can continue to work through fractured, sinful vessels, and attempted to persuade them to forgive both the evangelist and God. But inside ourselves questions were tumbling. "How can this happen, Lord? Why don't these men have a conscience strong enough to keep them out of trouble? They love you and preach a true word; why can't they live it? How can they wound your heart like that? What's the matter? What's missing?" So we said our usual, fervent, intellectual and righteous prayer, *"Help!"* And God answered.

First He said, *John, these people do not have an alert and functioning personal spirit. Their own personal spirit is not awake. They have a slumbering spirit.*

Immediately I wanted to know what that meant. Over several weeks of meditating, searching the hearts and histories of counselees, and seeking the Lord, He laid it out for me.

We are born with an alive and awake personal spirit. But that spirit needs to be met, welcomed, loved and nurtured through warm physical affection. If a baby growing from infanthood into childhood does not receive enough human touch, to that degree his spirit is not kept awake nor drawn forth into full functioning ability. He becomes a slumberer.

It was soon revealed that there are two kinds of slumbering spirits. There are those who never have been drawn forth to life, who early in infancy have fallen asleep and can no longer function. Secondly, there are those who did receive parental and other nurture and so were awake and functioning spiritually, but turned away from worship services, prayer and affection until their spirits fell asleep. In both, the heart has usually hardened as well.

If their spirits were totally inert, such people would of course be physically dead. It is in the areas of relationship to God and man and nature or to their own beings that these sleepers cannot function in their spirits. That means that they come to God mentally and emotionally but never really meet Him. They relate to the forms, to liturgy, doctrine, theology, law, or the plan of salvation, but not to His Person. They can share in emotions, weeping over the lost and about their own sins through remorse, but they are not able to commune with Jesus nor share His sufferings as St. Paul related in Philippians 3:10. They have no ability to empathize with Him or others. They are relegated and confined to the necessity of calculating and estimating with their minds what others think and feel.

One might ask, "What about the Holy Spirit? He is the very giver of life. His task is to make us alive. Why didn't such people come awake when the Holy Spirit came in?" Some did. But when I asked the Lord that question, He answered by telling me to picture a river. *That represents the Holy Spirit*, He said, *truly flowing through a man's life*. Then He said to picture a rock in the middle of the river, unmoved, the water cascading against it and around it. That rock represents the personal spirit of some people, hardened and incapable of participating in the flow of the Spirit's life. The Holy Spirit is there, flowing through the man's mind and heart, emotions and body, so he can preach brilliantly, work miracles and say mighty prophecies. But the man's own spirit cannot participate. It lies asleep, encased and non-functioning. Sadly, if the condition continues, it may demonstrate what Jesus meant when He said,

> Many will say to Me on that day, "Lord, Lord, did we not prophesy in Your name, and in Your name cast out demons, and in Your name perform many miracles?" And then I will declare to them, *"I never knew you; depart from Me, you who practice lawlessness"* (Matt. 7:22, 23).

The word "knew" in "I never knew you" is in Greek the same as the marriage word: Adam "knew" Eve. Jesus is saying, "I never fully *met* you."

The more we thought, the more this revelation made sense, and we could see it clearly in our counselees' lives.

But when we proceeded to teach about the slumbering spirit, we were shocked to discover the appalling fact that very few people in the Body of Christ knew what each person's spirit is supposed to do! It had not occurred to many that we have a spirit with specific definable functions. That drove us to seek and find what are the peculiar, distinct capacities and operations of the spirit.

The following section lists nine of the many functions of our personal spirits. We describe here what the spirit was designed by God to do, and by contrast what a slumbering spirit cannot do. What causes a person to fall asleep, and what can be done about it, will be answered later in this chapter.

We have come to see that the condition of having a slumbering spirit is one of the epidemic illnesses of our generation, increasing constantly as nurture dwindles and marriages and homes break apart. Everyone's spirit is asleep to some degree. Some fail to function in all nine areas, some in only one or two. None of us is fully awake, nor fully slumbering.

The first function of our personal spirit is corporate worship.

> But an hour is coming, and now is, when the true worshipers shall worship the Father in *spirit* and truth; for such people the Father seeks to be his worshipers. God is spirit; and those who worship Him must worship in spirit and truth (John 4:23, 24).

Those whose spirits are awake feel the uplifting presence of the Lord in a worship service. They feel His anointing pouring over them. Their spirit is touched and filled anew with His. Such joy and love well up that their soul sings praises to God. They can *abide* in His presence in great "joy inexpressible and full of glory" (1 Pet. 1:8).

Note "soul" and "spirit" and the tense in the first lines of the Magnificat: "And Mary said, 'My *soul exalts* the Lord, And my *spirit has rejoiced* in God my Savior" (Luke 1:46). When God moves upon us, He moves first upon our spirits. Our spirits rejoice in His love. That enables us to praise Him with a full heart, so the soul can then exalt Him. Because the spirit "*has* rejoiced," the soul *can* exalt.

Awakened people not only are carried by Him into worship, they sense and feel the swell of other people's spirits and hearts. They become suffused not only with His love, but in the love of all the fellowship. True worship knits hearts together because spirits are melted into one fire of love.

People who have slumbering spirits have often said to us, "I don't know what they are talking about. I never feel God's presence." Some feel momentary flickers but have no power to abide. They don't know how to bathe their needy spirits in His river, though surely "There is a river whose streams make glad the city of God . . ." (Ps. 46:4). We may ask a person whom we suspect has a slumbering spirit, "When you are in a worship service or a prayer meeting and others are raising their hands and praising God, do you feel His presence or do you just know by faith that He is there?" The answer slumberers invariably give is, "Oh, I just know He is there." One thinks of Jesus' words to Thomas, "Blessed are those who have not seen and yet believe" (John 20:29 RSV). These people do not experience the fullness of worship, and perhaps never have. At least they believe.

The second function of our personal spirit is to enable the person to have satisfying private devotions. Awakened people can enter His presence, bask in His love, and soar. They "mount up with wings like eagles" (Isa. 40:31). Words leap by inspiration off the pages of the Bible, and thoughts and images flow into their minds unbidden, by the gentle power of the Holy Spirit. Slumbering people on the other hand tell us, "I try to have devotions but it always runs dry.

I run out of words. I never feel anything." Sometimes they may decide, "If I can't pray very well, at least I can read the Bible." So they try to establish a discipline, perhaps to follow a lexicon through the Scriptures. But that too becomes a desert. Fairly soon they realize they have read the same sentences several times and not yet caught the meaning, even on the surface. Job 32:8 says that it is the *spirit* in a man which gives him understanding. In awakened people, the Holy Spirit moves through their spirits to cause understanding to spring forth in His Word; meanings and excitements leap off the pages. But for sleepers, reading is mechanical and barren because their spirits cannot respond to the Holy Spirit. If they continue with private devotions, it remains a duty without blessing.

We are accustomed to think that when a person receives the Holy Spirit, he immediately understands the things of the spirit. But there is no magic, only anointing to those who have ears to hear, and eyes to see. In this context, let us read,

> The *unspiritual* man does not receive the gifts of the Spirit of God, for they are folly to him, and he is *not able to understand them because they are spiritually discerned* (1 Cor. 2:14 RSV).

Comprehension is not a matter of brilliance of intellect. We know hundreds of brilliant spiritually asleep men who, like Nicodemus, can't grasp the simplest things of the Spirit, though technically they are filled with the Holy Spirit.

The third function of our personal spirit is to enable us to hear God. Turned-on and tuned-in people have dreams, or visions, or hear the Lord speak directly, as Numbers 12:6-8 says of His prophets. Awakened people may have intuitive hunches (empowered by the Holy Spirit). They receive revelations and thrill to walk hand in hand with God by His direction. Somnolent people say to us, "It's all Greek to me. I guess I have to believe these people who are always saying God keeps telling them things, but it never happens to me.

I never have a dream or see a vision. I guess I just plod along." It is by our spirit that God communes with us. He speaks into the ears of our spirit. These who "just plod along" have deafened ears and blind eyes because their spirit does not function.

The fourth function of our spirit is inspiration. Quickened people find ideas blossoming in their minds. They are creative. They discover new ways to do things. If they write poetry or compose music, it is redolent with the quality of life and blesses those who see and hear. Those in spiritual torpor do not often have fresh insights to share. If they write poetry, it is likely to be doggerel, or so perfectly scanned, metered and rhymed that it has no song; it is just metered, rhymed words.

I was alone in a church in our southland when the violinist who was at that time concertmaster of the local symphony came in to practice a piece he was to perform that night in the service. I didn't see him. Suddenly sounds burst the silence. They were technically perfect. The music was magnificent! But something was missing. It did not take long to sense that his violin was singing but his spirit wasn't singing through it. Later I saw reviews of his performances as a concert soloist across the country. They were all the same. Technically perfect. Marvelous fingerwork. Impeccable interpretation. But no spirit. His music didn't sing. His spirit was not awake; it couldn't sing the composer's songs through the instrument. He had technique without inspiration.

A friend speaks of two kinds of engineers in his office. Some, he says, have new ideas which carry the company forward in the excitement and thrill of the work. But others he calls "drones." They never have an original idea. They copy what others originate. Some are awake. Some sleep.

The fifth function of our personal spirit is to enable us to transcend time. Lest that seem mystical or mysterious, let's illustrate it by example. Two kinds of couples come to our office for marital counseling. The first possess awakened, functioning spirits. They are not confined to the pain of the

112

moment. Their spirits enable them to remember lovely memories of the past and to think of happy times to come. They have roots and hopes. They reach beyond present time to nourishing events of the past and dreams of the future. But the second class are dead to all that. Their spirits cannot project them backward or forward. They are enmeshed and confined to the pains of the moment. Present affliction is all they can think about and they want to flee.

The young man of whom I spoke in the beginning, who did not pay his bills, had this problem. If he wanted something in the moment, he charged it. But there was no way he could project into the future to see that there would be a time when bill collectors would insist on payment. He had no sense whatsoever of unfolding time. When bills arrived, those charges were so much a part of the unrecallable past that to him creditors were nuisances who had no right to bother him, rather than those trying to collect legitimate debts.

Perhaps the readers have wondered, as Paula and I have many times, how parishioners can sit under powerful preaching which warns of judgment coming for sin, who say and seem to mean, "Amen" again and again, and then so quickly and easily forget, and go out to sin as though judgment day had nothing to do with them at all! When I examined this in counseling, I found that these people did truly believe that we will all be held accountable for our deeds (Rom. 14:12, 1 Pet. 4:5). The puzzling thing was, "Why did that not have the force to convince them not to knowingly sin?" They acted as though there would be no record of anything they ever did. When the Lord opened my eyes to see spiritual slumber, I understood. Their minds could understand logically about final judgment, but their spirits could not receive that as anything more than words. It held no reality for them because they could not grasp any real sense of the future. Paula and I now see that no matter how anointed a teaching may be about the end times, to the slumbering spirit it is no more effective than putting a coin in a vending machine only to have it fall through into the coin return slot. We need to remember at this point that we are not speaking in an accusatory manner. We are simply describing the condition and its results. Perhaps if we can truly understand, we will find compassion. These people are simply incapable. It is not a matter of will-power or trying harder. They just don't have that part of their inner machine working to catch the coin when it is inserted!

The sixth function of our personal spirit is one of the three basic ones discussed in the first chapter, to enable us to commune with and communicate with others. Spiritually alert people meet each other through their spirits. We tune in to one another by empathy. Our spirit identifies with the other and feels what he feels. Many of us have had the experience of meeting someone for the first time and feeling like we have known him all our life. With that person we soon discover that we resonate. We hardly have to complete some sentences because the other has identified with us and has already leaped accurately to our meaning. Conversations leapfrog joyfully, quickly. It's fun. We come away refreshed, and we want to be with that one again.

On the other hand, we may have worked with a fellow for years, and have to admit in the end that we don't know him any better than we did the first day! We have just never "clicked." Conversations remained meticulous and guarded because he never seemed able to catch our meanings unless we spelled them out tediously. It was tiring to be around him. We were never able to develop friendship.

I am sure that we have all had the experience of visiting with someone, thinking that person was tracking with us, only to have him say something totally irrelevant, like out of left field somewhere. Perhaps we can see what happened by referring to spiritual slumber. He wasn't able to read our spirit. He was figuring out with his mind what to answer, and when the conversation entered an area he had to "read" to respond to, he couldn't. His mind was unable to track there, so he missed us.

People who have slumbering spirits are reduced to mental games. They never really can meet anyone. Their spirit isn't able to function in that way.

This means a corollary fact relative to so many divorces today. People whose spirits slumber cannot sustain relationships. Living with a slumberer is not only lonely but galling. For me to have sustained my half of our thirty-four years of marriage with Paula (as of January 12, 1985), I needed to be able to read where she is emotionally. I need each day to be able to sense when she wants a hug, or when physical closeness would be jarring to her. I need to stop chattering happily if my spirit senses her sorrow, to ask, "What is it, sweetheart?" Or, not to be silent and withdrawn when her spirit sends signals of needing to share. Often I have become so preoccupied and absent-minded, I've still missed that one more times than I've responded! On the other hand, she needs to be able to sense when my spirit is a thousand miles away, so as not to take my silences as a personal rebuff. She needs to know how to come after me in my spirit and call me to be present to her. The fact that we can do such things is one of the things which makes our marriage a blessing rather than a grind.

In counseling we hear so often how people whose spirits slumber miss each other. Out of their isolated unperceptive mental guesses, they do and say those things which are inappropriate to the other. After a while, that afflicts again and again. Living with a mate who tries to be nice, but cannot relate sensitively to us can become painfully lonely, more excruciating because we know the other was truly making an effort. We can see, as more and more homes break up, that they will produce more and more fractured people whose spirits never have been nurtured to life. More and more people are less and less equipped to make a go of marriage! Such unfortunates are reduced to impersonal, temporary encounters, because they cannot enter and sustain the inner sanctum of holiness between the spirits of a couple. We used to sing, "Take my hand, I'm a stranger in paradise," and little knew the poignance of what we sang! So many people are trying to live and have good marriages and families, but they are so woefully unequipped.

The seventh function of our spirit is to create the glory of marital sexual union. We learn from St. Paul that when a man lies with a woman he becomes "one with her" (1 Cor. 6:16).

> And don't you know that if a man joins himself to a prostitute she becomes a part of him and he becomes a part of her? For God tells us in the Scripture that in His sight the two become one person. But if you give yourself to the Lord, you and Christ are joined together as one person. That is why I say to run from sex sin. No other sin affects the body as this one does. When you sin this sin it is against your own body (1 Cor. 6:16-18 TLB).

Those are not mere poetic words. St. Paul was describing the fact of union. Those who have awakened spirits, and who have been consecrated to one another in a Christian wedding ceremony, can discover in their union a glory especially designed by the Lord for them to enjoy. In true union, the spirits of a couple interflow through their bodies, exhilarating and blessing one another. For this reason the Scripture says, "Adam *knew* Eve . . ." (Gen. 4:1 RSV). In marital sex rightly shared there is an intimate and precious knowing of one another, a cherishing and fulfilling meeting of whole being to whole being. That meeting depends upon the ability of the personal spirit of each to feel the other's presence and interpenetration of spirit.

Some couples have testified that while they were hugging and caressing the other, it seemed as though they could feel their own hands stroking their own chest through the other! Some men have testified to being exhilarated by great swirls of loving energy flowing from their wife's breasts, filling them with exalted love and cherishing for her. For this reason Proverbs 5:19 says, "As a loving hind and a graceful doe, Let her *breasts satisfy* you at all times; Be *exhilarated* always with her love."

Paula and I have been blessed to know, in all of our thirty-four years of marriage, the holiness and refreshment God created marital sex to be. It is my firm belief that if a man discovers the glory of the gift God has given to him in his own wife, which none other can have for him, he is greatly shielded from sexual temptation. The glory of marital sex happens by the fact that the Holy Spirit sings the love song of creation, for example, through my spirit to Paula and through Paula's spirit to mine. Our spirits alone cannot fully enrapture us to and in each other. But God can and does. When His Spirit flows through mine to her and hers to me, we are blessed and fulfilled and caused to love and cherish each other more than words or actions can express. That being a fact (to us because we know and experience it), then by logic alone we know that no sexual union outside of marriage can ever participate in the glory of sexual union! Our God is holy. The Holy Spirit will not flow into nor participate in unholiness. Therefore there absolutely cannot be glory in any union outside the marriage bed! Sex outside of marriage is strictly forbidden (Deut. 5:18, Exod. 20:14). The Holy Spirit will not thrill another's being through the spirit of an adulterer!

It is part of every Christian's protection to know that God's law is absolute. ". . . the advantage of knowledge is that wisdom preserves the lives of its possessors" (Eccles. 7:12b). No matter how lovely in face, figure and character a woman may be who is not one's mate, she positively cannot have or be glory, despite whatever feelings a married man may think he has toward her. Sexual union outside of marriage defiles both and confuses their souls. A wife tells her husband who he is by entering into union with him. Any other woman, however attractive, can only tell him a lie and confuse his identity. For this reason, Scripture says of those who have committed incest (applicable also to any other unlawful union), ". . . they have committed incest, their bloodguiltiness is upon them" (footnote: literally "confusion, a violation of divine order")

117

(Lev. 20:12b). And, he who commits adultery "destroyeth his own soul" (Prov. 6:32 KJV).

To our great sorrow, not everyone believes and adheres to God's laws as absolute. They throw their glory away. To prevent that tragedy, St. Paul wrote:

> For this is the will of God, your sanctification; that is, that you abstain from sexual immorality; that each of you know how to possess his own vessel [make love to his own wife] in sanctification and honor, not in lustful passion, like the Gentiles who do not know God; and that no man transgress and defraud his brother in the matter because the Lord is the avenger in all these things, just as we also told you before and solemnly warned you. For God has not called us for the purpose of impurity, but in sanctification (1 Thess. 4:3-7).

Not many understand and experience the glory even if they believe and have kept themselves only to each other. Couples may be blinded and prevented through simple lack of knowledge that sex can be a blessed meeting. Worse, many cannot enter that glory because their spirits are asleep.

People whose spirits have slumbered throughout their marriage have often expressed to us in counseling lack of interest in sex after a while. When early romantic zest wanes and newness wears off, they may lose sexual desire. For every one man who comes to our office to complain that his wife will not open to him sexually, we hear at least fifty women complain that their husband will not "give to [the] wife her conjugal rights" (1 Cor. 7:3 RSV). Why? Because if women's spirits are asleep, they tend to remain dutiful, and will give themselves, whereas men who have never discovered the glory of their wives commonly think it is a wife's duty to give to her husband but have little or no awareness that a husband has a duty to give to his wife! Trained in a sick culture, men too often think of their own sexual needs as a nasty bother to their wives, who may put up with it, but who would probably be just as happy if their husbands desisted. What a tragedy!

Whether male or female, slumbering spirits miss the glory of marriage. Having missed it, they become vulnerable to whatever person may entice them. All they know is physical titillation and emotional arousal. When someone comes along who seems to promise a little excitement, they fall prey to the attractions of sinful opportunity. Conscience, as we shall see, does not prevent them from committing sin. No memories of glory exist to call out warnings of loss. In the adultery, they may strike sparks to emotional tinder, starting romantic fires long since dead in their relationship with their mate. That kind of illicit union may seem so much better than what they have at home that they become thoroughly confused, thinking themselves alive again, whereas in fact their soul and spirit are dying. They do not know that Proverbs 7:27 says of the adulteress, "Her house is the way to Sheol, Descending to the chambers of death."

I think of a pastor I counseled. He was evangelical and a fundamentalist. But his spirit had never been awakened. He failed to find glory with his wife, not only in the marriage bed but in every other area of married life. The vacuum in his heart was inevitably filled by his secretary. He came to me in fear that the adultery he had already committed would be discovered. I explained how when a husband and wife fail to keep each other alive emotionally, the vacuum that causes can be filled by a love which is not real mate love but only confusion. After we prayed for forgiveness, I told him he not only had to break it off completely with the secretary, he could never be around her again in any kind of relationship. There was too much danger that he would fall again into sin. His response was, "Oh, I can't, John. This woman is life to me! I can't live without her!"

I implored him, "That's delusion, my friend! She is death to you! You can't live *because* of her!"

"But I've tried it, John," he argued. "I sink into emotional death without her. I can't let her go."

I persisted, "Your own wife was given to you to keep you

119

alive emotionally. You have to find your life with her. It is there that your spirit really wants to find life. This woman is only a poor substitute."

He insisted, "This woman is in my guts, John."

I insisted, "The love you have with her is not real. You will lose your family, your church, your ministry—"

He went around and around. Neither I nor the Lord won. He would not break free. He lost his church. For years his wife tried to stay with him, and finally left him. Since then he has been a broken man, wandering around looking for a place to serve. Truly "the way of transgressors is hard" (Prov. 13:15b KJV).

Were this case isolated, we could grieve less. Unfortunately we have ministered to literally hundreds of such cases. In 1983 we came across more instances of pastors in adultery than in all our previous thirty years of ministry!

The most common root we see behind such adulteries among Christians is the condition of the slumbering spirit. When we do not discover the glory of what God intended marriage to be, we also never know why God gave the law. Some even think God unfair, as though He does not want mankind to enjoy life. In fact God wants the highest and best joys in life for us and has designed the marriage bed as one of His highest fulfillments of that purpose. The law is to protect. But spiritually slumbering people are like people behind high wooden fences who have no awareness of what wonderful life is happening beyond the fence.

The eighth function of our personal spirit is to protect us from disease and to grant us buoyancy to throw it off quickly when we do have an illness. "The spirit of a man can endure his sickness, But a broken spirit who can bear?" (Prov. 18:14). "A joyful heart is good medicine, But a broken spirit dries up the bones" (Prov. 17:22). We have all known people who are seldom ill, or who, if ill, bear it well. Disease has no power over the emotions of such people. They soon throw it off, or if beset by a crippling or terminal condition, they remain vibrant and glowing. Their spirit sustains and overcomes. They never remain *under* the circumstances."

They bounce. On the other hand, we have all grieved for and been irritated at people who go down *under* every illness or setback. Flu or colds which hit the community and knock others down for a day or two last weeks with them. Crippling accidents or terminal illnesses destroy them. They wilt. Their trouble becomes the dominating center of their life, and everyone else's around them! Without the vibrancy of a functioning spirit, they have no see-through ability, no staying power, no stamina, no perseverance, no lasting joy.

The ninth function of our spirit is a good conscience which works *before* the event to keep us out of trouble, not merely afterwards to make us aware of sin. Conscience works by the ability of our personal spirit to empathize with others so that we are informed about their feelings, especially what may wound them. For example, if I see a brother my size wearing a jacket I like, what keeps me from stealing that jacket if he leaves it and no one is watching? The Ten Commandments tell me not to steal (Deut. 5:19), but the commandments are not designed so much to keep me from sinning as to convict me.

> Now we know that whatever the Law says, it speaks to those who are under the Law, that every mouth may be closed, and all the world may become accountable to God; because by the works of the Law no flesh will be justified in His sight; for through the Law comes the knowledge of sin (Rom. 3:19, 20).

At no time in Israel's history or ours has knowledge of the law alone been able to keep men from sinning. Israel knew, and failed. So do we all, if law is all we have.

Fear does not deter; people fall to adultery despite fear of discovery.

Love of the Lord should prevent sin, but servants on fire with love for Him sin anyway.

What keeps me from stealing my brother's jacket is that my spirit informs me how much I would grieve the Holy Spirit (Eph. 4:30), and pains me in advance by causing me to know my brother's hurt.

There are two kinds of conscience. Slumberers may well possess an active conscience which causes remorse *after* they sin. It operates by the law. It works well through the mind, by recall and emotions. But it seldom if ever works powerfully enough *before* the event to prevent it. It reminds us that *we* have failed the Lord and ourselves, but seldom if ever makes us aware *of our brother's hurt.* It makes us aware only that we failed to be what we set out to be. It seldom moves us to real repentance. Repentance happens when we are hurt for the sake of the Lord and others. Remorse remains self-centered and is seen in terms of our own failure to perform. Real repentance is a result of the gift of love. If I love someone, and my spirit is awake and alert, it checks me *before* I do a potentially harmful deed. Love constrains me because I cannot stand to hurt the one I love. If the brother is a stranger to me, the Lord in me loves him, and sends warning signals through my spirit not to do what might grieve the Lord and him.

If a man's spirit is in a stupor, it cannot warn him. It is as though that man wears blinders. If possible hurt to others begins to rise to consciousness, greed and desire block that out. But an awakened spirit sings out too loudly to be silenced without considerable effort. Perhaps it is for this reason 1 John 3:6 says, "No one who abides in Him sins; no one who sins has seen Him or knows Him." Really knowing Jesus in our spirit awakens such love in us for all others that we cannot bear to cause injury to another. If a man does sin, it is because in that area he does not actually in his spirit know and abide in Jesus.

"No one who is born of God practices sin, because His seed abides in him; and he cannot sin, because he is born of God" (1 John 3:9). Christians have long puzzled over that Scripture, knowing that Christians do occasionally sin. Perhaps understanding slumbering spirits may help to explain the mystery. When we are converted we are positionally born anew. But what we are seeing here is that in some areas of the inner being, that new birth has not yet been effective. We haven't yet worked out that salvation "with fear and trembling" (Phil. 2:12). Though St. John did not qualify being born of God by speaking of differing areas inside of us, we do see by our years of experience in counseling that every aspect in which a person's spirit slumbers is actually an area in which his spirit has not yet received the good news and the new birth. In those parts of his being, though positionally he is born anew once for all, in experience he is not, and thus he can and does sin, because his conscience does not function in certain areas. On the other hand, in all aspects of which a person's spirit is truly born anew and alive, indeed he cannot consciously choose to sin. His spirit will not let him. He makes plenty of blunders, and leaves undone what ought to be done, and still is plagued by wrong thoughts and feelings, but, in the sense of willful wrong choosing, he cannot sin. His awakened spirit has too powerful a tool through his conscience to suffer him to fall. Love overcomes him through his spirit, and will not let him choose to wound the Lord or other people.

However, if a man falls away from the discipline of the Way—worship, study of the Word, self-sacrificial giving to others, affection, etc.—his spirit can fall asleep. Conscience then fails. Most of the promises of God are conditional, dependent on our staying in a position to receive them.

Perhaps we can begin to see the dreadfully sick condition of mankind. As more and more homes have broken, increasingly fewer people possess fully awakened functioning spirits. Conscience therefore fails, and all manner of ills increase, among them adulteries, crimes, divorce rates, Christians speaking honor with their lips while their lives are far from His Way. Truly, when a nation has turned from God "their foolish heart was darkened" (Rom. 1:21b) and "God gave them over in the lusts of their hearts to impurity" (Rom. 1:24). A people whose spirits cannot function devolve generation by generation to more inhumane, bestial behavior.

As Paula and I began to see, and grieve more and more, we cried out to the Lord the second question, "Why are people's spirits slumbering?" The Lord gave us the second answer: *These people have never yet become human beings.*

Let us immediately make one disclaimer: we are not talking about humanism. Satan tries to copy all the glories of God. Humanism is Satan's copy of what God is accomplishing in mankind. Humanism is mankind, urged on by Hell, attempting to set itself at the center of the universe, trying by flesh (and by hidden powers of darkness) to become all that it thinks it should be. In short, humanism is nothing more nor less than the first sin all over again—man trying to be good without God. Humanism is an attempt to raise men to mankind's highest potential. In itself this is a lofty ideal, but by flesh without God, it is nothing but sin and idolatry.

We must however guard against letting our reaction against error turn us away from what is truth. Why should Satan try so hard through humanism to copy God's works unless something very important and right exists about being human? Something most important does exist. What is all of creation and Jesus' death and resurrection for? What is God's ultimate purpose? God is raising sons and daughters with whom to have fellowship (1 John 1:1-4)! God already had plenty of angels—beings without human bodies. The one new and abiding element that shall remain when all of creation is destroyed is the redeemed and glorified human body. Think on it. Heaven and earth will pass away. When fire has burned up and dissolved everything else in all creation (2 Pet. 3:10), only two things that were part of that creation will remain. One, His words, "Heaven and earth will pass away, but My words shall not pass away" (Matt. 24:35). Two, His own redeemed people. His words came from Heaven (John 14:10) and passed through Him to us. They were not born of earth but of Heaven. In this sense, like the angels, they were not part of this creation.

That leaves us, the only residue, born in but outlasting creation! Note the crucial factor. None of the material of this creation will abide—all matter will be burned up and destroyed—except the human redeemed and resurrected body! Elijah and Jesus took the earth of their human bodies into Heaven forever! It may be argued that our redeemed and resurrected bodies will be made of the new Heaven and earth, and that may be. Nevertheless, in at least Elijah and Jesus, there in Heaven forever is that bit of earth, transformed and glorious, but earth nonetheless. All of this is one way to say that it is humanity, not discarnate spirits, whom God is raising up as the new order of creation, the end of the entire project of creation.

So I asked Him what He meant by "human beings." As a man trained in anthropology, sociology and psychology, I know those definitions of homo sapiens. Here is the Christian one the Lord gave to me: *A human being is a person who has an alive and functioning spirit by which he empathizes with others, and cherishes what is in others more than his own life or interests.*

> Greater love has no one than this, that one lay down his life for his friends (John 15:13).

> . . . do not merely look out for your own personal interests, but also for the interests of others (Phil. 2:4).

By years of training and counseling experience, I knew what He meant by "These people have never yet become human beings." He was saying that such people are inhuman, "inhumane," because in their upbringing as children they did not receive that most essential nurture which was designed to make them human. *God placed us in families, knowing the risk, because only there, from fathers and mothers, brothers and sisters, relatives and friends, could we receive the nurture which alone could bring our spirit to fullness of life and function.* It is affectionate gentle touch which interpenetrates another through the physical body. It is rocking, cradling, nuzzling and fondling which awaken, draw forth and train each spirit to function socially. The love of God for us is as Spirit to spirit. That alone is not enough to make us human, wonderful as it is. If it were, why should He send us to earth at all?

The very purpose of our being here on earth is that right here, in the body, we may be loved to life in a way Heaven could not provide. God designed that we should find His love person to person, body to body, and so be drawn forth and trained to become human.

The human animal is the only species in all creation which will not become as its own kind if not raised by its own kind. Raise a horse among cattle and it will still run and whinny like a horse, not like a cow. If a cat is raised by dogs (as our loving dog raised our kitten when its mother died), the cat will not become confused and try to bark or lift his leg to urinate. It will meow and act in every way like a cat. But let a human baby lose its mother and be raised by wolves, as has happened in history, and the human will in most effects act like a wolf, running on all fours and baying at the moon. We do not become human by instinct, as other animals become what they are no matter where raised. Other animals, like dogs, may be helpless in the woods if raised in the city, but if they survive long enough, they regain by instinct what they were. But the human being does not. He is necessarily tribal. He is dependent on his parents and society longer than any other species in all of creation. The human animal must be talked to to talk, walked to walk, loved to love. We are culturally dependent.

We want to make it very clear that if our parents fail to give nurture, we are set into patterns of sin by our sinful responses. We can never be said to be unresponsible. We will be held accountable for our responses to those people who wounded us, but we are not accountable for the wounds themselves. The remedy for sinful response is forgiveness. The remedy for wounds is healing. If parents fail to provide affection, wounding happens, regardless of the response. Desperately needed faculties are crippled and dormant. That calls for healing with resurrection life in it.

No nurture is so vitally important to the human spirit as affection. Immediately after birth, we need holding and cuddling. A baby's spirit reaches out to nestle through that tiny body into the one who holds. That nurture is as necessary as food and drink. Without food and drink the body dies. Without touch the human spirit starves. With touch the spirit expands, learns who and what it is, relishes life, cherishes others, and becomes strong. Without touch, the spirit recoils from cold walls or wooden bars and finds no place to take hold of life. It shrivels and withdraws inside and closes its eyes.

God designed that the nurture we need should come through the primary people who called us to life, our father and mother. Both are essential to full, balanced nurture. Mothers have carried us inside themselves and fed us on their own breasts (hopefully). Fathers need to be actively present for the sake of their children during this time as well. From mothers we receive a special feminine quality of warmth, softness and sensitivity without which we would be bulls in china shops. But it is fathers who are primary in building structure and strength of character through which that warmth and sensitivity of spirit may flow.* He is the one who is designed to call the spirit forth with courage and vision to be, and the mother is to balance, support and encourage that process. Note: we do not say that the mother supplies *all* of the warmth and sensitivity and the father *all* of the structure and strength. We are speaking of *primary* giftings and responsibilities, which, when exercised according to the beautiful and perfect plan of God, are designed to equip and empower us to grow into the most of what we were created to be.

Scripture again and again addresses both fathers and mothers, but consistently gives fathers primary responsibility for raising children.

> And, ye fathers, provoke not your children to wrath: but bring them up in the nurture and admonition of the Lord (Eph. 6:4 KJV).

---

* We strongly recommend that the reader study the "Introduction" to *Crisis in Masculinity*, by Leanne Payne, for corroboration of these statements.

The NAS and RSV both say, "in the discipline and instruction of the Lord." We prefer the word "nurture." Note, the Word does not say "mothers . . . bring them up . . ." Nor does it say, "Parents . . ." The command is given specifically to fathers. Perhaps because mothers would have been there anyway, and it is fathers who have to be reminded! More likely because it is fathers who are primary in the raising of children.

> Behold, I am going to send you Elijah the prophet before the coming of the great and terrible day of the Lord. And he will restore the hearts of the fathers to their children, and the hearts of the children to their fathers, lest I come and smite the land with a curse (Mal. 4:5, 6).

Note again, the Lord addressed fathers. If fathers and children are not reconciled to each other, the earth will be smitten with a curse! But the promise is positive. He does not say all fathers will be turned to all their children, but enough, apparently, that the earth will not be fully smitten with a curse.

We founded Elijah House, and have taught across the country, and write books because we know beyond a shadow of doubt the crucial importance of fathers. Fathers must be awakened to know who they are to their children. Christians, and the world, must hear and respond to the many Elijah messengers who call fathers to their children or the curse will come, and the promise of Malachi will remain for a later generation with ears to hear.

> Hear, O Israel! The Lord is our God, the Lord is one! And you shall love the Lord your God with all your heart and with all your soul and with all your might. And these words, which I am commanding you today, shall be on your heart; and *you shall teach them diligently to your sons* and shall talk of them when you sit in your house and when you walk by the way and when you lie down and when you rise up (Deut. 6:4-7).

Notice how often the Lord says the same thing, concerning both fathers and mothers, but especially to fathers, since in each case He lists fathers first, and sometimes mentions fathers only.

> Hear, my *son*, your *father's* instruction, And do not forsake your *mother's* teaching; Indeed they are a graceful wreath to your head, And ornaments about your neck (Prov. 1:8, 9).

> My *son*, if you will receive my sayings, And treasure my commandments within you, Make your ear attentive to wisdom, Incline your heart to understanding . . . Then you will discern the fear of the Lord (Prov. 2:1, 2, 5).

Note how often the teaching of parents, especially of fathers, is directly related to "life."

> My *son*, do not forget my teaching, But let your heart keep my commandments; For length of days and years of *life*, And peace they will add to you (Prov. 3:1, 2).

> My *son*, do not reject the discipline of the Lord, Or loathe His reproof, For whom the Lord loves He reproves, Even as a *father* the son in whom he delights (Prov. 3:11, 12).

> Hear, O *sons*, the instruction of a *father*, And give attention that you may gain understanding, For I give you sound teaching; Do not abandon my instruction. When I was a son to my *father*, Tender and the only son in the sight of my mother, Then *he* taught me and said to me, "Let your heart hold fast my words; Keep my commandments and *live*" (Prov. 4:1-4).

> My *son*, give attention to my words; Incline your ear to my sayings. Do not let them depart from your sight; Keep them in the midst of your heart. For they are *life* to those who find them, And *health* to all their whole body. Watch over your heart with all diligence, For from it flow the springs of *life* (Prov. 4:20-23).

> My *son*, give attention to my wisdom, Incline your
> ear to my understanding; That you may observe
> discretion, And your lips may reserve knowledge
> (Prov. 5:1, 2).

> My *son*, keep my words, And treasure my
> commandments within you. Keep my commandments
> and *live* (Prov. 7:1, 2a).

It is clear that by God's command, by His plan and
provision, it is fathers and mothers who are commissioned
to train children in the Way. Sunday schools never existed
before the eighteenth century. We do not say they should be
discontinued. They need to be strengthened and improved.
But parents are not to relegate all teaching to Sunday
schools and thus abdicate their responsibilities. Sunday
schools can be one delegated arm of parental teaching, for
the *mind* and *soul*. But children's *spirits* learn more from
life than by rote. What children learn in Sunday school and
church may have little or great consequence, depending
solely on how the personal spirit is nurtured and taught by
experiencing life in the home. Hugs teach. Kisses instruct.
Discipline forms. Reproof harnesses rampaging energies.
Admonition builds checks upon emotions. Instruction
forms guidelines and channels for the flow of energies and
emotions. Without primal early training in the home,
Sunday schools merely weave inconsequential doilies over
volcanoes. "Foolishness is bound up in the heart of a child;
The rod of discipline will remove it far from him" (Prov.
22:15). Children become by experience what parents are,
not what they say, nor what Sunday school teachers or
anyone else says.

The moment a baby is conceived, his spirit needs his
father's presence beside the mother. As we saw in previous
chapters, the fetus is a person who knows by his spirit
whether the father welcomes him. Infants in utero know
what sex the father desires them to be. They hear what the
father says to the mother and react to the way he approaches
her. Already in the womb the spirit and character of a
father affect the formation of the character of his child.

The moment a baby is born he/she needs his/her father. Thank God modern medical practice encourages the presence of fathers at birth and allows the father to hold the newborn child as soon as possible. Immediately the father's spirit and strength encompass the child and draw his spirit to open, trust and risk, to venture vulnerability, to share, to nestle into another, to give and take. That is vital, basic training. A baby needs both the mother's sweetness and the father's warmth and strength. He needs to be made to feel welcome, secure in his belonging, at ease and at home in the earth.

Such touch brings healing. Many are the wounds of every person's spirit in becoming part of this sickened world. Loneliness and lostness from the wholeness of the Creator are a baby's immediately. Every trauma of mother and father for nine months have been his. Already he has known the shock of being cast out of the warm safety of the womb into the harshness of life. Touch is balm. Holding is healing.

Babies need fathers to walk and burp them in the night, to sing lullabies, to talk softly, lovingly, reassuringly. Fathers should feed, change diapers, rock and cuddle; everything that mothers do, fathers should as well, except breast feed—and had they been so equipped, they ought to have done that too! Infants need fathers to romp on the floor, play and laugh with them. Mothers are needed for all of this too, but most mothers do these things naturally. It is fathers who must be told how crucial their presence is. Mothers alone cannot fully draw children's spirits forth to life.

Marshall L. Hamilton, in his book *Father's Influence on Children*, (Nelson-Hall, Chicago, 1977) said:

> Studies of father absence report detrimental effects on children's aggression, dependency, degree of adjustment or "psychopathology," deliquency rates, moral behavior, success in the Peace Corps or military, premarital pregnancy rates, masculinity in males, and intellectual performance (p. 51).

A number of psychological problems and disorders, initially viewed as a result of inadequacies in the mother's behavior, appear to be influenced at least as much by the father's behavior in those studies where investigators have made the effort to study the father's influence [p. 141].

It is also clear that the model the father provides of political views, religious beliefs, and attitudes toward people of varied ethnic characteristics or national origins helps to determine at least the initial and often the lifelong attitudes of his children on these topics [p. 166].

The failure of the father to establish and effectively enforce guidelines has been related in varying degrees to male homosexuality, delinquency, schizophrenia, low self-esteem, lower levels of competence and unsuccessfulness [p. 167].

From a study by Tess Forrest in 1966:

She must learn paternal trust during infancy when she learns maternal trust. Especially from her father does the infant girl need confirmation of her desirability as a female and affirmation of her value as a different and separate person. His gentle tenderness communicates to her his pleasure in her femininity. Father, by comparison with mother, has a sharper eye, a firmer grip, a rougher cheek, a deeper voice. He is nonetheless equally tender, loving, warm and safe, and the infant girl can feel herself lovingly cradled by a man's arms and comforted by a man's voice. Contact with the father opens the door of the mother-infant dyad to the possibility and pleasure of triadic union and secondary dependency [p. 80].

To become like the father who is reasonably admirable and desirable is regularly associated with appropriate masculinity, popularity, and general good adjustment for the boy. If the father fails in any of these aspects, the risks of the son's incurring such

> problems as homosexuality, psychological disorders,
> or a delinquent pattern are increased, although there
> remain many ways in which adequate adjustment for
> the boy can be achieved [p. 78].

Boys and girls look to their fathers for their philosophy of life. From relating to fathers comes much of our zest for life, creativity, ambition, destiny and purpose. When children cannot drink life from their fathers, they are starving and crippled in spirit. To the degree of parents' failure, most especially fathers', children's spirits fall asleep. From then on they live by half-emotions and brittle thoughts, much like having good sails unfurled to catch the winds, only to flap listlessly without breath from then on, a ship hung in irons. They *cannot function*. The Body of Christ must come to comprehend the fullness of this tragedy. Children bereft of affection, most especially from their fathers, *cannot* meet God, embrace people or life or themselves fully. In this sense they have never become human. They cannot enter into another's heart by their spirit. They cannot love by spiritual sensitivity to the other. They are isolated, going through life's motions like zombies. Many are unaware that there is more to life than they have known. They are like eight-cylinder engines which have never run on more than two.

Since conscience cannot function except by remorse or fear, the result becomes callous disregard for life, progressively less and less regard for law. Before the First World War, the nuclear family was not isolated. Aunts, uncles, grandparents and cousins took up the slack when fathers were called to war and mothers went to work in war plants. Infants born then could still receive affection from primary relatives. It was a romantic and affectionate age.

Then increasing industrialization and mobility dehumanized and decentralized the family. By the time of the Second World War, many nuclear families had become isolated. Heads of families had gone to war and their infants did not know them at all. An entire generation fell asleep spiritually. Religion was still popular, but more and more by rote and rite, less in true piety. When the charismatic movement came, many who had no faculty for real encounter were filled by the Holy Spirit. Multitudes of charismatics who lacked the real hungered for more, but could not enter the holy of holies. Thus the charismatic movement has been characterized by immaturity and great pendulum swings from one imbalance to another. What is wrong is so simple. Slumbering spirits cannot truly meet God until healed by the Body. How to heal slumbering spirits is the missing key.

Consider that now entire generations of incapable people have filled divorce courts. Their children have less spirit yet, and exhibit more and more openly rebellion and debauchery. Crime rates soar. Perhaps now we can understand St. Paul's prophecy,

> But realize this, that in the last days difficult times will come. For men will be lovers of self, lovers of money, boastful, arrogant, revilers, disobedient to parents, ungrateful, unholy, unloving, irreconcilable, malicious gossips, without self-control, brutal, haters of good, treacherous, reckless, conceited, lovers of pleasure rather than lovers of God; holding to a form of godliness, although they have denied its power; and avoid such men as these (2 Tim. 3:1-5).

As we see it, the curse is already coming. "A curse without cause does not alight" (Prov. 26:2b). We fathers must shoulder the blame, and act to save our families before it is too late. Note "holding to a *form* of godliness, although they have denied its power." These people can mentally relate to doctrine and teaching. They can find comfort emotionally and logically in liturgy and the plan of salvation. These are "forms." Laws and rituals appeal to mind and heart. But they cannot embrace Him personally, for that requires a functioning spirit. When St. Paul advised, "avoid such men," we are sure he meant not to trust such people in closest fellowship, and not to place them in positions of influence or authority. Paul's command in Galatians 6:1 is, "Brethren, even if a man is caught in any trespass, you who are spiritual, restore such a one in a spirit of gentleness; looking to yourself, lest you too be tempted." Spiritually asleep people are not helped by making pariahs of them. They need welcome and embrace, holding and resurrection life. Perhaps no greater cry in our generation exists than to "prepare the way of the Lord" (Isa. 40:3 RSV) in the desert of the hearts and spirits of the slumbering.

In a moment we will share what can be done to awaken slumbering spirits, but let's first see how universally mankind knows this truth in heart if not yet in mind. Our most beloved fairy tales tell the story of slumbering and captive spirits! "Snow White and the Seven Dwarfs" appeals to generation after generation because we know deep within that it is about us. Snow White eats the poisoned apple—the poisoned fruit of life without affection—and falls asleep! The seven dwarfs represent our dwarfed talents. Who needs to be told who the wicked queen represents? Or the Prince Charming—Jesus! And how does he bring Snow White to life? By a kiss! It is love alone which can wake us from sleep.

How about "The Sleeping Beauty"? The princess pricks her finger on the distaff—work without expressions of love becomes drudgery—and falls asleep. All the servants and creatures in the castle fall asleep for a hundred years (as do all our talents and capabilities). Hedges and thorns surround the castle (much as we grow defensive prickly walls about our inner being). Prince Charming (Jesus) hacks his way through the thorns with his flaming sword (of truth), slays the dragon (Satan), and enters our castle. Again, it is by the kiss of love that the princess and all her court awaken.

Think about the frog who tricks a princess into keeping him by her bedside and feeding him until he bursts forth as a handsome prince—when he is kissed! We only hop and croak until our spirits are awakened by love to be the sons and daughters of the King. It is this sick world with its devils who have bewitched (put us to sleep) and turned us into frogs, caricatures of what we were meant to be.

Soon after the Lord taught us this key, Walt Disney produced a renewed version of "The Sleeping Beauty," and I wept through the whole thing! "Oh, God, come!" I cried. How we need that kind of revival!

How can we cause it to happen? How can we love slumbering spirits to life? First we need to discover the condition. It takes only a few incisive questions to discover, and the questions come from the list of nine functions of the spirit:

1. When you are in a worship service or a prayer meeting, do you feel the anointing of God flowing over you and through you, or do you only know He is there by faith?
2. When you have private devotions, do you enter into His presence? Can you abide in His presence? When you read the Bible, do the words leap with meaning off the page at times? Or does Bible reading run dry?
3. Do you ever hear the Lord or have spiritual dreams or visions? Does God talk to you?
4. When you are in a conversation, do you enter in and feel what the other person feels, or do you have to figure out with your mind what to say?
5. Are you a creative person? Do you have new ideas? Or do you always have to follow the manual?
6. Have you experienced a glory in marital sex in which you feel your mate's spirit flowing into yours?
7. Does your conscience warn you strongly before you do anything, and keep you out of trouble, or only work by remorse afterwards?

And so on. We seldom have to ask more than the first four questions to know.

When we see the condition, we explain what it is, and what its causes are. Almost every time, counselees readily and easily understand. They begin to exclaim, "Oh, this is why I could never—" and "No wonder—" and "How do I get this healed?"

We ask then, or review if we have already covered that ground, what their history was with their parents, particularly during earliest childhood. We look for the father's presence or absence in the first two or three years, affection, or lack of it, discipline, or lack of it, teaching and example, good or bad. We can then reveal to the counselee how his spirit thrived or starved, expanded or fell asleep.

It may be necessary to explain to a counselee how his spirit can hold resentment and judgments towards his parents when he is unaware of it. We help him to identify the fruits in his life which necessarily have roots. We assure him that just as he received salvation by faith, not by feeling, so he need not try to feel again what his spirit actually felt toward his parents; he needs only by faith to acknowledge that sins of resentment may be there, and receive forgiveness by faith. St. Paul said, "I am conscious of nothing against myself, yet I am not by this acquitted" (1 Cor. 4:4). Job said, "How many are my iniquities and sins?" (Job 13:23). David said, "Acquit me of hidden faults" (Ps. 19:12). And the Psalmist, "Search me, O God, and know my heart; Try me and know my anxious thoughts; And see if there be any hurtful way in me . . ." (Ps. 139:23, 24). We may quote some of these Scriptures in counseling sessions.

In prayer we do not pray for such a person apart from him or silently. We kneel beside him as he sits or kneels. We put an arm about his shoulders, and hold a hand; we know he needs human touch through which God's Spirit will do the work. Through touch the Lord supplies love which the person missed in infancy. We ask the Lord to minister to the inner child. We ask the person to repent and pray aloud concerning resentments. We pronounce forgiveness. Most importantly, we ask the Lord to enter and woo him to life in his spirit, to fill the vacuum. We pray that the Lord may restore to him as many years as the locust has eaten and the cankerworm destroyed (Joel 2:25). We ask specifically that the Lord awaken and draw his spirit forth to function with liveliness and enthusiasm. Sometimes we have to haul to death whatever death wishes and bitter-root judgments and expectancies have resulted from his being rejected or starved for affection.

After the prayer comes the most crucial part of healing. Other conditions may be overcome by a single prayer, or several. The counselor or intercessor may or may not be much involved in the process. And *perhaps* the other may recover whether or not he is in a good church or small group. Not so for the spiritually slumbering. The healing of this condition requires that the church be the Church! Some branch of the Church must be there as family to incubate that child in love, to provide what his natural family was not able to give him. It is not enough for slumberers to have what the churches usually call Christian fellowship. Sitting in rows fellowshipping with the backs of each other's necks on Sunday morning will not resurrect anyone. Church suppers, pastoral calls, church meetings and study groups will not get the job done. These are too detached, too distant, too unengaged at deep heart levels. It is good to have these as background and filler. But only rich personal encounter and involvement which reaches beyond secondary relationships to become immediate and primary can touch that slumbering spirit with life-giving power.

In Chapter Twenty-One of *The Transformation of the Inner Man* we discuss more fully the need in the Body for some to be fathers and mothers in Christ. Suffice it to say here that in the case of slumbering spirits, re-parenting is not just a nice option, it is the without-which-nothing. It does not always need to be consciously attempted, named or discussed. Sometimes it just happens. It is helpful if the one in the parent role sees what is happening and quietly allows and checks and guards until the other is whole enough to detach and go his way. Sometimes it is best to do consciously as St. Paul did, to make the other aware that ". . . I am again in labor until Christ is formed in you" (Gal. 4:19). It may be that the knowledge of a friend's willingness to risk and bear so much to carry us in love is the very thing that acts as a wedge to pry the heart's door open to receive.

Re-parenters come to know such love for their "child"; they experience first-hand what St. Paul meant when he said,

> For who is our hope or joy or crown of exultation? Is it not even you, in the presence of our Lord Jesus at His coming? For you are our glory and joy (1 Thess. 2:19, 20).

> Therefore, my beloved brethren whom I long to see, my joy and crown, so stand firm in the Lord, my beloved (Phil. 4:1).

> . . . for this reason, brethren, in all our distress and affliction we were comforted about you through your faith; for now we really live, if you stand firm in the Lord (1 Thess. 3:7, 8).

> For this reason, when I could endure it no longer, I also sent to find out about your faith, for fear that the tempter might have tempted you, and our labor should be in vain (1 Thess. 3:5).

One who struggles in love to re-parent another finally comes to see the Lord's tremendous love for him as He wooed him so patiently. Until then, one can give hardly more than lip service to the sacrifices of Jesus in loving us to life. But when we discover the cost to Him by wringing our own hearts for others, we fall on our knees, bursting with gratitude He did not give up on us. The healer is more healed in resurrecting the slumbering than the slumberer. Truly, "It is more blessed to give than to receive."

We suggest that our readers carefully read Chapter Twenty-One in *The Transformation of the Inner Man* so as to be aware of the limits and pitfalls, the clues when to enter and when to desist in such relationships. This work is not without danger and confusions. Nevertheless, the Lord did not call us to be safe, rather to lay down our lives sacrificially for others.

Slumbering spirits are awakened by the sacrificial love of a few and the support of the Body. Without the Body, the labor is too heavy and the dangers of fastening idolatrously too great. In one and the same chapter (Eph. 4) St. Paul spoke both of the importance of the few, the five-fold ministry of apostles, prophets, evangelists, pastors and teachers, and of the "whole body . . . building up of itself in love." Counselors should not work alone to resurrect the spiritually asleep, nor should the Body think it can do without those soldier specialists who risk themselves as counselors.

We cannot leave this subject without pleading to the entire Body to comprehend the level of risk such counselors endure. So often we as His Body have held up our noses in scorn when a counselor has fallen to confusion. But perhaps it was we who failed. Did we watch over and consult with our burden-bearing saints? Did we protect them by prayer? Did we see to it that when counselees misquoted their counselors or repeated things which ought not to have gone past closed doors, our counselors were defended and murmurers squelched?

Perhaps there is no more crucial finger to be placed in the dike which holds back the waters of destruction over our entire society than this work of awakening slumbering spirits. Either we, the Church, wake up to our task, or Satan rules a society filled with crime and divorce. Church, take the cry "Maranatha" (even so, come Lord) out of the mystical future! Here is where the King comes now, immediately, practically, to kiss His own to life—or we sleep on.

> Awake, awake, Clothe yourself in your strength, O Zion; Clothe yourself in your beautiful garments, O Jerusalem, the holy city (Isa. 52:1a).

Obviously we can't rush out to wake up the whole world. John and I (Paula) tried to take on the burden of that for a short time, and flattened ourselves before we realized that truly that was a job the Lord already came to do. It was a relief to know that we are to take responsibility only for those whom the Lord either points out or brings to us.

People may not be ready for intense ministry, or even aware that they need it. Often we have been called to soak them with general prayer apart from them while we quietly make ourselves available. The Lord will prepare hearts. We must never "accuse" a person of being needy or crash through his closed doors in a way that will cause ministry to appear as an attack.

Not all of us are called to intense counseling ministries. Not all are called to re-parent. But every Christian is a part of the family of God. In that family relationship we are all called to share the life we have been given. The Lord "comforts us in all our affliction so that we may be able to comfort those who are in any affliction with the comfort with which we ourselves are comforted by God" (2 Cor. 1:4).

We all slumber to a degree in some areas. We all have areas in which we have been quickened to life. As the Body shares in close relationship and unity, we will effectively impart life to one another. The Lord in us is the power. He has *only* imperfect vessels through whom to work, and yet His work is perfect.

Resurrection ministry does not have to be complicated. The following are testimonies of simple but tremendously powerful happenings we have seen in the Body of Christ.

In our community in the Baptist Church is a retired couple who will never retire from active service for the Lord because service describes *who* they *are* more than *what* they *do*. I doubt that they have any intellectual knowledge about slumbering spirits, but they have warmed and sparked untold numbers. They know and love the Lord and have made it a way of life to involve themselves in doing what He is doing. They have been mom and dad to many of the young couples in the church who are in the area without supportive families; their home is open and they know how to make people feel at ease and welcome. Every month they host birthday parties for people in the church, many of whom would have no other celebration on their special day. They have been concerned for the increasing number of children from broken homes whose fathers are gone and whose mothers are too burdened to spend quality time with them. Every day they go to the nearby elementary school to *be* there in the lunchroom or on the playground as loving grandparents for the children to identify with, to talk to, to drink from. Everett and Bernice know from deep inside that Jesus becomes flesh again and again through His people, so that when they hug a child, or speak a word of love and encouragement, Jesus' life and healing flow in immeasurable quantity, quality and power. They give themselves in other ways too numerous to mention. And they do so with joy.

In Cornerstone, the church our oldest son pastors, there was a young woman who conceived a child out of wedlock. When the time arrived for her infant son to be dedicated, Loren said to the congregation, "You all know the circumstances of this baby's birth. We don't know how long it will be before he has a daddy, and every little boy needs a daddy. If there is any man in the congregation who will promise to uphold this mother as she promises to raise her child in the nurture and admonition of the Lord, let him come forward now." Not *one* man came, but *every* man in the congregation! Such a promise was and is being fulfilled in simple ways: prayer for healing, support, provision, prayer that he be brought into the fullness of his life, watchful sensitivity to hug the little fellow whenever possible, to admire his person and his achievements, to extend a firm quiet hand of discipline when needed, to communicate to him that his belonging to the family is blessing and delight, to be available for counsel and help should the mother seek it. The little boy is growing more beautiful, as is his mother.

In Cornerstone there are home fellowship groups which include all ages. They are for the purpose of worship, Bible study, sharing, body ministry, fun, but especially for a sense of belonging in the family of God. Every single parent who consents is a part of one of the small-group families. As a part of this group they are no longer in isolation as they carry their heavy loads. Many churches are beginning to discover this anointed way of providing. Care extends beyond the meeting times. We have heard grateful testimony again and again along the line of, "I can't begin to say how much it meant when you came to help me with my children, to clean my house, to bring food, to hug up on me, to pray with me. I never knew what it was like to have a family before." The Lord awakens spirits and establishes them in love and strength through the personal involvement of those who lay down their lives for others.

One of the most astounding stories of growth under the Lord's anointing comes from Kansas. A professor who was head of his department at a state university was concerned for the large number of students who were far away from home, many of them having broken family ties because of rebellion or because homes had simply shattered beneath them, a good number of them looking for comfort and answers in wrong places and ways. He quietly let it be known that his home was open to anyone who just wanted a place to come and relax, have a cup of coffee, and visit a while. A few students came. Soon they were so at home they were talking about things that mattered. Sensitively the professor and his wife offered counsel and prayer. Those students brought friends. Soon the household took on the shape of a home fellowship, and groups were sharing counsel and prayer and Bible study. Many still came only for coffee and hugs. The home group overflowed into a school building and began to look more like a church. In a short while it was necessary for them to find a building to call their own. The professor found himself so busy pastoring he had to drop his job as department head at the university; then he dropped half of his teaching load, and was finally ordained as full-time pastor of a full-fledged church. Many of the young people who began as emotional basket cases are now the ones who have a basket full to overflowing to share with others. Some of the original group stayed with the church, but we have met a number around the country, who, when we have related this story, have said, "Oh! you're talking about the Mustard Seed! That's where the Lord saved my life!"

The beginning of resurrection ministry really can be so simple as saying, "I care. My door is open. My home is yours. Come on over and have a cup of coffee; we can talk if you like—"

Chapter Six

Spiritual Imprisonment

To Thee, O Lord, I call; My rock, do not be deaf to me, Lest, if Thou be silent to me, I become like those who go down to the *pit* (Ps. 28:1).

I waited patiently for the Lord; And He inclined to me, and heard my cry. He brought me up out of the *pit of destruction*, out of the *miry clay;* And He set my feet upon a rock making my footsteps firm. And He put a new song in my mouth, a song of praise to our God; Many will see and fear, And will trust in the Lord (Ps. 40:1-3).

You have seen many things, but have paid no attention; your ears are open, but you hear nothing. It pleased the Lord for the sake of His righteousness to make His law great and glorious. But this is a people plundered and looted, *all* of them *trapped in pits or hidden away in prisons*. They have become plunder, with no one to rescue them; they have been made loot, with no one to say, "Send them back" (Isa. 42:20-22 NIV).

The Spirit of the Lord is upon Me, Because He anointed Me to preach the gospel to the poor. He has sent Me to proclaim release to the captives, And recovery of sight to the blind, To set free those who are downtrodden, To proclaim the favorable year of the Lord (Luke 4:18).

There is a condition akin to, but worse than, spiritual slumber. A person can be spiritually imprisoned.

We discovered this condition while ministering to a lovely lady who is now our friend and co-worker and who has given us permission to use her name in her story. Jo Black came to us distraught because she could not enjoy the fullness of life. As the wife of a Lieutenant Colonel in the Air Force, Jo felt obliged to host parties and to attend many social functions on base. But she was never at ease. She felt awkward and uncertain because she found herself unable to feel what other people felt. She seemed like a square tire in tandem with all the round ones, jarring everyone with out-of-place sentiments and statements.

At the base chapel she had become filled with the Holy Spirit, but still had all the incapabilities slumbering spirits suffer. Nothing helped. Private devotions ran dry. Corporate worship was either only mildly enjoyable or boring, but never full of His presence. She thought of herself as a constant embarrassment to her husband, and couldn't imagine why he continued to appreciate and love her.

Worst of all, she said, was the fact that sex meant little or nothing to her. She would rather not have been bothered. Frank persisted in being a gentle and considerate lover, amazingly patient with her, and it hurt that she could not respond to such a wonderful man. If he hadn't been so kind and patient, she could have found some self-justification for turning away. But she couldn't fault him at all, and that filled her with self-disgust and remorse.

It was not that Jo had any physical problems. She was, and still is, one of the most beautiful women of face and figure Paula and I have ever known. "Disgustingly healthy," as Jo used to say. Never a headache or physical problem on which to blame her resistance to sex. She simply could not get into the act and feel anything but physical sensations, which after a while by themselves became boring and bothersome.

She wanted to find out what was blocking her. We asked our usual questions, and found lack of parental affection, especially from her father. After a while the Holy Spirit revealed a suppressed and forgotten molestation. So we brought to forgiveness every hurtful experience of any kind that we could find, and to the cross every practice in her nature. But Jo always returned to say, "I'm not any better, John. I still can't feel a thing."

In those days we knew nothing about spiritual slumber. We discovered spiritual imprisonment some months before slumber. Probably that history was the Lord's providence, for if we had known of spiritual slumber, we most likely would have leaped to the conclusion that it was the cause, and would have missed what was actually the problem, because the symptoms are so nearly identical. Failing to produce results, we would have become even more confused. We mention this because a number who have become aware of slumbering spirits have tried to set imprisoned spirits free as though slumber were all that was the matter, and consequent failure has caused them to doubt themselves and the key.

There came a day when Jo and I (John, ministering to her that day) were totally stumped. We couldn't think of another moment of her biography we hadn't looked at from a dozen angles. We couldn't imagine why she couldn't find any joy and zest in life.

I felt led to try an experiment. The Lord sometimes enables me by my spirit to identify with another's being by empathy so as to feel what they feel inside, and so find clues which could not be discovered otherwise. For a while, by the power of the Holy Spirit and permission of the other, I become as they are. I know him or her intimately, from within, as if I had lived their life. Not knowing anything else to do, Jo and I tried it.

When I have experienced that with others, I have been able to feel the presence of their spirit, their hurts and joys, through the Holy Spirit, obtaining a strong sense of the character and personality of the other.

When I identified spiritually with Jo, nobody was home! It was like stepping into a vacant hall. We have all felt the emptiness of great buildings when we have entered alone. Jo was as empty as a vacant cave! Her own spirit did not seem to be there. It was not that Jo was inhabited by any foreign spirit; I would have sensed the presence of evil. Her Christian life and the Holy Spirit, whose presence I *could* feel, had kept demonic things from attacking her. It was the opposite of demonic inhabitation. Other than the Holy Spirit, nobody was there, not even Jo!

I exclaimed, "Jo, where are you? I can't find you."

"You tell me, John. You're the counselor. I don't know."

Again I was stumped, more so than before. I had never experienced anything like this.

Sometimes help comes from strange places. I had been reading J.R.R. Tolkien's *Lord of the Rings*, a three-volume series. In the third book, *The Return of The King*, Merry, a friend of Strider who had by then been revealed as the returning king, had been struck down by one of the black wraiths, servants of Sauron (the Satan of that fantasy). Merry's spirit was wandering in nether glooms, more and more lost, as he slipped into a coma from which none had been known to awaken. Calling for the herb athelas, crushing it in boiling water until its fragrance filled the room, Strider, now become King Elessar Evenstar, took hold of Merry's hand and sent his own spirit seeking Merry's. At length he found him in the visions of his inner spirit, and escorted him back to life. (Let those who have reservations about such fantasies hold them in check; they merely gave me an inspiration. The Lord can use anything for His own good purposes.)

Recalling that story gave me an idea. So, in the same way, having sought and gained the Lord's permission, I sent my spirit with the Lord's, who is our returning King, to find Jo. He did it by a vision. Whether the vision was merely a representation, a parable of some other reality, or whether in some sense I saw spiritual reality as it was, I have no idea. Whatever it was, it worked.

I "saw" our wonderful Lord walking down a steeply sloping dark tunnel. He did not carry a torch or lantern. He was himself the light. I followed Him. The experience was much like following a car down a narrow lane at night, watching the headlights momentarily shine on walls or bushes, leaving darkness behind. I watched the light of Jesus illuminate the walls as He passed. We came to a huge dungeon door, ancient and rusted, locked. Before the Lord it opened by itself. Scriptures raced through my mind, ". . . behold, I am alive forevermore, and I have the keys of death and of Hades" (Rev. 1:18). I knew we were entering that kind of place! "He who is holy, who is true, who has the key of David, who opens and no one will shut, and who shuts and no one opens . . ." (Rev. 3:7). "All authority has been given to Me in heaven and on earth" (Matt. 28:18). He hadn't needed to insert a key; He himself is the key! The door flew open at His authority. "The gates of hell shall not prevail against it" (Matt. 16:18b KJV). It was confirmed to me in a flash that Jesus meant to speak of the Church on the attack, not on the defensive, breaking open the gates of Hell to invade and set its captives free! We were entering a dungeon of Hell, and I knew it!

I watched as He walked across a dirty floor. Phantasmagoria of Hell fled before His presence! There, in a corner, huddled in a fetal position, manacled by wrists and ankles attached by chains to a wall, was Jo. She appeared ghastly white and blue, emaciated and starved, tiny as a child. With His beautiful nail-scarred brown hands, He deftly, gently broke the shackles off of Jo. He picked her up, cradling her softly against His chest, and I thought, "He shall feed His flock like a shepherd: he shall gather the lambs with his arm, and carry them in his bosom, and shall gently lead those that are with young" (Isa. 40:11 KJV). I wept for joy and the beauty of it.

The Lord carried Jo out of that place. I described aloud for Jo what I was seeing. Later she told me that she felt every moment of it in indescribable joy and anticipation.

As He carried her, He breathed His own breath into her, while Genesis 2:7 and countless Scriptures about the wind of the Holy Spirit (as in John 3), and Elisha breathing his breath into the Shunamite woman's dead son (2 Kings 4:18-37) cascaded through my mind. Then He set her on her feet, and, taking her left hand in His right, began to walk out of the tunnel with her. As they walked, Jo began to grow, like the Wonder Bread advertisement of some years ago, from a little girl to the grown woman she is. Then He passed His hands over her body, and wherever I could see skin, it turned from deathly pale to glowing pink.

The vision ended as I saw Him turn her loose to frolic in a lovely meadow as He watched, beaming with joy and pride.

After several minutes of silent basking in the glow of His presence, I said, "Jo, I don't pretend to understand that at all, but I know something wonderful has happened. Let's wait and see."

Jo left for a two-week trip. The next time I saw her, she was beaming! She could hardly wait to tell me! "John, guess what! I'm out, and I'm alive! I can feel! People on the airplane started pouring out their troubles to me, and for the first time I felt like I had something to say to them. I felt what they felt. I knew what to say. I don't feel like a stranger anymore. I enjoy visiting with people. Best of all, I really enjoy sex now. Sometimes I even go after Frank. And [with a chuckle and a gleam in her eye] he can't believe it. He's wearing himself out!"

Twice Jo fell back, not fully into prison but into slumber and incapability. It was a simple matter to call her to life again. She learned to exercise a discipline of saying each day, "Lord, I choose life!" People began to stream to her door. Of course the Lord brought to her person after person who had suffered the same kind of imprisonment. She delighted in seeing the Lord set them free one by one. Jo came on staff as one of our counselors. She formed prayer groups and started Bible study classes on base. She was on fire for the Lord, so glad to be free and whole!

Nevertheless, all this drove me to the Scriptures. By then I had been down so many seemingly good blind alleys, I wasn't going to have anything if it couldn't be found in the Word of God. It was not hard to find. It could hardly be missed. Jesus said it in Luke 4:18 (quoting Isa. 61:1). This was one of the very purposes for which He had come!

> The Spirit of the Lord is upon Me,
> Because He anointed Me to preach
> the gospel to the poor. He has sent
> Me to proclaim release to the *captives*,
> And recovery of sight to the blind,
> to set free those who are *downtrodden*.

What was Jo but that, captive and downtrodden? I had always interpreted those verses figuratively, as referring to inner freedom, or as about criminals in prison eventually going free. They still could mean those things. But Jesus was revealing a literal meaning I had never thought of.

Then he revealed many other Scriptures, most of which are listed at the head of this chapter. Note, however, how precisely Psalm 88 describes the condition:

1. ". . . my life has drawn near to Sheol" (v. 3).
2. "I am reckoned among those who go down to the pit" (v. 4a). This is not merely our expression, "It's the pits," but a very real literal pit for our spirit!
3. "I have become like a man without strength" (v. 4b). This was exactly Jo's condition.
4. ". . . they are cut off from thy hand" (v. 5), aptly describing the way Jo felt.
5. "Thou hast put me in the lowest pit, In dark places, in the depths" (v. 6). Jo knew that as real, not poetic.
6. "Thou hast removed my acquaintances far from me; Thou hast made me an object of loathing to them" (v. 8a). This was the social condition Jo had lived in all her life.
7. "I am shut up and cannot go out" (v. 8b). This was Jo's prison. She was shut up, and unable to get out.
8. "My eye has wasted away because of affliction" (v. 9). Jo grieved every day because she couldn't live.

9. "I have called upon Thee every day, O Lord; I have spread out my hands to Thee" (v. 9). The reference is that God didn't seem to hear, and didn't answer the Psalmist. Nor did He seem to hear Jo.
10. "Wilt Thou perform wonders for the dead? Will the departed spirits rise and praise Thee?" (v. 10). Whatever that Scripture means literally, to Jo it described how dead she felt, how vacant and "departed."

And so on. The entire Psalm described her condition.

Seeing it in Scripture was not enough. I knew by then I could read into Scripture what I wanted to see. So I asked Him both to teach me more and to give me so many undeniable experiences of undying fruit that it would be much farther around the barn to deny this revelation than to accept it.

He began to teach me. He explained that when a person experiences overwhelming trauma in the womb, that person may rebel against God. The person then, while still in utero, turns back from life, wanting to flee and hide, not wanting to be born, not wanting to have to come out of the womb and risk life. He reminded me that when we bury our talent, even what we think we have is taken from us (Matt. 25:14-30). Then He quoted the Scripture, "The thief comes only to steal, and kill, and destroy; I came that they might have life, and might have it abundantly" (John 10:10). He said, *John, you and so many others in My Body have fastened on the words "kill" and "destroy" because you could understand these from your own experience. But have you ever considered, what does Satan want to steal? It is my sheep he wants to steal. Many have understood that, and thought it meant only to carry their souls into Hell in the end. But that is not all he can do. Christians are normally hidden (Col. 3:3), and protected (Ps. 91 and 34:7), but when children rebel against Me, they open doors to Satan. His minions can then come about that person in the womb, or sometime later in life, and imprison his spirit. From then on he cannot live and function, as you saw with Jo.*

He went on to explain that there is a hidden meaning in another familiar Scripture: "If you have not been faithful in the use of that which is another's, who will give you that which is your own?" (Luke 16:12). He said, *John, did you ever stop to think, what is it which is your own which is to be given to you?* The answer was many things, of course. But He applied it in this instance this way, *Turn that Scripture around. If a man is faithful in that which is another's, he will be given that which is his own. Jo, imprisoned as she was, was trying her best to be faithful with that which was not hers, My kingdom. She was trying to serve. By her faith and obedience, then, I could give her what was hers, her own spirit, set free to live life.*

I never did understand whether some portion of our spirit is actually carried away from us physically, or whether we are somehow imprisoned deep within ourselves. The latter, I suspect. The other seems too weird, even for my imagination.

The Lord then brought case after case of imprisoned spirits. Though my best way to set people free remains to do it by describing by vision what He does, the scenes of captivity are almost always different. One person I saw in an old ramshackle cabin, locked in and chained to a bunk bed in a corner. It turned out that the man had experienced such a cabin in his life, had feared it irrationally, and saw the whole scene with me as I prayed, sometimes in advance of my describing it, exactly as I was seeing the drama unfolding. One man I saw, appropriately, frozen in an iceberg. His heart was indeed frozen. Paula once saw a vision of a woman in a birdcage, unable to sing, and another of a man in a hole in the ground, covered over by grass. He called out again and again in a weak voice, but none of those who walked by could hear. Such prisons I take as parables, though it seemed to me that in Jo's case I was seeing something much closer to actual reality. The fact that the pictures seemed appropriate, and that many could see and experience even while I described it, was not enough. I knew the powers of suggestion.

What became more and more convincing was lasting and undeniable fruit. Hardshell cases began to change before my eyes. More importantly, like Jo, they came back to exclaim, "I *heard* a beautiful symphony this week. I thrilled to it! It was always just nice noise before," or, "I saw a sunset! For the first time I really saw it. I felt it. I never knew how much of life I have been plodding through, dead!" "John and Paula, visiting with people has stopped being a weariness. I can tune in with people now. It's refreshing to visit." "Hallelujah! I can experience God's presence. He's real! I can *feel* Him!" None of these things had happened before. It did in fact become easier to admit we had found a real key than to try to explain it away some other way.

Spiritual imprisonment is diagnosed both by observing symptoms and by the operation of the gifts of knowledge and perception. When we want to rule in or rule out possible imprisonment, we ask the same list of questions as for slumbering spirits, and then several more. Since sexual felicity is a telling key for spiritually imprisoned people, we usually ask whether sex is just something to do or whether it is filled with joy and glory. We ask,

1. Do you ever feel hollow, empty or vacant, like something is missing?
2. Do you ever feel deeply lonely, alone, way off somewhere, even in the middle of a crowd?
3. Do you ever feel persecuted, tormented or afflicted when on the surface no one is bothering you? (Demonic spirits do torment the spirits of captive people, and they feel it like a subcurrent river of pain without knowing what it is.)
4. Do you suffer from the sense that there are talents and powers and energies in you which you can't reach, as though they are locked away from you?
5. Do you ever feel desperate and lost and futile inside when on the surface everything seems to be going fine?

6. Do you ever feel like trouble and danger are all around you, when in fact everything and everyone around you is perfectly safe?
7. Do you ever have unaccountable inner rages? Do you get furiously angry at something, when actually there is nothing to be angry at? (The spirits of imprisoned people rage against the chains which bind them.)
8. Do you have trouble staying awake at services which are quite lively and exciting? Just when the pastor is preaching a really good sermon, do you find it difficult to keep your eyes open? (Satan is a hypnotist.)

If we still are not certain, or want other corroborations, we may ask a few other questions, such as

9. Do you, or did you, ever suffer vertigo (dizziness)? In the presence of the power of the Lord in a worship service, have you felt weak or dizzy? (We do not know why this phenomenon occurs, but it is common for imprisoned people to break out in a cold sweat and/or become dizzy when others feel uplifted, warmed and joyous under the Lord's anointing. Perhaps by empathy they feel the nausea of their captors' pain in the presence of Jesus, but we do not know.)
10. Have you ever suffered any dyslexia? (Imprisoned people commonly but not always have had some degree of dyslexia in childhood, or currently suffer from it.)
11. In the midst of a powerful time of worship, do you feel at peace and joyous, or nervous and unaccountably upset? Do you feel agitated, or calmed, when others around you pray and thank Him for being present?

    Perhaps this reaction happens because like blind Bartimaeus they want to call out all the louder when Jesus passes close by (Mark 10:46-52) and/or perhaps their demonic captors are made nervous and fearful by His presence, and they feel it.

Frequently, counselees' answers reveal quite clearly whether or not they suffer imprisonment. Sometimes, however, questions and answers remain inconclusive. It is then that we enter prayer and wait upon the Lord for discernment. Sometimes He reveals the condition instantly, sometimes not. In His wisdom, He may know it is not time to answer clearly. He may want us to discuss the biography of the person more fully; there may be clues He wants us to have in mind which we would not bother to seek were He to answer too soon. So we visit some more, asking the Lord to reveal in our sharing what He wants us to see. Before we ask the above questions, it should be understood that we will have obtained the history of the subject's family, and as much of the early life as the person can recall or remember from memories shared by other members of the family.

If we suspect slumber or imprisonment, we will search out as much as can be discovered about the circumstances surrounding conception. Was the person invited, or did he happen? Were the parents happy to be expecting, and happy with each other? Was the mother a smoker or a drinker at the time of the pregnancy? What number child was the person? Did the parents have strong desires for a baby of either sex? Were there separations due to business or war?

Sometimes a person is not a slumberer. He may answer all diagnostic questions in such a way that it is obvious he is not asleep spiritually. But further questions reveal that he *is* imprisoned. Such people suffer more than those who are both asleep and imprisoned. They feel and sense many things keenly in their spirit, which only increases bafflement and pain when they find themselves locked away from ability to live life. Satan being the hypnotist he is, they may fight to stay awake, becoming more and more fatigued and strained. Usually, however, people are both asleep and imprisoned.

When spiritual imprisonment seems certain to us, we explain the condition and what causes it. Before prayer, we make the counselee aware that his own sins are involved. We discuss rebellion, shrinking back, amniosis (See Chapter Thirteen in *The Transformation of the Inner Man*), and the necessity to forgive Father God and be forgiven for resentments against God and life on earth. We insist on verbal statements in reply to the questions, "Do you choose life? Are you willing to pay the price of pain and vulnerability in order to choose and risk life anew every day?"

Prayer begins with simple petitions for inner healing, as outlined in the first chapters. We make sure that full prayers of forgiveness are said, both for the counselee to forgive, and to be forgiven, to accomplish fullness of reconciliation to being a person on earth.

Having healed and forgiven everything we have discussed which might have opened the door to powers of darkness to imprison, we ask the Lord to set the person free. We have never felt it enough merely to ask that it be done. We take action immediately by praying it through until the person knows himself to be free. Usually, as we have indicated, that requires an experiential involvement in some kind of visionary prayer in which we are engaged in the activity with the Lord. We are sometimes called into spiritual warfare, standing to hold back the powers of darkness alongside the Lord as He sets the person free.

Setting a person free from spiritual captivity by prayer is one of the most exciting and rewarding adventures one can have! There is no way to adequately describe how the experience moves from something one could be imagining, having no more reality than pictures in the mind, into an intensely real, emotionally stirring experience. Somewhere in the process of the prayer, though one may have started out thinking himself involved in nothing more than his own fantasy world, reality breaks through, and one finds his spirit leaping with joy in the Lord. Perhaps since the visions and prayers serve as a vehicle for the Lord for His purposes in His desire to set His children free, it may matter little how accurate or real or fanciful our prayer visions may be. What is important is that lasting fruits result. People are very really set free.

Most often, when people are freed from inner prisons, it is as though they set out to make up for lost time. They are often more on fire for the Lord than others are. They find themselves ministering with great faith and joy. Others seek them out till one wonders where all the people are coming from.

Jo served with us in Elijah House until her husband was transferred to Loring Air Force Base, Maine. Jo had become as a daughter to us, and was heartbroken at first. "All the way up there in Maine!" she said. "Mountain Home, Idaho, would have been too far already!"

But we said, "It's time you were on your own, Jo. The Lord will go with you."

Soon after she arrived at Loring, a women's group invited her to give her testimony. It turned out to be electrifying. Women and then men swamped her for prayer help and counseling. She phoned, "John and Paula, I can't do this."

"Yes, you can, Jo. The Lord will be with you."

She started study and prayer groups. Then a local pastor, leaving town for a while, asked her to fill his pulpit. Again she phoned, "I can't do that, John and Paula. I'm no preacher. How can I, a woman, step into a pulpit as a preacher?"

We asked her, "What does Frank say?"

"Oh, he's all for it. Says he'll be right there to support me."

"Well, then, go to it; the Lord will be with you." Again the Lord blessed her, and everyone was pleased, including Jo's family.

Somehow a family in Connecticut whose husband and father was dying of cancer heard that this woman in Maine could pray and God would answer. They called Jo, pleading with her to come down there to heal their father. "John and Paula, I can't do that. What if nothing happens? I'm no magic faith healer. What will I do?"

"What does Frank say?"

"He says to go on, my prayers can't hurt anything."

"Give it a try, Jo. The Lord will go with you."

When she arrived, she found the family gathered in the house, already bickering over distribution of the estate. The man, who had been large and strong, now lay withered and frail. Jo thought, "Oh, what can I do?" There was no way to phone us, and she could hear the refrain inside her head anyway, "The Lord will be with you." She sat by the bed and began to pray. Then, led by the Holy Spirit, she crawled onto the bed, cradled the man in her arms, and sang to him in the Spirit as she rocked him like a baby. After a while he fell sound asleep, the first real rest he had been able to find in days.

The next morning Jo returned to find the man much improved; he had eaten a meal and was sitting up in bed. But the family gathered in the next room, still fussing audibly with one another. She heard the Lord say clearly, *Call them to repentance. They are killing their father.*

"No, Lord, I can't do that!"

Tell them, Jo.

She called them all to his bedside and said, "You are killing your father by your continual fighting with one another. The Lord wants you to repent." They got down on their knees and she led them through prayers of repentance, forgiveness and reconciliation. As they said, "Amen," the sick man exclaimed, "The fire is gone! There is no more pain!" Several of the family received the Lord.

Jo says she wishes she could report that the man fully recovered and that everyone lived happily ever after, but that didn't happen. Jo returned home. Some in the family returned to their old ways. The man died several weeks later. *But he never suffered pain again!*

The Lord continues to use Jo and her family. The Air Force has sent them to Africa, where Jo and Frank know, "The Lord goes with you."

We tell Jo's story because we know that many who have been imprisoned feel ineffectual, as though they have already blown the mission of their life. Far from it, their experience, and the glory of being set free, has equipped them as few others. They *know* the reality of evil. They *know* the mercy and grace of our Lord. They do not have to strive to believe. They know *whom* they have believed. People are drawn to their fire.

Our spirits may have known this key all along. As "Snow White" and "The Sleeping Beauty" tell the story of slumbering spirits, there are many fantasy stories of princes and princesses who are held captive; the stories "Bluebeard" and "Rapunzel" are two examples. Such stories seem fresh to every generation. They hold a fascination for us. It could be that our spirits know about imprisonment while our minds remain unaware or tend to scoff.

In grade school, we never tired of playing a game variously called "Stink Base" or "Prisoners' Base." Two teams faced each other across a field. Each had its own line and its own prison. Combatants dashed across the field towards each other, attempting to lure the other side into chasing them. Whoever came most recently from behind his own line had the "power." Whomever he touched became his prisoner. No one could interfere as he conducted his prisoner to the area blocked out as the prison. Now the other team sought to set their teammates free. If someone could run through without being touched and grab the hand of a prisoner, both could walk back to their line unharmed. Whichever team held the most prisoners at the end of the game was declared the winner.

Even as a child, though admittedly more mystical than most, I "knew" there was something more to that game than met the eye. It spoke to something deep within me. I "knew" something was "true" about it.

Whoever comes freshest off the base line of prayer truly does have the "power." There *are* real captives. We do run into enemy territory to grab captives' hands to set them free. Since Jesus is with us, in us, we are safe to walk hand in hand to freedom. One difference: there will be no

Christian captives in Satan's camp when the warfare is ended! We win! Because He has already won!

Perhaps some cautions need to be voiced. First, this work is not for beginners in the faith. One must have such trust in the Lordship of Jesus that he is neither afraid of nor distracted by powers of darkness, nor foolhardy. The prayer warrior must know obedience to our Lord, so as to walk in and out, with Him leading, not chasing off to fight irrelevant battles. Second, the prayer warrior must have both a lively imagination and one disciplined by experience in Christ. He must on the one hand be able to receive whatever impressions the Lord would give him, and on the other be disciplined as a soldier not to add to or become entangled in any other pursuits than the one at hand (2 Tim. 2:3, 4). His imagination must be firmly under the control of the Lord Jesus Christ, and none other. Emotions likewise must be disciplined not to run amok. The same for the mind. Paula and I have never experienced harm nor encountered any real danger to ourselves in this work, but we also know that our Lord did not engage us in it until we possessed that kind of self-control and discipline.

We want also to beware of leaping to conclusions that this or that person is imprisoned. Time is a friend. If the person has been imprisoned for a number of years, one more day may not hurt much, as we wait and observe, pray and think. The Lord can confirm, and will do so.

On the other hand, if the person is not imprisoned, I doubt that our prayers could damage much more than our pride. No one wants to appear foolish. But it is possible the counselee could become more turned off and wounded in the end if what we prayed about was not his condition after all.

All cautions observed, nothing ought to deter us. How many people are there who are leading strangled lives, who know there is something more if they could only get to it? Such people would rather we try than guard our reputation. So what if we miss? At least we loved enough to risk, and though superficially some may be angry if we fail because we were wrong in diagnosis, they know at heart level at least we loved enough to attempt something for their sake.

This is the very work for which Jesus came to earth, to "Set the captive free." Let us respond and serve, and let the Lord who is foolish enough to use us cracked vessels live with the results! He is big enough to do that, only we do not want to use our freedom as a pretext for evil or foolishness. God's children—so very, very many of them—need to be set free.

Chapter Seven

Depression

Rejoice with those who rejoice, and weep with those who weep (Rom. 12:15).

Like one who takes off a garment on a cold day, or like vinegar on soda, Is he who sings songs to a troubled heart (Prov. 25:20).

Unfortunately, in zeal to heal while remaining woefully uninformed, Christians have often unwittingly done those things which torment rather than ease depressed people. The Body of Christ needs to learn first of all what *not* to do in their efforts to help those suffering in depressive states, and, second, what *can* be done which will complement whatever professional treatment may have been prescribed.

We need to understand what depression is, and what it is not. Though we recommend that the reader acquaint himself with the many valid medical definitions of depression, we do not intend to present those here. Our purpose is not medical. We do want to say emphatically that there are very real medically discernible chemical factors involved in depression, and that all who counsel without medical qualifications need to respect and observe medical counsel, advice and prescription. No Christian non-medical counselor should ever say, "Throw your pills down the drain," or "Quit seeing that psychiatrist." If a depressive under our ministry begins to improve, and we suspect that drugs may hinder more than help, we can send our counselee to the doctor to describe his improvement and ask the doctor about the advisability of reducing the dosage. Or, if we have opportunity, we ourselves can consult with the physician. No one should ever practice medicine without a license. To give medical counsel without training and licensing is legally reprehensible, to say nothing of being theologically erroneous.

It is not lack of faith to take medicine! Ecclesiasticus 38:1-8 (though as a part of the Apocrypha not regarded by Protestant churches as part of the scriptural canon, still regarded by all of Christendom as inspired by the Holy Spirit and to be respected) says,

> Honor the physician with the honor due him, according to your need of him, for the Lord created him; for healing comes from the Most High, and he will receive a gift from the king. The skill of the physician lifts up his head, and in the presence of great men he is admired. The Lord created medicines from the earth, and a sensible man will not despise them. Was not water made sweet with a tree in order that his power might be known? And he gave skill to men that he might be glorified in his marvelous works. By them he heals and takes away pain; the pharmacist makes of them a compound. His works will never be finished; and from him health is upon the face of the earth.

We do not think it lack of faith to ask a mechanic to overhaul our car engine, or a lack of trust to follow a recipe in baking. Neither should we, having prayed for healing, fear to take whatever medicines a doctor may have prescribed. If the Lord has power to heal, He has equal power to overcome any dosage no longer needed. Most physicians are happy to reduce dosages. Let the Body hear!

The first caveat is *not* to give medical advice! Few readers can imagine how many times we have heard of Christians arrogantly bragging about how they told someone to flush their medication down the toilet and to have faith, and how often we have heard of consequent damage, only to hear those same self-important counselors blame the results on the counselee's "lack of faith." That kind of arrogant foolishness needs to be repented of and firmly abandoned.

Depression is both physical and psychosomatic. In each case, however psychosomatically it may have been induced, depression is a very real physical condition. On the other hand, whether the depression originated in something chemical or was induced by organic shock to the system, or originated in some other cause, it holds tremendously intense psychological realities. Later on we will list many psychological causes for depression. It needs to be held firmly in mind that such a list does not overlook nor rule out simple chemical imbalance. These things overlap and interact.

We do intend to present a Christian definition of depression. It is our intention to equip Christians to minister to depressives in those ways in which every common lay person can minister, without impinging upon any professional medical field. It needs also to be remembered that in presenting a spiritual definition of depression, we are not intending to invalidate or treat any other definition as of lesser value. Many psychiatrists whom we have taught in our Christian counseling seminars have been able to lay our Christian definition of depression alongside their medical perspectives with no apparent conflict or difficulty.

In short, depression is a condition in which our personal spirit has died to its capacity to sustain the person fully, either emotionally or physically. Were the death of a spirit's capacity to function complete, death would be the result. "Remember Him before the silver cord is broken and the golden bowl is crushed, the pitcher by the well is shattered and the wheel at the cistern is crushed; then the dust will return to the earth as it was, and the spirit will return to God who gave it" (Eccles. 12:6, 7). In depression a person's spirit still sustains the body, though far less successfully than normally; it has no capacity to sustain the person psychologically. No matter how stridently duty calls, the depressive has no energy to perform. He cannot feel joy. Conversations which once were refreshment become a weariness. "Oughts" and "shoulds" impel him to make responses he can no longer feel or possess inner drive to accomplish. "Thou hast put me in the lowest pit, In dark places, in the depths" (Ps. 88:6). "I am shut up and cannot go out" (v. 8c). Whereas when not in depression, he may have been able to reach into inner reservoirs and call up reserve energy to make himself feel and act, now the reservoir is empty. He is emotionally bankrupt. There are no more emotional energy funds in the account. There is only perplexity, guilt, despair, bleakness and blackness.

Despondency is not the same as depression. We all have highs and lows. Normal people know that tomorrow they will feel better. They know they can still call upon inner reserve funds by listening to music, or hiking in the fields or going to a party or a prayer meeting—whatever they have learned to do which refreshes. Even if the normal "pick-me-ups" fail, they know that a night or two of rest will renew them. The key factor is that they still possess *hope*. The most telling fact of depression is *despair*. Depressed people are not only without hope, they *know* that tomorrow will not be better. Knowledge gained by bitter experience has taught them that tomorrow will be as bleak as today. It is not a matter of valid or invalid reasoning or positive thought. Facts—solid irrefutable events—nail the feet of tomorrow's bird of hope to the floor. There is no way to think or reason that somthing good will someday appear. The candle of hope is totally extinguished.

The first fact every ministering Christian must hold constantly in mind is that a depressed peson *cannot* help himself. Recovery is not a matter of thinking more positively, making a series of positive confessions; making oneself feel better, getting rid of a demon, nor getting enough rest or changing one's diet. Recovery is a matter of rekindling and resurrecting that deadened spirit. No person in depression can kindle his own fire. He must be brought out of the pit by others or not at all. He must be resurrected by the prayers of others. He *cannot do it alone.*

Sometimes depressions mysteriously lift, seemingly unaccountably. One wonders who may have been pumping the handle of prayer unseen and unknown, whether some chemical lack or imbalance was suddenly overcome, or whether the Lord, who moves in mysterious ways, simply sent a ray of light. For whatever reason, depressions sometimes slowly or suddenly unaccountably depart, but the point is that the depressive had nothing to do with it, and knows he didn't. Overcoming depression is not a matter of willpower.

Once we see that a depressive cannot do anything to move himself out of his condition, we will have the key to stop most of the mistaken ways by which we may have been trying to help depressives.

In a moment we will list many important things that should not be done, but first let us consider some diagnostic clues which will help to determine at least on a lay level whether or not a person is in fact in depression. Neurotic depression is not the same as psychotic manic depression. Neurotic depression is distinguished by lack of energy. The skin is often flaccid and gray, and the eyes commonly appear vapid and flat. Looking into the eyes of a depressive is to look into a sea of nothingness. One sees no drive, no flickers of interest, no sparks of emotion, no lust, no greed, no joy, no humor, no sparkle. Only emptiness.

Depression is also a matter of deepening degrees. Toward the depths, shoulders sag and steps shuffle haltingly. Hearing is not impaired but appears so, due to slowness or entire lack of response. Hair loses it shine and body, and finally hangs in greasy streamers. Sometimes stale body odors are present.

Manic depressives swing from euphoric highs to depressive lows. But at the bottom of the pendulum, they still retain vast energies. Looking into their eyes is not the same as peering into a neurotic depressive. A manic depressive's eyes seldom appear flat, and never vapid. Looking into them is to stare at a freight train hurtling towards you at a hundred miles an hour. The skin still has color and the step does not falter nor do the shoulders sag. A manic depressive may feel depressed but he knows in his heart that he will swing out of it again, and part of his anger is at the instability itself which he cannot control. To be stuck at either pole would seem preferable to the constant swing, even though at *conscious* levels, high or low, such a person may forget and think the high or low is all there is to life (chronic manic depressives are constantly being surprised consciously when no emotional condition lasts, either high or low).

Neurotic depressives often require little or no diagnostic skill on the part of the one ministering to them. They know they are depressed and can usually express that fact most clearly. Sometimes, having said they are depressed, they will volunteer enough symptoms to confirm easily the accuracy of their own self-diagnosis. If not, a few simple questions will quickly confirm the diagnosis: "How long have you felt this way? Do you wake up every morning feeling impossible? Is every little decision a major burden to you these days? Do you find that you can't make yourself do the simplest household chores (or tasks on the job) which you used to do easily? Do you hate yourself for it and sink further? Do people tell you to cheer up, and you don't know how, and then hate yourself for hating them?" Most depressives will unhesitatingly say, "Oh, yes," to all or most of these questions, grateful that you understand.

Depressives are usually emotionally honest. Depression is not a sign of weakness. Strong people fall into it. People who are determined not to hurt others find the pit of depression far more often than aggressively hurtful people. It is as though they were strong enough to prevent themselves from attacking others until unexpressed emotions rebounded to attack their own energies. Depressives are usually people who have had the emotional strength to face reality as it is, though they have tended to see the cup as half empty rather than half full. They are not in delusion. Their sight may be out of balance, full of the negative, but they have not lost track of reality. A psychotic may happily pronounce that two and two are five, but a neurotic depressive says, "Two and two are four, and I can't stand it another minute!"

Once diagnosis of depression is corroborated, ministry is totally different from that appropriate for a non-depressed person. (It should be stated here that we are addressing the matter of ministering to the neurotic, *not* the psychotic. The psychotic belongs in the hands of a professionally trained counselor.) One must do everything in reverse to what one would do in relation to a non-depressive. The key scripture is, "Rejoice with those who rejoice, and weep with those who weep" (Rom. 12:15). To weep with those who weep means to empathize, to enter in and feel with, to walk where the other is. What might benefit a normal person, one must *not* say to a depressive. What encourages a normal person will further depress a depressive. What lifts the heart of the normal will crush one already in the pits. All the techniques or personality charms we have found effective elsewhere belong nowhere in ministry to depressives. We have entered an entirely different ball game, which has its own rules. Success in healing comes only to those who learn the rules. Ministering to the depressed calls us to death on the cross so that none of our practiced ways for general ministry intrude and interfere.

This means that the Body of Christ must most importantly learn what *not* to do in proximity to persons in depression. Having taught in many seminars the following list of things not to do when counseling depressives, we are sad to report that the universal response has been, "Oh, my, I've done all the wrong things. I see I have meant to help, and I've actually been cruel. God forgive me." Let us hope we can at least lessen the burden we have unwittingly been to those in depression, by being careful to observe the following:

1. Do not say, "Cheer up!" A depressed person is totally unable to cheer himself, or to respond to cheer. It is not a matter of willpower. He is simply incapable of doing so! Trying to brighten and failing depresses him more. Your command not only tells him you fail to understand, it plunges him further into isolation.

2. Do not take a depressed person to a party. Parties may be good antidotes for momentarily despondent people. The fellowship and fun may refresh them. But that same comradeship and enjoyment only inundate a depressed person with feelings of guilt for being a wet blanket, and then perhaps also into jealousies and angers that others can enjoy life while he can't, thence into further guilt and anger at himself. We see from this why the Scripture says, "Like one who takes off a garment on a cold day, or like vinegar on soda, Is he who sings songs to a troubled heart" (Prov. 25:20). Again, joining the party is not a matter of will-power; it is not blameworthy that he can't put on a face so as not to hamper the merriment. Your taking him to a party has put the depressive in an untenable position which only causes his differentness to stand out like a thistle bush among the daisies.

3. Do not preach to a depressed person, or

4. scold, or

5. teach. Depressives know they cannot do what you preach because they know as St. Paul did "that nothing good dwells in me, that is, in my flesh; for the wishing is present in me, but the doing of the good is not" (Rom. 7:18). Failing energies drastically limit a depressed person's attention span. Words become a weariness. ". . . excessive devotion to books is wearying to the body" (Eccles. 12:12). Even normal people tire of wordiness; to depressives wordiness becomes oppressive by fatigue. Exhortations prove to him that you fail utterly to understand. You still think there is something he could and should do to help

himself if he would only try. You fail to grasp that his spirit is dead, incapable of functioning. He can turn all the knobs on his gas range and no burners will turn on. Your words show that you do not fully believe that his pilot light has gone out. He feels condemned.

6. Do not give advice. "Have you tried this? Well, if you would only—" All such well-meant remedies drive the depressive further into bleakness. Most likely he has tried everything his advisors can think of and more. Advice participates in the same delusion as exhortation. Nothing a person in the pits can do will propel him out of it and he knows that. The telling mark of depression is helplessness and hopelessness. Only someone who has experienced depression can fully appreciate the futility, the total blackness of the pit of despair. "I am reckoned among those who go down to the pit; I have become like a man without strength, Forsaken among the dead, Like the slain who lie in the grave . . ." (Ps. 88:4, 5a). Exhorters and advisors are to depressives what Proverbs 28:3 says, "A poor man who oppresses the lowly Is like a driving rain which leaves no food."

7. *Do not attempt to exorcise a depressive!* Depression is not first demonic. It is not primarily a matter of invasion by a foreign entity. Since it is a psychological and spiritual condition in which one's own personal spirit has sunk into death to ability to function, attended by all manner of concomitant fears, anxieties, guilts and frustrations, a demonic spirit of *oppression* may take advantage of the lassitude of mind and heart to oppress a depressive into further darkness. But the depressed person does not need even to be made aware of that possibility. One can silently bind and cast away any oppressive spirits and call for the Lord's angels to surround and protect him. "For He will give His angels charge concerning you, To guard you in all your ways" (Ps. 91:11). "The angel of the Lord encamps around those who fear Him, and rescues them" (Ps. 34:7). If someone treats the condition loudly and overtly as a demon and pronounces an exorcism, that spirit of oppression is

cast away. For a short duration, perhaps for a day, or even a week, the person may seem to be out of depression, and may give such testimony that the church rejoices in another seeming victory. But such a victory seldom lasts. If the condition in the heart and mind which invited the oppressive still remains, the person will soon plunge into the full depths again. The depressive will eventually feel worse than ever, and, when nothing good persists, he may conclude, "There, I knew it, even God can't help me. The devil's got me for sure. I'm doomed." "And they have healed the brokenness of My people superficially, Saying, 'Peace, peace,' But there is no peace" (Jer. 6:14). To make the depressive aware of demonic presences increases fear. Such people already know they are helpless. They know they have no power. To tell them that demons are present is like saying to a paper hanger busily slapping paper to the ceiling that malaria-carrying mosquitos are buzzing around him and he had better mash them or else, or like shouting warnings to a hog-tied man that he is about to be thrown into the water.

8. Do not take a depressed person to a prayer meeting. We all fall into the pits occasionally, and prayer meetings are usually great medicine for weary hearts. A good worship service lifts us. "Like apples of gold in settings of silver Is a word spoken in right circumstances" (Prov. 25:11) and "Like the cold of snow in the time of harvest Is a faithful messenger to those who send him, For he refreshes the soul of his masters" (Prov. 25:13). In the days when Proverbs 25 was written, a particular fruit called the kitchilika was grown in backyard gardens. It was somewhat like a cross between an orange and a grapefruit, looked in color like an apple, and was commonly squeezed for juice as a refreshing drink for weary traveling guests. Snow at the right time brings forth flavor, as frost is needed in the state of Washington to give its apples their tart and delicious flavor. Just so, the Word of God and prayer refresh non-depressive people. But depressives no longer possess a functioning spirit with which to catch and hold

either the Word or the presence of God. They are incapable of joining the corporate worship which lifts everyone else. It only depresses them further because they cannot help seeing the benefit others receive while they feel nothing but increased sadness, anger and jealousy.

9. Do not take a depressed person to a comedy, or for a hike in the woods, or a picnic, or for a swim at the beach for all the same reasons that parties are taboo.

10. Do not exhort a depressive to find help in private devotions. Do not expect him to be able to leap into the arms of the Lord for comfort and healing. Devotional practices are first and best helps for a normal person. But for the depressed they are torture. Depressives no longer feel that they can pray, especially for themselves. Agnes Sanford in first stages of depression could still pray for others and they would be healed, but she had absolutely no faith in her prayers for herself.

> O Lord, the God of my salvation, I have cried out by day and in the night before Thee. Let my prayer come before Thee; Incline Thine ear to my cry! For my soul has had enough troubles, And my life has drawn near to Sheol. . . . Thy wrath has rested upon me, And Thou hast afflicted me with all Thy waves. . . . My eye has wasted away because of affliction; I have called upon Thee every day, O Lord; I have spread out my hands to Thee. . . . But I, O Lord, have cried out to Thee for help, And in the morning my prayer comes before Thee. O Lord, why dost Thou reject my soul? Why dost Thou hide Thy face from me? (Ps. 88:1-3, 7, 9, 13, 14).

Depressives have become convinced God will not hear their prayers. Again, therefore, to subject them to meetings in which their eyes can see the faces of others suffused with His presence while they feel only the blackness of apparent rejection is to them nothing but torment. To expect that the Lord will come to them in private devotions reveals that you fail to comprehend they can no longer abide in His presence. The powerful presence of the Lord which refreshes others only oppresses them.

How long, O Lord? Wilt Thou forget me forever? How long wilt Thou hide Thy face from me? How long shall I take counsel in my soul, Having sorrow in my heart all the day? How long will my enemy be exalted over me? Consider and answer me, O Lord, my God; Enlighten my eyes, lest I sleep the sleep of death, Lest my enemy say, "I have overcome him," Lest my adversaries rejoice when I am shaken (Ps. 13:1-4).

One might ask, "How could His perfect and gentle presence ever oppress anyone?" The Lord's presence in reality never oppresses, but depressives are fully capable of perceiving blessing as oppression. This is the closest depressives come to delusion. ". . . with the pure thou dost show thyself pure; and with the crooked thou dost show thyself perverse" (Ps. 18:26 RSV). Remember it is the same sun arising in Malachi 4:1 which destroys the wicked completely, while in verse two it is a sun of righteousness rising with healing in its wings. I (John) can remember being so foolishly angry a number of times at my parents or brothers or sister that when one or all of them with a fully good heart came to offer affection to me, it seemed full of guile and oppression, something not at all to be received, until the anger had run its course. Just so, the eyes of a depressive wear glasses that see rejection and "I ought to be rejected" when love is purely poured. They cannot receive His goodness and mercy when they most need it, often thinking perversely that they don't deserve it because obviously they have failed, whereas when not in depression they would have grasped easily that they never did have to deserve His love. Jealousy of others who obviously enjoy His favor continually attacks and oppresses depressives; also when the depressive is in crowds and groups his energies are too low to withstand the impressing energies of others around him. I (John) can remember that when I suffered migraine headaches, I could not stand Paula's presence. I wanted her nearby. But my spirit was somehow more sensitive under the pain to movements around me. Sounds strummed on the nerves of my body as if raking me with briars. People under depression have lost energy to respond, but the energies of others crash like high and demanding waves on their shores. They cannot stand to be in crowds, especially under the powerful energies of prayer or high emotions. For that reason,

11. Do not take a depressive to a worship service, or

12. the theatre, ballet, or opera, or

13. a ball game or other sporting event.

14. Do not attempt to heal the memories of a person in depression. Often some ancient and unhealed memory is a primal cause for the depression, but that can only be healed *after* the subject is out of depression. Inner transformation is death and rebirth in the inner man. At best it requires strength of spirit as we undergo whatever degree of trauma such change by inner death and rebirth requires. (See Chapter Six, "Breaking the Cycle," in *The Transformation of the Inner Man* for a fuller exposition of the process of death and rebirth in inner healing.) Depressives cannot withstand the pressures of inner transformation. We must lift the depressive out of the pit and then not fail to heal the inner heart so that guilts, angers, hates, rejections, or other woundings and sins do not entangle and re-imprison him in depression.

15. Do not visit overlong with a depressive. Be sensitive to his energy level and attention span.

One might ask, "Well, then, what is left that one *can* do for a person in depression?" A great deal. But one must know what, and be confident in the Lord that we truly can "do all things through Him who strengthens me" (Phil. 4:13).

In the process of revealing what can be done, we will also continue to list what one should not do.

16. Do not smile. Wipe the smile off your face. "Weep with those who weep." We must enter in where the other is before we can carry him out. We do not have to become what he is, but we must empathize until he knows that we know, and that we can share what he feels, without judgment or blame. Smiles tell him that we are not where

he is, and more cogently, that we fail to commiserate and probably cannot, and are therefore to be avoided. There are inner steel doors which when shut are not likely to open again for a while.

Do commiserate. Sit down and begin to share all the *worst* things. "I know how you feel. Every morning the sky is black. Every decision is too much. You can't make yourself do the little things you used to do easily. You hate yourself and then you hate others because they can do everything so easily, and then you hate yourself for hating them. And nobody understands. They say, 'Cheer up,' and try to make you feel better, and you can't. You know tomorrow isn't going to be any better. You've tried everything and nothing works."

By now the depressive will be sitting in the palm of your hand. He knows you are not in depression, because he can see it. And he believes you have been there because you understand and you aren't saying and doing all the foolish things everyone else has tried on him. At least some of his loneliness is eased. You aren't likely to reject him by being stupidly unaware of where he is. And since you are obviously out of depression, a tiniest glimmer of hope may for the first time enter his mind.

A psychiatrist friend, Dr. John Lefsrud of Edmonton, Alberta, knowing how vital hope is to the depressed, greets depressives at the entrance to his clinic with his own firm and compassionate presence, addresses them by name and says, "Well, what are you going to do when you get out of here?" He doesn't demand or wait for an answer. By his professional status and the question, he is purposefully implanting a seed of hope.

Within the above paragraphs were several other implicit recommendations.

17. Do not stand when the other is sitting. You may have little awareness of posture relative to status, but a depressive most likely will. Your standing will elevate your presence as a weight over him. Sitting, relaxedly, in a chair on the same level with him says you are entering in

sensitively, on his level. I (John) learned this the hard way. A lady friend brought her husband who was in the early stages of depression and whom I had never met. He was a proud man; for him to have any emotional problem was already demeaning, and it was downright insulting to be expected to talk to a counselor. Only the pressure of his wife forced him to come at all. We had recently left the pastorate to begin a counseling service on faith and were using some low-slung chairs a friend had given us for counselees in the office while I used a rickety old high-backed thing for an office chair. Already needing something to pounce on to justify anger so he could escape, that was his opening. "He who is estranged seeks pretexts to break out against all sound judgment" (Prov. 18:1 RSV). To him it was patent that I had purposely chosen such chairs and such a seating arrangement to debase my counselees and elevate myself, and after telling me all about that in no uncertain terms, he flounced out, leaving his mystified wife wringing her hands, while to me there was no mystery at all, only regret.

18. Don't sit too close. Do not invade his space. With normal people I like to be close. In prayer, especially, I will kneel beside the other, and place an arm over the other's shoulders. Such closeness is to be avoided when ministering to depressives. Their jangled nerves cannot stand such proximity.

19. Do not minister to a depressive in a group or even two by two. If more than one ministers, let one sit in front, holding whatever attention is required, and let others sit behind the counselee, present but out of demanding consciousness. The Lord sent them out two by two (Luke 10:1). Ecclesiastes 4:9-10 says, "Two are better than one because they have a good return for their labor." Normal people are best helped by many. "But in abundance of counselors there is victory" (Prov. 11:14). Presence of many avoids confusing romantic notions; it avoids latching onto one person as healer rather than the Lord. But the depressive cannot stand the freight of too many people's unconscious demand for response simply by being visibly

present. If more than one ministers to a depressed person, they should try to arrange things so that assistants are comfortably out of range. Depressives can only handle one, and that usually not for too long.

20. Do not close the door. Closing a door in a counseling office, or finding some enclosed private place to speak of intimate matters, is comforting and assuring to normal persons. It says you respect their need for confidentiality. But to a depressive it may spell entrapment. He may need to feel that he can get out if he needs to flee. Your leaving the door open says you will respect that. And it also tells him you do not intend to put him through a spate of internal searches he can't now stand. That open door is a mark of your sensitivity to him. It relaxes him.

21. Do not be humble. Do not say, "I *may* be able to help you." Do not say, "Is this how you sometimes feel?" With normal people we do not want to seem presumptuous or prideful. We ask rather than state. We try to show respect for the other's privacy and initiative. We may mask our own inner confidence behind "may" and "I think I can," for humility's sake. Depressives, contrariwise, need to hear nothing humble, no "I think I know how you feel," no "ifs" whatever. They need to hear "I *know* how you feel." But then you must prove it by commiserating. If a counselor has never been depressed, he must borrow someone's experience and speak as though he has been there. It is vital to the other to establish trust and confidence. When the time is appropriate, a counselor can say, *"I can get you out of there,"* but not "I think—" or "I may—" or "It is possible that—" Agnes Sanford remembered what she thought to herself when a young man approached her to minister to her when she was in depression, "If this young man says one 'if,' I know I'll never get well." The depressive at that moment is like a man being rolled into an operating room about to undergo surgery, totally dependent on the doctor. If the doctor were to try to be humble saying, "I don't know whether I can take this gall bladder out or not," I guarantee most pre-ops would be on their feet running bare-bottomed

pell-mell out the hospital door! We want absolute sureness in our doctor any time our life is dependent on his skill. Depressives know they can't revive themselves. If you offer to help, it will be all up to you or not at all. Knowing that, they want to hear no lack of confidence, no "ifs," no lack of positive assurance of success. They want to know that you know how they feel before they venture one iota of trust in you. Your assertion and your proof that you do know is tonic to their tortured soul, for they have borne the burden of trying to make others understand them and failed often so completely that your assertion that you already know how they feel and then the fact that you proceed to prove it is restful beyond measure.

22. Do not explain or talk too long. Once you commiserate enough to see that they are willing to place themselves in your hands because you understand them, stop talking and say, "I can get you out of there."

23. Do not say, "You can get out of depression," or "I can tell you how to get out of your depression." That is the surest way to blow the whole mission and slam the doors shut. Their healing must rest squarely and solely on your shoulders. A depressive is emotionally paralyzed. When the four men let down the paralyzed man in front of Jesus, He looked up, and "seeing their faith, said to the man, 'Rise . . .'" (Luke 5:17-26). A depressed person will be resurrected from the pit by the rope of your faith, not at all his, and from the beginning he and you must be assured of that.

24. Tell him you know how to pray over him in such a way that *he will be healed.* But immediately hasten to add, "By my faith, not yours." *Do not let him think for a moment that you think he must do something,* anything at all, to claim his own healing. With normal people we want to minister in such a way that their own faith is so involved that in the end we can say as Jesus did, "Your faith has saved you; go in peace" (Luke 7:50). But a depressed person knows that if anything is up to him, it won't work. And he will be looking both for you to fail, and to succeed with him,

by being alternately sure you will fail and hopeful you won't.

25. Explain to him that he is like the paralytic who was let down before Jesus, and that you will pray over him a prayer by your faith, not his. Then pray over him. But in this case *do not lay hands on his head*. His energies cannot withstand the weight of your hand physically and his nerves are too battered. Lay hands *lightly* on his shoulders while standing behind him. Standing behind gives closeness while respecting distance.

26. Do not pray too long. Pray vividly, imaginatively, and positively. Remember not to say, "If it be Thy will." This is not the time for uncertainty. Nothing is surer in Jesus than that the Lord came precisely to set us free from such inner prisons, as He said in Luke 4:18: "The Spirit of the Lord is upon Me, Because He anointed Me to preach the gospel to the poor. He has sent Me to proclaim release to the captives, And recovery of sight to the blind, To set free those who are downtrodden, To proclaim the favorable year of the Lord."

I pray seeing and describing the frame of the other as transparent, seeing through to visualize the candle of his spirit as having gone out, now being rekindled by the Lord.

27. Do not let the other measure success or failure by feelings or any immediate signs. I hasten to say, "I know, Lord, that [name] may not feel anything at present. We are not doing this on the basis of feelings, but on the basis of my faith, and I know it will work. Sooner or later, maybe today, maybe next week, but certainly in the near future, this person will begin to feel better, like suddenly seeing a blade of grass popping up through the snow. I'm going to hold him in my heart, Lord, and I will keep on praying until he is totally free and out of depression. I know it will work, Lord, and I thank and praise you for it."

28. Do not end the session with the prayer. Say immediately, "I want to see you again."

29. Do not say, "Can you come to see me again?" or "Would you like to see me another time?" With normal people we

assure respect of their wishes by such questions. Depressives are sure that no one could love them (or ought to) and certainly no one wants to be around them. "I want to see you again" is thus healing to their expectancy and to their dread of rejection.

Explain that sometimes we need to pray several times for the inner pilot light to come on and stay on. I sometimes say, "Our inner being is like an old Ford motor on a cold day. Sometimes it conks out or coughs again several times before it keeps running by itself. We may need to pray several times, but in the end I know it will work." Make another appointment.

30. Do not leave anything indeterminate. Make a specific time and date. "I would like to see you on Wednesday at 2:00." If you say, "Come when you can," he won't. Nail it down.

31. Do not expect the depressive to come to you. If the miracle has not already happened, he won't. To get dressed to go somewhere is too much, let alone the fear of failure. Rather, you go to him. If you don't already know, say, "Where do you live? I'll come and get you." Normal people want to be given some latitude and privacy to feel free to keep an appointment or not. Depressives must have assurance that you will take full responsibility to come after them, and that you want to. They may say, "Oh, don't put yourself out for me," but do not believe them. Put yourself on the line for them.

32. Do not fail to keep the appointment. That is absolutely imperative. If grandmother dies, bury her next week. That depressive's life now hangs on your dependability. If you fail to show up, no matter how valid the reason, nor how reasonably his *mind* says "I understand, it couldn't be helped," his *heart* will conclude, "I knew it. It isn't going to work. I'm let down and rejected again, as I deserve to be."

33. In your prayer do not hand the person over to God. Agnes Sanford, known the world over as the pioneer into rediscovering healing among mainline churches, the discoverer and forerunner of healing the inner man,

post-graduate depressive and authority on how to minister to depressives, lost Ted, her husband, by death, and promptly sank into another depression herself. She came to Paula and me, then pastor and wife in the small town of Council Grove, Kansas, in the little First Congregational Church, United Church of Christ. We were overawed that this great pioneering saint would come to little us wanting help. We thought it humble and appropriate to say in prayer, "We place Agnes in your hands, Lord. We release her to you. We know you will care for her, Lord Jesus, because you love her." Agnes sank immediately into the blackest pits of depression. When I next saw her, she let me know how Paula and I had failed her. Agnes could still pray for others and they would be healed. She could still teach and be powerfully effective. She had faith for others and not one whit for herself! She had already tried God alone for herself and she and He (in her thinking) had failed. To hand her over to God was to doom her to failure. She needed to be carried by others, and had come to us for that and that alone, which was the very thing our false humility and fear prevented us from doing for her. I immediately repented and said, "Oh, Agnes, we'll be glad to do it for you. We'll be glad to carry you in our hearts. We'll love you to life. That's a delight. You're not a burden. You're a joy." Agnes quickly rose out of depression. I continued to carry her in a heart of love (see Chapters Twenty-One and Twenty-Two of her autobiography *Sealed Orders*). Agnes not only was delivered from depression, she mellowed and became freer and wiser, happier and more relaxed as the years passed.

Never release people who have been depressed too soon into God's hand alone. You must carry them even as St. Paul wrote in Galatians 4:19, "with whom I am again in labor until Christ is formed in you." Note the "again." People, strong and sure in Jesus, ministering saints as Agnes was, can temporarily lose it and need to be carried awhile. Do not give up. Persevere. Resurrecting the other may take a long time. One woman whose relatives called me (John) for help was so depressed she had been in bed two long years, with bedsores on her body. Her mother-in-law was running her household and caring for her and the children. I ministered to her as we have outlined. It took persistent visits, two a week at first, then once a week for over six months, before she rallied enough to rise out of her bed and begin to assume her position as a wife and mother. It took many more months of counseling to discover and heal the many hidden roots behind the depression.

34. Do not carry the burden of the other alone. You must minister one on one, but apart from the person in depression, call friends and prayer warriors to help you carry the burden. Wisdom may dictate whether to tell the depressive or not. Some already feel guilty that you have to expend so much effort, and reproach themselves if they do not quickly arise. They do not want to burden anybody, which is a part of why they went into depression and which must be unlearned eventually. But for the presence of such wrong thinking, one may not feel it wise to inform the other of the many who are praying. On the other hand, some persons would take such information as a mark of love and be encouraged. We should act as we sense each individual needs.

35. Do not enlist the prayer help of the "wailers." We do not need the moaners and the groaners whose psychic energies may afflict the counselee. Draft prayer warriors who are bright, positive and happy.

36. Do not overlook simple practical matters as a depressive begins to come out of it. "Oh, you have a new hairdo." "You look better today." Body language, dress, sparkles in the eyes, many things will be clues as the other begins to resurrect. We can help that process of re-entry in two ways. One, to notice, affirm, and compliment when a tiny practical step has been taken. "You're wearing a shirt and tie and a nice suit again. You look great. That's good to see." Two, we can encourage the person to try his wings again in many little ways.

A young man ministering to Agnes years ago (not myself), seeing that she was beginning to come alive, said,

"Agnes, what did you used to like to do before you became depressed?"

"Oh, I used to like to write. I'm an author."

"Well, try your hand at it again. Don't knock yourself out, but see if you can get some enjoyment out of it again.'

Agnes wrote a full three-act play, the story of Saul and Jonathan and David. Behind her depression had been many angers no Episcopal rector's wife ought to express. The more people she slew on stage the better she felt, until entire armies had been slaughtered! Some people play piano or guitar, or garden, or hike, or birdwatch, or fish. Whatever practical interest was there, encourage renewal.

37. If the person begins to fall into a transference, i.e., thinks he or she is falling in love with you, do not cut that counselee off. With some, you can explain what a transference is (See Chapter Twenty-One, "Fathers and Mothers in Christ," in *The Transformation of the Inner Man*). Some are not willing to hear that their love for you has unreal or confused elements. That places the burden squarely on your heart. Keep your own heart clear. Know that that kind of love from the other is not romantic or mate love no matter how convinced the counselee may be that it is. Know most surely that your own love for the other is neither romance nor mate love, that yours is that of the Lord for one being redeemed, or like that of a parent for a child, and that the other's love is a temporary, overly intense fastening upon you as the umbilical cord of their life's blood. Someday that cord will be cut and you will be the best of friends, but never lovers.

There is a great danger in this area. More counselors have fallen by not recognizing and handling transferences than any way Paula and I know of. So much so, one could almost say, "Flee the battle in the first place." But Christ does not call us to be safe, rather to minister and risk ourselves as His own example showed. One rhema application of a word from Scripture has been of great assurance to us, "Where no oxen are, the manger is clean, But much increase comes by the strength of the ox" (Prov. 14:4).

Things may get messy and fraught with danger as we serve, but the Lord would not have us be Pharisees who guard their own untouchableness, but servants who bear the burden and the heat of the day.

Be sure to persist until the other is free from depression, its root causes discovered, and the other fully transformed and walking in his new life. Do not terminate either the counseling or the relationship until the counselee is able to stay free by himself. Our minds can grasp quickly that we are loved, but the heart must test and try and be assured again and again and again before it settles, firmly fixed, a question not needing to be raised again, that it is loved. Security becomes courage to live when the question of love is settled.

In transferences the counselee places his counselor in a seemingly idolatrous position, for temporarily he drinks from the counselor what normally ought to be obtained only directly from God. In or out of transference, a person rising out of depression walks for a while not in his own spiritual strength but in the piety of his helper. One could liken this to being born again. In physical birth we are encased in our mother's body and life. During that time we are not idolatrous, though all our life's sustenance is mediated through her being. We are not responsible for ourselves; another is. To surrender such control of ourselves when we are adult *is* idolatrous, for our Lord wants us to stand on our own feet, dependent only on Him. But it needs to be understood that people in depression are no longer capable of functioning as responsible adults. This is not to say they have regressed to become as little children again, only that they have become currently incapable. They need to be carried for a time within the ambiance of another.

The relationship is thus not idolatrous. But therein lies danger, for the counselor may so enjoy carrying the counselee—for ego, power, lust, the need to be needed, possessiveness, the idolatry of being like God to another—that he may unconsciously, even consciously, be unwilling to release when the time is ripe. Or the reverse may be true:

the counselor may be so worried, wearied or bothered by the responsibility that he cuts off the relationship too soon, and the counselee feels rejected and plummets again. Or the counselee may be tempted to hang on too long or cut off too soon. Most often it is counselees who become confused. Counselors must hold the line, informed and aware.

The worst and most common danger is sexual. Whether men counsel women or the reverse, or persons of the same sex counsel one another, either or both may become sexually or romantically aroused and confused. Mates of either or both may feel that spiritual adultery is going on, i.e., when one or both drink the kind of love and sharing (apart from sexual concern) which properly belongs only to mates. That may in fact be happening. Society, looking on, may impute scandal into an innocent love relationship, or rightly see spiritual and/or physical adultery and react. Tragically, it often happens that the couple do become sexually involved.

For all these reasons, when counselors see that counselees, in all kinds of counseling, whether depressives or not, are latching on, they should keep wise colleagues closely informed and watchful. Counselors must be humble enough to hear and heed the warning notes of such friends. If love is a fire, it is of great benefit to resurrect and warm hearts to life, but no wise person plays with it. It must be wisely and completely contained and checked continually lest it break out in unwanted places. In short, we must not fear to risk, but neither should we fail our Lord's service by lack of caution. Let wisdom and restraint prevail. The responsibility rests on the counselor's shoulders to make the counselee aware he is loved, while holding that love in proper limits, without making the counselee feel rejected.

The Lord sent me one time into a hospital room where I found a lady tardily recovering from a heart attack. Whether the depression caused the attack or came afterwards, the result was that she no longer wanted to live. I assisted the medical people by ministering to the physical heart by prayer, and then began the longer task of resurrecting her from depression. Several months later she was nearly free of depression and had overcome many of the original causes for both.

I was escorting her in my car to a prayer meeting. She was a physically beautiful woman, about the age of my mother, married, and a grandmother. I could sense that she was summoning courage to ask me an embarrassing question. Finally she drew a deep breath and blurted out, "Pastor, if I asked you to go to bed with me, would you deny me?"

Hurt for her, for the pain and confusion she had put herself through, and ashamed that I had not spared her by wiser counsel, I thought a while and finally said, "You know that I care for you, but it's not that kind of love, my friend. As the Lord's servant, I must not, so I would have to deny you, but I would not reject you." Though shocked, I was trying in my own immature way, by my answer and by my manner, to tell her that I would hold the line for her, that I did in fact have a love for her, and that I still accepted her and did not disrespect her for asking. I knew something was going on which was not really sexual at all. I wanted to keep the door open for further counsel. She would need to talk about it. There was a depth of transference and confusion.

I knew that something powerful had so impelled her as to overcome the great propriety with which she had always conducted herself. It was later discovered that though she might actually have seduced me had I been less secure in Christ and in my love for Paula, at a deeper level she was testing me. If she threw off the ladylike performing mask and appeared seductive, would I still be able to love, like and respect her? My answer, whether wise or foolish I still wonder, at least satisfied her deeper questions. I would not let the relationship go astray; she could rest about her feelings. She concluded then (it was later revealed) that she was indeed loved truly, and properly, and could risk becoming whole and free.

I share this story that others may see that sometimes

when relationships seem to be going the wrong way, underneath they may not be at all—and certainly need not. At that moment her life hung both on my determination to live righteously in Christ, and upon my willingness to let Jesus find and minister behind seeming wrong to the reality emerging within her. It was later disclosed that a stepfather she trusted and loved had made sexual advances. Though twenty years older than me, she had put me in his place and was testing; was it safe to let any father figure love her? Could her love seduce a father figure? Could she be loved without that love turning to sex improperly? That matrix of never answered questions had lain causally below every depression to which she had fallen prey. All of that was what was actually behind what seemed on the surface to be only sexual lust.

By this story I would advise counselors, especially in ministering to depressives, *not* to react to what *seems* to be happening. "And He will delight in the fear of the Lord, And He will not judge by what His eyes see, Nor make a decision by what His ears hear" (Isa. 11:3). Equal errors could have been made in the above story; on the one hand to fall to temptation, on the other to have acted self-righteously as though that person were reprehensible and only to be scolded, rejected, and condemned. Both would have missed what was actually happening. We must hold circumspectly to the way of the Lord concerning our own life, but minister compassionately and patiently towards the other that the Lord may have opportunity to reveal the actual heart's song.

We approach the causes of depression by that story for the reason that the most common and basic cause of depression is a combination of performance orientation and hidden unresolved emotional factors of guilt, fear and resentment and rejection. Most likely had a person been able to elevate that nexus of sores to conscious awareness, depression would not have happened. When depression lifts, the heart begins to seek ways to send to the surface signals of the original causal hurts and sins. Performance orientation, as it did before the depression, still prevents simple open admission of guilt or trauma. So the inner spirit finds gambits, like dreams, or stories, or seeming seduction. It is the counselor's task to catch the clues and the Holy Spirit's to reveal what they mean.

Performance orientation can best be understood by reading Chapter Three in our book *The Transformation of the Inner Man*. In short, performance orientation occurs when a person does not receive enough unconditional love and affection, taking into the heart instead the message, "Only if you measure up to the standards around here will you be loved or belong." Since we all need love to live, fear rules the heart, fear of rejection. The result is either compliance—"I will do whatever seems to gain your approval because I understand that I must do so to win your love"—or rebellion—"If I have to perform for love, I won't at all, and that will punish you." If the person is one who tries to perform for love, then he is filled with striving. He is never sure he has done enough to merit love. He is always measuring and judging how well he has done. Whatever affection does come his way never fully convinces him he is loved, because he thinks, 'If they knew what I'm really like, they couldn't love me." Since being loved has become equated with being "good," every performance-oriented person fears discovery. He cannot let others see what is repulsive or reprehensible, either on the outside in behavior or on the inside in his nature, for fear of rejection. This locks him into playing roles while feeling innerly more and more isolated. The longer he performs, the more subconscious anger is fomented; he is angry that he has to perform for love instead of being loved simply because he exists. He develops an inner need to blow the good-guy image in order to discover whether he will be loved anyway (which is what was behind the grandmother's seductive proposal to me).

In relation to depression, this means that performance-oriented persons strive too long too hard to perform, until the inner being gets tired of the game. The unrecognized thought of the heart is, "This isn't working. I don't feel a bit more loved than when I began (whatever the person set out to accomplish). I quit." The spirit goes on a sit-down strike and dies to willingness to perform at all. Depressions of this type can happen seemingly overnight, though observant people could have seen the signs long before. Burn-out depressions are never as sudden as they seem.

A performance-oriented person can also try to win love by performing, and failing, perhaps not at all in the eyes of others, but in his own, feels dejected and unloveable. If loved ones give affection, he feels guilty; he hasn't deserved it, or "They couldn't really mean it," because then he would have to live up to it, and feels unable and unworthy. Under that kind of inner turmoil, he performs badly, feels worse, so performs less well and fails again and so sinks stage by stage down into the pit of depression.

A performance-oriented person can plummet into depression from either end of the scale. Over-achievers get tired of the effort, and successes threaten to reveal to them that they don't feel a bit more loved or secure. The result is inner capitulation. On the other hand failure is seen as tantamount to lack of love and rejection which creates more failure, which in turn becomes the downward spiral of failure and feelings of ineptitude until depression becomes the bottom of the pit.

Performance-oriented people also fall prey to depression by dint of isolation and guilt. If a performer knows he must confess his sins to another that he may be healed (James 5:16), he may dutifully do so, but very carefully and in controlled fashion, so that listeners may conclude that he is being open, honest and real, whereas in fact he has only played a carefully controlled role. The real inner, raw, unprepared unthought-out volcanic matter of inner turmoil is never let loose even to himself, much less to others. Most often, performance-oriented people will not even enter the role play of self-realization by confession. They are convinced that no one could love them if they ever knew what was inside them. All this means that the healing balm of forgiveness is not allowed at the core of the inner man where memories are stored. Further it means that the closer others become, the more diligently the performance-oriented person must work to keep up the front. Thus ancient guilts eat out the energy and strength of the performer. While he pours himself out for others, his own inner bank is being drained of resources until finally it is as though he skates over thin ice and plunges into the cold water of depression. Whether the resultant depression is sudden or slow in arrival, the cause is not whatever "final feather broke the camel's back." The cause lies in ancient guilts and loneliness never yet healed by the cross and blood of Christ.

Agnes Sanford was called upon to minister to a missionary lady sent home from the mission field overseas due to an unrelenting state of depression. Agnes ministered to her as we have outlined, until the lady was willing to talk about the possible causes of her depression. Though the lady was an evangelist, preaching the free gift of God's love to the heathen, she herself was so performance-oriented that at heart level she had never really believed God could love her if she didn't serve well or if she did some awful thing. At last it came out that at sixteen years of age she had had an affair and lost her virginity. Her performance-oriented nature had prevented her from telling anyone. She had tried to confess it in secret to Jesus and had striven to believe she had been forgiven. But she had never been able to forgive herself, and didn't see in her heart how anyone else could forgive her either, much less God.

Agnes exclaimed, "Oh, there we have it. It's an old unforgiven guilt way down in your heart."

"What do you mean, 'unforgiven?' I've been preachin' salvation to the heathen for fifty years! I *know* God has forgiven me."

"Yes," Agnes replied. "Of course the grown one knows you're forgiven. It's that sixteen-year-old girl inside you who has never felt it." If I remember Agnes' story correctly, the lady would have said something like, "That's preposterous," but the truth of Agnes' words reached too deep and touched that hurting heart until the grown one burst into tears and knew the truth of what Agnes had said.

"But how can God forgive that little girl now? That was over fifty years ago."

"What if you could imagine you were just sixteen and it was the very day after you'd done it and could walk right up to Jesus and tell Him all about it? Would He be able to forgive you?"

"Oh, yes, yes. Of course He could."

"Let's do it."

So they prayed just that way, asking Jesus to walk up to that young girl and tell her He forgives her, just like He did to that other woman so long ago to whom he said, "Neither do I condemn you; go your way" (John 8:11).

The lady who had preached forgiveness to the heathen for fifty years had now received it herself, and her depression was gone, never to return. It had no more lodging place in her heart. And the performer knew at the deep level of her heart that she really was loved when she hadn't done everything rightly.

Performance orientation could be said to lie in some degree behind every person in depression, even though it may not be the primal cause. The first cause, some blow or loss, guilt or rejection, is like the spark, but the performance orientation is the tinder. Or the wound is the seed, but performance orientation is the fertile ground where depression may quietly grow. It may not be that all depressed people are at root performance-oriented, but in more than twenty-five years' counseling experience, Paula and I have never yet found a depressed person in whom performance orientation was not a major factor causing the depression. It is of course not true the other way around— not all performance-oriented people are headed for depression. But I tend to believe that each other cause might not have concluded in depression were not performance orientation a contributing factor.

Other causes may be the following (not necessarily in order of importance or in order of frequency):

One may be an ancient guilt, such as was true in the missionary's story. Counselors need to comprehend one thing most clearly. People, performance-oriented or not, may go through the proper steps of confession and still retain guilt. If they have confessed in private as the missionary did (which by the way is unscriptural, there being no command anywhere in the Bible to confess sins in private, but clear directives to confess to others, as in James 5:13ff), the question remains in the person's heart whether mankind could forgive if anyone knew. Most likely the inner being remains as unconvinced of forgiveness as the heart of the missionary was. The Lord truly forgives; sometimes we do not receive.

If a person has confessed to others, he may not have let the balm of priestly authority reach his own tortured heart. Sometimes the only way performance-oriented people have known parental touch was by punishment, and so punishment has subconsciously become connected with knowing oneself to be loved. Such people can unknowingly be punishing themselves by refusing forgiveness, thus grabbing a false sense that God does love them because look how He is punishing them! Hebrews 12 thus twists in their minds to confirm that God loves them because He seems to be punishing them as they punish themselves.

Most often in cases in which guilt has produced depression, what Paula and I find is that the other truly believes that God has forgiven, but he has never effectively been able to forgive himself. Needing love and needing to convince himself he loves others, he could not forgive himself because to his mind had he loved he never would have done such a thing, and of course he doesn't deserve to be forgiven. Paula and I have sometimes heard performance-oriented people say when asked to forgive others, "Well, I could forgive him if he just deserved it, but he did that on purpose!" Just so, such people judge and refuse to forgive themselves. Grace for them has to be deserved. Performers' hearts block out the fact that grace means "undeserved favor"—at the very moment their minds may believe firmly in unmerited grace! Even non-performance-oriented people may do the same kind of blocking themselves out from forgiving themselves. We have all bought to some degree the idolatrous lie that we ought to have been gods, and hate ourselves when our sins prove we aren't.

All this leads to another caveat. Counselors *must not* believe counselees too easily when they say they know they are forgiven. Fruits, not protestations of faith, reveal what is there. If the wound is still there, something hasn't happened, most likely forgiveness. Further questions, in different ways, may reveal what is actually lodged in the heart: "Do you look back at that incident with deep peace, even gratitude that it happened, or with a shudder?" "Do you like you?" "How about liking that twenty-year-old you were when you did that?" "How do you feel about that guy who did that to you?" "Can you imaginatively take that younger person you were into your arms easily?" "Would you just as soon forget that one and get back up here to be this present one?" And so on. Somehow the person needs to be led to complete forgiveness of all involved, even to forgive God for letting it happen (2 Cor. 5:18-20), most especially to forgive and accept himself!

Childhood wounds sometimes fester until youthful energy wanes or present stresses break down resistance, depression being the result. Again, present stresses may seem to be the cause whereas they may only be the spark that lit the fuse to a bomb long ago set to detonate somewhere sometime.

Common wounds are: deprivation of affection, most wounding in earliest childhood; early loss of loved ones as in parental death, divorce or separation; being rejected and given away to desertion, orphanages or adoption; the loss of a favorite grandparent or brother or sister, or even the family dog; major illnesses in early childhood, especially the kind that necessitated long isolation. Or there can be too much responsibility too soon, as when parents are alcoholic or immature, and an older child takes responsibility to care for the younger ones, often without adequate provision.

Pre-natal and birth traumas, as described in earlier chapters, can later produce depression. Earliest wounds are more likely to produce depression than later wounds. Childhood traumas after infancy can be dealt with consciously at the time, or be remembered and wrestled through, whereas earliest wounds are often unknown to the conscious mind, and incapable of being recalled, but by that far more powerfully effective in the unconscious. It is not true that what you do not know cannot hurt you. The reverse is more nearly true—what we do not know and cannot see within us *can* hurt us.

One could set it as a principle that whenever people think to protect others by not sharing troubles with them (at all, we mean; there is wisdom in choosing right moments), they actually hurt their loved ones worse by leaving them to struggle in their spirits with feelings to which they can attach no names. It is often just this kind of unknown grief, guilt, fear or rejection which so devastates the inner man that depression is the result. Truth sets us free. We make crooked the straight paths of God when we obscure, thinking to protect.

Loss of a job, retirement, too many changes too rapidly, like retiring and quickly moving to a new locality away from old friends and church fellowship, can result in depression. Women whose lives have centered in being mothers may slump into depression when children leave the home. Retirement may spell uselessness, especially to performance-oriented men. Business failure may load guilt on inner volcanic suppressions.

Death of a mate, or worse, divorce, may cast one into depression. Loss of a loved one means revolution in terms of long-practiced endearing actions and supports. There is no mate to share a gladness with, to laugh with at a comedy, to weep with over losses. Little rituals of comfort so long practiced, such as having a cup of coffee ready when he comes in the door, or her fingers kneading sore shoulder muscles at night, or snuggling together in bed after a long hard day, now, by their absence, speak volumes of loneliness.

Depression seldom hits as severely in those who have the gift of tears, or the ability to rage. It is the stoic, the philosophic controlled ones who unwittingly add fuel to later fires of depression. Nice people become depressed over losses and griefs more often than people who can take things out on others. Aggressive people do not store up so many hurts which turn inward to attack the holder. Quiet, disciplined people determined not to hurt, not ever to bother or be a burden, are the people to watch after loss. It is these who can slip most often into depression, though aggressive people can too.

Postpartum depression is common. Often, though not always, what happens is that a woman may have been so wounded as a girl that in her hidden inner heart she did not want to live. She may have grown beyond whatever the wounding was and happily sought marriage and pregnancy. But secretly part of her did not want to bring forth life. The little one in the womb may have triggered into her hatred of herself in the womb. During the pregnancy, all of her energies were preempted by nature to produce that new life. Once the baby was delivered, it was as though a taut rubber band snapped back to the other pull upon it, the hidden desire to end life, not to love and produce life. Now the burden of that new dependent life becomes unaccountably just that, a burden rather than the clean joy she thought it would be. Sometimes physical chemistry is a causative factor in these cases, but we tend to honor the speculation that if there were no a priori predilections to sorrow and death, the woman's vitality would beneficially alter her chemistry, especially as the love the baby gives to her and the needs of nursing would draw her to life. Again, we have noted that it is most often performance-oriented women who suffer more than normal postpartum symptoms.

A physical or great psychic shock may throw someone

into depression. Hysterectomies, the loss of a limb or an eye, or a disfiguring accident are often followed by depression.

Trauma or stress too long sustained, such as shell shock, may lead into depression. The head of a local TV station was brought to us, so far under depression he walked with a shuffling gait, led by the hand like a child, shoulders sagging, eyes vapid. The TV station had fallen on rough times—debts, hectic schedules, friction between personnel, etc.—and he had tried dutifully to carry it all on his own heart and shoulders. Though it was the work load and emotional stress which acted as the catalyst, the cause lay in his childhood. He had been raised by a domineering, thoroughly performance-oriented, success-hunting mother, and his father was ineffective. From neither was there affection and nurture. So long as the TV station seemed headed towards success and stability, he could withstand and even relish the pressure. Unconsciously he was being mama's good boy, succeeding despite all the odds, and rewarding himself emotionally with feelings of magnanimity. He could accept this tycoon he had become. It told him he was loved (and mama and papa could love him too). A few reverses were sustainable. But when failure seemed imminent, his own sense of worth was shattered. Looming failure sucked inner worth like a relentless vampire until all drive was gone and depression claimed its victim. It was necessary not only to lift him from depression, but then to penetrate behind the business failures he saw as the cause, to what in fact did eat away his inner being.

"Trips" of any kind sustained too long may swing the pendulum to depression. Even heightened joys, one after another, can end in a crash, when the inner being, seeking balance, finds something to be sad about. Many saints have been amazed and dismayed to find the pit of depression claiming them just after weeks and weeks of glorious adventures, mystic heights and great victories in the Lord. Everything seemed to be going great, and then seemingly out of nowhere there came feelings of depression. It is natural and healthy to swing to an opposite balance. But if some unhealed thing, from which perhaps we fled into serving the Lord so long and arduously, lies beneath the surface, we may land on the down side heavily enough to fall through into waiting glooms, and not find ourselves able to swing up again. Counterbalancing emotions are okay. We need them. What is not good is when we can't bounce back up because the low hooked into some depressing thing in us waiting to happen.

The shortest way to speak of causes is to say that if some great wounding, fear, anger, hate or guilt rampages unchecked within, any kind of shock or wound may propel us beyond itself into the depths of depression.

Depressives *can* be helped. We need only know how, and persist in prayer and counsel.

Two aspects need to be addressed before we leave the subject. *One*, we have not said much about anger. Some counselors see anger as a major cause, suspecting that it lies behind most depressions. One friend walked into the room of a client who had so fallen into depression, again and again, as to need hospitalization, and bluntly asked, "Okay, what are you angry about this time?" It worked. The patient blurted it out, and began to recover. If it is true that anger often lodges in the hearts of depressives, we need to remember that performance orientation is the key. Anger expressed properly is healthy, as Jesus looked around at them "with anger, grieved at their hardness of heart . . ." (Mark 3:5), and often rebuked the Pharisees and scribes in sharp words. Performance-oriented people suppress anger. So do we all at times. Most of the time we will find, however, that it is performance orientation that has locked anger inexpressibly into the heart until it festered and sickened the spirit of the holder.

Two, "What about catching the signs and preventing depression?" and, "What can relatives and friends do who live with depressives?" People who have had more than one depression can learn to recognize the signs. So can their relatives and friends. Several antidotes can check the slide. Encourage the person to talk, to get it "off the chest."

Draw the person into sharing. Change things. Break treadmill routines, have some fun, take a short holiday, get together with some friends who make you feel good, who are not a responsibility, with whom one does not have to put on a face or keep a guard up. Get into a prayer meeting (before depression sets in, all the no-nos in the first part of this chapter may be good medicine). Take the person to a counselor. Best of all, give lots of warm physical affection and look for excuses to give positive affirmations and compliments. If some family members are part of the problem, find a little space and time away from them for the potential depressive.

If the person has already slid into depression, family members need to go about family routines as though they are not terribly upset. Above all, avoid haranguing and scolding when the depressive fails to perform. Family members can unobtrusively pick up some of the chores the depressive is dropping. If the family carries on solidly, the guilt of the depressive is lessened. Normally such behavior would tell a person he is unwanted and not needed, but the depressive is likely to be more relieved than hurt.

In a hospital, about to undergo an operation, we are not at all helped by a nurse who exclaims, "Oh my, you look a wreck! Oh, you poor thing!" But if she proceeds about her business calmly and briskly, composed in her own self, we get the message, "Well, I must be okay, she doesn't seem too concerned. Everything's going okay, I guess." Depressives need that kind of "world-in-place" atmosphere about them. High tensions and clattering noises fray the nerves of normal people; to depressives they are wearying and nerve-shattering in the extreme, especially since as performers they have always taken emotional responsibility to hold things together, and now they can't.

Nature is good for people on the slide or already in the pits. I love that old hymn which sings so truly:

Into the woods my Master went,
Clean forspent, forspent,
Into the woods my Master came,
Forspent with love and shame.

But the olive trees were not blind to Him,
The little gray leaves were kind to Him;
The thorn tree had a mind to Him,
When into the woods He came.

Out of the woods my Master went,
And He was well content.
Out of the woods my Master came,
Content with death and shame.

When Death and Shame would woo Him last,
From under the trees they drew Him last;
'Twas on a tree they slew Him last
When out of the woods He came.
—*Pilgrim Hymnal,*
Pilgrim Press, Boston 1831

Ever since God blessed Adam and Eve to till the garden, nature and mankind have been intended to care for one another. What soul is there so dead that his spirit finds little repose and refreshment in nature? Some are blessed by the sea. Nothing eased Agnes Sanford so much as being by or on the sea. Some are refreshed by woods or prairies or streams or lakes. Forests sing to my tattered nerves a song of eternity and rest in God's goodness. Rippling grasses on the prairie or golden waves of ripening wheat soothe my over-busied soul and calm my spirit. The gentle prickling touch of grass on the feet or the searching warmth of dust between the toes, the kiss of tufts of breeze upon the cheeks, or lying flat and watching lacy shapes of white on blue form ships and dragons in the skies—all these things are tonic to weary souls and depressed spirits. People on the slide need large doses of quiet nature before it's too late. Even nature on the rampage can have a therapeutic effect. Having been raised on the prairie, I absolutely love and cherish and relish and get thrilled and turned on by a wildly crashing thunderstorm. I'm exhilarated and refreshed, and when it's over, feel like singing praises as I walk in the smell of new, wet earth and see the sparkle of drops falling from wet leaves. All the earth wears a mantle of freshness, and so does my spirit.

Some may have been frightened in a storm or depressed even more by nature's quietness. Know what is good for each, and apply it.

Finally, performance-oriented counselors will try to remember the thirty-eight no-nos above, in precise order, and strive to apply them exactly—and become despondent in the process! But the secure will catch the principles of sensitivity and common sense, notch the cautions into the memory bank, and let the love and compassion of the Holy Spirit move through their eyes and voices and hands to lift the weary depressed to resurrection life again.

For all those who find themselves exclaiming, "Oh my, I've blown it. How many depressed people have I already hurt?!" let's forgive and love ourselves and go on. Medical doctors, with the best of intentions, bled George Washington to death, but the field has matured, and so can we.

Chapter Eight

Defilements, Devils and Death Wishes

Do not be deceived: "Bad company corrupts good morals." Become sober-minded as you ought, and stop sinning; for some have no knowledge of God. I speak this to your shame (1 Cor. 15:33, 34).

Beloved, while I was making every effort to write you about our common salvation, I felt the necessity to write to you appealing that you contend earnestly for the faith which was once for all delivered to the saints. For certain persons have crept in unnoticed, those who were long beforehand marked out for this condemnation, ungodly persons who turn the grace of our God into licentiousnes and deny our only Master and Lord, Jesus Christ (Jude 3, 4).

Occasionally I have visited with someone, perhaps a total stranger, and felt for no exterior reason at all that I wanted to smash his face in! A few times, upon examining my own heart, I have found that that particular type of person has triggered into long-forgotten animosities toward someone else, festering in my heart. It was good to have those hidden feelings revealed so that friends could overcome them in prayer. I had been guilty of projectionism, which is what happens when an inner turmoil locates its enemy out there somewhere and projects its steam on some person who did not merit it at all. Thus I defiled him.

But occasionally I have known in my spirit that the desire for violence, to hit that guy, did not originate in me at all. Later, as I had opportunity to counsel with him, I found that he percolated with violence, not so much that he wanted to inflict it as that his spirit continually sent out signals to others to do violence to him! Such signals originate from a martyr attitude born of bitter-root judgments and expectancies to be struck and hurt by others. It was that which emanated from him which defiled me and created those feelings and thoughts within me.

Have we not all had occasions of being next to someone who radiated sexual uncleanness? Women tend to be more keenly aware of this than men. Many times wives have walked away from some chance meeting to fill their husband's ears with warnings about "that fellow," usually to the husband's bewilderment. "Hey, you just met that man! How can you know all that about him? Don't you think you're being a bit hasty and judgmental?" Later on he may discover that the fellow had seduced half the women in his office! She felt defiled in his presence. She knew. Wise husbands have learned to give some credence to such perceptions, at least to look for the outcropping of possible weeds in the garden.

Haven't we all met some people who instantly caused us to feel on guard? I remember hearing my friend who was a pastor raving about a teacher who had come from another country, who was teaching in his church. I was curious, and strangely worried in my spirit. My friend sensed that and arranged for us to have breakfast with him and his traveling companion. I liked the teacher. My spirit could trust him. But what an evil presence radiated from his companion! My spirit sang out inside me almost audibly, "Enemy! Enemy!" I felt unclean inside myself in his presence, unsettled and wary. I knew him to be a wolf in sheep's clothing.

I warned my pastor friend. But he could not hear me. The teacher returned home. His companion stayed, and ripped that congregation to shreds! According to him all art works and musical scores had to be thrown out of every home, unless they had the face or name of Jesus on them. They were of the devil. He pronounced curses over most of the congregation when they would not surrender to his wishes. Women in the congregation were told they would have uterine cancers if they disobeyed him, or if they merely disagreed. The congregation finally rose up and threw him out, along with my pastor friend, unfortunately. But worse yet, nearly a third of the congregation, the babies in Christ, were defiled by his spirit and left to join him in delusion.

In this story we see the operation of the gift of perception of spirits on the basis of our spirit's ability to feel what is in the other, to sense and identify defilement. We may possess that gift purely from God, but it grows by experience, "But solid food is for the mature, who because of practice have their senses trained to discern good and evil" (Heb. 5:14). The import of this story, however is not to teach about the gift of discernment, but the danger to those whose spirits either are not keen enough or not sufficiently mature to beware. That man's spirit so infected and defiled the simple that they found themselves thinking in ways and saying things they never would have allowed otherwise.

> Leave the presence of a fool, Or you will not discern words of knowledge. The wisdom of the prudent is to understand his way, But the folly of fools is deceit (Prov. 14:7, 8).

> For a fool speaks nonsense, And his heart inclines toward wickedness, To practice ungodliness and to speak error against the Lord, To keep the hungry person unsatisfied And to withhold drink from the

thirsty. As for a rogue, his weapons are evil; He devises wicked schemes, to destroy the afflicted with slander, Even though the needy one speaks what is right (Isa. 32:6, 7).

Incidentally, in about a year that man suddenly contracted intestinal cancer, and was dead in six weeks! One thinks of Herod, who was eaten by worms (Acts 12:23) and the magician whom the Holy Spirit blinded through Paul on the island of Salamis (Acts 13:1-12).

The tragedy in my friend's church was one of defilement. As I had found myself thinking strange thoughts in the presence of the people in our first examples, so these people found themselves thinking in that wolf's ways. We are not speaking of hypnotic spells nor of conscious thought-control techniques. That man himself was unaware of the demonic source of the influence of his spirit, though he had learned to depend on his ability to influence people. Later we will return to expound about the devils behind the scenes; for now, we focus purely on what emanates from our own personal spirits. The immature Christians in that church either lacked perception or experience or were simply overwhelmed. They were unaware of their defilement. They believed their thoughts were their own.

Early in our ministry, Paula and I served in a church in a small town which was the center of an agricultural area. The local banker held mortgages on nearly every business and farm in the community. He was also a member of our trustees' board (in that denomination, trustees held the purse strings). Between meetings, individual trustees would come to me privately at night like Nicodemus to say of my ideas to start the church moving, "We know you are right, John. Come next meeting, you watch. We are going to be right with you." I am sure they meant it. They really intended to stand for the Lord and His servant. But what invariably happened was amazing to watch. The banker would enter the room, not saying a thing. Those trustees fairly fell over themselves to agree with his position! Money could rightly be said to be enough to explain the whole thing. But I knew something else was at work, because I felt it in my own being. I found my own thoughts tumbling and jumbling. Without a word being said, I felt the influence of his presence. It was strong. It defiled. Of course it was not he alone. The god of mammon radiated through him. I had to take hold of myself, center in Jesus, and meditate on His Word several minutes before my mind and heart would clear. Then I could see again where I stood, and the rightness of it. My trustee friends were too new in Christ. They were not well enough protected. They were carried away, ". . . tossed here and there by waves . . ." (Eph. 4:14b). Could it be that St. Paul also meant by "waves" what our teenagers a few years ago called "vibes"? Whether or not this is true, our trustees were constantly overcome by defilement.

Thank God it works the other way, too. Haven't we enjoyed visiting some people because we were refreshed by them? Don't some people somehow make us feel cleaner? I gave thanks to God for the little old "mothers-in-the Lord" He gave me in several congregations. When "the burden and heat of the day" (Matt. 20:12 KJV), would threaten to become too much, I would call on one or more of them, ostensibly to minister to them. The truth was I needed to visit with them a while to let their wholesome saintly presence wash through me. I could feel their chastised-by-life wholeness permeating their homes with peace. It hardly mattered if on the surface they seemed disturbed by some petty family problem, and I could indeed minister to them. Their sweet spirits cleansed me.

Defilement is a powerful force behind many of the sins of any people. But we do not write to cause people to be afraid to mingle. Far from it. We are overcomers, more than conquerors (Rom. 8:35-39). We teach to make aware. Wise ones learn spiritual hygiene. Often I have come home from ministry "trailing clouds of little imps" rather than Wordsworth's "clouds of glory." Paula and I have learned to pray, asking the Lord to cleanse us from all defilements, "Wash us clean, Lord, from whatever we may have picked up today. Lord, we release to you all the burdens and problems, and everything which entered or latched on to our spirits today. Cleanse us, Lord." It is amazing how a simple long hug from Paula chases wrong things away. It is as though the Lord through her spirit pours wholeness and such light that everything else simply flees from my spirit.

Sometimes in the night I am sure my spirit wars for the Lord. I think this is so for many who serve Him. Dreams are sometimes evidence of the warfare we have been engaged in during the night. It has been my experience to awaken brown and bugged, feeling like I want to shrug something off. Prayer helps, and often fully cleanses, like taking a refreshing shower. Sometimes, however, I can't do it by myself, and prayer with Paula won't get it done either. If Paula puts her chest against mine (sans clothes) and just rests quietly, I feel the song of her spirit soaring through me, and pretty soon I'm all right again—and usually don't want to get out of bed quite yet! I hope I do sound a bit suggestive; I wish more couples would learn to refresh one another as God intended.

Paula and I are not different from anyone else. All people feel these defilements of which we have testified. The Body needs to learn how to handle them by prayer and by the presence of loved ones.

A word of caution should be added. The Hebrew people were very much aware of defilements, too much aware. Old Testament law mentions many things which defiled, and what to do about them—not at all repeated in the New Testament, which ought to tell us something! Many foods defiled (Lev. 11). Giving birth defiled (Lev. 12). Some diseases made people unclean (Lev. 13). Accidental or purposeful ejaculation defiled, and so did women's menstrual periods (Lev. 15). Immorality, idols, touching dead bodies—hundreds of things defiled. Jesus found Pharisees performing four hundred absolutions a day just to wash away defilements. The word "kosher" comes from those days of careful washings and preparations designed to avoid defilement. Simon the Pharisee was convinced

Jesus was no prophet or He would have prohibited that woman of ill repute from defiling Him by touching His feet (Luke 7:36-50).

Jesus countered this by letting His disciples eat with unwashed hands, and by teaching directly,

> "Not what enters into the mouth defiles the man, but what proceeds out of the mouth, this defiles the man." Then the disciples came and said to Him, "Do You know that the Pharisees were offended when they heard this statement?" But He answered and said, "Every plant which My heavenly Father did not plant shall be rooted up. Let them alone; they are blind guides of the blind. And if a blind man guides a blind man, both will fall into a pit." And Peter answered and said to Him, "Explain the parable to us." And He said, "Are you also still without understanding? Do you not understand that everything that goes into the mouth passes into the stomach, and is eliminated? But the things that proceed out of the mouth come from the heart, and those defile the man. For out of the heart come evil thoughts, murders, adulteries, fornications, thefts, false witness, slanders. These are the things which defile the man" (Matt. 15:11-20).

Once for all Jesus did away with exterior fears of defilement and consequent rituals to cleanse. No Christian need fear defilement from outside by *things.*

But He retained warnings of inner defilements: ". . . out of the heart come evil thoughts, murders, adulteries, fornications, thefts, false witness, slanders. *These are the things which defile the man."* Not what touches us from outside but what we *feel inside* and *do outside,* immorally or idolatrously, is what defiles.

Therefore, when we become aware that what is in the spirits of others can defile us, we need to counterbalance that with simple faith. We do not need to fear, only to pray away whatever we sense invading our heart and mind through our spirit's involvement with others. "Greater is

He who is in you than he who is in the world" (1 John 4:4). Above all, Christians must not retreat from the world.

We must learn not to celebrate the strength of the flesh. When Paula and I first began to travel, we would enter a church or home, or town or area where we were to minister, and soon discover many false currents. Sometimes there were streams of rancor and division because of what had been happening in the home or church or among the leadership, or waves of unbelief or scoffing from the audience. In the beginning, in our immaturity, we let that get to us. We would think, "There is no way we can minister here" or, "This is going to be tough. I don't know whether we want to tackle this or not." We reaped according to the small measure of our faith. When we grew in faith to know in real terms that He *has* already won the victory, we realized that we were already victorious! In the beginning, we would pray up a storm and have a grand time chasing demons all over the place. It did clear the air, but it left us puffed up with ourselves and our soldierly power and quite distracted from the King of kings. We learned there is a better way to accomplish the same cleansing. We might, along the way, still say a short, "Clear the air, Lord," but that is relatively unimportant. We have learned that when we *know He has* already won the victory, *we carry that power with us.* He transmits it and it flows through us. Now we ignore the devils and start praising Jesus. Pretty soon they can't tolerate that and depart, leaving Jesus with all the glory and them with none at all because nobody paid them any attention.

Nevertheless, let each soldier fight with whatever weapons he has faith to use, ". . . according to the measure of faith" (Rom. 12:3 RSV). I am sure it was better to have battled as we did than to have abandoned the field altogether, until we learned a better way. Sometimes today we still chase demons, but no longer because we are afraid they will get the better of us. We know the battle is the Lord's and the victory is His.

Sometimes I am tempted to be upset with brothers who begin every meeting by rebuking the devil and commanding him to leave; my spirit senses there is no need. The Lord reminds me then that my brother will grow beyond that as the Lord teaches him in His own time and way. "And if on some point you think differently, that too God will make clear to you" (Phil. 3:15 NIV).

It is good to be aware of defilements for another reason, though, and this is to protect the unaware and the immature. St. Paul wrote most of his letters to protect the Body from the defilements of the circumcision party. He wrote specifically to excise the corruption in Corinth through incest (1 Cor. 5). Because we are members one of another, and when one suffers all suffer (1 Cor. 12:26), we know that immorality defiles all, and besides being a bad witness, could lead the weak into seduction. In 2 Thessalonians 3:6, he wrote to "keep aloof from every brother who leads an unruly life and not according to the tradition which you received from us." He did not want the weak contaminated by exposure to uncleanness. One must remember, however, that abandonment of a brother is to happen only if all the other steps of Matthew 18 and Galatians 6:1 have been undertaken but the brother still refuses correction. We try first with everything in us to heal before we abandon a brother to learn the hard way.

St. Peter wrote,

> For if after they have escaped the *defilements* of the world by the knowledge of the Lord and Savior Jesus Christ, they are again entangled in them and are overcome, the last state has become worse for them than the first. For it would be better for them not to have known the way of righteousness, than having known it, to turn away from the holy commandment delivered to them. It has happened to them according to the true proverb, "A dog returns to its own vomit," and, "A sow, after washing, returns to wallowing in the mire" (2 Pet. 2:20-22).

211

The word is that of an elder to protect the young in faith. We have that responsibility, even as in Ezekiel 33:1-6:

> And the word of the Lord came to me saying, "Son of man, speak to the sons of your people, and say to them, 'If I bring a sword upon a land, and the people of the land take one man from among them and make him their watchman; and he sees the sword coming upon the land, and he blows on the trumpet and warns the people, then he who hears the sound of the trumpet and does not take warning, and a sword comes and takes him away, his blood will be on his own head. He heard the sound of the trumpet but did not take warning; his blood will be on himself. But had he taken warning, he would have delivered his life. But if the watchman sees the sword coming and does not blow the trumpet, and the people are not warned, and a sword comes and takes a person from them, he is taken away in his iniquity; but his blood I will require from the watchman's hand.' "

We write, however, mainly about healing. Whether they come from people's spirits or demons, defilements wound. When one recovers his way from defilement, whether he only felt it and took warning, dipped his toe or took a fateful plunge, confession is the first step. We need to confess to the Lord our vulnerability. Listen to the wisdom of Isaiah when the glory of the Lord filled the temple, "Woe is me, for I am ruined! Because I am a man of unclean lips, And *I live among a people of unclean lips*" (Isa. 6:5). Even if no iniquity can find a lodging place in us, we live in the midst of a "crooked and perverse generation" (Phil. 2:15). We imbibe their corruption merely by being among them. It never hurts to confess, "I am unclean, Lord. Wash me." "If we say that we have no sin, we are deceiving ourselves, and the truth is not in us" (1 John 1:8).

Having confessed, we need to receive, to let forgiveness cleanse. St. John wrote, ". . . if we walk in the light as He Himself is in the light, we have fellowship with one another, and the blood of Jesus His Son *cleanses us* from all sin" (1 John 1:7). Did the reader ever wonder, as we have, why St. John didn't simply say, ". . . as He Himself is in the light . . . and the blood of Jesus His Son cleanses us . . ."? Why mention "fellowship" in that context? He said in verse 9, "If we confess our sins, He is faithful and righteous to forgive us our sins and to cleanse us from all unright-eousness." The context was forgiveness. Why did he place that seemingly irrelevant phrase about fellowship in that text? Because it is not merely the blood of Jesus which heals. The blood cleanses. But it is not the task of the blood alone to heal. It is fellowship which heals and restores.

Remember when the woman touched the hem of Jesus' garment (Luke 8:40-48) and wanted to slink away unnoticed? She had been physically healed. But Jesus wouldn't let her escape. His questions made her come forward and confess her condition in a culture which regarded issues of blood as unclean! He wanted her to confess publicly why she was there! Being touched by her had defiled everyone near her in the crowd. By biblical law she was not supposed to be there at all (Lev. 15:19-30). No wonder she wanted to keep her presence a secret. Why then did our gracious Lord make her embarrass herself like that? Confessing in front of *everybody?* Because Jesus knew physical healing was not enough. He knew that whatever the embarrassment to her, she must be restored to the *fellowship* of her fellow citizens. Only their acceptance and embrace could heal twelve years of suffering and ostracism! Let us hear the lesson, Body of Christ. We must not terminate ministry with confession and application of the blood. That is redemption and restoration, but it is not yet healing. To be received with open arms, to be held and told words of love, is healing. We need arms and hands which touch and hold. When our mind hears wonderful, freeing words, our heart may still tremble. Our spirit may still languish. Touch soothes the heart and restores the spirit. Tears of joy in fellowship tell us we are truly loved. That heals.

How much ought to be confessed, as in James 5:16, "to one

another," and how much simply in private to Jesus alone is probably best told by the seriousness of involvement in sin, or by what it takes to make us whole again. Simple struggles in the heart can probably best be tossed off in flash prayers during the day. It is actions, especially those which have involved others, which need to be confessed in public. Most often, though, there is no need to say the names of others involved. Our confession should protect those who may not be ready for any degree of public disclosure.

We can make nuisances of ourselves and wear out our friends if we think absolutely everything has to be talked out with someone! Martin Luther's confessor finally cried out in exasperation, "Martin, will you quit wearing me out with these little peccadilloes! Go out and do some mighty sin and then come back here, but quit wearing me out with all this!"

Certainly, sexual sin must be confessed. So should violation of the law by theft, lying and so on. These and similar things require oral confession. Simple sins of heart and thought He quietly cleanses as we go.

So far we have spoken only of inadvertent personal defilement by the presence of others. Some people set out to seduce willfully, consciously. Whether to sex, or theft, or gambling, or lying, or whatever, they not only want to persuade with words, they set out to influence spirit to spirit. They may be unaware of the power of their personal spirit, but they know they have influence, and consciously they try to use it. They want, as it were, to weave a spell over us. Countless times many of us have cleansed brothers' and sisters' hearts in church or counseling, only to see them overcome by seducers who purposely set out to defile them. St. Paul became so angry about this kind of thing while battling with the circumcision party that he cried out, "Would that those who are troubling you would even mutilate themselves!" (Gal. 5:12). Haven't most of us who minister in any capacity experienced the same frustrations and angers? Defilement is no rare thing. It is a part of every Christian's daily battle to walk His way. We need to become more aware of defilement, in order to snatch some from the fire (Jude 23).

St. Paul told us to admonish one another (Col. 3:16). Proverbs 27:6 RSV says, "Faithful are the wounds of a friend; profuse are the kisses of an enemy." "Blows that wound cleanse away evil; strokes make clean the inmost parts" (Prov. 20:30 RSV). Sometimes we must have courage to rebuke. ". . . reprove them severely that they may be sound in the faith" (Titus 1:13). The trouble is, usually we become so agitated and tense ourselves about having to rebuke that by the time we screw up our courage to act, we blast a canary with a cannon! A word to the wise would have been sufficient, and we knew it, but couldn't control ourselves enough to say only what was necessary. Or we can't summon enough fortitude and so manage to fire only a BB against a bear! There is no other way to learn to rebuke rightly and wisely than to suffer the pain of trial and error. The Body must learn. It really can't be taught from a "how to" book. The Holy Spirit teaches by experience. We must simply plunge in and learn to do it.

It is seldom the one being defiled who needs a sharp rebuke. He requires warning and strength from us by love and acceptance. Maybe some talking *with*, not *at*, will help him see what he was already beginning to see anyway. *It is the defiler who needs the sharp rebuke!* I wish I had stepped in to sound off against that wolf in sheep's clothing in my friend's church. Perhaps my brother pastor would be a sane man today had I spoken not only to him but to the wolf. Perhaps some would-be wolves would have been saved too.

Whatever level of rebuke we undertake should be followed with healing hugs where possible. Lest we sound like apostles of embrace, I want to mention here that healing can take many other forms, such as sitting down to dinner together, or playing a game of pinochle or golf. Once a brother pastor and I could not get along. So we went out to dinner together at the "Clinkerdagger" in Spokane. That restaurant has a balcony which hangs out over the Spokane River, providing a tremendous view of it cascading gloriously during spring runoff. We wanted to enjoy that scene while we were having dinner. But the waitress said, "I'm sorry, gentlemen, the only place I have left is the love set." That is a two-seat bench, table in front, affording the very best view of the river. Not thinking of anything else, we said, "Oh good, we'll take it. That's just what we wanted!" She brought our order. When she returned to pour coffee, there we were, in prayer, holding hands! She was certain we were gay! When we saw the look on her face, we exploded in laughter. That conspiracy of humor, our private joke, we knew was the Lord's way of healing and knitting us together.

Demons may be behind many defilements. We are not willing to say "all." That gives Satan not only too much credit but attributes to him an omniscience and ubiquitousness (knowing everything and being present everywhere) he does not have. Only our Lord has that.

When demons are the factor, it is usually easily discerned by those who are gifted by the Holy Spirit. The telling mark is the change in the people. Not only do they think and talk in ways foreign to themselves (which can happen solely by human defilement), they have about them a presence which is not their own. The timbre of their voice betrays something else acting in them. People influenced by people still seem somehow self-contained and in control of themselves, whereas people influenced or controlled by demons (not necessarily inhabited), enter a level of stridency or irrationality. One can almost see the demonic leaking out the corners of their mouths. They sometimes come up with ideas and information you know they could not have thought of or known without help. It often happens that spiritually sensitive Christians discern the presence of something demonic by feelings of nausea, or a sense of twistedness and oppression which causes pain or pressure in the chest or head.

When demons are present in such instances, we commonly are not dealing with mere low-echelon spirits. It is "principalities . . . world rulers of this present

216

darkness" (Eph. 6:12 RSV) with whom we have to do. Realization of this should cause us no fear. From the lowest imps of darkness to the Devil himself, the least Christian has the victory easily, for "they overcame him because of the blood of the Lamb and because of the word of their testimony" (Rev. 12:11). Such movies as "The Exorcist" do us the disservice of teaching the weak that Satan has awesome power he in fact can no longer wield, except against those who do not know Jesus, or Christians who give him that power by believing he has it.

Demons inhabit or influence people. *Principalities wield power*, usually *from outside people*, by turning the force of defiling currents upon them, or setting up blockages. World rulers manipulate archetypal forms of thought over people to control emotions and stifle free thinking (see the first part of Chapter Sixteen in our book *The Transformation of the Inner Man*). Archetypal structures are typical ways of thinking within the mentality of mankind which are a part of the overarching flesh we all share. Some common archetypes are racial prejudice, subjugation of women, greed, war and aggression, religious stereotypes and religious dogmas.

When people begin to practice ways of feeling and thinking which enter the field of an archetype, opportunity is given to principalities to control them by enmeshing them in the web of such thought forms. Football players wear helmets to protect their heads from impact. To understand archetypes, one needs only to reverse the function of such a helmet. Instead of protecting from harm, archetypes shield from the light of God and prevent sane rationality. Instead of being lined with padding to cushion from blows, archetypes are themselves the blow, from tentacles of defilement flowing through the corridors of the brain to chain and enslave the person to wrong thoughts and feelings.

Archetypes are devices by which principalities defile and control, under the tutelage of the world rulers of this present darkness. I hurt and ache when my brother can't wait to tell me the latest "nigger joke." I grieve not so much for the black people our Lord causes all sincere Christians to love, though of course such things wound every black brother and sister. I grieve more for the imprisonment of the prejudiced brother's mind and heart. He has no idea of the extent of the invasion upon him. He possesses no awareness of the control that defilement has upon his life. Martin Luther King, Jr., did wonders for blacks in America, but probably greater service by far to the rest of us by leading the fight to break the bondages of archetypal defilement!

Do we not all yearn for our liberal brothers of the cloth who unwittingly spout doctrines of demons (1 Tim 4:1)? They are defiled. Totally unaware of it, they have become mere puppets, spouting doctrines of foolishness, thinking these things are their own wise thoughts. The insidiousness of the defilement is that they think they alone possess the cleanness of truth, that those of orthodox faith are still trapped in yesteryear's defilements! Only the Savior, the Word and the Holy Spirit set us free. ". . . where the Spirit of the Lord is, there is freedom" (2 Cor. 3:17 RSV). "For God hath not given us the spirit of fear; but of power, and of love, and of a *sound mind*" (2 Tim. 1:7 KJV). Many of our liberal brothers, mentally deprived and blinded, do not have life, thinking all the while that their mess of fleshly thoughts, which are actually wielded by the prince of the power of the air, are life. Only the Son is Life. "You are from God, little children, and have overcome them; because greater is He who is in you than he who is in the world. They are from the world; *therefore they speak as from the world, and the world listens to them*" (1 John 4:4, 5). It is mainly by archetypal control through principalities that men are defiled, and their defilement defiles others in the world.

Paula and I are not alone in having attended church conferences with high hopes, only to watch the conference gradually turn to rancor. After a while it took no great gift of discernment to see, as each speaker raised his voice more stentoriously, in matters of discussion which didn't in fact amount to a hill of beans, that more than fallen humanity was expressing itself! Demonic powers defiled the assembly until they could raise their strident voices through the men who pridefully thought they were serving only the Lord's cause. The result was divisiveness, leaving men seeking their own tents to nurse petty grievances in isolation. Haven't most of us grieved to see such things? And haven't we all known that such futile dissensions over the law should be avoided (Titus 3:9), but all too often couldn't stop ourselves when we too found ourselves drawn into the battle?

I (John) attended a denominational conference with a brother pastor (it could have been any denominational or non-denominational gathering). At the conference, one of the main speakers became more and more what he thought was anointed to call that group back to the "good old ways." It is always good to call God's people back to His good ways. These "good old ways" turned out to be fleshly traditions beyond which most of that body had matured. Mistaking zeal for anointing, he carried on more and more vehemently. Soon the entire audience was silently engaged in spiritual warfare. Some were rebuking the horde of defiling spirits which were coming over the audience. Others were loudly saying "Amen," caught up in his defilement and delusions, while their spirits wrestled with the disfavor they felt from all the others. The result was not edification and unity, but rancor and division.

On the other hand, it works the other way. In 1959 Agnes Sanford was invited to speak in an extremely legalistic fundamentalist college. Knowing she would be engaged in spiritual warfare because her message would likely unseat vast powers of darkness, she called for help. Father Wilbur Fogg, Episcopal rector, his wife Alice and I went there to be in the audience to intercede. Agnes began her message by calling out, "Brothers and sisters, do you believe the Word of God is true from cover to cover?" The response was a unanimous loud chorus, "Amen, Sister!"

"So do I. Do you believe that God created the world exactly as Genesis 1 says He did?"

"Amen!"

"So do I. Do you believe He created the world in six days and rested on the seventh?"

"Amen!"

"So do I. Then I have some news for you, my friends. If you really believe God created the world just like the Bible says, then you can't believe He did it in six of our earth's twenty-four hour days, because the Bible doesn't say that He did!"

Not one amen, not a sound! Stunned silence! The battle was on. We hit our prayer knees, fast!

Then Agnes opened the Word to them, much as Jesus did for Cleopas and the other disciple on the road to Emmaus (Luke 24:13-35). She showed them that our sun and moon were not created until the fourth day (Gen. 1:14-19); therefore that when God spoke of the first "day" and "night" He could not have been referring to our earthly twenty-four-hour days, which come from our planet's turning about our sun, but of some other kind of day and night, of a time-span only He knows, probably aeons long! Her logic was straight and compelling. But that was not where the battle was. Angels of heavenly light were bursting into the room as she spoke that teaching. Wilbur and Alice and I could almost physically see shackles of steel falling off the minds of the congregation. Their jaws hung open and their eyes were staring, while light shattered archetypes of imprisonment in their minds. That was the breakthrough. From that point on, for three days, Agnes took them from mansion to mansion heretofore closed to them in the Kingdom of God.

In Council Grove, Kansas, where Paula and I served for several years, the Roman Catholic priest and I became best buddies. It happened that he had an advanced case of multiple sclerosis, so the bishop stuck him in that small town, thinking to keep him out of harm's way. His body may have become crippled, but his mind and spirit certainly were not. He soon had that place jumping. He could no longer drive, so sometimes I became his chauffeur. One time he wanted to go to a meeting in Wichita of the entire priesthood of the Roman Catholic diocese of Kansas. The Roman Catholic bishop of all Kansas was to be the main speaker. I enjoyed the dinner, and then began to become strangely excited in my spirit as the meeting was to begin. I "knew" something was in the wind. Something great was brewing. Warfare was on, and the good guys were winning! I was too young then; I didn't have any part in the battle, but I could sense it was going on. Nothing out of the ordinary happened until the bishop stood up to speak. He said what was probably the ritual collect of the day, crossed himself, and began his talk by saying, "Brothers, I have news for you. Marthin Luther was right!" The silence was deafening! Light was bursting everywhere!

Had the bishop spoken only in his flesh, he probably would have lost his congregation! But God had gone before. Angels and the prayers of intercessors had already claimed the victory. Jaws dropped open and eyes crossed for a moment but hearts and minds did not close. They were *with* him. They were hearing, eagerly. He went on to teach all the fundamental facts of the gospel which Luther had rediscovered and said, "We were blind, brothers, we were blind." On the way out, probably the only Protestant pastor in that entire conclave, I overheard group after cluster of priests muttering together, "Never thought I would ever hear a bishop of ours saying things like that !" "How did he ever get up the courage?" But I felt no negative reactions. There may have been some negativity among some, but I am certain the majority were delighted with his word. Heaven had won a major victory. "You are already clean because of the word which I have spoken to you" (John 15:3). His Word cleanses. But warfare in prayer opens ears to hear and eyes to see. Defilement blocks. Intercession prepares the way of the Lord in the desert (Isa. 40).

Political demagogues spout streams of catch phrases designed to latch on to un-thought-out demonic defilements

221

over people. Hitler gained control of Germany that way, most likely unaware that he was himself a slave of dark powers. Lynch mobs in our southland were incited and controlled by the same kinds of inflammatory speeches, wielded from behind the scenes by principalities. In March 1984 our President Reagan was appalled to find congressmen and senators foolishly debating many irrelevant issues concerning his proposed amendment to allow prayer in public schools. He could not understand how men of logicality and the highest social and political standing in our nation could spout such irrelevant foolishnesses, and said so in a moment of commentary. Perhaps we *can* understand. World rulers wanted above all to block prayer. They concentrated energy to make foolish the wise. How? By wielding archetypes of fear of control, by reaching into hidden latent childhood wounds and resentments against parents, teachers, pastors, etc., and connecting them to false places in the mind. Thus they caused men of usual wisdom to be proud of their confused thoughts. "Professing to be wise, they became fools" (Rom. 1:22).

Here was a direct confrontation with powers of darkness concerning defilement in our time. Christians all over America were massed to pray as an intercessory army. We knew the battle was joined. Why did we not win? "My people are destroyed for lack of knowledge" (Hos. 4:6). God and His hosts will not invade and control; the Holy Spirit will not override anyone's free will. Powers of darkness will; it is their modus operandi. Who among us prayed as a warrior against the hosts of darkness over the nation's capital? I could wager that many did. But who directed the battle, sword of truth in hand, against the archetypes of thought-control and the principalities who wielded them?

Teacher of this very thing that I am, one of the Lord's prophets who see where the battle really is, who teaches others, knowing the battle was on, I forgot! Why? Defilement and demonic strategy. Paula and I found ourselves engaged in more pressing spiritual warfare here. I have no doubt that Satan purposefully distracted us, and doubtless many others who could have seen and dislodged the demons' filthy hands. One almost could have heard Satan saying, "Gorbag, you and your troops run up there and keep all those intercessor types who really know how to do spiritual warfare occupied and distracted, lest they get onto our game there in Washington, D.C. and put a stop to us." The moment I saw the newspaper announcing defeat, I knew what had happened. Satan had kept the knowledgeable warriors busy elsewhere while he won the victory there—temporarily.

Does this say he has power? No. Merely strategy. Delusion is his power, by defilement. In direct confrontation he flees. "But resist him, firm in your faith . . ." (1 Pet. 5:9a). "Submit therefore to God. Resist the devil and *he will flee from you*" (James 4:7). The devil wins whatever temporary victories are his by strategy, by bothering and distracting or lulling to apathy, above all by avoiding discovery. He knows he cannot win when Christians discover his presence and his tactics.

Sometimes he controls entire nations by defilement. Presently we are all watching how he manipulates the nation of Iran through the Ayatollah and religious fanaticism. He wields archetypes and fans emotional sparks by bonfires of hate and war, even as centuries earlier he caused Islamic warriors to sweep across Africa and into Europe, fired by zeal to convert or kill. Defilement!

"How can a young man keep his way pure? By keeping it according to Thy Word" (Ps. 119:9). "I have hidden your word in my heart that I might not sin against you" (Ps. 119:11 NIV). While puzzling one day how so many Christians who know His Word cover to cover can yet sin against Him again and again, so easily it seems, I asked the Lord. He made me aware of that word "heart," that the Word did not say they laid it up in their *minds*, but hid the Word in their *hearts*. So I asked Him what it is to lay the Word into the heart, "How does the Word move from head to heart? How can I make sure it travels there and abides?" His reply was first just one word, "Love." He went on to teach me that only those whose awakened spirits *really love Him and who move out to love others in Him are those who truly laminate His Word to their hearts.* Until it is *lived in love*, it does not move from head to heart. He made it most clear to me that such love must be a direct meeting and cherishing of Him personally, ". . . lying close to the breast of Jesus" (John 13:23 RSV), or it does not bond Word and heart together.

How shall we resist becoming defiled by the world, the pride of life and the lust of the eyes (1 John 2:16)? By letting Jesus love us. By soaking ourselves in His love, and then *pouring that love to others as a life style twenty-four hours a day!* Those who selfishly want Him only for themselves, only for the hope of heaven, will be defiled, again and again. But those who pour His love to others bond His Word to their hearts and sit, walk and stand in Him.

We have insisted many times that we need the human embrace of fellowship in the Body. We would never lessen nor contradict that teaching. But it must be clearly understood that we cannot benefit fully from the Body unless the Lord is the first love of our hearts. Some cannot find Him unless the Body so loves as to enable their spirits to awaken and find. But if a child of God fastens on to the Body and thinks that is enough, or for any reason will not let go and move on to Him, eventually He himself will sour the relation to all others. He is rightly a jealous God because He loves us. If we forget for a moment all the other insights we have shared so far and merely reflect, we will remember that it was at those times we let our love grow cold that we fell away or were tempted. It is that simple. However, for ability to enter warfare, in order to protect the weak, and to heal the wounded, we need to know all these other things.

Now let us turn to speak of death wishes. We include death wishes in this chapter because it is the weight of defilement which one way or another lies behind every death wish.

We do not know whether our spirit came to earth from Heaven, having had some form of pre-existence there, or whether it begins with conception, breathed into creation

224

at that moment. Sometimes I lean one way or the other, certain by biblical hints, or theology, or by experience, that it must be this way or that. I do tend most of the time to think we must have been with the Father and that our Lord asked us to come, but no one knows for sure. One Scripture in this regard I find fascinating to meditate upon: "As you do not know how *the spirit comes to the bones in the womb of a woman with child,* so you do not know the work of God who makes everything" (Eccles. 11:5 RSV).

However, our spirit knew the beauty and wholesomeness of Heaven. Our spirit remembers what it was like to be at one with the Creator, whether through millenia of heavenly dwelling or in a moment of creation. St. Augustine said, "Thou hast made us in Thyself and our hearts are restless until they find their rest in Thee."

Imagine then the effect upon a pure and pristine spirit upon becoming part of this earth's corruption! One way to envision the effect is to remember yourself as a landlubber taking your first ocean voyage, or a landhugger flying in a tiny airplane for the first time, caught in a thunderstorm, bouncing around wildly. Consider the nausea, the sickness. Remember the yearning to return to solid earth again. Recall how you cried out, "Oh, why did I come on this trip?" Remember how you hung over the rail or used the air-sick bag and wished so fervently it were all over! How embarrassed you were. Even if you were not forced to flee to the restroom or use the air-sick bag, remember how you did not want others to look too closely at you? You were sure they could see the bile splashing up behind your eyeballs! You were mortified. You kept telling yourself you would be okay after awhile, just hang on. If you can recall all that, you have only mildly described the feelings of your spirit in your first moments and days bouncing around in the womb in the midst of the defilement of the world.

Think of this simple fact: Heaven is not spinning and rotating around the sun. Everything here is, however. We have come from quietness into a wildly gyrating universe. Did the reader ever venture onto one of those Mad Hatter teacups in Disneyland or Disneyworld, or the "Scrambler" at a carnival? Did you ever wonder why those harum-scarum rides possess such an attraction for us? One reason may be that they trigger the first memories of our spirit below our mind's memory! They allow us to feel consciously what we first encountered when we began. That relieves us by making conscious what was hidden.

In homes where children are longed for and loved, reception begins to heal first frights and nauseas, even in the womb. When traumas surround and invade the womb —fightings, bickerings, loud noises, hurtful emotions—the spirit of the child cannot overcome the nausea of general defilement we all suffer by being here in this sickened world. The result is the cry, "Stop the bus! I want off!" We don't want to be here. Our mind may not know that, but that has become our spirit's determination. We have become determined to die because that is the only other option to having to live all the way through what has become to us an unbearable world.

Death wishes once settled into us manifest themselves in many ways. First, they may be the underlying cause behind abnormally dangerous and tenacious childhood diseases. The personal spirit does not sustain the body normally nor easily throw off disease because it doesn't want to. It wants to act out our death wish. Our energies run counter to themselves. Many parents have come to us for counsel and prayer, distraught and fearful because their child or children are either constantly ill or tremendously accident-prone. We always want to know the family history: Did the child come as an afterthought, or was the conception desired and sought? How did the pregnancy proceed? Was it a difficult time physically for the mother? How did the parents relate to each other during the pregnancy? What economic, job-related, or other pressures were on the parents? Were there any great tragedies, deaths, or other traumatic happenings during that time? What kind of birth experience was it? Were other children jealous of the new baby or did they welcome the child? Was there postpartum depression? Did any tragedies or traumas happen shortly after birth? And so on.

Most of the time we find readily identifiable causes behind death wishes in infants. These can be healed as we have discussed in previous chapters.

We do not grow out of death wishes and leave them behind. If they are not dealt with, they remain, awaiting only proper stimuli to send sickness and trouble pulsing through life.

Death wishes affect coordination and confidence. Some people go through life haltingly. Some looked pinched, as though life had never been full of zest and gusto. Some people have haunted looks in their eyes, which say to my heart, "I'm in here somewhere; won't someone please come and lead me out to life?" Some have wistfulness in their eyes. Consciously they want to live, but they can't find the turn-on switch. Death wishes are one form of inner vow (see Chapter Eleven in *The Transformation of the Inner Man*).

Paula has a body naturally built for athletics. But she too suffered an early spiritual confusion. Hers was not a death wish. Rather, it was a message, as related earlier (in Chapter Two), that she had no right to live. What that caused was an athletic blockage. Instead of stepping into a tennis swing wholeheartedly, she held back so that her body was always out of position. Her swing would then be an awkward, lunging swat rather than an easy, coordinated stroke. Her body position always took power from her swing, so that she was never properly behind and flowing through any athletic movement. I used to watch in puzzlement as it seemed she wasn't able to throw herself into the game, only role-playing. Last summer (1983) a dear friend ministered to the depths of her spirit, finding she had been deeply wounded in the womb. At once the mystery was resolved. Her spirit had enjoyed no freedom to flow into fun and games. That robbed her body of its natural coordination. Now she is learning in playing tennis to step into a swing with her whole being. And she is enjoying aerobics classes. It is a joy to watch her becoming more "here," her spirit flowing through her body in athletics.

Being an athlete and counselor, I watch the way people move. I observe how their mental intentions flow into athletic exertions. I study the way people walk, how they hold themselves, the "tells" in their hands and body positions. Once one takes hold of this key of early death wishes, it becomes amazing how easily one can learn to detect their operation in people's movements. Particularly one can see it in the overly controlled, pinched walk of mother-dominated people. One can see how they have never been freed to let go and flow freely into life. There have been too many checks and rules. Movements are therefore curbed and cribbed. They have no abundant life. Every body movement and posture proclaims that fact.

Death wishes affect voice tones. I can hear in the way a man sings whether his spirit has been free to choose life. Some so lack authority they rob their diaphragm of power. Or they place the sound in wrong places on the palate, and so sound ineffectual, breathy, breathless or childish. Some sound hard and thin. In trained voices it is much more difficult to detect what is in the personal spirit. Their coaches have worked on those deficiencies. Untrained voices still reflect what conditions hamper or aid volume, pitch and intensity. When one catches the keys, such perceptions lose mysticality and become easy common sense.

Death wishes are often behind "losers." We mean the kind of person who should have everything going for him, mentally, emotionally and athletically, but who somehow frequently manages to snatch defeat from the jaws of victory. Such people proceed to the brink of success but no farther. At the moment when it seems a breakthrough to success cannot possibly be thwarted, something happens. Either they do something foolish, or from some unlooked-for, seemingly impossible direction, something blocks or destroys. Often the entire project crumbles. Wise men build securely on strong foundations; the foolish build on sand (Luke 6:46-49). The difficulty is that these people do not consciously know what is the area of sand on which they have built.

Not every propensity to lose has a death wish behind it. We can have self-fulfilling loser tendencies from parents' words like, "You'll never amount to anything," which our heart has believed and continues to act out, or from excessive performance orientation (see Chapter Three in our book, *The Transformation of the Inner Man*), or from many other quirks in our nature. One man I counseled who kept losing just when victory seemed imminent had a father who continually failed. The root in this son was that something in him had accepted a lie that he must never outperform his father! Therefore he unconsciously continually sabotaged himself.

Today (April 18, 1984) I visited with a young man whose parents had conceived him out of wedlock and were forced to marry because he was on the way. He had been born with his belly burst open around his umbilical cord. Questioning revealed that he had received the message that he was an unwanted burden and ought to die so the parents could be free to enjoy life. That death wish had manifested itself in an inability to take hold of his powers to accomplish. Again and again he had nearly flunked out or quit projects when he possessed the mental ability to be at the top of the class. His death wish continually robbed his conscious mind of power to achieve.

Death wishes most commonly affect sexual fulfillment. At taproot level, such people have never accepted being bodies. They view their bodies as necessary evils to be put up with so long as they still have to be here. They may learn to engage in sexual activity with their mate, whether for duty or whatever amount of enjoyment they have attained. But the glory is far from them. Their spirit is not free to cascade gloriously through every cell to ravish the other with love and joy. Usually people who have hidden death wishes tell us they would rather not be bothered sexually. Akin to slumbering spirits, they also cannot meet the other through their body.

As with slumbering spirits, those who have hidden death wishes also have dwarfed talents. The spirit may be awake, but unfree to engage and venture life. I often am caused to see such people visually in prayer as frosted buds, unable to burst open the sepals and unfold to full bloom. In prayer I "see" the Lord causing the person to bloom gloriously. I watch, and describe aloud as that bud becomes a beautiful flower. Such people need a great deal of encouragement to continue to expand and choose life as they are set free.

Everyone who has a hidden death wish has anger at God in the depths of his spirit. His mind may be so unaware as to be affronted at the very idea that anyone could be angry at God. Behind this is the common delusion that the object of our anger must deserve it for us to be angry. Of course God doesn't deserve our anger, but that does not keep us from it. "The foolishness of man subverts his way, And his heart rages against the Lord." (Prov. 19:3). We are angry at God for separating us from Him, for putting us in this messed-up earth, for letting us fall, for "not being there" when we needed Him in the womb. Of course He was there, but our angry hearts could not believe He was.

When we want to detect a possible death wish, and/or we want to convince someone that he really is angry with God, Paula and I use the following series of questions. These questions are not to be answered by long thought but by the first feeling or thought which comes to mind. If a question cannot be answered without a long time to think, that itself is already a telling answer.

I usually explain to the counselee that I do not know whether we began in Heaven or at conception but that for the purpose of this series of questions, let's imagine that we existed in the heavens. All questions are to be answered silently if the person so wishes. We will discuss them later.

1. Suppose we are sitting in a group in a heavenly place enjoying the angels and the saints, the Lord enters and says, "I would like three or four

volunteers to go to earth." Would you have been one of the volunteers?

2. If Jesus had presented himself before you, had said your name, and asked, "Will you go to earth for me?" would you have responded, "Oh, boy, yes Sir, right away, Hallelujah!" or "O.K. (drat!)"

3. If you had to come to earth but were given your choice, would you choose the time and place in which you were born, or some other century or country?

4. Would you choose to be born to your parents, or some other?

5. Would you choose your father? Or some other father?

6. Your mother?

7. Would you choose to be a boy or a girl?

8. Would you choose your face?

9. Your body?

10. Your mind?

11. Your character and personality?

12. If you are a woman, are you beautiful? Pretty? Attractive? Desirable? Loveable? Would someone choose you? Should they? If you are a man, are you handsome? Good-looking? Attractive? Desirable? Loveable? would someone choose you? Should they?

13. Do you like you?

14. If Jesus walked up to you in the present moment and said, "I'll give you your choice. You can either go all the way through life or straight up to Heaven with me right now," which way would you choose?

As we ask these questions, we tune in our spirit to the other's spirit to sense by empathy what he really feels. Sometimes people are incapable of being fully honest. We may sense more accurately than they can express what they actually should have answered.

After completing the list, we say, "In whatever degree you would not have volunteered for life on earth or would have agreed only reluctantly to come, in whatever degree you would not have chosen your time and place or either or both of your parents, or you would not have chosen the sex you are, in whatever degree you would not have chosen your face, your body, your mind or character, in whatever degree you do not think you are beautiful or handsome, loveable or chooseable, in whatever degree you don't love you, to that degree you are angry at God. You are saying inside that He could have done a better job creating you. In whatever degree you would choose to go straight to Heaven rather than live life here, you are telling God you don't like it here."

In counseling, to help people understand, we may use an analogy, such as, "Suppose you prepare for your child a beautiful nursery full of toys and interesting things, and put him in it, but five minutes later he comes running out and says, 'I don't like it in there.' How would you feel as a parent? Are you honored? Or dishonored?" We can then add, "Do you see that when we do not like the earth which is our nursery and we do not want to stay here, we dishonor the gift of Father God?"

Or, "Suppose you give your child a little red wagon. He isn't too happy with it, and seldom plays with it. If he does, he leaves it upside down in the snow. How do you feel as a parent? Are you honored or dishonored? But suppose (something entirely fictitious) he loves it so much that he takes other children for rides in it, washes it, waxes it and puts it in the garage. Now how do you feel as a parent?" Some have laughingly said, "Soaped," realizing how few children would be that responsible. All, however, get the point. Such behavior honors the giver. So we say, "The news we have for you is that you, in your body, your mind, your face, in every way you are, you *are* the little red wagon God has given you. If you do not love it and care for it, you dishonor God. You are angry at God for what He created you to be." "Thou shalt love thy neighbour *as thyself*"(Mark 12:31 KJV). We are *commanded* to love ourselves.

One of the most strikingly overlooked aspects of our faith is our need to be reconciled to God. We seem to think that we should never be angry at God because He of course does not deserve it. More importantly we think that there is no way we could forgive God because He has not done anything wrong. We forget that many times we have mistakenly held things against others who never did what we thought they did, and yet we needed to forgive them. Forgiving them did not mean that they had done something requiring forgiveness, only that we needed to clear our own hearts. Just so in the matter of being reconciled to God. He is not to blame, but that did not keep us from pouting at Him, and must not keep us from forgiving Him.

The early church had little confusion about forgiving God. St. Paul wrote incisively about it, as a command:

> Now all these things are from God, who reconciled us to Himself through Christ, and gave us the ministry of reconciliation, namely, that God was in Christ reconciling the world to Himself, not counting their trespasses against them, and He has committed to us the word of reconciliation. Therefore, we are ambassadors for Christ, as though God were entreating through us; we beg you on behalf of Christ, *be reconciled to God* (2 Cor. 5:18-20).

Note, St. Paul did not say, as we might expect, "reconciled Himself to the world," as though all that was needed was that He should forgive us. It is true that He did need to forgive us; He accomplished that in Jesus Christ. Here, however, the context makes it clear St. Paul was speaking of both sides, God forgiving man and being reconciled to man, and man forgiving God and being reconciled to Him. "We beg you on behalf of Christ, *be reconciled to God.*"

If we could have voiced our cry in the vertiginous nausea of earth-sickness as we came out of Heaven into this corrupted world, our cry in the womb would have been, "God, how could you? I didn't bargain for this! You didn't tell me it would be this hard! Where are you?" Or, "Lord, you sent me here with a job to do for you (Eph. 2:10), and then you put me in this messed-up family, and now I'm all mixed up! I can't even remember what I was supposed to do. Now how can I do the job? And how is that fair?" Or,

"Where were you when I needed you? No conscientious earthly father would have let his child fall this far without doing something about it. Don't you care?" Never mind that He does care and has acted at horrendous cost to himself. At the moment we are far from able to believe that.

We suggest the reader tackle reading both Job and many of the Psalms with an eye open to the honesty of their cries before God. Try Psalms 38 and 39 for honesty of description; this is how far I have sunk, Lord, "Do not forsake me, O Lord; . . . Make haste to help me" (Ps. 38:21, 22), Psalm 44:9 for honest complaint, "Yet Thou hast rejected us and brought us to dishonor . . ." or Job, contending with God, "But I would speak to the Almighty, And I desire to argue with God" (Job 13:3). "Though He slay me, I will hope in Him. Nevertheless I will argue my ways before Him (v. 15). "Only two things do not do to me, Then I will not hide from Thy face: Remove Thy hand from me, And let not the dread of Thee terrify me. Then call, and I will answer; Or let me speak, then reply to me. How many are my iniquities and sins? Make known to me my rebellion and my sin. Why dost Thou hide Thy face, And consider me Thine enemy" (vv. 20-24)?

Job's complaint is the cry of everyone, of our own spirits before God, if we only knew it. Every one of us has stored resentment against God. It is not very acceptable to think angry thoughts at God, so we won't admit we have them. But they are there.

It is this hidden storehouse which serves as access to demonic powers to defile us. It is for this reason we have placed defilement, devils and death wishes in one chapter. Defilement from outside, from people, from things or devils, cannot lodge in us *unless it finds interior fertile soil*. Here is the soil of birth for all manner of evil in all of us, these hidden thoughts that, after all, God is unjust and uncaring, "at least for me, whatever He may be for anyone else, or He would not have put me here in this situation of my life, and left me in it! It isn't fair!"

Perhaps the most basic thing we can do in counseling is to lead people into prayers of forgiving God and being reconciled not only to Him but to being who they are themselves. Every person needs to accept being what God has created him to be. Several years ago, Paula and Loren and I conducted a seminar in Spokane especially for professional counselors. Its purpose was to teach professionally trained people how to minister in Christ through forgiveness and death on the cross. Many clergymen, psychiatrists and psychological counselors attended this seminar. As was our custom, we divided the attendees into small groups so that immediately after each teaching, they could delve into each other with freeing ministry in prayer. They were to learn by putting into practice what had just been taught orally. We have done this with many groups and found it most effective. Usually people have leaped into honest confessions, prayers and tears for one another with great healing results. To our chagrin, we found that these people could not and would not open up honestly to one another. Here were professionals whose daily occupation was to listen to counselees opening to them to confess lurid details frankly and honestly. It was their business to hear confessions. But these same counselors could not open up and confess honestly to one another!

For several days I puzzled and grieved before the Lord. What was the matter? Then the Lord revealed the answer. It was not, as I had supposed, professional reserve and jealousy. This group had in it more than the usual number of people who absolutely could not accept themselves. Not liking what they found themselves to be as infants and children, they had struggled and hastened to grow up. They had worked hard to escape from being that child they had been. That struggle to mature had brought them to the place where they could help others; no way were they willing to look back! In some ways confession involves making oneself a child again, being vulnerable and open, trusting as a child trusts. They could not confess to one another (though they insisted that others do so every day) because they were adamantly unwilling to enter the risk of being childlike again! ". . . whoever does not receive the kingdom like a little child shall not enter it at all" (Luke 18:17).

We led the group through the above list of questions. Their answers were nearly unanimous. They did not like themselves. They would not have chosen to come to earth. They saw that they were angry at God for creating them. They realized they had been unable to accept themselves.

Herein lies an important evangelical and theological point. We saw by this experience with those professional counselors that many Christians have accepted Jesus as Lord and Savior precisely to escape being what they are.

It is okay to want to change. Jesus does come to transform us. But these people had missed the crucial first step. Jesus had come to them and *accepted them just as they were, without change.* The sweetest meaning of Jesus' being born in a filthy and smelly stable is that He comes into us at our worst, accepting us before we change in any way, "even when we were dead in our transgressions . . ." (Eph. 2:5). These people had missed that. They were not about to accept that awful child they had once been. They had used Jesus and the cross to escape.

We asked these counselors to imagine that runny-nosed, mess-in-the-diapers screeching little kid they had been, standing tear-streaked in front of them, and to reach down and take that little one into loving arms. *Not to clean him up first and then love him, but to hold and comfort him just as he was.* We made sure they were not allowed to improve that little person in any way in order to love him. They were to love him and accept him as Jesus had, just as he was, without change. If he would never become any better, they would still love and cherish him.

We led them through a process of repentance. "Lord, we repent for rebelling against being born here on earth where you put us. We repent for not liking and accepting what you created us to be. We repent for rejecting earth and ourselves and all of earth's experiences. We couldn't trust your lordship, that you knew what you were doing. We forgive you, Lord Jesus Christ, and Father God, for creating us and putting us here. We repent for rejecting ourselves. We accept our bodies. Reconcile us to ourselves. Reconcile us to our time and place, our position in this earth. Thank you, Jesus."

That seminar turned from the worst to the greatest in one session! People broke through everywhere into genuine joy to be alive, to be here in the body, children of God on earth. It affected health, coordination, outlook on life, marital relations, sex, ability to worship, simple enjoyments like food and play, etc. Some went home to look for old pictures of themselves as children with the intent to reinforce the prayers already said with more precise visualization.

We had found an important key. How many millions of people are there who have tried to grow up too fast because they wanted to escape being a snot-nosed kid? One can never make it that way. That unacceptable kid continually makes trouble in the heart. We do immature and foolish things because within us part of us has not grown up. Psychologists speak of this as fragmentation, or lack of integration, and as dated or fixed emotions. St. Paul spoke of it as ". . . a different law in the members of my body, waging war against the law of my mind, and making me a prisoner of the law of sin which is in my members" (Rom. 7:23). We are at war with ourselves because part of our inner being throws tantrums at not having been accepted. First Corinthians 13:11 says, "When I was a child, I used to speak as a child, think as a child, reason as a child; when I became a man, I did away with childish things." We can never do away with childish things by stuffing them away to hide them, by pretending they aren't there, by scrambling to cover them. We must accept ourselves with the same compassion and unconditional love the Lord has for us. Then we will be able to present ourselves nakedly, trusting Him, acknowledging our sin. It is only as we are "rooted and grounded in love," His love which "surpasses knowledge," that we grow into full maturity (Eph. 3:14-19).

So very many Christians want to use salvation to escape from being what they were, whereas Jesus would have us forgive ourselves and accept ourselves just as He has. That is not only redemption, it is inner integration. One little lady to whom I was ministering could not stop being immature and foolish until she saw her hatred for her own inner child and decided with me in prayer to receive her and love her. She had been bothered by inner voices which would not go away. The temptation for me had been to cast away a foreign spirit. In this instance, that was not required. Once she accepted her own person, I asked, "Where are the voices?"

"Gone, Pastor, I am at peace." The voices had not been demonic; they had only been a way her inner child could throw tantrums for attention.

Behind all such inner turmoils are death wishes. When we cannot receive and love our inner child, that easily becomes a death wish. Satan finds in that rejected little one fertile soil for his seeds of defilement. That battle is over when we join Jesus in loving and accepting ourselves just as we were, in every moment of our life.

It goes without saying that behind every suicide attempt, however manipulative, is nevertheless a death wish. The successful have only managed to act out what their inner spirit wanted all along—escape.

Once we diagnose the presence of a hidden death wish, we overcome it by prayer ministry. "Do you want to be whole? Do you choose life?" We make the person say it, decisively, even as Jesus so often asked those who came to Him to declare what they wanted. We ask Jesus to minister to the inner child, wooing him to life. We take up authority to break whatever inner vows not to live may have been formed. We pray for integration of spirit, heart, mind and body, that all inner parts may accept and work harmoniously with one another. We pray for bodily coordination, that the spirit may flow freely into action unimpeded, through all parts of the body. We ask the person to exercise an ongoing discipline of daily choosing life.

It is amazing what such simple ministry accomplishes. Our files are full of letters from persons testifying to new freedom to enjoy the abundant life Jesus came to give. We are confident the Body of Christ can easily learn to discern defilements, to see how principalities wield defiling archetypes, and how these things create and then work through death wishes. We *can* set one another free!

Chapter Nine

Identifications and Shrikism

For lack of wood the fire goes out, And where there is no whisperer, contention quiets down. Like charcoal to hot embers and wood to fire, So is a contentious man to kindle strife. The words of a whisperer are like dainty morsels, And they go down into the innermost parts of the body. Like an earthen vessel overlaid with silver dross Are burning lips and a wicked heart. He who hates disguises it with his lips, But he lays up deceit in his heart. When he speaks graciously, do not believe him, For there are seven abominations in his heart. Though his hatred covers itself with guile, His wickedness will be revealed before the assembly. He who digs a pit will fall into it, And he who rolls a stone, it will come back on him. A lying tongue hates those it crushes, And a flattering mouth works ruin (Prov. 26:20-28).

For we all stumble in many ways. If any one does not stumble in what he says, he is a perfect man, able to bridle the whole body as well. Now if we put the bits into the horses' mouths so that they may obey us, we direct their entire body as well. Behold the ships also,

241

though they are so great and are driven by strong winds, are still directed by a very small rudder, wherever the inclination of the pilot desires. So also the tongue is a small part of the body, and yet it boasts of great things. Behold, how great a forest is set aflame by such a small fire! *And the tongue is a fire, the very world of iniquity; the tongue is set among our members as that which defiles the entire body, and sets on fire the course of our life, and is set on fire by hell.* For every species of beasts and birds, of reptiles and creatures of the sea, is tamed, and has been tamed by the human race. But no one can tame the tongue; it is a restless evil and full of deadly poison (James 3:2-8).

A woman came to us, bringing her husband. Her problem, she said, was that she could not stop ruling the roost. Her husband would never rise up to stop her. She dominated him completely, but was tired of it. She said she could never rest in him, and she wanted to. Could we find the cause and set him free to be a man?

It did not take long to discover that he had been raised by a controlling mother and older sisters. He was accustomed to being dominated. It was the way he had learned to identify love. Now, if his wife bossed him around, he knew she cared for him. The role was familiar and comfortable, though demeaning. That was the price one paid for peace and love.

Her father, as one would suspect, was a weak man, dominated by her mother. Neither parent could show affection. Both were controlled by performance orientation. But the father was a gentle and kindly man, whose feelings were constantly lacerated by her mother's vicious tongue. From the age of six until she left home at eighteen, her most vivid memory of her father was that from time to time he would come to her and begin to tell her of the awful things her mother had said to him. He would break down and cry and put his head on her shoulder and she would comfort him. This was the only physical experience of love she knew. It became her identification of love, that of being a strong woman to comfort a weak man.

As she matured she became such a beautiful woman that she won a major beauty contest in one of our eastern states. At forty-plus she still retained such striking beauty, she could have won a Mrs. America competition. In her twenties she went to work for a leading sports figure. In that position she met many of America's top athletes. Her beauty won her many dates with men of great physical stature and strong character. Somehow she could never become romantically interested in any of them, though they pursued her ardently. Then she met the man who became her husband. He was about the same height as she, was not athletic, not broad-shouldered, but was gentle and kind. It happened that recently he had been jilted by his fiancee whom he had loved dearly. His heart was broken. On the first date, as he began to share his hurt, he cried, and laid his head on her shoulder.

Who could miss seeing what happened? She identified love! He needed her. Now she could know herself as a loving woman comforting a weak man. None of the strong men had been able to trigger into that identification. She had no built-in ways of relating to strong men who didn't "need" her. This familiar role she could identify, accept, and walk in with a sense of worth and belonging. So she married him.

Need relationships are never stable nor permanent. Participants realize eventually that they want more than to be needed, or the weak one develops enough gumption to want to change. The strong one then has to learn to relinquish that role or be upset and displaced. Warfare ensues. Old roles must die. New bases for relating must be found. Some marriages survive, especially those in which Jesus is Lord. Most relationships based on need fracture as individuals mature because they cannot accept the changes that have occurred. The mate may not be able to give up the old identifications and consequent roles, nor appreciate the new.

My task (John's) as a counselor was to make this wife aware of her need for her husband to be weak. I explained to her how she had learned to identify herself as a loving person by ministering to a weak man, and asked her whether she could face the fact that she really did not want him to be strong, though she thought she did. She protested vigorously that she was tired of the whole thing, that she wanted nothing so much as for him to be strong for her. But I could see that her heart was far from what her mind believed. In no way, by teaching and counsel, could I cause her to see what she actually in her heart was determined to maintain.

So I did what counselors have learned to do in such situations: I started a fight! Counselors know how to ask a few questions, well aware that the answers will provoke a battle. In the ensuing argument, what is truly the inner content of the heart will often surface. The counselor can see behind masks then to what actually transpires between the couple. Sure enough, this pair were soon at it hammer and tongs. Before long his sensitive heart broke and he wept. Instantly her entire mood and behavior changed. She had what her heart wanted. She became the comforting strong one, taking his head on her shoulder, crooning sweet things to him.

"There," I cried. "Do you see it? Do you see what you just did? You weren't satisfied until you re-established the kind of relationship in which you could identify yourself as loving. You needed him to be the weak one who cries, so you could be the strong one to comfort him. Do you see that though a part of your mind and heart wants him to be strong for you, the ruling part of you is determined not to allow that?"

"Oh, yes, John, I see it. I see it. Oh, what am I going to do!?"

There followed much counsel and prayer for the transformation of the inner man. She needed to see her family's generational pattern of domineering women and weak men. She needed to confess her hatred of both her father and mother, and be forgiven. Most of all, she needed to haul that false identification of love to death on the cross. He needed to see the same things in his family patterns, his own hatreds of his father for being weak, and of his mother for domineering, likewise his sisters, and his own false identification of love and the false comfort of abdicating leadership.

Paula and I want to point out two things of spirit and resultant character structure: first, the power of identifications, and second, shrikism.

As our spirit encounters life, it seeks nurture. As babies instinctively search for a nipple and learn to suckle, so the spirit seeks touches of love. God has designed us so that our spirits find love and thus power to live through warm physical affection. He himself flows through us in His Spirit when we give and receive affection. The primal drive of our spirit is to find and live in the way for which it was created.

When we do not receive expressions of affection, which are food and nurture to the spirit, we latch onto whatever substitute we can find. We then identify love not by affection and open-hearted interplay of "I-thou" interchange spirit to spirit, but by whatever form love seems to take. It is as though we latch onto the package rather than the contents. If we can't have the true contents, the package becomes all-important. Since the form love comes in replaces love itself, and never satisfies, we must secure more and more.

For this reason, plus what we all inherit in Adamic sin, love in all of us becomes something warped and twisted. All love which has not died on the cross and been born anew is use, manipulation, exploitation, demand and control! The world honors love and ideally accepts all forms of love as good. Father love, mother love, mate love, filial love, neighborly love, etc., all are accepted as beneficial. But none are pure. All unregenerate love is carnal and sick.

There is only one letter's difference between mother love and "smother" love. That "s" dies only with surrender to Christ on the cross. Our Adamic inhuman nature causes us to pervert love to its opposites. *True love lays down its life for others, but unregenerate love lays down the lives of others for itself.* A father who thinks that because he loves he is encouraging his son to play football, or his daughter the violin, may in fact be squelching the life of his son or daughter, whose talents may lie elsewhere. A mother who interferes with her daughter's marriage because "I just love her too much to see her suffer" may in fact destroy her daughter's life for her own image of motherhood, under the false name of "love."

As each girl grows, her life with her father and other primary males builds into her images of what a man who loves her should do and be. Those subliminal images define to her what love and hate are. That set of images (especially as it is composed of forms love came in rather than affection itself) and her drive to have those images fulfilled spell captivity rather than freedom for her mate. The same for a boy with his mother. He too owns a set of prerequisites his wife must fulfill. *True love sets the other free to become all he or she can become. Carnal love imprisons the other so that he cannot become who he is.* For example, a girl may have learned that her father would make all her decisions and bail her out of all problems. In effect, that way of loving may have smothered her life. She may have resented it, but it is the only package by which she has learned to identify love from a man. She may marry a wise and free man who instinctively senses when her demands would reduce her to being a child curled up on her daddy's lap. He insists she make her own decisions and stand to the consequences. She may interpret that which is true love as unlove and rejection. Unless he is very strong in himself, her "packages" can force him from expressing his own wisdom to act out the roles she unconsciously sets for him. We sense what the other wants. When there is no freedom not to be that for fear of seeming to reject, love imprisons.

One wife who came to us reported that her father was a hardworking farmer. He arose early and labored in the

fields until sunset. He was a kind and loving man, but after
his evening meal he would tumble exhaustedly into bed, so
she hardly ever saw him. The one time he was truly present
for her was when she would become ill. He would postpone
his chores, stay home and fix delicious chicken soup for her.
He would sit by her bed, put his warm strong hand on her
forehead, speak reassuringly to her, and linger until he was
satisfied that she was all right. That was how she grew to
identify love, according to the package in which it came.
She learned to wallow in such attention, milking every
headache and fever for all it was worth.

Naturally, she married a workaholic like her father, kind
and gentle but gone most of the time. The first time she
developed a migraine, she went to bed and waited for the
chicken soup. But it never came. She remonstrated and
called out for help, but her young husband only said,
"You're a big girl now, take some aspirin. You'll get over
it." Then he left for work.

She was devastated! "This man doesn't love me!" Of
course he did, and her mind accepted that within a few
months, but it took her heart years to learn to recognize and
receive as real love what he had to give in his own way. She
had to consciously bring to death in prayer the power of
what that childhood "package" had trained into her heart.
And she had to walk in a discipline of choosing to believe
that she was loved, until the Lord developed within her new
eyes with which to see and interpret her husband's unique
expressions of caring for her.

Countless images in our hearts form the package of love
—for me, the way mom cooked a meal, took care of me when
I was ill, ironed clothes and stored them in the right dresser
drawers, played the piano, got us ready for school, packed
lunches, saw to it that our hair was combed. Even the "spit
baths" in the car several blocks from our destination and
the "unnecessary" worrying over cuts and bruises, bothersome as they were, spelled love. All these things and
countless others formed the package Paula had to fit or I
believed she didn't love me—except for the spit baths!

Paula's father was strong, present when he was home, loving, witty, and caring. By the time her mind was formed, he was wise by experience. When she married me, I was still a wild-eyed immature mystic searching everywhere except the right places for truth. No way could that boy fill the man-sized image she identified as love.

We had boxes the other had to fit. Until our packages died on the cross, we pushed and pulled, demanded and were disappointed. Every few months we would hassle our way through the fogs and confusions until what lay bare was that each of us felt the other didn't really love, or at least wasn't expressing it. And then we would have to confess to being hurt by that. Each of us had thought we were trying harder to love than the other one, and to be told we hadn't been perceived as trying at all was the cruelest cut of all! It was the packages. We could not perceive as love what the other one did do because that hadn't been a part of our package. More powerfully, we *could* perceive as *unlove* what the other one *didn't do* which he didn't do for the same reason, not part of the learned package love came in in our families.

It should be said that in families where copious amounts of physical affection have been daily fare, it is usually the case that so much security has been generated in the personal spirits of all that offspring do not latch onto the "packages" so intensely. They are more able to read love in what the other does. Alternatively, in families where little affectionate touch was experienced, there is likely to be little flexibility. Given the predictability of human nature, the maxim is, to the degree of lack of affection, to that degree there is rigidity in identifying love. However, it should also be stated that when a person who has experienced much affectionate touch in early years marries a mate who is reserved and unable to demonstrate caring with warm hugs and freely expressed admiration and affirmation, that contrast over a period of years may undermine security and put a crippling strain on flexibility. This occurs unless the person is walking in very close relationship with the Lord whose grace sustains and maintains. Also, in some, affectionate touch can have become a "package" in itself: "People hug the ones they love. My husband never holds me unless he wants sex; therefore I feel used, not loved." But the maxim still stands. Where the spirit has been so nurtured in the early years by affectionate touch, there is that initial base of security and flexibility which will enable more easily forgiveness, compassion and the forbearing of the other in love until the Lord can melt the heart and empower change in one or both.

Images and demands are present in every person, whether secure or insecure. For that reason, many couples have come to us and said, "We don't understand. We have a mystery. Before we married we felt free with each other. We could discuss anything. We never fought." (Slight untruth here; memory can play tricks.) "It was fun to be together. Then we got married. We were at each other's throats from the honeymoon on. We battled about everything. We couldn't be ourselves anymore. Every word had to be guarded. It wasn't fun to be with each other anymore. It was like living in prison. Then we were divorced. It felt so good to be free. After a while we began to date each other again, and found out we like each other. So we started to think about re-marrying. Man, we were into the hassles all over again! How come? Aren't we meant for each other? Are we supposed to be friends but not married?"

The answer? Identifications. Pictures. Packages. So long as they were not married, they had some emotional distance. They could still be their own persons. The closer they drew to each other, the more their unseen inner needs took over to have their images of love fulfilled. They would then measure and judge each other's performance and feel trapped and cheated. Unregenerate love has no way other than separation to overcome the vast world of unconscious demands that individuals can impose upon each other.

In this sense, the cruelest thing Christianity has inadvertently done is to teach the Christian ideal of marriage without teaching Christ. Our movies, novels, neighborly examples—every way our own good marriages cannot be hid but are as a city set on a hill—all have painted vivid pictures for the non-Christian world as to what their married life ought to be like. That image has become their death knell, because it becomes part of their world of demand. They cannot live up to such images without Christ, and so the demand and the attempt to respond do nothing more than imprison. We are not saying we should not be examples, as though failing would make it easier on unbelievers! Our example should be part of what convicts and creates hunger for Christ. We *are* saying that we Christians need to comprehend the dynamics. We ought to be aware, standing by ready to evangelize and pick up the pieces. In other words, it is better that men and women hear the gospel and begin to die to their demand worlds inside the healing milieu of the Lord and His Church. But if people have *not* surrendered to Christ, they *will* learn the hard way, and our example will be part of what makes it tougher. We need then to evangelize by healing and restoring hearts and marriages.

Unfortunately, many Christians have thought themselves totally changed by conversion, which in fact only began the process. And so they too have not only continued with their inherited unconscious demand worlds, they have added to them everything they presently are learning in Sunday school and church! They draw the prison lines even tighter! Christ said of lawyers what sometimes also applies to us Christians: "Woe to you lawyers as well! For you weigh men down with burdens hard to bear, while you yourselves will not even touch the burdens with one of your fingers" (Luke 11:46). It takes a lot of dying with Jesus before our "ought" and "should" worlds quit attempting to compel our mates to be what we want them to be rather than what they are meant to be by God's gift. Strangely, when we finally die to self, we discover to our delight that what the other actually is blesses our hearts far more than what we thought we wanted.

There is no other way out of our morass of unconscious demands on each other than death to them through prayer and discipline. Jesus is the answer, not in a once-for-all conversion but in a conversion which continues anew every day as we discover more of what needs to die.

Let us posit one distinction as vividly as we can. When we become convicted by the Holy Spirit that we are sinners and we receive Jesus, the natural proclivity is to think that all the evil in us died on that cross. That is fine. It did. But two facts must be faced. Experientially, not all of that evil has yet found the death it has died positionally. Paula and I have said that repeatedly in all of our books and tapes. But now let us be clear concerning the second fact. Not only the bad in us must die; so must also the good. Much of our nature we have viewed as good. What is wrong with the kindness we naturally have? Or our natural generosity? All the God-given natural talents which have been ours from day one? What is wrong with them? Nothing, except they are all veined with impurities of sin. We may have taken it for granted those good things died and were reborn at conversion and that all the impure motives died out of us then. But not so.

When I received Jesus, let's say that I recognized ten talents or God-given abilities within me. Suppose that in two areas I recognized I had become so rotten I needed a Savior. "Praise be to God, Jesus died for my sin. I'm born anew. I'm washed clean. Now I'll take the eight good qualities, add the two redeemed, and thank you, Jesus, I'm on my way, whole again." The Lord allowed that for a while. Then, because He loves me, He sadly said, *John, there aren't any eight good ones. It's all sin.*

The incisive message of this chapter is first that all those pictures and ways of loving in which we were raised are sin, and need to die. Those good things which became part of us as we grew up—loyalty, fondness, gentleness, gratitude, courtesy, whatever else—all are corrupted by sin, and must find their death on the cross. For example, family loyalty seems good. It *is* good. But suppose a pastor properly chastises our brother and sister. Uncrucified loyalty is still carnal, belonging to the old world. If we listen to it, we attack the pastor self-righteously, thinking family loyalty has made our case just and right. Mothers may justify screaming at their children because, "after all, I guess I just care too much," whereas true mother love in Christ would have respected the child and called him to account without railing. What really operated was parental pride, masked as love. A husband's jealousy may cause him to attack someone who befriends his wife, thinking it is love and righteous possessiveness which impels him. In truth it was undealt-with angers and fears dating back to the time when his parents separated. *We have no pure motives.* There is nothing purely good which dwells within us (Rom. 7:18). All our righteousness is as filthy rags.

For this reason Jesus said, "If anyone comes to Me, and does not hate his own father and mother and wife and children and brothers and sisters, yes, and even his own life, he cannot be My disciple" (Luke 14:26). The word "hate," like "love," is used in many ways. I love the Lord, I love Paula, and I love a hot dog—all differently. No way could Jesus have meant to license us to hate anyone in a wrong way. He means that we are to hate that continuing carnal influence through our families and ourselves which would press the old wineskin's ways upon the new. All the ways we learned to do all the good things of family have to be hated and put to death on the cross so that the new way of Jesus can be ours. This teaching can be found in fuller form in our book, *Restoring the Christian Family*, in Chapter Eighteen, "Renunciation, or Cutting Free," or in our tape, "Cutting Free." Let it suffice in this context to grasp that it is all those good things in us, which comprise the package we have identified as love, which must die on the cross, and the sooner the better. We do this simply by praying for that crucifixion to happen, as we see our packages one by one, day by day. Jesus then accomplishes that death in us, the easy way if possible, the hard way if necessary. And He gives everything back to us, redeemed.

One man who came often to our home to visit had been raised by an extremely critical mother. She was incapable of giving affection, and she lashed him with her tongue continually. That became his identification of love, to be scolded and harangued. If he came alone to our home, within a few minutes he would be saying, "I'd better call home and let my wife know where I am, or boy, I'm going to get it." When they came to visit together, we would notice that he would say little barbed things calculated to provoke her, until finally she would explode and lash out at him. That satisfied his need for assurance of love. He would throw up his arms as though to ward off blows. The comically tragic thing was that he stands six foot seven and she is only five foot two! She was no threat at all! His way of knowing he was loved was to provoke her to attack. Then the little boy inside the grown man could ward off blows and feel loved again.

We share this story to demonstrate the difference between learning the easy way or the hard way. This man could not hear our attempts to show him the true agenda in their battles. If he could have, they could have prayed them to the cross and laughed together at themselves. Since he could not, what could have been jovial became deadly serious. The only way our loving Lord could set them free was to sicken them into disgust and loathing for the game. Their battles became worse and worse, until there was nothing left in him which unconsciously wanted to be hassled. He could no longer identify harangues as love, only hate. Their marriage survived, but only after reaching the pits of disgust after which they truly wanted to die to self.

Sometimes identifications of love are built so strongly by fantasy and projected so powerfully as demand that they totally block out recognition and acceptance of love that is very genuinely and warmly given. For instance, a girl grows up with a father who is hyper-critical, demanding, insensitive and self-centered. She comes to the belief that men will not notice her, care about how she feels, affirm her or provide for her, but will use her to serve their selfish ends. At the same time she builds a picture of what she desperately thinks she needs from a man, and dreams that someday she will marry a husband who will stay at home with her, listen attentively to all she has to say, bring her flowers and candy, take her to exotic and exciting places, tell her she is beautiful, and do all the romantic things for her that she has heard about in movies and books. She marries a man who, in spite of his own childhood woundings, tries to do what he thinks will bless and please his wife. Her birthday approaches. She begins to build pictures of what a perfect celebration she will have. She imagines the man of her life coming home from work early to take her to dinner and a late show. Dinner will be in a fine restaurant with candlelight and soft music and no one to rush them or break in on their privacy. They will hold hands in the show and go for a moonlight drive around the lakeshore afterward. He will tell her how lovely she is and she will smile and sigh and feel goosepimply all over. "The Day" arrives and she gives him hints: "You could *surprise* me with . . ." All day long she rehearses the wonderful evening they will have. About five o'clock he calls to say he will be delayed; he is sorry, but it can't be avoided, and he will arrive as soon as possible. Two hours later he comes breathlessly in the door with a beautifully wrapped gift and a box of chocolates in his hand (she is crazy about chocolate), an awkward apology on his lips (he was never good at saying "I'm sorry"), and they hurry to the restaurant. Service is slow and irritation mounts as it becomes apparent that they won't be able to get to the show on time. Attempts at conversation degenerate rapidly to accusation and defensive response and finally to brooding silence. Her dream is shattered and she sinks under a black cloud of "He never thinks of me," leaving his gift and the chocolates unopened and forgotten. "What's the use?" he thinks. "I can't win."

So much for identification. The second factor we want to discuss is shrikism. A shrike is a bird which impales its victim on a thorn and then tears it apart muscle by muscle.

In human terms, a shrike is a person who so gathers all the righteousness to himself or herself that everyone else must act out wickedness. Then in the very act of seeming to try to help, the shrike actually destroys the other bit by bit. Worse, the shrike actually thinks he or she is truly trying to be loving and helpful.

In the story with which we began the chapter, the wife had become a shrike. She needed to destroy her husband so that he would be weak and she could be the strong one. As a result, her very ministrations to him, the comforting and crooning, actually demeaned and debased him. Her attempts to love were in effect a shrike's demolition of his manhood, "muscle by muscle."

One of the most powerful forces at work in creating and maintaining shrikism is the fleshly way we counterbalance one another in all relationships. For instance, if one mate is overly talkative, the other becomes silent. It is not that the mate has nothing to say. Being half of the other, the need to counterbalance causes him or her to retire. If one is very extroverted and aggressive, usually the other balances by becoming quiet and introverted. If one won't discipline the children, the other tends to over-discipline. The counterbalancing is not a conscious attempt, but a deeply unconscious one that happens simply because of our oneness in marriage.

In the beginning of our marriage, I was the super-spook mystic, always having dreams, seeing visions, and having far-out experiences. Paula was as mystically gifted as I, but dared not express it. She became the down-to-earth, practical one. The wilder I became, the more sensible and controlled she became; conversely the more determined to be a rock of common sense she became, the more head-in-the skyish I became. We were driving each other off balance.

Behind that driving was shrikism in each of us. Paula had grown up with brothers with whom she competed in sibling rivalry. They were good in sports, fun-loving and mischievously adventurous, so she excelled with high marks at school and in trying to be more dependable and wise than they. Subtly it was built into her to ace a man out in the act of ministering to his mistakes. She would be the solid righteous one in whom the family could take comfort. That would have been fine except that her role required someone to play the opposite. Her heart could not purely want me to be wise and stable. She unconsciously needed me to stumble about and make mistakes.

I fit that pattern excellently. I had grown up with a critical mother. Taught to be obedient and dutiful, not only to the gentle but also to the overbearing (1 Pet. 2:18), I determined to do the right thing no matter whether abused or complimented. I became the martyr who would perform, take the abuse, and go right on serving anyway. It was good to be willing to serve no matter what, but my role needed a persecutor. My judgment was that the woman is the vicious one who attacks the nobly suffering man. So my game was to venture out on the frontiers of faith, a pioneer searching where no one else dared to go, already suffering "the slings and arrows of outrageous fortune," taking up "arms against a sea of troubles" (*Hamlet*, Act III, Scene I), only to find myself not only seeming to be unsupported by Paula, but in my eyes attacked and criticized. The criticism, which I could not help but recognize as good for me, also proved again my long-suffering "righteousness."

The essence of shrikism is that it establishes personal righteousness at the expense of others. Not all performance-oriented people are shrikes, but all shrikes are performance-oriented. Having bought the lie that they must perform well to be loved, yet insecure about their performance, they are driven unconsciously to contrast themselves with others; others must look bad in order for the shrike to look good. The shrike fears rejection more than anything else, yet in his striving to outperform everyone, he gathers righteousness to himself. Without knowing it, he does the very things which make him almost impossible to live with. His end is rejection.

Wanting love, the woman in our first story ministered to her husband, unaware that, in her need to be the strong one helping a weak husband, she was disembowelling him, until in the end he could only hate her. He became vulnerable to any woman who could make him feel strong and capable. Sure enough, he had an affair, and his gorgeous Christian wife could not understand how he could have chosen *that* creature over her! Fortunately they sought counsel in time, and their marriage was saved.

There was a man who was an extremely competent engineer but who nonetheless lost one job after another. He had been raised with two brothers. Tremendous demands were put on the children to perform chores around the house, but there was no parental affection. Dick was soon bigger, stronger and faster than his brothers; at least he could outwork them. The scraps of parental praise he received for outperforming the other two became his identification of love. It was also the making of a shrike, for feelings of self-worth and being loved required someone else to perform less well than he. Soon after Dick would go to work in an office, his superior intelligence would enable him to master a job others had taken months to learn. Being a generous, loving person, he would set out to help his fellow employees, unaware that he was putting them down. People felt demeaned and accused. Soon he would be the center of dissension in the office. Eventually the boss would come to say, "Dick, you're a great worker, you're intelligent and well trained, and I'll give you a high recommendation, but somehow you don't fit in this office. I'm going to have to let you go."

Dick went through three positions in the first several years we knew him. I attended a banquet with him at which his current boss was the speaker. Three times Dick interrupted his boss's speech to correct him with "helpful" suggestions! He seemed to be totally unaware that his "help" undermined his boss and his own position. I visited in Dick's home. He continually berated his wife as she prepared supper, fussing around her kitchen, "helping."

He had no idea what he was doing to his wife's sense of worth. His ability to feel loved and okay depended on his being able to outperform his wife in her own kitchen. Dick was also a trained pianist. His children were taking lessons. I watched him sit down beside them, lovingly wanting to help. Within a few minutes the children would slink away in tears while Dick sat there playing magnificent solos.

Shrikes often have loving outer natures. They go out of their way to help others, and can't understand why others reject them. They usually become noble martyrs who keep trying to help anyway.

Shrikes take their place among the noble saints of the church. They usually work more diligently than anyone else. But they can be detected by the fact that people around them who are usually competent and confident become fumble-fingered or forget to show up. People in proximity to shrikes perform less well than they normally do in proximity to anyone else. In this case, the cause is defilement, as discussed in Chapter Eight.

All of us are afflicted with shrikism. It is latent in every person insofar as all of us have some degree of performance orientation and have competed in a form of sibling rivalry at home or in school. We all live from an inner wellspring of well-being. If ours is drained and we fail to fill it from Jesus, then we either puff ourselves up or knock a hole in someone else's reservoir. That person needs our help. So we help him and thus make ourselves feel big and great again. That is shrikism, making oneself feel okay at the expense of others.

Presently there is an epidemic of shrikism in the Church, especially among women, though men also can become shrikes. Many have been raised in homes lacking in affection. Competing with brothers for scraps of parental attention, they learned to win the game for love at home by being more righteous than their brothers. Unaware that that has remained an active pattern, they may have come to the Lord first in the family. As they became more pious and devoted, tending also in their immaturity, like me, to become more and more mystical and religiously experience-centered, usually their husbands unconsciously counterbalance by becoming more and more earthy and then worldly. That hooked into the earlier game of sibling rivalry. These wives, being new children in the family of God, then prayed fervently for their husbands to be converted, unaware how their hearts sabotaged their prayers. They were again involved in sibling rivalry, their new righteousness dependent upon contrast with "that awful man." The more pious and holy they became, the more sinfully their husbands reacted. Shrikism then became an active option. The wife was not that good. The husband was not that bad. She was not that pious and prayerful and he was not that worldly and callous. Their counterbalancing of one another was driving them to positions that were polar opposites.

"Job's comforters" did not help. Her church friends praised that saintly woman who continued by the grace of God to live with that heathen sinner. His friends could not understand how he could stand to live with that "crazy super-spook" and her "hypocritical religious fanatic friends." Many prayers were said by the wife and her friends, who couldn't understand why God would not save that wretched creature. The dynamic of counterbalancing and shrikism stood in the way of his heart. He also wanted the Lord, but accepting the Lord had become tantamount to surrendering to her rather than to Him. Quite apart from the blockages of pride, a man senses in his spirit something wrong about that. Besides, he is afraid he will become like her and her friends. Her example is not at all evangelistic to him.

Sometimes it happens the other way around, with the same results. We have ministered lately to several men who lost their wives when they came to the Lord and heard His call to ministry. The same counterbalancing dynamic and the same kind of shrikism took effect.

Such polarism need not result. Spiritual people need to climb down off the pedestal. Let them be earthy and real, human and vulnerable at home. What is often aggravating is that the mate of a new Christian feels, often rightly so, that the Lord has become a rival. Mate love has been transferred to the Lord, where it does not belong, and the unconverted mate feels aced out by a love no one can compete against and win! New Christians tend to broadcast, "I have a new and vastly satisfying love; I don't need you anymore." Let the Christian drink humbly from both the affection and the wisdom of the non-Christian mate. The non-Christian is sanctified through the believing one (1 Cor. 7:14). By faith a believer can draw God's wisdom powerfully from an unbelieving mate.

Jo, whose story is told in Chapter Six, "Spiritual Imprisonment," soon soared to great and glorious heights in the Lord, while Frank still desisted even from attending church. But we were grateful to the Lord that no such polarism or shrikism developed. Jo continually asked Frank's advice for help for her counselees. Never have I heard wiser counsel than the Lord gave her through Frank! She asked him the questions of faith or about the Bible which stumped her. She honored his headship in every way. She did not believe that if he would accept Christ as Lord, only then could he act as her head. She activated him in that position he already held (Eph. 5:22, 23). She gave herself to him more warmly and womanly the more she knew the Lord. One day she said chuckling, "Frank keeps sitting there thumbing through his Bible, muttering to herself that he *has* to learn to understand this thing!" It was not long before he was such a solid churchman that several airmen in his company began to attend base chapel saying, "If Frank Black says there is something to this, then there must be."

True faith separates us from continuing carnal influence from our families, but it never separates us from them personally. If distance is resulting seemingly from the faith of one and the lack of faith in the other, it is nothing but delusion to believe that our Lord Jesus is causing that separation. Not He but flesh, most likely counterbalancing dynamics and shrikism, is causing harm to the family. Let Christians repent of elitism, specialness, "spookism," and every other "ism" one can think of, and return humbly to the arms of the mate God gave them.

We do not have to fear being overcome by what the mate is. We are more than overcomers. No one is all evil nor all good. By faith we can follow St. Paul's prescription in Philippians 4:8: "Finally, brethren, whatever is true, whatever is honorable, whatever is right, whatever is pure, whatever is lovely, whatever is of good repute, if there is any excellence and if anything worthy of praise, let your mind dwell on these things." We can by faith draw from our mate the best rather than the worst.

The following are the sharpest questions we have found to determine whether shrikism is at work through ourselves:

> Do people around you act out their best selves, or their worst?
>
> Is your mate becoming a better person, or worse, by living with you?
>
> Are you drawing wisdom and goodness from your mate, or less than he/she is capable of?
>
> Could you really rejoice if your mate came to the Lord? Or would part of you have to try harder to become a better Christian than your mate can be?

"Do nothing from selfishness or conceit, but in humility count others better than yourself" (Phil. 2:3 RSV). Janet Wilcox, our in-house counselor who lives with us, is fond of saying, "Humility is nothing more or less than the direct result of seeing things as they are." The final check for shrikism is therefore, "Which do you see first and most easily, the other fellow's faults, or yours?" or, "In an argument do you seek to bless and protect the other's heart while finding truth together, or do you seek to prove him wrong and you right?"

Mercifully, there is a difference between the general shrikism to which we are all occasionally subject, and being a confirmed shrike. A confirmed shrike is one in whom the drive to establish oneself is so all-consuming that shrikism is the basic stance of life. These people live in and for a picture of themselves. They work at it twenty-four hours a day, though they may be totally unaware of it.

Dick had become a confirmed shrike. Everywhere he went his behavior was the same, with the same results. His wife eventually grew tired of being treated as an inept child in her own home, and left him. When she finally individuated enough to be her own person, her repressed angers erupted like a volcano. No matter how friends pleaded, she pressed with vitriolic intensity for divorce. She had had it. He would never change. Now, since we become what we judge (Rom. 2:1), and in her eyes Dick could do nothing right, she shrikes on him from a distance through his children, while she plays the role of the righteous divorcee.

The following is a list of symptoms by which to detect the presence of a shrike. Though we speak here in the context of church life, the same applies in offices, clubs, athletic teams, etc., wherever society is.

Shrikes always have a reason, an excuse, or an alibi to justify what they do. The fault is never theirs. If true accusation is inescapable and they must admit they did a wrong thing, someone else has put them into an untenable position. They *had* to do it. Unconsciously, to them blame is tantamount to not being loved; they cannot conceive that someone could love them despite their faults, so they must never have any faults. The shrike cannot perceive that most people already see his faults and love him anyway.

Shrikes falsely perceive what others do and impute to them wrong motives. One divorced woman we knew was greatly ministered to by her church. They gave her groceries, helped her with her yard, brought cut wood for her stove, assisted her in finding a job, prayed for her, carried her in their hearts, and withstood her assaults. To hear her tell it, that church is filled with hard-hearted and self-centered people who never do anything for anyone else unless it is to make themselves feel good or to enhance their own reputation. She could not perceive any of their efforts truly as love for her and imputed her own false motives to their good works.

That leads us to the next symptom. Shrikes often impute *their own* unconscious motives to others and bitterly charge them. The divorcee of whom we have just spoken (we'll call her Alice) was always running about doing things for others. But she was tragically unaware that her motives for serving others were mixed, often rooted in her own unhealed insecurities. She continually projected what was in her own heart onto others, and attacked it as if it were in them. St. Paul wrote to Timothy concerning this kind of shrike: ". . . they also learn to be idle, as they go around from house to house; and not merely idle, but also gossips and busybodies, talking about things not proper to mention" (1 Tim. 5:13). Shrikes do attempt to do works for the Lord, but inasmuch as they are so out of the flow of the Spirit, it devolves to mere "dead works." (Heb. 6:1). Their many works become more of a bother than a help; thus in this sense they are "idle."

Shrikes carry tales. They are usually the gossipmongers of the church. Their ability to feel good depends upon contrast to the failings of others, so they make sure everyone knows about everyone else's faults. Commonly, however, such gossiping is masked, even from themselves, as "concern." "Let's pray about so-and-so, they have been doing this and that." By defilement, solid people who normally would not gossip at all often surprise the pastor by being carried away by shrikes. Shrikes do not believe they are gossips, and hotly deny it. One shrike told the same story to the pastor and every elder in the church, always with the identical refrain, "I haven't told anyone else. And I'm only telling you so you can pray." When confronted by the group, each one revealing how she had told them the same thing, she could not believe it and would not admit it. She insisted that they had gossiped to each other and were putting this on her. She had done no such thing. She was a good person and they all knew it. The very idea!

Shrikes cannot arrive at a knowledge of the truth. The simple truth they are incapable of hearing is that they are loved unconditionally. Their extreme performance orientation and pitiful attempts to establish their righteousness so they will feel loved and secure are the very things which block them from comprehending or receiving that Jesus can love and accept them without all that labor. Shrikism is thus one of the "various impulses" St. Paul wrote about when he said that there "are those who enter into households and captivate weak women *weighed down with sins,* led on by *various impulses,* always learning and *never able to come to a knowledge of the truth"* (2 Tim. 3:6).

Though St. Paul mentioned women, we have seen the same thing in men. In one small group in which we shared was a man who repeatedly raised carping questions. Most thought he merely loved to argue. He would jump into a quarrel at the drop of a hat. What we discovered actually lay behind his constantly irrelevant questioning and bickering was the heart of a shrike. He would prove his superior biblical knowledge at the expense of everyone else so that he could be the true one setting everyone else straight. After a while all of us perceived what was going on, and our hearts bled for him. Shrikism is a wicked trap, a construct of Satan to keep souls away from true fellowship with the Father and Son and from one another.

Shrikes re-write history. One woman was raised by a father who could not give affection. He demanded performance. She saw him fly into a rage and beat mercilessly on her beloved older brother. She could not admit anger at her father. That would be sinful, and she must be a perfect lady in order to be loved. By the grace of God she married a gentle, kindly man not at all like her father. That very fact threatened to expose her real feelings toward her father. From then on, her husband could do nothing right, while in her mind her father became more and more saintly. She had also competed with her brothers, who could work in the fields alongside her father, whereas she could not. Therefore in front of her children she had to appear to work much longer, more dedicatedly, and more nobly self-sacrificingly than her husband did. Over the years, incipient shrikism became more and more confirmed.

By the time counseling started, I had known the family for many years. I knew the actual facts of their life together. Each time I tried to help her face the truth, the next time I saw her she had gone back over the incidents we had discussed and re-worked them all, thoroughly convinced that the fabrications she now told me were in fact the true history. These new stories ". . . you could not have known about because I never told anyone before, wanting to protect his reputation. . . ." The new "revelations" always made it appear that she had nobly protected that evil man from discovery. Eventually, her versions of their life together came to bear almost no resemblance to fact. She remains convinced that her story is the only true one and that, poor martyr she is, no one knows all that she has suffered. When someone remarked to her that though she had divorced him, he had never wanted it, and always had loved her, her reply was, "Why, of course, he never had any grounds. I was a perfect wife to him." This despite the fact that all of her children and grandchildren honor and love him and have little to do with her since she rips them as viciously as she does him. Such people are to be pitied and fought for in prayer.

Shrikes enlist armies. They find cronies in the church who will beleive they are as good as they are trying to appear to be. They keep these friends supplied with "evidence," concoctions of half-truths twisted to put the pastor (or whoever needs to be shot down) in the worst light. "But these men revile the things which they do not understand; . . ." (Jude 10). "These are grumblers, finding fault, following after their own lusts; they speak arrogantly, flattering people for the sake of gaining an advantage" (Jude 16). "If only all those people knew what is really going on! We've just got to hold this church together. I'm sure glad you're standing true and straight. Someday it will all come out and you'll see I was right all along. That awful man! But we've just got to love him. Let's pray for him." They really believe they are champions of the faith, not realizing their own need for others to be wrong so they can be right has twisted their perception of reality. ". . . in which are some things hard to understand, which the untaught and *unstable distort*, as they do also the rest of the Scriptures, to their own destruction" (2 Pet. 3:16b). St. Peter was speaking of difficult passages in St. Paul's letters, but his words aptly describe how shrikes misunderstand events in the life of the church, and twist them to their own destruction, since whoever reviles the Lord's anointed is in trouble with the Lord.

Shrikes perceive attempts to help them as attack. One day in my office a husband was attempting to reach his wife's heart. She had made sure everyone in the church knew what an awful man he was. Time and the Lord had vindicated him and she had left that "bunch of backsliders" to find a "true church." Now we were attempting to save their marriage. Sitting beside her, full of love and zeal to reach her, he gently took hold of her arm as he pleaded with her to hear him and me. But she flounced away and exclaimed, "Did you see what he just did? He hit me!" She was firmly convinced in her mind that his touch was violently intended. In her heart she knew she was lying, of course, but her spirit was so completely engaged in the effort to establish herself as righteous and him as wicked that the slightest pretext would do.

Shrikes are always controlling. They haven't the security and trust to let things happen as they will. They cannot be at rest and trust that others will like them. They either must be the center of attention or so manipulate that they are in control of what is happening. A man who was semi-retired was hired by a church to design and build a new entrance and front to the church building. The change also was intended to expand seating capacity and beautify the rear of the sanctuary. He was doing a magnificent job and loving it. Another man, a trustee, manipulated other trustees, whispered in the ear of the pastor, and finally made things so difficult that the first man gave up in disgust and left the church. The trustee then finished the work, unaware that what really impelled him was not concern for the work but sibling rivalry and the need to be in control. This man continually disrupts the life of the congregation.

Shrikes cannot rest. They are chronically exhausted, if not physically, then emotionally. The reason is that they must forever work for love. The more diligently they work, the "behinder" they become, for their labors turn people away: So they redouble efforts. The losing game goes on and on.

Shrikes resist inner healing. After all, nothing is wrong with them. It's those other people. If they do allow themselves to be ministered to, it is only so far as they remain in control, revealing nothing which might lead to real inner depths of sin. They are role playing the righteousness of humbly being ministered to. One shrike used to tell me about the dumb mistakes she had made. But her confessions were intended to show how her good and loving heart caused her to continue to do kind things (stupidly) for undeserving people.

Shrikes usually have slumbering spirits. Not all do, and certainly not all who have slumbering spirits are shrikes. Insofar as they do have slumbering spirits, they read what is going on in worship services and meetings from within their own mentality instead of by the true mind of the Holy Spirit. Thus they are apt to receive distorted versions, and repeat those to outsiders.

There are many other symptoms, but whoever picks up the basic keys of fear, performance orientation, striving and sibling rivalry, and connects them to the need to establish one's own righteousness at the expense of others, will soon compile his own list. What is important is that the Church learn to recognize and minister to the many shrikes in its midst.

Setting a confirmed shrike free is the most difficult work we have encountered. The success we have experienced has come about only by the long hard route of patience, persistence and forbearance undergirded by prayer, but we continue to search for a simpler way. The problem occurs not only in the fact that such people find it extremely difficult to admit fault. It is that shrikism has become the basic stance and drive of their entire life! Even if the shrike sees it and loathes it, it is so ingrained in every way he thinks, feels and acts, that dislodging it may take years of painful self-discovery and crucifixion. Added to that is the fear and confusion: "If I die to the only way I know, then how shall I live? In what new mold can my energies flow?" To have an inner bitter-root judgment or expectancy is to suffer from one sick area of the total being. One can root that out and go on. The same for inner vows, or prenatal wounds and sins. But shrikes are not merely sickened in one area while remaining somewhat whole in others. They suffer an ailment of the personal spirit which has built their entire soul structure and way of meeting life as a wrong answer to the threat of isolation and fear, loneliness and rejection.

Replacing shrikism calls for radical and total death on the cross. That death cannot be accomplished unless the personal spirit finally catches what the mind received in the first conversion experience—that Jesus loves us—unconditionally! The spirit has long been programmed to earn love. It is a total revolution to upset that lifetime of learning. The shrike's spirit may catch glimpses of being loved, but the strongman of the self can quickly rebuild familiar tracks to run in. In short, our self has a life of its own, and fights not to die; shrikism becomes the fortress and stronghold of the nature of the self.

Shrikism as a general tendency in all of us is fairly easy to heal. We deal with the root causes in the same way that we pray for any other condition inside of us. Confession, repentance, forgiveness, absolution, death on the cross and resurrection to new life is the simple route to wholeness.

Once we have recognized the problem and the basic ministry has been accomplished, the discipline of walking in the new way can be a delight. We laugh at ourselves as we say, "Oh, there I was, shriking again" or, "Hey, you're shriking on me again." "Oh dear, I was, wasn't I? Forgive me."

Confirmed shrikes need longsuffering friends who will indeed stick closer than a brother (Prov. 18:24). These must be people who are able to express affection when the shrike least deserves it. They must be generous, open-hearted people who are not turned away, upset or defeated by slights and insults. Again and again we have counseled with those who wanted desperately to change. Ministry was well received and initially effective. Yet the fabric of healing was ripped apart by loved ones in the home who had learned by hurt over a period of years to close themselves off behind defensive walls, to hide and throw retaliative barbs. Often a wife's newly born intentions have crashed against the steel walls of negative expectation and judgment of a husband who feels that he has "had it." "She'll never change." His attitude sets her up for a fall into old familiar patterns, reinstating the program she has just rejected. Loved ones in the family of the shrike must be open to ministry to enable them to deal with the sin in their own hearts which caused them to reap such a relationship, and defensive attitudes developed in themselves which refuse the shrike room to change. By prayer they must be given enough strength of spirit and sovereign gift of trust and courage to open again to the one who has repeatedly wounded them so that they can give unconditional love and affection, which are essential to healing.

Those who minister to shrikes must be people who have the ability to confront and rebuke, lightly but firmly, again and again. Shrikes must be told when they are shriking, in no uncertain terms. They have to be taken off the pedestal of righteousness again and again, *coupled with such acceptance and affection* that the inmost spirit finally accepts the idea that it doesn't need that display of righteousness to be loved, and will not be rejected when wrong.

Paula and I were not confirmed shrikes, but we had plenty of it in us. We learned to confront each other consistently when we were at it. It often seemed not to work in the moment. Paula or I would steam off in a huff, certain the other had misread us. But the Holy Spirit had us, and sooner or later we would have to admit the truth and "fess up." As we learned not to locate the "enemy" in the other person, but to discipline ourselves to choose compassionately to unite with the other person against their bondage, words of confrontation became more and more effective. As we learned to affirm the other before the confrontation—"I love you, appreciate you, but this is what you are doing"—we discovered that our attempts to help one another were more readily received. And as we developed a personal relationship with the Lord so that our own sense of worth and well-being was dependent first of all upon Him, we were not bound to take either the attacks or the bumbling attempts of the other to "help" as personally threatening. The Lord himself could more and more enable us to discern the concern in a criticism, the truth in a lie, the hurt of the other in a quick sharp answer rather than first the intent to hurt. Praying together became a way of lifting problems to common ground at the foot of the cross and releasing our imperfect perceptions of truth to Him who is the Truth. We found that unwillingness to pray together concerning a misunderstanding or disagreement or anger was a sure sign of our individual unwillingness to give up the game of proving the other wrong and nursing our own offendedness.

For confirmed shrikes, we must not assume that because we have prayed several times about the deepest things in the personal spirit, they ought therefore to have been healed. We must pray over the same areas again and again, until the spirit, in which it originates, is finally and totally healed.

Preface
SECTION III
Spiritual Sins

In this section, it is not our purpose to catalogue and fully describe all the various forms of occult involvement and other spiritual sins. Many authors have already done that. Any competent clerk in any Christian bookstore can refer the reader to several good books on the subject. Our purpose is to teach the Body of Christ how to heal whatever wounds have been inflicted upon the personal spirit. Therefore we will chronicle and describe some of the more important occult sins so that sufficient understanding serves as a base for comprehending what should be healed and how to do that.

All occult involvement wounds our personal spirit. We need not only deliverance and forgiveness but also healing. As counselors, we are called to see what are the conditions in the history of the person which made him vulnerable to temptation and attack. We need to heal not only the effects of sin, but the causes. It is to that end that we include this section on spiritual sins in what is basically a book about inner healing.

In our ministry we have discovered a great gap in the Body's understanding in this area. Too many who minister have rightly applied the blood for forgiveness, the cross for death of occult practices, authority for exorcism and the Word of God for teaching, but then have prematurely rejoiced as though the entire work of redemption had been accomplished. But clients may retain the same deep wounds which originally caused their fall and more great bruises in the spirit as a result of their occult sins. The Body needs to learn how to persevere until the work in the other is complete, and the person is not only free but whole again.

Chapter Ten

Occult Involvement

Occult involvement is unequivocally forbidden by the Lord:

> When you enter the land which the Lord your God gives you, you shall not learn to imitate the detestable things of those nations. There shall not be found among you anyone who makes his son or his daughter pass through the fire, one who uses divination, one who practices witchcraft, or one who interprets omens, or a sorcerer, or one who casts a spell, or a medium, or a spiritist, or one who calls up the dead. For whoever does these things is detestable to the Lord; and because of these detestable things the Lord your God will drive them out before you. You shall be blameless before the Lord your God. For those nations which you shall dispossess, listen to those who practice witchcraft and to diviners, but as for you, the Lord your God has not allowed you to do so (Deut. 18:9-14).

The word "occult" means "something hidden" or "the act of hiding something." In astronomy, when the sun's rays hide a star, that is termed an "occult occurrence." In that context the word "occult" bears no negative connotations. It is merely a descriptive scientific word. In religious circles, however, it means, "Of the nature of or pertaining to those sciences involving the use of the supernatural (as magic, alchemy, astrology, theosophy, and the like)" (*Oxford Universal Dictionary*, Clarendon Press, 1933).

Magic in this context does not mean those tricks done by quickness of hand and eye which are often accomplished by modern-day performing "magicians." Such tricks are properly called "legerdemain." To practice magic means to ". . . influence the course of events by compelling the agency of spiritual beings, or by bringing into operation some occult controlling principle of nature" (ibid.).

Magic thus has two dimensions. In the first, magic means the operation of principles by our own psychic energy to accomplish our own purposes. In this dimension the user of magic operates alone, employing only his own psychic power to influence and harness nature to his purposes. He may himself be operated unwittingly by demonic principalities, but for the purpose of our distinction, he is unaware of it or at least not consciously inviting any other agencies or powers than his own. In the second dimension, the wielder of magic consciously invokes the aid of other beings. This kind of magic is thus also necromancy, spiritism, sorcery, and sometimes mediumism.

Necromancy means the art of using objects to consult with the dead to obtain knowledge of the future or to cause things to happen. Spiritism is a term used by many co-terminously with spiritualism, which is the practice of attempting to confer with alleged spirits of departed persons. Mediumism refers to the practice of a spiritualist in contacting such spirits, sometimes in allowing the use of his own body, specifically his vocal cords, for alleged departed spirits to speak through.

Concerning spiritualism, the Lord is both concise and stern: "As for the person who turns to mediums and to spiritists, to play the harlot after them, *I will also set My face against that person and will cut him off from among his people"* (Lev. 20:6). The Word is far more stern concerning the mediums themselves: "As for a man or a woman, if there is a medium or a spiritist among them, they shall surely be put to death; they shall be stoned with stones, their bloodguiltiness is upon them" (Lev. 20:27). The command is given also in Leviticus 19:31: "Do not turn to mediums or spiritists; do not seek them out to be defiled by them. I am the Lord your God."

Alchemy, the second word listed above from my dictionary, does *not* refer to the popular notion of men with pointed hats seeking the four implausibles:

1. To turn baser metals into gold;
2. To find the universal solvent (an acid which supposedly could dissolve anything);
3. The elixir of youth (a potion thought to bestow eternal youth on whoever drank it. Some historians believe that Ponce de Leon was searching for such an elixir when he became one of the discoverers of Florida);
4. A machine of perpetual motion.

Alchemy is an ancient science, far antedating the rise of the Hebrew nation. Under persecution from Christians and others, alchemists masked their actual purposes behind the four searches listed above, causing the public to esteem them foolish seekers after the impossible, Their true purpose, however, was nothing more nor less than the quest for perfection of the soul!

Perfection in this context does not mean maturation into Christ-like moral and ethical virtues, such as are listed in Colossians 3:12-17. Rather it means a discipline and purging of the soul's faculties until one can discover and harness the power of one's own personal spirit to accomplish miracles, without the intervention of God. The quest is for power, to release the power locked within our personal spirit. Latently, every person does possess such power. For example, science has learned how to destroy everything within a twenty-five mile radius by unleashing power through splitting or fusing tiny atoms. If such infinitesimally small things as atoms can be caused to release such awesome power, consider what may be locked within one solitary person's spirit!

When sin entered Adam's heart, the Lord had to shut down and hide the power He had built into him, lest one man alone be more devastating than many H-bombs! "For the creation was subjected to futility, not of its own will, but because of Him who subjected it, in hope that the creation itself also will be set free from its slavery to corruption into the freedom of the glory of the children of God" (Rom. 8:20, 21). It is as though God turned the rheostat down from bright to dimmest dim, in both nature and mankind, lest the power He placed there be used by corrupt minds and hearts. Ever since the Fall, Satan has worked to release the powers of mankind before their time, thus leading to all the occult strivings which God has forbidden. In time, in God's wisdom, He will restore mankind to fullness of glory, as St. Paul wrote:

> But if the ministry of death, in letters engraved on stone, came with glory, so that the sons of Israel could not look intently at the face of Moses because of the glory of his face, fading as it was, how shall the ministry of the Spirit fail to be even more with glory? For if the ministry of condemnation has glory, much more does the ministry of righteousness abound in glory (2 Cor. 3:7-9).

But until sin has been destroyed from the heart of mankind, God will not restore men to power. Satan, knowing what damage would result, seeks to restore the psychic powers of men, even as he promised Jesus power (Matt. 4:8 and Luke 4:6).

Dunce caps, which were pointed conical hats some of us as children had to wear as part of our punishment while sitting in a corner on a stool in grade school days, originated from the pointed conical hats alchemists wore during the Middle Ages. Alchemists appeared to be fools; thus whoever had to wear the dunce cap was ridiculed for being a fool. But alchemists were neither fools in that sense, nor did conical mean comical. They were in dead earnest. Theirs was the first sin re-enacted: the attempt by study and practice to become like God, wielding His kind of power.

The story of Aladdin's lamp, a bed-time story, beloved by many generations, is actually an alchemist story. Aladdin searched through three successively deeper caverns. Alchemists speak of arcane, esoteric (interior, hidden) searches through three successive inner caves of the being, the mind, the heart and the spirit. In the deepest, Aladdin found a magical lamp. At the depths within a man's spirit, alchemists thought to find wondrous knowledge. Still today lamps remain universal symbols for knowledge. When Aladdin rubbed the lamp, a genie would appear and do wondrous things, whatever Aladdin requested. Rubbing produces heat by coefficients of friction. Alchemists wrote of the "argent," which meant the golden heat of fire by which the spirit within would be excited and enabled to do wondrous things, in response to the will of the alchemist.

In the Introduction to *Hermetic Philosophy and Alchemy* (M.A. Atwood, the Julian Press, New York, 1960), Walter Leslie Wilmhurst wrote of alchemy,

> If we speak of it as an Art, it is because it is usually so called in the literature of the subject, but it is rather an exact science—and a divine science at that, "holy Alkimy" as its professors have called it—one involving deep knowledge of the *mental, psychical and spiritual* elements in man and of the way in which they may be practically *controlled and manipulated.* . . ." (p. 7)

Again, on page 26,

> Simply stated, Hermetism, or its synonym Alchemy, was in its primary intention and office *the philosophic and exact science of the regeneration of the human soul from its present sense-immersed state into the perfection and nobility of that divine condition in which it was originally created.*"

Humanism, which is the attempt of mankind, without God, to become everything man was created to be, is nothing new. Alchemists of countless generations have made our modern humanists look pale. On page 42 Wilmhurst said of alchemy,

> It views man, i.e., the soul or true ego of man, as in process of restoration from the terrible calamity of his "fall," in the course of which process development under the operation of the forces and laws of nature has partially redeemed him from chaos and disorder and brought him to a point from which, *by the right application of his intelligence and will,* he can cooperate in *effecting his complete regeneration* [italics in all three extracts mine].

Alchemy is thus Gnostic, embracing the heresy that one can be saved by right knowledge. Alchemy is therefore also Pelagian, perpetuating the heresy that one can save oneself without accepting Jesus Christ as Lord and Savior.

Alchemists were fond of speaking of the "lapis lazuli," or white stone (actually a rich azure or sky blue). When discipline and training had progressed sufficiently, when purification warranted, the subject would be placed in a hypnotic trance, in which in some mysterious way his soul was to be congealed into the white stone, or "Philosopher's Stone." His spirit and soul, guided by the mesmerizer, were to travel through regions and "ethers" to become one with all. All knowledge of all mankind was thus to be "on tap." Alchemists sought by science and discipline to become the white stone by which they could have all knowledge and wisdom.

Mankind and Satan have always copied what God does. By alchemy these men were trying to *achieve without God* what our *Lord promised to give* through the Holy Spirit. "But the Helper, the Holy Spirit, whom the Father will send in My name, *He will teach you all things,* and bring to your remembrance all that I said to you" (John 14:26).

St. Peter wrote to ". . . those who reside as aliens, scattered through Pontus, Galatia, Cappadocia, Asia and Bithynia" (1 Pet. 1:1). Throughout all that region were many alchemists. St. Paul encountered Elymas, who as a magician was most likely also an alchemist, on the island of Paphos, and called down blindness upon him when he would not stop making "crooked the straight ways of the Lord" (Acts 13:10). To new Christians in those days, alchemy may have seemed a welcome lure, a shortcut to power to insecure "aliens." Whether or not St. Peter knew of alchemy and consciously addressed 1 Peter 2 to overcome its influence, certainly the Holy Spirit did. Note in St. Peter's letter the references to "stones."

> Therefore, putting aside all malice and all guile and hypocrisy and envy and all slander, like newborn babes, long for the pure milk of the word, that by it you may grow in respect to salvation, if you have tasted the kindness of the Lord. And coming to Him as to a *living stone*, rejected by men, but choice and precious in the sight of God, you also, as *living stones*, are being built up as a spiritual house for a holy priesthood, to offer up spiritual sacrifices acceptable to God through Jesus Christ. For this is contained in Scripture: "Behold I lay in Zion a choice *stone*, a precious *corner stone*, And he who believes in Him shall not be disappointed." This precious value, then, is for you who believe, but for those who disbelieve, "The *stone* which the builders rejected, This became the very *corner stone*," and, "A *stone* of stumbling and a rock of offense"; for they stumble because they are disobedient to the word, and to this doom they were also appointed. But you are A chosen race, a royal priesthood, a holy nation, a people for God's own possession, that you may proclaim the excellencies of Him who has called you out of darkness into His marvelous light; for you once were not a people, but now you are the people of God; you had not received mercy, but now you have received mercy. Beloved, I urge you as aliens and strangers to abstain from fleshly lusts, which wage war against the soul (1 Pet. 2:1-11).

Jesus is the one chief and true corner stone, the only perfected soul or white stone. Note: alchemists would arduously build themselves into perfected stones, by science and hypnotism. St. Peter called for Christians to *be built* ". . . as living stones, *are being built up* as a spiritual house . . ." Alchemists would build themselves as *individuals*. Christians are to be built *as a spiritual house*, a chosen *race*, a royal *priesthood*, a holy *nation*, a *people* for God's own possession (not to possess themselves for themselves).

Whether St. John on the island of Patmos was aware of alchemy or not, the Holy Spirit certainly was, and so the Lord promised, "He who has an ear, let him hear what the Spirit says to the churches. To him who overcomes, to him will I give some of the hidden manna, and *I will give him a white stone*, and a new name written on the stone which no one knows but he who receives it" (Rev. 2:17). In Hebrew culture a white stone was given to a man who had been forgiven great sins. The wearing of the stone was a sign of his having been forgiven. But the Holy Spirit may also be saying something like, "To him who overcomes I will *give a perfected soul;* no one has to study alchemy to *achieve* it." We are all in process of being transformed into His likeness, which will finally be accomplished in "the twinkling of an eye" (2 Cor. 15:52) as a gift, not something accomplished by alchemic science or its modern counterpart, humanism.

By peering into his white stone or perfected soul, an alchemist thought himself able to know things at a distance or in the future. These are of course gifts given only at God's discretion through two of the nine gifts of the Holy Spirit, the gifts of knowledge and of prophecy. Today carnival fortune tellers mimic alchemy by pretending to gaze into their "crystal ball." The crystal ball is none other than a cheap imitation of the philosopher's lapis lazuli, or white stone.

The philosopher or alchemist of course never achieved his desired end. He found nothing but counterfeits, which Simon knew when he saw the true wonders the apostles performed and cried after them that he might be given this power too (Acts 8:9-24). But alchemists or "wizards" did find enough results to astound the common people, as Simon ". . . formerly was practicing magic in the city, and astonishing the people of Samaria, claiming to be someone great" (v. 9). By what they did accomplish, they deluded themselves that they were on the right track.

See what the magicians of Egypt could do. Most likely they were adepts of alchemy, but whether or not, they duplicated the first signs of Moses and Aaron! Their rods also became serpents, though that of Aaron swallowed theirs (Exod. 7:12). Aaron stretched out his hand and "lifted up the staff and struck the water that was in the Nile, in the sight of Pharaoh and in the sight of his servants, and all the water that was in the Nile was turned to blood. And the fish that were in the Nile died, and the Nile became foul, so that the Egyptians could not drink water from the Nile. And the blood was through all the land of Egypt. *But the magicians of Egypt did the same with their secret arts* . . ."(vs. 20-22). "Aaron stretched out his hand over the waters of Egypt, and the frogs came up and covered the land of Egypt. *And the magicians did the same with their secret arts*, making frogs come up on the land of Egypt" (Exod. 8:6, 7). When Aaron caused gnats to plague Egypt, ". . . the *magicians tried with their secret arts* to bring forth gnats, *but they could not* . . ." (v. 18).

It was in Greece that philosophy flourished and within it the science of alchemy. With this in mind, perhaps we can see more in the familiar passage of 1 Corinthians 1:17-25,

> For Christ did not send me to baptize, but to preach the gospel, *not in cleverness of speech, that the cross of Christ should not be made void.* For the word of the cross is to those who are perishing foolishness, but to us who are being saved it is the power of God. For it is written, *"I will destroy the wisdom of the wise,* And the cleverness of the clever, I will set aside." Where is the wise man? Where is the scribe? Where is the debater of this age? Has not God made foolish the wisdom of the

world? For since in the wisdom of God the world through its wisdom did not come to know God, God was well pleased through the foolishness of the message preached to save those who believe. For indeed Jews ask for signs, and *Greeks search for wisdom;* but we preach Christ crucified, to Jews a stumbling block, and to Gentiles foolishness, but to those who are the called, both Jews and Greeks, Christ the power of God and the wisdom of God. Because the foolishness of God is wiser than men, and the weakness of God is stronger than men.

In chapter two St. Paul continued,

And my message and my preaching were not in persuasive words of wisdom, but in demonstration of the Spirit and of power, *that your faith should not rest on the wisdom of men, but on the power of God.* Yet we do speak wisdom among those who are mature; *a wisdom, however, not of this age, nor of the rulers of this age, who are passing away;* but we speak God's wisdom in a mystery, the hidden wisdom, which God predestined before the ages to our glory; the wisdom *which none of the rulers of this age has understood;* for if they had understood it, they would not have crucified the Lord of glory; but just as it is written, "Things which eye has not seen and ear has not heard, And which have not entered the heart of man, All that God has prepared for those who love Him." (vv. 4-9).

When we understand what alchemy taught and strove to accomplish, we comprehend more fully why St. Paul said so clearly ". . . the wisdom which none of the rulers of this age has understood" and ". . . that your faith should not rest on the wisdom of men but on the power of God." Only Christ, not men's wisdom, can restore us and perfect us.

We err if we regard magic or alchemy as mere foolishness. God has made it foolish, as St. Paul said, but God would not have forbidden it so sternly were it only harmless mistaken imagination! Probably most who become involved are mere dilettante dabblers, encountering little else than their own imaginations.

But there is a reality, terribly real. It is for the damning sinfulness of that reality that God destroyed the inhabitants of Canaan before Israel, and repeatedly scolded, warned and disciplined Israel. The punishment of God upon wizards (adept alchemists) was no less severe than for mediums. The same Leviticus 20:27 which we quoted earlier from the NAS reads in the RSV, "A man or a woman who is a medium *or a wizard* shall be put to death; they shall be stoned with stones, their blood shall be upon them."

So far we have discussed magic and wizardry or alchemy. Some wizards are solely alchemic wizards. Some, however, add sorcery to their sins. Not all sorcerers are also alchemists just as not all alchemists are also sorcerers. Sorcery is a particular form of magic or witchcraft. Sorcery is that second kind of magic which contacts and uses other spirits and powers in order to manipulate nature or cause things to happen. There is no such thing as white magic. Satan uses such things as the modern T.V. program starring "Samantha" to beguile us by cute nose-twitches that some magic is innocent and fun. All magic is sin. However, in so-called white magic the operator at least thinks he is doing good. His intentions may be benign, however shot through with sin. Not so with sorcery. Sorcery is black magic. Its intent, methods and ends are evil, for selfish purposes only. Sorcery is never for others but *against* them, for the sole gain of the sorcerer.

Satanic cults use sorcery against the church. They "pray" in chants and rhythms to cause unaccountable mechanical breakdowns, temper flareups, gossiping, adulteries, etc. It may seem something too far out to believe that men and women in the twentieth century can engage in such evil, seemingly superstitious activities, much less be effective in it, but Paula and I have been in direct prayer warfare against witches' covens and warlocks and we know by experience the kinds of things which can happen. During one such battle, Paula was pregnant with Andrea. An unseen powerful force pushed her so strongly that she almost tumbled down the stairs. It was not imagination.

It was an actual attempt to harm her. Our eldest son Loren was working for a Christian psychiatrist friend, who at the time was building a house on a cliff in a remote area above the Spokane River, plus a boat dock and garage below, beside the river. Loren was doing some of the carpentry work. One morning in prayer I felt a premonition from the Lord. Asking what it was, I was given a vision of Loren swinging down from a high place, using long yellow lines, with great danger all around. Before Loren left for work, I called to him and asked, "Loren, are you going to be working up high today, or down below?"

"Down below, today, dad, I'll be working on the boat dock."

"Well, just be careful today, will you? You know me and my premonitions." And I told him about the vision.

That day, Cynthia (the doctor's wife) and two of their daughters came out to inspect their new house. Cynthia squatted by the edge of the cliff to examine something about the foundation. A powerful, invisible hand hit her in the back with such force it tumbled her over the edge of the cliff! She hit on her heel and then lit on her back halfway down the cliff on a ledge. The girls took a long yellow extension cord and lowered it down to Loren, who had clambered up that steep, shale-covered cliff side to reach Cynthia. Loren was a weight lifter at the time. Having tied the electric cord about his waist, he took Cynthia in his arms, trying desperately not to move or jostle her spine, for fear it was broken, and stepped down that steep incline balancing percariously with Cynthia in his arms. Thank God he was always blessed with the agility and balance of a cat. With the girls steadying him by pulling on the cord, he made it safely all the way down, and put Cynthia in the back of the station wagon, which he had "happened" to park at the bottom instead of on top as usual. At the hospital it was determined that Cynthia had fractured three vertebrae, but not one had slipped out of place! Any one of the three could have sliced her spinal cord! Her right heel was sheared off. But the heel and back were so soon healed that within three weeks she was swinging happily along on crutches without a cast!

Her accident had been no accident at all. Cynthia had been a student of ballet. Her balance was excellent. There was nothing imaginary about the blow which toppled her. At the time, her family and ours had been involved in spiritual warfare together against witches and warlocks.

Seven of us had been invited to conduct a teaching mission on the island of Vancouver. I would teach, and they would lead prayer groups. No sooner had we arrived at St. Mary's Priory, Victoria, than a committee came to say, "Thank God you're here. There is a coven of witches headed by a warlock on an island nearby who have been hating a boy to death. He is dying of a mysterious blood disease and the doctors don't know what it is or what causes it. But we do! It's those witches!" Before we could say anything, word came that the boy had died. We decided to go to battle in prayer and put a stop to the activity of that coven.

That began the war. People in the village on the island reported that some had seen apparitions of this man flying over the village! Many were terrified of him and the coven. Few dared to cross him.

After we returned home, we continued in spiritual warfare. In a few days I began to feel drained. In a month or so, prophetic people were telling me that I needed more protection about me. Friends in an audience where I spoke sat with tears streaming down their faces. Afterward I asked, "Was what I said so bad it made you cry?"

"No, John, we could see in the Spirit that you are being hit, again and again, moment by moment, day after day." Truly, I felt like a punching bag, black and blue all over, though nothing physical showed.

I went to speak at a Christian camp. There, a friend who is gifted as a Christian masseuse saw the hurt and ache in my body. She said, "Maybe it would help if you let me give you a rubdown." Leery of that but willing to try anything, I first made sure someone else was present. Then we spread a blanket on the grass and she began to massage my back.

Again and again she came to the same spot midway down my spinal column on the right side. She seemed puzzled. Finally I asked, "What is it? You seemed disturbed about something."

She replied, "I don't know, John. I've never encountered anything like this. There's something evil here."

We sent the other person to find a woman we knew at the camp who possessed a keen gift of discernment. When she arrived, the masseuse said, "Marilyn, there is something in John's back. I don't know what it is. I want you to take it away." We told Marilyn nothing more than that and gave her no indication where on my back whatever it was might be.

Marilyn prayed in the Spirit for a few minutes, and then grabbed forcefully exactly on that spot in my back, and jerked something out and away from me, screaming in fear of it! We asked her what it was. When she had regained her composure, she said, "It was a spear, an evil thing of Satan, sticking right there in John's back!" Lest that seem impossible, or implausible or fanciful, listen to the Scripture: ". . . in addition to all, taking up the shield of faith with which you will be able to extinguish *all the flaming missiles* of the evil one" (Eph. 6:16). Perhaps one reason the Lord let that happen was so that we could know beyond doubt that the Scripture sometimes means what it says exactly as it says it, not merely poetically. Those darts are real. No one can tell me otherwise. I had felt the sickness of it in me. I felt it when Marilyn pulled it out of me. And I knew the relief and the health which flooded into me again. Spiritual warfare is real!

Subsequently I heard from someone on that island that the warlock and his coven had suffered a terrible car wreck. He wasn't being seen flying over that village anymore! His power had been broken.

Agnes Sanford was in England. A pastor came to her complaining that three warlocks had combined forces to try to hate him to death. He was feeling the attack physically every day. She asked the Lord what to do, and in this case He said to her, *Pray that the forces be reversed.*

So she did, visualizing their streams of attack being returned upon themselves. The very next day all three warlocks were found dead! The Lord had let them reap their own hate. Well does St. John say, "Any one who hates his brother is a murderer" (1 John 3:15a RSV). Hate truly does murder. Sorcerers know how to send spirits to afflict their enemies.

When covens exist they seek actively to attack whatever churches seem to have life in them. For a while, Satanists decided to make the Rathdrum prairie adjacent to Coeur D'Alene their headquarters. Satanists may not be consciously aware of it, but many of their rituals are sorcerer's rites. Horrible, weird things began to happen. Animals were found gutted, or with sexual or other parts excised. One of our friends, a nutritionist who traveled regularly through the region to supervise nutrition programs in schools and hospitals, was advised unofficially by an official in the sheriff's department to carry a gun in her glove compartment, and that she should not step out of her car for any reason while she was in that area. He advised her not to travel alone, but if she had to, never to stop her car. He warned her that if a chain of people appeared before her across the road, she was not even to slow down. If she hit someone, she was not to stop, nor to report it! She was to have her car repaired and say nothing. Another acquaintance of ours, in that same time period, encountered such a human chain across a country road in front of a tree which had been felled. Having been similarly advised, she gunned her car, turned off the road, and bounced across a field as fast as she could go to a neighbor's house.

I ministered in Canada to a lady who had been conceived and dedicated in the womb to be a child of Satan! Her parents and other Satanists continuously used her in unspeakably degrading sexual rituals. Dung was used for the bread of communion. St. Paul wrote, "Do not participate in the unfruitful deeds of darkness, but instead even expose them; for it is disgraceful even to speak of the things which are done by them in secret" (Eph. 5:11, 12). St. Paul's teaching is woefully appropriate today! Decency forbids me to relate further details of the incredibly debasing activity which surrounded this child, to which they subjected her! Amazingly, something within her resisted throughout. Appeals to the government finally delivered her from such abuse, and the Lord subsequently saved her. Now she wanted inner healing for all those years which still plagued her memories through nightmares and terrors.

We have ministered to a number of erstwhile Satanists, who have all related similar debaucheries involved with the most debasing forms of sorcery. We share this much so that the Body may once and for all take its head out of the sand! It is blind foolishness to think that because most modern men have learned not to believe "foolish super-stitions," such horrible Satanic rites do not exist today, or are only ineffectual fantasies and foolishness. Believing that Satanists and their black sorceries do not exist will not make them go away! These evils are rampant and on the increase as our world more and more turns from the truth of God's Word.

> And just as they did not see fit to acknowledge God any longer, God gave them over to a depraved mind, to do those things which are not proper, being filled with all unright-eousness, wickedness, greed, malice; full of envy, murder, strife, deceit, malice; they are gossips, slanderers, haters of God, insolent, arrogant, boastful, inventors of evil, dis-obedient to parents, without understanding, untrustworthy, unloving, unmerciful; and, although they know the ordinance of God, that those who practice such things are worthy of death, they not only do the same, but also give hearty approval to those who practice them (Rom. 1:28-32).

The Body of Christ must learn how to set free and heal those our Lord would snatch from Satan's sorcery. Dismissing it as foolish imagination will accomplish nothing. We must know how to minister victoriously against the reality which ensnared them. And we must know how to set free and heal the wounds of those whom the Satanists have afflicted.

When we were young in faith and first into spiritual warfare, Paula and I used to be jumped on in the night in our sleep. This experience is common to many Christians. A demonic thing would enter our room and jump on me, paralyzing me instantly. I could not move a muscle. I could hardly breathe. Knowing that Jesus who is in me is stronger than he who is in the world, I would begin to pray, silently repeating, ".Jesus is my Lord. Jesus, you are Lord." In a minute or two, I could say Jesus' name aloud, and begin to throw that entity off. Sometimes in the process, my struggles would arouse Paula, who would join in the fray, until we were freed and the house was clean again. A few minutes later we would be sound asleep again, and the same or another demonic thing would jump on Paula. She would go through the same struggle, awakening me, and we would pray again. Now, years later, we are never so attacked, perhaps because the Devil knows our faith is too strong. We know, first hand, what St. John meant when he wrote,

> I am writing to you, fathers, because you know Him who has been from the beginning. I am writing to you, young men, *because you have overcome the evil one.* I have written to you, children, because you know the Father. I have written to you, fathers, because you know Him who has been from the beginning. I have written to you, young men, because you are strong, *and the word of God abides in you, and you have overcome the evil one* (1 John 2:13, 14).

Several years later, one of our United Church of Christ missionaries on sabbatical from Africa related several stories of natives being killed by what they called "the black wraith." He described the same experience we had suffered. We had been protected by faith. Strangely, we had never been really afraid, only annoyed. We knew by faith the devil could not kill us. We had been able to fall asleep immediately afterwards, sure of our Lord's protection. Those natives had died because of fear. Their fear had empowered the demons and the witch doctors behind them with more power than they should have held. The missionary from Africa, and others from Haiti (in other denominations) reported also about the power of witch doctors to afflict people with pain, with troubles and accidents from a long distance.

One of our friends, a pastor, had a beautiful blonde daughter who was recruited by a team to travel to Haiti for missionary work for a summer. The pastor spoke of it when Paula and I were visiting him, before she left. My heart sank. I knew there was danger for her and that she should not go. But how could I communicate that? I knew that she would encounter witchcraft and be unprepared to handle it. The pastor hardly believed in such things. It ought not to be assumed that anyone traveling to Haiti would be in danger; of course not. This was a specific warning for her. She did cross such forces of evil, and came home with a rare disease no medical doctors seemed able to cure. I am sure the family could not believe me when I tried to tell them what was really causing it. Recently, Paula and I heard that a traveling exorcist came there and, having perceived a demonic thing afflicting her, cast it away, and she is well again.

Is it enough? Those who have had similar experiences will already know that what we say is true. Sorcerers can wield demonic powers to afflict; demonic things can physically attack people.

Astrology was also listed in my Oxford Dictionary as one of the occult practices. Many Christians have thought astrology not to be one of the evils the Lord prohibited. But the Word of God is clear. Isaiah scolded Israel for turning to sorcerers and astrologers,

> Stand fast now in your spells And in your many sorceries With which you have labored from your youth; Perhaps you will be able to profit, Perhaps you may cause trembling. You are wearied with your many counsels, Let now the astrologers, Those who prophesy by the stars, Those who predict by the new moons, Stand up and save you from what will come

upon you. Behold, they have become like stubble, Fire burns them; They cannot deliver themselves from the power of the flame; There will be no coal to warm by, Nor a fire to sit before! So have those become to you with whom you have labored, Who have trafficked with you from your youth; Each has wandered in his own way. There is none to save you (Isa. 47:12-15).

Astrology participates in the sin of divination. Divination is the practice of peering into the future or the unknown. It is Satan's copy of the gifts of knowledge and prophecy. Sometimes in God's wisdom He does not want us to know things, much as wise earthly fathers conceal from their children information about sex until he knows they are mature enough to deal with it. "It is the glory of God to conceal a matter, But the glory of kings is to search out a matter" (Prov. 15:2). When the Lord does want us to know, He may choose one or many ways to involve us "kings" in the glory of searching out whatever it is, according to His knowledge of our maturity. "I have many more things to say to you, but you cannot bear them now" (John 16:12). He knows when to hide knowledge and when and how best to reveal it.

Divination breaks His providence. Divination happens when we fail to trust God. We want a handle on life. We want to know what is coming so as to be prepared for it. To use our minds and computers to project what is probable and to be prepared is not yet divination. That is not yet an improper taking thought for the morrow (Matt. 6:34). That is to use the God-given natural wisdom God expects us to maintain. Divination occurs when we want more than that. When we attempt to find security in assurances by knowledge gained illicitly, that is divination. The key behind the sin of disobedience in divination is fear and lack of trust. We install something else as god to us when we can no longer trust blindly the hand of God. "Who is blind but My servant, Or so deaf as My messenger whom I send? Who is so blind as he that is at peace with Me, Or so blind as the servant of the Lord?" (Isa. 42:19). The Lord's servant is willing to see nothing and hear nothing, trusting in the Lord.

Fortune-tellers, palm readers, tea leaf readers and so on are all diviners, forbidden by the Word of the Lord, "There shall not be found among you . . . one who uses divination, one who practices witchcraft, or one who interprets omens . . ." (Deut. 18:10).

There is a fine line between seeking the Lord's guidance, and unconsciously attempting to turn that into divination. Again and again the kings of Israel sought out the Lord's prophets, saying, "Inquire of the Lord for us." Sometimes their hearts were right, and sometimes so full of fear they were attempting to involve His prophets in divination.

Common everyday listening can be turned by a wrong heart to divination. Paula and I visited a farmer friend in Arkansas. As we drove in, we asked him what was wrong; his bean crops looked very unhealthy. He explained that by his experience and natural wisdom he had planned to plant wheat that year. But he had been trying to do everything by listening to God and he was sure he had heard God tell him to plant beans. It turned out that the kind of weather which occurred during that growing season would have been good for wheat but was terrible for beans. Now he was going deeply into debt.

On the surface it seems like trying to listen to God about all things is good. But God does not want to reduce us to slaves or robots. He has given us good minds and He expects us to use them. Moreover, questioning soon revealed that our friend had been fearful of failure. He would use "listening to God" to be overly certain. That became the sin of divination. Had God wanted to steer him away from one crop to another, the Lord would have taken the initiative to speak, and would have confirmed by at least two witnesses. But our friend's fearful heart sought to turn God into his diviner. The Lord let him listen to a wrong voice, as both discipline and teaching. That was a tough way to learn, but it was certainly written on our friend's heart to listen when God wants to speak but not to push God to be his diviner.

The same mistake and consequent dire results have happened to many in the Body of Christ.

In the same way, there is a fine line between prayer and magic. When we discover the laws of God's universe and hear the promises of God, we can claim those promises and activate those principles by prayer with such a wrong heart that we have actually merged into magic rather than prayer. Magic would take hold of God's Word and so claim His promises as to try to manipulate or force God to do what we want. True prayer is petition, humbly respecting the free will of a Father who may in wisdom say "No." Authority in prayer to accomplish something can and ought to be expressed, but only after careful listening to God so that it is the Holy Spirit who acts in and with us as we express what is also the Father's will. But when we grasp His promises and insist that He do what we want because He promised, "And Lord, your Word is true, so we know you have to," we are actually trying to manipulate God. Our prayer has become magic! We are operating His principle to obtain what we want!

Oral Roberts has rightly discovered the principle of "seed faith." What we say is not meant against him, whose ministry we honor. But we can improperly use seed faith until it becomes a kind of magic. When a servant of the Lord sends a nickel, for example, enclosed in his letter asking for help, he is working the principle of seed faith on you, whether or not he is aware. The force of that principle to cause you to give him a gift in return is magic. The key of discernment is courtesy. The way of the Lord respects the free will of all men. Such a gift as a nickel or a penny, sent in that context, works to overcome our free will by the force of the principles of law. It disrespects our right to make up our minds freely whether to give to that ministry.

I used to listen to a well-known teacher of healing and would occasionally hear the Lord saying in my spirit, "This teacher is teaching magic." The teacher was urgently insisting that if we apply faith, God *must* heal. Please, dear Body of Christ, never try to get a handle on God! God doesn't *have* to do anything! To try to make Him do anything is magic; magic is the operation of principles or laws of God to accomplish our own selfish ends. Even healing in this context is our own selfish end. It might not be God's will to heal in that moment, though later He might. We cannot force Him to act on our timetable. To operate a car is not magic. In that, we are only cooperating with the laws of nature as an engine propels by the laws of combustion. Our own energy is not added to it. We are not interfering. Magic interferes by the will of the magician, forcing a thing to happen by occult or hidden principles.

In this regard, the teachers of the recent faith movement unwittingly have led many who are sincere Christians into the operation of magic. We plead with the Body of Christ to repent, to pray for all who have stumbled into this kind of magic, and above all, not to condemn people or fracture the unity of the Body by rejection. We all pioneer, in frontiers of faith, stumbling by trial and error into maturity. Let us love one another, be reconciled and healed.

Theosophy is a claim to have esoteric knowledge of the interplay of natural elements and the world of the spirit (not in this instance meaning only our own personal spirit, but the spiritual world which pervades all things). Theosophists commonly see their view of life as deeper and more profound than recognized religious doctrines. Orthodox dogmas they view as mere exoteric outworkings or expressions of the deeper truths only they, the enlightened ones, are privy to. Again the sin is Gnostic. They believe they are being saved by their esoteric knowledge. These "masters" or "illuminati" then feel it incumbent upon them to teach "lesser lights" the way. But they are impelled by principalities of delusion. They teach doctrines of men:

> You hypocrites, rightly did Isaiah prophesy of you, saying, "This people honors me with their lips, But their heart is far away from Me. But in vain do they worship Me, Teaching as doctrines the precepts of men" (Matt. 15:7-9).

Worse, unwittingly, they teach doctrines of demons. "But the Spirit explicitly says that in later times some will fall away from the faith, paying attention to deceitful spirits and doctrines of demons" (1 Tim. 4:1).

Theosophists, like alchemists, also are Pelagian and humanistic, though they would prefer to call themselves theistic, being normally quite religious. Rosicrucianism, the works of Madame Blavatsky, and others are examples of theosophy. Theosophy attempts to discover truth by experience. Unfortunately, not the God-given experiences we Christians are benefitted by, under the tutelage of the Holy Spirit, checked by the Word and by brothers and sisters in the faith. They seek experiential apprehension of false doctrines in secret "mandami" and psychic experiences. They seek to lead "initiates" into deeper and deeper "mysteries."

The aims of theosophy are not much different from those of alchemists. They differ only in method, not enduring the alchemist's rigorous self-disciplines and inner searches to produce the white stone. Theosophists also seek integration and wholeness, to be restored to the pristine perfection of Adam. However, we know that "no one comes to the Father, but through Me" (John 14:6). Man and Satan have continually sought any way other than death on the cross to be born anew and restored to the Kingdom. Perhaps we should say that Satan has continually sought any ploy, any device, any teaching, anything which will lure men away from the tough way of the cross to the wide and smooth road of destruction. Always he appeals to man's desire to become who he is supposed to become; this is the very same temptation set before Eve's wondering person and nascent eyes! The temptation is always for a person to achieve perfection in himself, sometimes with the help of others but essentially on his own, without God.

The root therefore of every occult sin is pride! One primary reason for the cross is to humble us. God's plan is to divest us thoroughly of pride through continuous application of the cross. "Where then is boasting? It is excluded. By what kind of law? Of works? No, but by a law of faith" (Rom. 3:27). The essence of all occultism is to become something in oneself, to have and wield a power which elevates oneself, even as Simon wanted people to think of him as someone great. Regarding that sinful proclivity, St. Paul wrote,

> For if anyone thinks he is something when he is nothing, he deceives himself (Gal. 6:3).

> And if any man think that he knoweth anything, he knoweth nothing yet as he ought to know (1 Cor. 8:2 KJV).

> Let no man deceive himself. If any man among you thinks that he is wise in this age, let him become foolish that he may become wise. For the wisdom of this world is foolishness before God (1 Cor. 3:18, 19a).

Among the occult practices listed in Deuteronomy 18:10 and 11, there remains only mediumism (to be discussed in the next chapter) and "one who casts a spell." Friedrich Anton Mesmer, who was born May 23, 1733, and died March 5, 1815, was the modern rediscoverer of hypnotism. Friedrich believed in "magnetism," supposedly derived from astrological forces. He attempted to use magnetic forces for healing. It was through hypnotism primarily that he thought he could apply such "magnetism." After him, hypnotism was called "mesmerism." Today his name has become part of our daily vocabulary. When we become enthralled with a performance or a person, we say we were "mesmerized." In biblical days hypnotism was spoken of as "casting a spell," and a hypnotist was called a "charmer."

Hypnotism is strictly forbidden. Christians should need no reason; obedience should be enough. But one reason for the prohibition is that we are not to surrender our will to any other than the Lord Jesus Christ. A second reason is that such surrender opens inner psychic doors which should be open to no one but our Lord. A third is that none other than Jesus can be trusted to rule our will. It is not true that hypnotism cannot cause one to act against one's will and is therefore supposedly safe. If a hypnotist can discover and lay hold of an inner hatred, resentment, anger or fearsome usable latent but powerful inner drive he can use that to cause a person to do all manner of ill, evil or embarrassing things he never would have thought himself capable of doing in his right mind.

At a seminar, I was teaching on some other subject when a question necessitated an answer concerning hypnotism. I explained how the Word of God forbids it, and that the use of it in parlor games is entirely foolish and reprehensible. I said that no Christian counselor or psychiatrist should use it, that if he wanted to discover something in a client, let him ask questions or let the Holy Spirit reveal it by gifts of knowledge and discernment. I explained that hynotism could reveal what the Lord is not ready yet to heal, whereas the Holy Spirit will reveal each thing only as the other is prepared for healing. Concerning its use for orthodontal operations for people who cannot stand to undergo anesthesia, I said I could not say, only that the Word of God forbids its use.

Immediately after, I sat down to lunch directly across the table from an oral surgeon who was then the president of the national association which teaches doctors how to use clinical hypnosis! He told me he agreed fully in every way that such warnings were valid and necessary. Only, he did use hypnotism for patients who could not be anesthetized. Ten years later, that man came to me and sadly said, "John, the Lord has shown me the hard way. Never again will I use hypnotism for any purpose whatsoever!" Crowds surrounded us and carried me away, and I never found opportunity to ask what had happened. What had he experienced which filled him with such sadness and determination? At another conference, when the subject came up, a psychiatrist testified that he also had used hypnotism in the past and never would again. Again, there was not sufficient time to discover fully why. But we should not need to know. Obedience to God's Word should be enough. Praise

God that He is revealing His Word to professionally trained servants.

At a School of Pastoral Care, Dr. Morton Kelsey, a Christian psychologist, was asked about hypnotism. He also testified against it and reported that a counselor had hypnotized a counselee. He gave her a post-hypnotic suggestion that she would never smoke again. It worked. She stopped smoking. Two weeks later she jumped out the second-floor window! The counselor concluded he had removed her steam valve without healing her inner pressures. Morton Kelsey observed that it was not merely unwise use of hypnotism that made it wrong, but the use of it at all.

There are many other forms of occult involvement, but perhaps all could be subsumed under the headings we have discussed. Our purpose is not to chronicle or expose all the various forms of occultism to the light of God's Word. It is rather to teach the Body of Christ about occult involvement so as to enable healing.

All involvement with occultism wounds. God did not build us for it. Our system is wrenched, whether we operate it or have it used on us, wittingly or unknowingly. Involvement in occultism is like forcing a lovely soprano voice to sing bass. That harms the vocal cords. Our bodies and spirits do not naturally flow in occult ways. Shakespeare knew this, concerning all sin, and caused Lady Macbeth to say it most clearly,

> Come, you spirits,
> That tend to mortal thoughts, *unsex me here*,
> And fill me from the crown to the toe, top-full
> Of direst cruelty; *make thick my blood*,
> *Stop up the access, and passage to remorse*,
> *That no compunctious visitings of nature*
> *Shake my fell purpose*, nor keep peace between
> The effect of it! *Come to my woman's breasts*,
> And *take my milk for gall*, you murdering ministers,
> Wherever in your sightless substances,
> *You wait on nature's mischief!* Come thick night,

And pall thee in the dunnest smoke of Hell,
That my knee knife *see not the wound it makes,*
Nor Heaven peep through the blanket of the dark,
To cry, "Hold, hold!"
(*Macbeth,* Act I, Scene 5, italics added)

Sin, especially occultism, destroys the wholesome flow of the spirit in action in the body. Shakespeare caused Macbeth to say it in that familiar passage from Act II, Scene 2,

Methought I heard a voice cry, "Sleep no more!
Macbeth does murder sleep," the innocent sleep,
Sleep that knits up the ravelled sleave of care,
The death of each day's life, *sore labour's bath,*
Balm of hurt minds, great nature's second course,
Chief nourisher in life's feast . . .

Remember that the play begins with three witches who *defile* Macbeth by false prophecies of glory. The unfolding drama of Macbeth is a revelation and teaching of the twisting effects upon God-given conscience and courses of thought by sorcery. We suggest that any who would counsel and heal the effects of occultism would profit by studying the play *Macbeth* with an eye to seeing how occultism perverts nature and mankind from their natural courses.

A common first result of occultism is disturbed sleep. Insomnia, fretful sleep and nightmares are caused by many things, but one of the causes Elijah House counselors routinely look for is past or present occult involvement, or whether the person is under occult attack. Questions soon reveal whether the person has ever been involved. Many people assume falsely that occultism could not be the cause of their difficulties because they never practiced anything occult regularly. They may have forgotten the the one time as a child when as a lark they went with some friends to see "Aunt Fanny," who took hold of their hands and enthralled them by knowing things which had happened to them and by telling them about what would happen in their future. Or how they used to have fun playing with the Ouija board.

Or today, playing that devil-created game called Dungeons and Dragons, which directly involves the players in occult practices. Or the few times they tried to hypnotize one another or played at holding a seance. However innocuous it may seem, sin is sin, and sets in motion forces which must later be dealt with in one way or another. It is not that God is that repulsed or upset by children's playful dabblings. He understands. But the laws of the universe are neither compassionate nor indulgent. However gleefully we may step off the roof of a tall building, the results are disastrous. It only takes one time. God is compassionate (see Psalm 103). He was not angry at our childish adventures. But just as gravity cannot be denied, neither can God revoke His laws because foolish children do not understand. How foolish it would seem to us if a child thought he could swim unaided by scuba equipment in an underwater cave for five minutes. We would *expect* him to drown. No one would try to blame God. Whoever understands the law concerning occultism is not surprised or offended when dire results crop up years after the event. Only now are we beginning to see the awful effects upon Vietnam veterans who came into contact with Agent Orange years ago. Results from one instance of occult activity in childhood may afflict someone horribly in adulthood. Counselors need to see that we are dealing with legal cause and effect. Dabblers in the occult do not generally immediately reap what they have sown, but it is inevitable that one day they will.

Disturbed sleep due to occultism can be healed first by forgiveness for whatever degree of involvement the person experienced, and second by closure. Occult dabblings, however insignificant, open doors to occult forces. Playful explorations give access to powers which otherwise would have no means of entering the individual: "Oh, that there were one among you who would shut the doors, that you might not kindle fire upon my altar in vain!" (Mal. 1:10 RSV). Whatever the proper exegesis of that verse is, we see it in application by the Holy Spirit in healing occult effects. Christian counselors should pray that the Lord may shut all the psychic doors of the person, especially when the fire of prayer is lit.

Third, disturbed sleep can be healed by hiding. "You have died and your life is hidden with Christ in God" (Col. 3:3). A Christian normally is obscured from Satan, guarded by the angels of God. Demonic powers cannot see where to afflict him, nor how to prevent his plans. But occultism exposes a person to view. In Tolkien's fantasy, *The Lord of the Rings*, whenever Frodo put on the *magic* ring he carried, he became invisible to everyone—except to the powers of darkness! He had entered by magic into their world and now they could see him more clearly than if he were only his natural self. Just so, by occultism we enter Satan's world and his minions see us. We heal such exposure simply by praying that the person be re-hidden.

Sometimes I will say, "Lord, as the angels reached out and gathered Lot in and blinded those men in Sodom so that they groped for the handle all night and could not find it, so I haul this person into the Body of Christ and I blind all the powers of darkness. They can no longer see my brother (or sister). From now on he is hidden from them. I obscure all the pathways over which they have tracked him. 'Let their way be dark and slippery, With the angel of the Lord pursuing them' " (Ps. 35:6).

Fourth, we pray for physical healing. We ask the Lord to pour His healing balm throughout their body and spirit, healing and removing any devices the devil may have implanted.

A second effect of occultism is that the person may be pestered by hearing annoying inner voices. Sometimes that has natural psychological causes. Sometimes, nevertheless, there may be occult causes as well, or occultism may be the only cause. Questioning and discernment are needed to determine which. If one is not sure, it does not hurt to pray away occult influence, just in case. If occult influence was not the cause, at least one rules that out by having taken care of the possibility. The same four steps are taken in prayer. We add a fifth as well. We rebuke the spirits and voices, cast them away, and command them in Jesus' name to be silent. Occasionally such prayer catapults us into a full-blown exorcism, of which we will speak more fully in the next chapter.

A third common effect of occultism is recurrent accidents or tragic happenings. Sometimes after we have checked out and prayed away bitter-root judgments and expectancies by which the person is continually mysteriously defeated or reaps tragedy (see Chapter Fourteen in *The Transformation of the Inner Man*), the person still retains an uncanny ability to snatch harm out of the arms of safety. The Holy Spirit may then reveal that because of occult involvement some time in their life, the powers of darkness know how and when to cause just the right wrong action which tumbles their house of cards. We have all suffered damaging coincidences, such as someone's choosing to phone us just as we were stepping out the door for an important interview—causing us to miss our appointment! Or committing ourselves to a course of action which turned out to be wrong for us, only to learn moments too late that bit of information which could have saved us all that pain and trouble, only then to discover that a strange set of circumstances kept that knowledge from arriving on time. Or if something doesn't happen in time, all our plans will come to naught—such as a company remembering to pay a debt so we can do some special thing, or a person remembering to recommend us for this or that. Christians are constantly being surprised at the Lord's providence and timing. Just the right set of coincidences happen to turn everything to roses. For occultly hindered people it happens the other way around. If there is any loophole, if anything can foul up the works, it will happen like clockwork! They never seem to luck out. They become fond of saying, "You know, if it weren't for bad luck, I wouldn't have any luck at all."

We stop Satan's game by the same steps outlined above, only we add to the prayer a direct command that his inroads into the person's life be stopped. We command him to take his hands off their life. Perhaps it should be added that the most common cause of such accidents and hurtful happenings is a curse. By this we mean that some power of darkness or person involved in sorcery may have placed a curse on his life. We simply break the curse by the authority and the name of Jesus. Second, the curse may be that the person unconsciously cursed his father and mother in his bitterness and judgments against them. Jesus reminded His followers that "Moses said, 'Honor your father and your mother;' and 'He who speaks evil of father or mother, let him be put to death' " (Mark 7:10). The death we die is to our abundant life. Cursing our father or mother, in that sense, puts a curse on our life. Nothing will go fully right from then on. We insert this here because we know that if a counselor discovers and casts away occult destructions but does not uncover and bring to forgiveness whatever lay between a person and his parents, the troubles most likely will not stop. Unforgiveness would retain the curse on the person's life, continuing to give Satan access.

A fourth result from occult involvement may be affliction and physical illnesses. A person may feel bothered and tormented. Or he may be subject to recurrent rashes or minor illnesses for which medical doctors can't find the right cure. Again, there may be many psychosomatic or purely medical causes, but on the other hand it may be unwise to overlook the possibility of occult influence. One woman in our prayer group only recently had been complaining of inability to arrive at full healing and health. There was always something nagging. I "saw" occultism in the family history and prayed for it to be stopped. Last night (May 1, 1984) she handed me a letter full of rejoicing that our prayer in the group had set her free.

Sometimes physical afflictions happen not because of past involvement but through effects of present spiritual warfare. Agnes Sanford ran afoul of a batch of witches' covens in a foreign country. It was as though she had stirred up a hornets' nest. The conflict was affecting her through headaches, weariness, blocked moments in her teachings and fits of despondency and feelings of futility. She called me for help. Under anointing, knowing everything else had been tried, I told her to "Try getting out into nature. Walk in the woods. Roll on the grass." She tried it, and it worked, especially rolling on the grass. It was as though all those negative effects drained out of her into the earth. She wrote back that some people thought she was one crazy lady, but she sure felt better!

I might interject here that my Osage Indian ancestors used to say that one reason the white man loses track of who he is and does wrong things is that he lives too far away from the earth. His houses and streets isolate him from the good earth. Indians purposefully sat on the earth and slept on the earth whenever possible for the reason that they knew it was good for them. Nature camps have been established for city children because of sociological studies made concerning the effects of a lack of wholesome natural environment. We recommend as one antidote for occult influence, besides all the ways we pray for healing, large doses of time outside in the good earth. When counselees have piled in on me, one after the other, and I feel defiled, I may take ten minutes between appointments to walk out into the garden and let my fingers work in the soil. It drains away that defilement which by then I can no longer successfully pray away.

A fifth symptom of occult attack is lapses of memory, blocked thought patterns, inability to remember where one has put things or what one is doing, and loss of one's stream of thought while speaking. Having suffered effects of hypoglycemia at one time, and acute stress at others, I know firsthand that these symptoms can be the result of physical and psychological causes. Nevertheless, discernment may also reveal occult causes. Neither cause need rule out the other. Perhaps one would be able to overcome the physical causes were occultism not tipping the scales, or be able to withstand occult attack were not one already so exhausted or stressed. However, sometimes effects can be there by occult interference when no physical reason exists.

When Agnes Sanford and I first began traveling together as a team, it was for that reason. Opposing spirits had been blocking her thoughts and constricting her throat, severely restricting her ability to speak. I seldom spoke, usually only in the mornings. I was not there for that purpose. We would pray together during the day. At the meetings, I would read the Scriptures and say a prayer, Agnes would teach, and afterwards I would close with prayer. During her talk I sat in the audience close by where I could watch her, interceding the entire time. So long as I remembered to attend to my duties instead of being caught up in what she was saying, power flowed through her without interruption. She had also been plagued by tension headaches, partly from the stress of so much speaking and the burden of intercession, but also from occult opposition. I was there to protect her so that she might be free to concentrate on the ministry. Many speakers have learned to enlist prayer warriors at home, and some have intercessors as part of their traveling team, as a wall of protection, as in Psalm 8:2: "From the mouth of infants and nursing babes Thou hast established strength, Because of Thine adversaries, to make the enemy and the revengeful cease."

A sixth effect of occult involvement is constant family turmoil and tragedies. Satan often attacks the Lord's servants through afflictions upon their families. Church members should learn to pray regularly for their pastor's family. Traveling teachers, prophets and evangelists need groups who dedicate themselves to prayer on their behalf, especially to watch over their families, since their frequent absences from home leave their families vulnerable and subject to bouts of resentment at his absences.

Apart from servants in service, if occultism has been engaged in at any time in life, family doors have been opened which ought to have remained shut. Hear again the Lord's word concerning those who have been to seances: "I will . . . *cut him off from among his people*" (Lev. 20:6).

The law of sowing and reaping goes into operation. When a man turns to the occult, in effect he cuts off himself and all those in his charge from the Lord. That is the seed he has sown; therefore that is what he must reap. Powers of darkness take advantage of that to add to the discipline of the law the ravages of turmoil and tragedy. Guilt which fails to find its ways to the cross then becomes a handle demonic powers can pump. We stop such interference by the same applications of forgiveness and healing, hiding the family. But let us remember the lessons of our first chapter. There is need for much healing of wounded spirits, lest we go through the proper motions but fail to hug and heal as my father did after he spanked us. Torn and tattered feelings and relationships need to be mended. It will not do to rebuke Satan's hosts away, only to leave the door open through unhealed wounds and remembrances.

A seventh common symptom might be subsumed under previous effects but deserves mention on its own. Sometimes it seems as though there is an unending drain on family finances. Just about the time the mother and father hope to lift their heads above water for a while, sudden unlooked-for expenses plunge them under again. Every light at the end of the tunnel is somehow snuffed out or proves to be a false hope. The key thing is that expenses arrive in the most outlandish, unfair, mysterious ways! Life does not flow evenly. Budgets are so disrupted as to be impossible to adhere to. It is as though there is a curse on the wealth of the family. If the family is not tithing, of course there is, and that needs to be corrected first,

> Will a man rob God? Yet you are robbing Me! But you say, "How have we robbed Thee?" In tithes and contributions. *You are cursed with a curse,* for you are robbing Me, the whole nation of you! Bring the whole tithe into the storehouse, so that there may be food in My house, and test Me now in this, says the Lord of hosts, if I will not open for you the windows of heaven, and pour out for you a blessing until there is no more need. Then *I will rebuke the devourer for you,* so that

it may not destroy the fruits of the ground; Nor will your vine in the field cast its grapes, says the Lord of hosts. And all the nations will call you blessed, for you shall be a delightful land, says the Lord of hosts (Mal. 3:8-12).

Sometimes, however, the family may be tithing faithfully, and hurting all the more because now it seems that God's promises fail to be true. "I'm doing my part! Why isn't God coming through? This isn't fair. I know He has a reason, but how come when things go wrong He always has an excuse and I never have one?!" So the latter effect of occult involvement is more important than financial loss; there is nothing the devil would rather do than break our trust in the faithfulness of God.

Sometimes in prayer by vision I have seen a great lake of blessing God has stored up, which He wants to pour down, but the curse has turned the funnel of reception upside down. The waters of blessing splatter off the sides like an umbrella and only a trickle comes through the small opening. In faith, we take the devil's hands off the supply line, and see the funnel properly situated, reaching out to catch the floods of goodness and channel them to His child and His family.

Healing is needed not only for the family for all the strains of financial loss but between them and God. They need to be enabled to say words of forgiveness to God, as St. Paul urged, "on behalf of Christ, be reconciled to God" (2 Cor. 5:20b). The same reconciliation with God could also be applied for all the other hurts we have discussed, but here it is specifically required in that a specific promise of God *seems* to have been broken.

An eighth result of occult involvement is not merely to be expected, it is an absolute requirement that it *will* happen, by law. That is the descent through generational sin of trouble and harm to generation after generation to come (Deut. 5:9). We only mention this here, since it will be discussed more fully in Chapter Thirteen.

There are many other results but these are the most common.

The Body of Christ needs to become aware, to know its power and its authority. The calling is urgent:

> God takes His stand in His own congregation; He judges in the midst of the rulers. How long will you judge unjustly, And show partiality to the wicked? Vindicate the weak and the fatherless; Do justice to the afflicted and destitute. Rescue the weak and needy; Deliver them out of the hand of the wicked (Ps. 82:1-4).

The power is given:

> And Jesus came up and spoke to them, saying, *"All* authority has been given to Me in heaven and on earth" (Matt. 28:18).

> And these signs will accompany those who have believed: in My name *they will cast out demons*, they will speak with new tongues; (Mark 16:17).

The least Christian wields the fullness of power and shares the joy of the battle. The kings and nations upon whom we shall execute the vengeance of God are of course first the demonic powers.

> Let the godly ones exult in glory; Let them sing for joy on their beds. Let the high praises of God be in their mouth. And a two-edged sword in their hand, To execute vengeance on the nations, And punishment on the peoples; To bind their kings with chains, And their nobles with fetters of iron; To execute on them the judgment written; This is an honor for *all* His godly ones. Praise the Lord! (Ps. 149:5-9).

Chapter Eleven

Spiritualism and Exorcism

> As for the person who turns to mediums and to
> spiritists, to play the harlot after them, I will also set
> My face against that person and will cut him off from
> among his people (Lev. 20:6).
>
> As for a man or a woman, if there is a medium or a
> spiritist among them, they shall surely be put to death;
> they shall be stoned with stones, their bloodguiltiness
> is upon them (Lev. 20:27).

Spiritualism holds great appeal for those who have
insufficient faith or who lack biblical knowledge. The
lonely who have lost a loved one, who cannot simply believe
they will share eternity together after this short life, see
spiritualism as a means to have some contact with that
loved one and reassurance from him. They may have little
or no conscious awareness that God forbids it. It seems good
to them to ease an aching heart by such contacts. There may
be other reasons to turn to spiritualism. There may be a
great need to find a lost bank box key or last will and
testament. "If we could only contact Uncle Will, he could
tell us. What's wrong with that?" Some have great fear of

death, or more accurately, fear of vanishing into nothingness after death. Not having fullness of faith in our resurrected Lord, in their hearts, though their lips may confess faith, they feel that they need experiences which seem to grant assurance that something real does exist beyond the grave. Seances seem to provide the evidence that they want. But God provides better ways to answer such needs, and nothing in any instance can make spiritualism right.

Spiritualism is the practice of attempting to contact and communicate with those who have departed this life. One who practices making contacts and becomes one through whom contacts are made is called a medium.

As we see by the above Scriptures, spiritualism is strictly forbidden by the Word of the Lord. Our Lord does not explain why it is forbidden, except to say "You shall have no other gods before Me" (Exod. 20:3), which implies that we human beings cannot contact a departed spirit without entering into some form of idolatry. But God does not have to explain himself. It is enough that He forbids it.

However, we can easily see some of His reasons. The first is the idolatry mentioned above. We may give to spirits allegiance and obedience which ought to be given to God only. For example, we have known people so hooked on spiritualism that they would not make any decision without first consulting the spirits. That relegates to spirits (usually demons masquerading as Uncle Bill or Aunt Betsy) what ought to be given only to God. "Commit your way to the Lord, Trust also in Him, and He will do it" (Ps. 37:5). "Commit your works to the Lord, And your plans will be established" (Prov. 16:3).

A second reason is defilement. Some scholars of the Word maintain that upon death, a person's spirit is immediately taken into chambers in Heaven. They say spiritists can never contact a departed soul. These scholars say people only contact that satanic "angel" who watched over the person all of his life who can therefore perfectly counterfeit his ways and voice and proclaim things which seemingly only the departed person could have known. Such scholars therefore maintain that whoever attempts to contact a relative only becomes contaminated by demonic spirits. As we will explain later, we question whether that explanation covers all the facts; there may be cases in which persons do actually contact the spirit of a departed person. But in either case, defilement is the result. By such contact, one opens doors of his spirit which ought to remain closed.

On earth before death, as we have expounded in Chapter Eight, living persons can defile us by their presence or by what emanates from their spirits across space apart from us. But people do have bodies. Their spirits must abide within their own bodies. This is not so with a departed spirit or a demon counterfeiting a presence. These do not have bodies. That means that they can attach themselves to a living person or enter and inhabit and perhaps eventually possess him or her altogether. Thus a person who attends seances not only is defiled but may become demon possessed.

Often, those who try to contact spirits only fool themselves, or as mediums are only charlatans attempting to beguile their clients for money or some other advantage. Children frequently play foolish parlor games, attempting to hold seances. Because nothing real seems to happen, some have thought there is no reality at all to spiritualism, and have simply scoffed.

However, spiritualism is forbidden for more reasons than idolatry, defilement, exposure to demonic contamination, etc., all of which can happen even if attempts to make contact with departed spirits are unsuccessful. God so sternly countermands it because of the possibility of becoming involved in relationships with ghosts or demons who lead astray. Our Lord would not have become greatly concerned about mere imaginative foolishness. Many only fool themselves. Nothing of more reality happens than the sin of trying. Nevertheless, even misfired attempts open forbidden doors and sow to later reapings of judgment.

Even childish games like the Ouija board cause great harm. Sometimes, however, mediums and seance participants do invoke and make actual contact. It is the stark reality of such things that arouses our Lord's anger.

Contacted spirits, whether in fact a departed person or a demonic counterfeit, are not to be believed. Demons want to begin by telling a person on earth, through the vocal cords of the medium, some simple easily verifiable facts, such as where a lost item treasured by the family can be found. They do this to establish belief and trust. Once so established, they can thus lead the person gullibly into delusions and baser and baser deceptions and doctrines. Continued contacts increase footholds in the person's spirit and soul until finally he is fully snared and on his way to Hell. There are many "spiritualist churches" who name Jesus as Lord and continue to believe they are fully Christian while treading the broad path to torture in eternity. Satan blinds their eyes (2 Cor. 4:4) to Scriptures like Leviticus 20:6 and 27, careful to encourage them to pray to God and to continue in their "church." He knows that if once the veneer of being good Christians is stripped away, his deception will be exposed for what it is. Therefore Satan wants them to continue with all the trappings of Christianity while his own "trappings" remain operative in their lives, their true nature unsuspected.

As mentioned earlier, some scholars maintain that since the departed go to Heaven or to Hell, mediums can only contact counterfeit spirits, whose intimate knowledge allows them to fool those who contact them. In the main, and most often, I think those scholars are correct. But perhaps one ought not to be too dogmatic about pronouncements that mediums and those who attend seances *only* contact counterfeits. When Saul became agitated before the great battle he was to fight the next day against the Philistines, and no prophet would speak God's word to him, he arose and rode all through the night behind enemy lines to find the witch of Endor. He knew that to turn to mediums was forbidden, but he was desperate and frightened. He himself had ". . . cut off those who are mediums and spiritists from the land" (1 Sam. 28:9). But being mentally disturbed, like many today who know better, Saul decided to contact a medium anyway. Saul asked the witch to call up Samuel. Nowhere and in no way does the Scripture indicate anything imaginary, or that Saul did not in fact speak with Samuel. Rather, the account is straightforwardly factual:

> When the woman saw Samuel, she cried out with a loud voice; and the woman spoke to Saul, saying, "Why have you deceived me? For you are Saul." And the king said to her, "Do not be afraid; but what do you see?" And the woman said to Saul, "I see a divine being coming up out of the earth." And he said to her, "What is his form?" And she said, "An old man is coming up, and he is wrapped with a robe." And Saul knew that it was Samuel, and he bowed with his face to the ground and did homage. Then Samuel said to Saul, "Why have you disturbed me by bringing me up?" And Saul answered, "I am greatly distressed; for the Philistines are waging war against me, and God has departed from me and answers me no more, either through prophets or by dreams; therefore I have called you, that you may make known to me what I should do." And Samuel said, "Why then do you ask me, since the Lord has departed from you and has become your adversary? And the Lord has done accordingly as He spoke through me; for the Lord has torn the kingdom out of your hand and given it to your neighbor, to David. As you did not obey the Lord and did not execute His fierce wrath on Amalek, so the Lord has done this thing to you this day. Moreover the Lord will also give over Israel along with you into the hands of the Philistines, therefore tomorrow you and your sons will be with me. Indeed the Lord will give over the army of Israel into the hands of the Philistines!" (1 Sam. 28:12-19).

Whether or not Saul would have been defeated and killed anyway the next day had he not visited the medium,

Samuel made the pronouncement of his death because whoever consults a medium will be cut off!

So we see that at least this Bible story makes it clear that sometimes mediums do in fact truly contact the departed. Samuel lived in Old Testament times. Perhaps Christians cannot be disturbed as he was, since we live in a different time. On the other hand, perhaps we ought not to be too absolute in our assertions where the Bible is not. The visit of Samuel to Saul was unquestionably real. Perhaps some other contacts are real also. If so, that does not make any visits permissible. They are sin, forbidden by God, and that should be enough for any believer.

It is an interesting footnote that the witch of Endor prevailed upon Saul to eat a meal before he left. Not only was it the custom to urge hospitality and to give a meal whenever possible; the woman was terrified that Saul, who had been cutting off all mediums, would recollect himself and do so to her. When he ate her food, he ate her salt. It was one of the strongest customs of the day that a person could not harm another whose salt he had eaten. So by offering kindness, she thought to save herself from the king. Apparently it worked. Whether or not Saul would otherwise have harmed her, he did not. In just such ways, however, by being warm and kindly people, those who are involved in the sin of spiritualism sometimes think to save themselves. "Look at all the good, kind things we do. Certainly God could not reject us. We aren't wicked." But in the final judgment neither the witch of Endor nor any other well-meaning, loving but misguided spiritualist will be able to escape the judgment of God. Sin is sin, no matter how nice our character or kindly our intentions.

One time, while making routine hospital calls, I (John) came into a room in which I soon discovered that the lady to whom I was ministering, who was on her deathbed, was a long-practicing spiritualist. I began to witness to her of the saving grace of the Lord Jesus Christ. Yes, she would receive Him as Lord and Savior; had she not always known Him in her spiritualist church? Yes, I supposed she knew *of* Him. Now I would have her *receive* Him, be forgiven and be born anew. She would do that too, she said, and received Him in prayer as her Lord and Savior. Then I said, "Bessie, now that you have received Jesus as Lord and Savior, you will have to renounce your workers and let them go." Some spiritualists entitle the spirits they think they contact on the other side as their "workers." Some workers are regarded as good and others as evil and not to be trusted. (When I entered the room, her eyes had widened and she had exclaimed, "Oh, you are surrounded by the very best workers!" I knew instantly she was a spiritualist and so I had responded, "Yes, Bessie, that is the Lord Jesus Christ and all His company." That had begun our conversation.)

Bessie demurred, "Oh, no, I need my workers."

"No, Bessie, you don't need anyone but Jesus."

"No, no, I need them!"

At that moment the glory of the Lord came upon us. The Lord himself was approaching her. But Bessie was writhing in pain and drew back in abject fear of Him. I saw what the Lord was doing and so spoke again. "Do you see, Bessie, it's those spirits that are afraid of Him. You have nothing to fear. You belong to Him. He loves you. Just let those workers go, and it will be all right."

"Oh no, I couldn't."

Again the glory of the Lord came, more intensely. Again Bessie blanched in terror. "Let those workers go, Bessie. Jesus loves you. It will be okay."

"No, no, I can't."

"Yes, you can."

So we went around and around, several times. Finally, apparently the grace of God touched her with His empowering love, and she said, "Okay, I'll let them go." With that I commanded every spirit, whether ghost or demon, to leave her, except the Holy Spirit, and forgave her the sin of spiritualism. Bessie relaxed and the glory of the Lord came again—and stayed! Bessie was no longer afraid. Her fear had not been hers, but the terror of the demons within her. She was at peace. When I left, I looked back to see a joyously serene expression on her face. Her family reported that she passed away soon after, calmly and peacefully.

Unfortunately, not all such cases are that clear and simple. There are gray areas in dealing with spiritism. Others may use these words differently, but we employ the word spiritualism to refer specifically to conscious attempts to contact departed spirits, usually in seances through mediums. To us "spiritism" is a larger word, referring also to attempts to contact nature spirits, or being open to being contacted by spirits as is true of Peter Caddy's group at Findhorn, Scotland.

I share here (quite reluctantly, in obedience to the Lord) several stories from our family history, knowing that most every family holds in memory many similar happenings. I share them to make several points. It must be understood that these are not testimonies. We are not proud of ourselves for them and do not see them as giving any glory to the Lord. We do not share them to encourage others to try to have such experiences, nor to think of them as admirable, rather to say that as Spirit-filled Christians we need to disallow and so far as possible avoid such encounters. Not because they are unmistakably bad or forbidden, but simply because we do not know; they are in the gray areas, and we need to be careful to keep our garments unspotted from the flesh (Jude 23).

Our family (John's) has always been mystical. Many strange things happened within it. Once my mother was in great pain in a hospital bed. Recalling how her mother had been a comfort to her as a little girl when she was ill, in a moment of regression into childhood, she wished her mother could be there to comfort her. In the next instant it seemed to her that Grandmother Potter, long deceased, was there, standing by her bed, and the next second it seemed mother was standing by the bed and grandmother was in her body, taking all the pain for her. After a few minutes of relief, Grandmother

Potter was gone and my mother was again in the hospital bed.*

It is of course only Jesus who bears our pain for us. Some might think He allowed grandmother to return to help her daughter. Others, including me, are more inclined to think that either my mother fooled herself or was deluded by some spirit posing as her mother. But no one knows.

The point is, however, that here is a gray area. We are not completely sure either way. Perhaps the greatest danger is that some who suffer or some who have never had such an experience might think, "I wish something like that would happen to me." That may open doors or encourage attempts which ought not to be made. As a Spirit-filled Christian I would never seek that kind of experience, and have prayed that the Lord bring to death all my mystical nature and to put the cross between myself and my mystical family heritage. But suppose that in visiting and swapping stories, I share such stories as this? Can it not tempt my weaker brothers? I think that in gray areas like these, the advice of Paul regarding not eating meat lest his weaker brother be tempted ought to be observed by us all (Rom. 14:13-22).

Our Lord Jesus as the Word who was with God was the very Creator God (John 1:1-14, Col. 1:15 ff., Heb. 1:1-3) who gave the law to Moses. Yet we see Him on the Mount of Transfiguration conversing with both Moses and Elijah (Matt. 17:1-8). Elijah had not died but was translated. Moses had died. Since our Lord never sinned (2 Cor. 5:21),

---

* Since in some of these stories my Grandmother Potter is mentioned, it ought to be stated that Grandmother Potter was a staunch, Bible-reading believer. She would have had nothing to do with spiritualism, and I never knew her to be very mystical. She was quite down to earth. A strict fundamentalist teetotaler, she would have been horrified to learn that the Hadacol medicine she loved to take for colds and coughs was about ninety proof!

and was found here speaking with a departed person, apparently not all contacts from heaven to earth are forbidden! Spiritualism occurs when men try to contact the residents of Heaven. That we must never do. We mention this in no way to attempt to excuse spiritualism; we seek rather to ease the hearts of some who have been troubled by experiences in which the departed have seemed to come to them uninvited. Even the fact that our Lord embraced such an experience is, to me, a part of the grayness. The lines are not always clear.

Here is another story from my family history. My mother purchased a used recliner chair. Having brought it home, she was cleaning it before use. While reaching deep between the cushion and sidewall, she suddenly heard what she understood to be her mother's voice (several years after her death) saying, "Reach deeper, Zelma." She did, and found an extremely valuable diamond ring, which the jeweler later sized to fit her. She wears it to this day, sure that it was a gift from her mother.

My mother did not attempt to contact anyone. This happened *to* her. But by what agency? Did God allow, so that it really was grandmother's spirit who spoke? Or was it a demon, attempting to convince my mother so as to weaken true faith and lead her astray? Some would be adamantly convinced either way. Surely there are gray areas which no one fully understands.

For Spirit-filled Christians, I am more concerned about the gray areas than about spiritualism itself. Spiritualism is a known evil. We can easily recognize it and avoid it, determined to obey His Word. But the gray areas spark immense curiosity. Scriptural guidelines are not so clear. We have seen some counselees move step by seemingly innocent step into greater and greater off-balancedness, if not into outright deception and sin. Many have by mystical occurrences unwittingly been caught in idolatry, looking for consolation and guidance from sources other than the Holy Spirit. It is for these reasons that I expose our family stories. I know from years of counseling that almost every family can share similar stories. I am not counseling fear and withdrawal but rather caution and propriety. Let us be determined to keep our way pure according to His Word (Ps. 119:9). Then if something like the above stories happens to us, we can simply release it to the Lord, ask forgiveness if in any way we have been open to what we ought not to be, praise God for the experience and go on in Him, wise enough not to share stories where the immature might be tempted into false adventure.

In my office as a prophet and as a pastor I often knew beforehand about a death coming within my congregation. that was easy to understand as part of the gift of knowledge. "Surely the Lord God does nothing Unless He reveals His secret counsel To His servants the prophets" (Amos 3:7). That knowledge called me to intercede. Often I was in prayer for the person when the call came to tell me of his death. That was my function as a pastor and a prophet. But sometimes things would happen that were not so easy to understand. One time when trying to determine what to say in a funeral sermon, I entered quite a wrestle because I knew so many things both good and bad about the person, which the community also knew. I was alone in my office, praying about it while my left hand lay extended on my desk. At last I decided the Lord would have me focus only on His grace, and, since I could not ignore all things about my friend's life because the congregation expected me to say something, I would speak only briefly, with compassion. My eyes were still closed, head bent in prayer. A hand clasped my left hand and squeezed, unmistakably meaning the same as when we give a gentle squeeze to express affirmation. I "recognized" the presence of my friend, the departed person. What in fact did happen? Was it indeed the ghost of my friend, affirming my choice? Was it the Lord, assuring me? Or was it something trying to delude and lead me astray? I did not seek to contact anyone nor to experience anything. It happened, *unbidden*, *to* me. I am sure many pastors have puzzled about similar experiences.

Here again is a gray area. What shall we make of it or do about it?

I share this story to testify to what I have done. I have prayed that the Lord preserve me from all false experiences, that the Lord bring to death all fleshly mysticism and close in me anything that ought not to be open. On the other hand, I have prayed that if the Lord wants me to be vulnerable to such things, that He protect me and "lead me not into temptation." I know from counseling that many pastors are "pestered" by experiences they cannot quite put away in definite boxes, and they hesitate to share them anywhere, for fear of what people might think or do.

One time I was visiting my mother, who at that time was emotionally upset and in danger of making some wrong decisions. Though people travel thousands of miles to counsel with me and I am internationally known for my expertise as a counselor, I of course could not get to first base with my own mother (Matt. 13:57). Exasperated and grieving, I walked away into another room. No windows or doors were open. No water was running anywhere in the house. Suddenly I felt the presence above me of my Grandmother Potter who I "knew" was weeping for my mother. A drop of water fell onto my brow and ran into my eye, so real and so copious I had to take off my glasses and dry out both them and my eye! There was no moisture on the ceiling, no physically explainable reason for it! What happened? Was it in fact a tear? Why? Why would the Lord allow such a thing to happen to one who has spoken against spiritism and spiritualism and is determined to walk circumspectly before the Lord? I know I risk my own reputation (and perhaps my beloved family) even by telling such stories. But I risk it for a most cogently compelling reason. I know that there are many, many pastors and lay people in the Body who have encountered similar experiences, who have not told anyone for fear of being labeled a "kook" or weird, or even being thrown out of their church as a spiritist or spiritualist! Fifteen years ago I renounced all mysticism and said to the Lord, "I want no experience of any kind unless it happens only by the Holy Spirit." Since then I have not experienced anything like these stories, so perhaps one reason they happened was my immaturity in Christ. But that's precisely the point of our sharing. How many Christians, especially the newly born, have had similar things happen to them, and who has known to listen to them without blame? Who has known how to minister to them or recognize the need?

Suppression and isolation are not good. *It is healing to share in the right places.* Small groups *in churches are right places.* Friends can discern and pray. We must take away the aura of judgment and condemnation and share properly, inside the Church, where our brothers and sisters can pray for us and protect us. Whether such happenings are recognizably good or bad, loneliness from a mystical experience can wound the spirit.

I have debated and prayed a long time before deciding to share these stories and believe that there are burdens of confusion and wondering that need to be lifted from a great many of our brothers and sisters. The risk of our reputation is worth it for their healing. I do *not* expect nor hope that the Body can answer the questions of those who have had similar experiences. I certainly can't; not even of my own. To dwell on these matters would likely be a delusory distraction, keeping us from concentration on more appropriate and fruitful pursuits. This side of Heaven there will always be ". . . more things in heaven and earth, Horatio, than are dreamt of in your philosophy" (*Hamlet*, Act I, Scene 5). But we can end the loneliness and the wondering whether those who have mystical experiences are crazy or weird, by our acceptance of such people and our willingness to hear and to support in prayer. Having come out of an extremely mystical heritage, I know first-hand the ravages of loneliness which strange experiences can engender! I know the hunger for sharing in safe places within the Body. I know the need for mystical Christians in our midst not to feel isolated, but to feel themselves enfolded in the love and prayerful balancing concern of people who may never have had such experiences.

Mystics in our midst are often involved in gray-area experiences. They need earthy people to stand by them and with them. Earthy people also need the challenge of hearing experiences outside their ken. Too long, an atmosphere of fear and ridicule, scorn and judgment has prevailed, silencing and isolating those who are mystical. We tend to fear what we do not understand. So many times brothers and sisters have come to us greatly wounded because they did share a happening, only to find themselves under condemnation and greater isolation and loneliness than that which impelled them to speak in the first place! We plead with the Body not to be arrogant and insensitive, especially when called upon to warn a brother or sister.

I do not condone or whitewash such experiences or those who have them. I only plead for healing. The mystical in this pragmatic age are left vulnerable to many things by isolation. The Body needs to gather around and protect the mystics in its midst, lest they be carried off into delusion, or be shut down by unwillingness to venture, and become unfruitful even in the clearly valid gifts of the Holy Spirit. For, isolated, they become too bruised and lonely to function even if they remain willing to do so. Let us be determined to be healing emissaries of Jesus first rather than swift swords of judgment—though if healing love is present, swift swords can also be healing instruments.

Great healing is needed for those who have been involved in spiritualism and/or spiritism. All the effects and prescriptions for healing listed in the previous chapter pertain here as well, with several additions and emphases.

First, spiritualism, far more than most other occult things, exposes participants to the sights and inroads of the powers of darkness. Whether people actively participated or were somewhat innocently involved by others, they need to be more assiduously hidden from the eyes of devils, and more rigorously shut off in all centers of their soul from access by the devil.

Defilement is more severe. Unclean spirits may have attached themselves, or have entered them. Exorcism is most likely required in such cases.

Deposits may have been left in the mind. Thoughts and emotions, recollections of seeming to have talked again with a dear one, may plague and clamor to be accepted and to be repeated. Sometimes people are convinced that departed ones have commissioned or commanded them to do something which would prove lack of loyalty or love if denied. The entire plot of *Hamlet* revolves around his belief that his dead father has appeared to him and commanded him to take vengeance on his brother for killing and usurping his throne and his wife. Honor seems to be at stake. Misplaced zeal tears at them to act, usually in wrong ways for a wrong cause, as vengeance should not be Hamlet's but the Lord's.

Such deposits should be broken by the voice of authority, dispelling spirits' words by His name. Demons usually want to stir people to do some great wrong thing to right some supposed great wrong—or even to do some seemingly right thing to prevent or correct some wrong happening. Many times Christians have been convinced that if they could only convey a forgiveness seemingly from the other side, a person could come to rest about a guilt, or perhaps that if they could express for a departed person a love that person failed to express while on earth, someone's longing heart might be healed. But those longings are not to be fulfilled by spiritualism. The Holy Spirit has other and better ways to address those needs. When needs as these seem to have been fulfilled through spiritualism, a counselor must even appear to wound in order to heal. "Mary, that message came from spiritualism. I know it has been a comfort to your heart. But it's a false comfort. Don't you see that you still question; your spirit is not at rest, even though your mind has latched onto that message? Let's let go of that message. We don't have to know whether or not it could have been something your loved one would have wanted to say to you. Our Lord is our only true comfort.

Let's listen only to Him, and wash ourselves of all defilement. Okay? Will you pray with me about it?"

Remembrances of messages or experiences nag continually at the mind and heart for acceptance. A brother or sister may come from a seance and say to one who has never even thought of attending anything spiritualistic, "Dad came to us last night, and he wants all of us in the family to know he loves us, and he wants you, George, as the eldest, to watch over the rest of the family, especially David who he says is heading into trouble." That may seem innocuous, even helpful. But George probably would have taken responsibility anyway. The message confuses. If David does head into trouble, George's mind and all the rest of the family's thoughts may be plagued with thoughts that perhaps spiritualism is okay after all. If George does watch out especially for David, he is necessarily bothered by the apprehension that after all he may be doing the bidding of a spiritualist's counsel, so that even a right duty in the family is tainted by questions of uncleanness. If a prophet were to have given the same counsel to George, and David were kept from trouble, God would receive the glory. But who gets the glory if circumstances are otherwise?

Those who pray for deliverance and healing should petition for cleansing of the counselee's mind and heart, that all memories may be washed clean from suggestion and temptation. Counselors should avail themselves of the cleansing power of God's Word.

> The law of the Lord is perfect, restoring the soul; the testimony of the Lord is sure, making wise the simple. The precepts of the Lord are right, rejoicing the heart; The commandment of the Lord is pure, enlightening the eyes. The fear of the Lord is clean, enduring forever; The judgments of the Lord are true; they are righteous altogether. They are more desirable than gold, yes, than much fine gold; Sweeter also than honey and the drippings of the honeycomb. Moreover, by them Thy servant is warned; In keeping them there is great reward (Ps. 19:7-11).

A counselor would be well advised to read several passages like that to the counselee, and to assign daily reading of Scriptures like all of Psalm 119, John 12 through 20, or the Letter to the Romans. Jesus was not speaking figuratively when He said, "You are already clean *because of the word which I have spoken to you*" (John 15:3). His Word is the power unto salvation (Rom. 1:16).

Demons love to incite family troubles by supposed messages in seances. One purporting to be a departed sister may say, "Watch out for Martha; she is telling tales about you where she should not," or "Dan's wife is making eyes at your husband. Be aware." To mask the intents of creating suspicion and sowing seeds of unrest and division, the demon behind the scene may throw in some good advice, such as "Be compassionate," or "Try to forgive," knowing that the person will be more likely thereby to treasure the message without suspecting it. The demon knows those seeds of suspicion and division will do their dirty work in the heart anyway. The person may try to throw the message off, but in the back of his mind questions and resentments may continue to gnaw away.

Let us be clear about the difference between the Lord's words and those from flesh and demons. A prophet of the Lord may also give warnings, perhaps even with the same admonitions or counsels to be compassionate and to forgive. When the prophet speaks, it is the Holy Spirit speaking through him. His words carry the Lord's anointing. They affect the heart with His purposes. They bring forth good "for it is God who is at work in you, both to will and to work for His good pleasure" (Phil. 2:13). When a gossiper spreads stories, flesh is at work, "A worthless man digs up evil, While *his words are as a scorching fire.* A perverse man spreads strife And a slanderer separates intimate friends" (Prov. 16:27, 28). Flesh may or may not be impelled or aided by devils; the slander may come only from flesh. But when it comes by the agency of spiritualism, it always has behind it and working through it demons and their defilements. It carries Satan's "anointing" and worms its way into people to pander to the basest motives of flesh. God's Word calls forth His righteousness within us. Satanic words seduce to the worst of the flesh within mankind.

It is important that we comprehend this distinction, for many have said, "I don't see what's so wrong about that word from the spiritualist. My pastor said the very same thing to me, in the same words. I just took it as confirmation." Not so. Those words from the spiritualist are not identical to those from the pastor even if identical in word, expression and tone. It is the distinctive power and source of each which is the deciding factor. God needs no confirmations from the Devil. His Word is only sullied by the leaven of additions from evil sources. We are to keep our hearts and minds, souls and spirits *only* unto Him who is the fountain, who has the Words of life (John 6:68).

People who have been involved in any form of the occult should be urged to renounce it, aloud, before others, in prayer. For those involved in spiritualism, it is not merely a wise urging but an imperative. The spoken word contains power, most especially in confession, as in James 5:13-19, which is the command to confess our sins before others.

It is important in all prayer concerning occult involvement to make use of the blood of Christ, especially for those tainted by spiritism and spiritualism. The blood, the Word and the cross are the most powerful weapons of our warfare in healing those involved in occultism, especially spiritualism.

Since Leviticus 20:6 says, "As for the person who turns to mediums and to spiritists, to play the harlot after them, *I will also set My face against that person and will cut him off from among his people,*" there are therefore two prime effects of spiritualism which ought to be addressed by healing prayer. The person needs to be restored to the favor of God. Reconciliation should be voiced in prayer until the person knows he is again within God's good graces. Moreover, blessing ought to be reestablished. A person may feel accepted again but perhaps only as a third-rate citizen who is again allowed access to God, but of course no good thing would ever come his way again. Therefore the person must have God's blessing pronounced over him until he again believes that God's angels and saints go before him to seek his good and he could again be entrusted with an important task. His confidence as a child of the King for whom the King provides needs to be reestablished.

Second, those involved and now repentant of spiritism and spiritualism must be restored to their families and to the Family of God. From the moment of occult sin, the irresistible forces of the law of sowing and reaping act to cut a man off. That curse of the law has been stopped on the cross of Christ. God nailed all the demands of the law to the cross and canceled all those legal requirements (Col. 2:14). As with all sin, spiritualism demands retribution. Forgiveness does not mean God overlooks sin but that He pays the price of our redemption from sin by taking it in pain upon himself. Nevertheless, that awesome complete and glorious price He paid waits upon prayer to apply it. The counselor or healer must not fail to pray for full and complete termination of the effects of spiritualism! We say this because to our great chagrin and the Body's continuing harm, we have all too often heard of those who have spoken of their dereliction and consequent repentance only to have their hearers fail to pray or do anything about it! That is almost as grievous as the sin of the involved one. Prayer is the first access of the grace of God to mankind. Understanding is not enough. Acceptance is not enough. Only prayer applies the blood and the cross and completes the work.

Any kind of occult involvement sends harm through family lines for generations to come. So does spiritualism. Those who pray are called also to stop the descent of harm through generational sin. We will speak of that in Chapter Thirteen.

Though any kind of occult involvement may result in demonic oppression or habitation, demonization is almost certain in the case of spiritualism. Spiritualism, especially on the part of the medium, is not only an attempt to contact spirits. While in sorcery an attempt is made to work with and through demons, spiritualism gives direct invitation to enter and work *through* one's own body. Thus, more than in any other occult involvement, spiritualism results in demonic habitation.

There are those who believe that no Spirit-filled Christian can be inhabited by a demonic power. We have not found this to be historic fact, no matter how appealing the theology that the Holy Spirit and demons cannot inhabit the same area. The fact is, it happens. We have exorcised hundreds of Spirit-filled Christians, some of whom have been not only Spirit-filled for many years but well-recognized, powerful servants of the Lord! How this can be so, I cannot fully explain, but that it has been is for us an incontestable fact of many years of grueling experience. Thank God it is likewise incontestable that once the Holy Spirit enters, all other spirits *inevitably must leave.*

Sometimes, in deference to the beliefs of some, we have simply said that a believer has become "demonized." That makes no distinction as to where the demon is, whether inside or outside the person. Perhaps those who believe a demon cannot inhabit a Christian are correct in that in those deepest regions of Christ's indwelling through His Spirit, no demon can abide. It may be that the demon we exorcise merely inhabits some more exterior area of a person's character and personality.

Therefore, we use several terms to distinguish degrees of being demonized. The first level we call "infestation." By that we do not mean that the person is inhabited but that satanic hosts swarm about him like a stirred-up hornet's nest. Through uncrucified areas of his flesh, they can occasionally activate and sometimes motivate him to wrong actions. They hook into him in unguarded areas, from outside his person.

The next degree is simple habitation. A demon has entered but is ineffective. It is as though, to use an analogy, white corpuscles have encysted it as though it were a tubercular infection. Temporarily at least the strength of the person's character has fought it down, unable to cast it out, but able to render it largely ineffective. After one receives the Holy Spirit, His power forces the demon to surface, be revealed and cast out.

That was my case (John's). Raised in an extremely liberal church, I was well instructed morally but not grounded in the Word nor in a personal relationship with Jesus Christ. In my search for reality, I had dabbled in studies some of which I did not even recognize as occult in the years before the Lord found me. Along the way a demon had entered. I was not aware of any symptoms other than fatigue. Surely that demonic thing must have at least blunted sensitivity, warped my theology and my sermons, and postponed the Lord's capture of my heart. But the strength of His hold upon my as yet unregenerate old man was apparently enough to corral and render that devil mainly mute. I received the Holy Spirit in October of 1958. Great glory and joy surrounded all that happened at first. But then in November that demonic thing could no longer maintain its place, and surfaced.

I know by what I experienced how dreadful is the pain and terror demons feel under the application of the true light of God and His blood and cross. As that demon surfaced, I was no longer comfortable and capable of rejoicing in the presence of a powerful servant of God. It had been a joy to visit with Ed Bender, then pastor of the Open Bible Church of Streator, Illinois. It became fraught with fear. Wilbur Fogg, my Episcopal rector friend, playfully tossed holy water at me one day while I was chatting with him in the sanctuary of the Episcopal Church. To that demon whose emotions registered as mine, that was a moment of stark terror! Those globules of water sailing toward me appeared as mountains of smashing fire! In the exorcism, done by Wilbur and his wife Alice, the mention of the blood of Jesus caused actual physical pain and the cross engendered sheer terror. I felt it when that demon could stand it no longer, and left me.

I have since ministered to many hundreds of people whose history was similar to mine. Perhaps those who maintain that Spirit-filled people cannot be inhabited by demons are correct in the sense that Spirit-baptized persons cannot remain inhabited, as the person comes more and more into the fullness of the Holy Spirit. But people certainly can still be inhabited for a while after receiving the Holy Spirit, because I was, and so have many to whom I have ministered deliverance.

Many people have wondered how it can be that immediately after a highly anointed time—or sometimes during a greatly blessed service—unholy desires pester the emotions, or base thoughts course through the mind, or even curse words. Sometimes families and churches explode into rancor and divisiveness during or immediately after a tremendous revival movement in the church. Secular psychiatrists have told Paula and me that after a great revival has come through an area, their offices, more than at any other time, are filled with desperate clients. This is because we neither understand our nature nor the function of the Holy Spirit.

Picture it like an old dry well. Sticks and leaves, spiders and insects litter the bottom. Now let a great rain fill that old well with water. All that trash, along with its living inhabitants, rises to the surface of the water. In the same way the water of the Holy Spirit forces to the surface whatever rotten old things have been lying dormant in our natures. We may have become freshly so refilled and anointed that we want to think we must really be holy, else the Holy Spirit couldn't be that much with us and in us. But that attitude is only delusion and false pride. The first function of the Spirit who is called Holy is to convict of sin. He himself dislodges and causes those old things to rise up within us. He is neither surprised nor offended. He knew all along. We are the only ones astonished at what is revealed. The following diagrams may help:

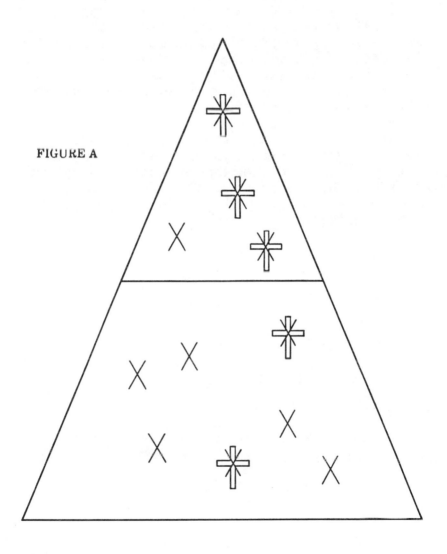

FIGURE A

The top portion of the triangle represents our conscious mind. Each X represents a wound or sinful aspect of our nature. The superimposed crosses stand for problem areas we have already recognized and successfully reckoned as dead on the cross (Rom. 6:11). The bottom section pictures our hidden heart or subconscious areas. The line between the two signifies our common unwillingness to discover what is actually in our heart.

Our personal spirit, the breath of God in us, wants to reveal the remaining troubled areas to consciousness to be seen. ". . . all things become visible when they are exposed by the light, for everything that becomes visible is light" (Eph. 5:13). But we are normally unwilling to admit or face the unknown in us, so we push those things down and build walls, as in Figure B.

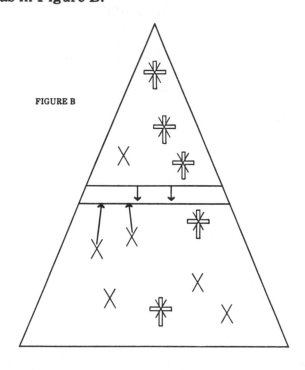

FIGURE B

So long as our spirit does not obtain sufficient power, our conscious mind can win the battle. We gain a false peace, while the inner one smolders like a volcano. We shut off our inner voice and will not hear, though our spirit sends signals through dreams and insights, and perhaps by psychosomatic illnesses.

But let a person be filled by the Holy Spirit, and the spirit gains ability to act with undeniable power. Or let a wife or husband or relatives or friends touch the heart with real love, and power transfuses into the spirit of the person. The personal spirit now possess sufficient power to demand a hearing. The Holy Spirit is wise, and will not drive us into a mental breakdown. But our own spirit can act like a tempestuous child, demanding by a nightmare or by some kind of emotional outburst that we recognize that particular sin or admit that we do have some problem in our life. Thus the battle is on, as in Figure C.

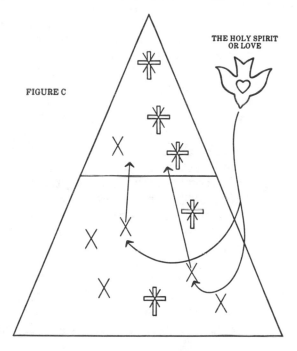

FIGURE C

THE HOLY SPIRIT
OR LOVE

This explains why, as so often happens, family and church battles occur immediately *after* great and anointed times. Our inmost being, as St. Paul said, delights in the law of God, and has been blocked by the war in our members, but thanks be to God in Jesus Christ (Rom. 7:22-25) we have been given power to break through. When the Church or mates or friends or we ourselves fail to understand the process, we may think Satan is attacking because he is angry at the recent victory. We may shout Satan away and wrestle ourselves under control again, only to miss the blessing which simple confession, forgiveness and inner healing prayer could have wrought. Not Satan primarily, but flesh, was at work. At such times, we need to learn to hear one another compassionately, not frightened or disturbed as though something out of place were happening. In this instance, troubles do not mean that the anointing is leaving but rather the reverse, that the anointing is proceeding to the task for which it was sent.

Let the wisdom of the Lord forewarn and prepare. Let the Body look not so much for times of great uninterrupted peace and blessing after the Lord has moved upon a congregation. That rarely happens. What usually occurs is that that new surge of power not only dislodges fortresses of flesh but sometimes forces infesting and inhabiting demons to surface. Had the Church understood, it could have rejoiced, and administered healing, thus prolonging and deepening the move of the Lord in its life. Unfortunately, His people are often destroyed for lack of knowledge, and since they do not understand the process, they also do not comprehend what is happening in their own natures. That means then that those sinful things which are surfacing find no proper access to the light of knowledge for what they are. Often, frightened Christians think, "Oh no, how can I have such a thought—or this kind of feeling—when the anointing is on us all?! I must be terrible!" So they repress that thing, and rebuke the devil. Simple confession would have brought joyous healing: "Yes, Lord, I see I have that thing in me. Show me its root. Lead me to friends who can set me free." The rule is that when urges from within are denied access to proper action, they *will* come up, some way, somehow—perverted and destructive! In this way, movements of the Lord in congregations grind to a halt by rancor and disunity where counsel, confession and prayer ought to have proceeded to sanctification and transformation.

Both the hidden perversions in our sin nature and whatever demons may have been connected to them become dislodged by the power of the Holy Spirit. It will not do only to cast away the demonic and think of the problem as only exterior warfare with demons. Demons cannot inhabit a person without a house of character to hide in. It is that sinful area—an unforgiveness, some practice of "getting even," or an arrogant way of dominating or cowing others by fleshly strength, any kind of practice in our old nature— which is now being called to death on the cross by the present agency of the Holy Spirit. If we only cast away the demonic, seven worse demons are apt to return and the person's last state will be worse than the first (Luke 11:24-26). What is important is to haul that house the demon has lived in to the cross where Jesus promised to destroy all the works of the devil (1 John 3:8). We shortchange ourselves and fail the work of Christ when we think that because people have been born anew and filled with the Holy Spirit, the work is all done. It is only begun. Each visitation of God in the Church will plunge His people into dealing with whatever is caused to surface!

Some time ago, early in the history of the charismatic movement in this century, the many newly Spirit-baptized, especially from mainline erstwhile liberal congregations, discovered that Satan is indeed real, and that there are in fact real demons. Most of us who lived through that time (mostly in the 1960s) can remember how frantic some of us became with this new discovery. For a while, everything had demons in it! They were everywhere! Everyone who was anyone in the kingdom had to be into deliverance. Spit and vomit buckets appeared in prayer rooms, along with paper towels and napkins. As is usual with homo sapiens, we rushed off balance into the weird, to the extreme. We suggest the reader listen to our Elijah House tape entitled, "A Sensible View of Exorcism." Fortunately, most of the Body has matured through that time. But let us chronicle some of the lessons we learned—or should by now have learned:

Exorcisms do not have to involve shouting and screaming, rolling on the floor in convulsions, and vomiting. Sometimes that happens, as in the case of the boy who lay in convulsions when exorcised by Jesus (Luke 9:37-43). However, some demonstrations happen only because some people are susceptible to suggestion and some are emotionally demonstrative. A lot of what went on early in the charismatic movement happened because we expected it to. That gave Satan a playground. Exorcisms can be done by quiet authority and faith, without hyper-emotion or physical demonstrations. The point is that mature exorcists need not send undercurrent messages to the exorcised to act out unnecessary emotional or physical demonstrations. Sometimes such reactions happen, but we ought as healers to mature in our task until we are neither needlessly allowing it nor unconsciously setting the other up to act in such ways.

In the early years of our ministry, exorcisms became prolonged struggles in which the exorcised acted out all manner of weird behaviors. Then the Lord taught us that all that strange activity could happen only because we believed Satan possessed that kind of power! Our belief structure presented him with a circus arena to put on a show. We learned that Satan could even delight in losing battle after battle to us. He knew he would lose anyway, but he could have a ball with us before exiting, so long as we were willing to let him have all that attention and let him glory in all that supposed power. When we learned that they really "overcame him because of the blood of the Lamb and because of the word of their testimony" (Rev. 12:11), and that Satan has no power any longer, having been totally defeated and stripped by our Lord Jesus Christ, our faith no longer gave the devil a theatre to perform in. Now exorcisms are usually short, simple and easy.

Usually, this is the case, but not always. One night friends at a meeting in California were teaching about exorcism. They asked me to come up and offer some words of wisdom. I shared as we have here, that all such emotionalism and weird behavior is not necessary, and that exorcisms can be conducted with dignity and authority. The Lord, in His humor, caused the first man, at the first word of authority, to slide out of his chair onto the floor in convulsions—and we were into a dramatic battle!

We do not need to command demons to name themselves, nor is it wise. Whoever said that the devil would tell the truth? Jesus said that he was a liar from the beginning and the father of lies (John 8:44). We know of Christians who have spent all night in exorcism, casting out, by their own subsequent account, more than two hundred demons from one individual. Sometimes that may in fact be the case. We are convinced that, unfortunately, most often what did transpire was that the expectancies and the methods of the exorcists invited the Devil to play with them all night! If we need to know the name of a demon (and it is truly wise and powerful to know a name), then let us ask the Holy Spirit! What have we to do listening to the Devil? Or giving him permission to speak and act through a person? Paula and I command the Devil to be silent. We give him no permission to put on a show through the flesh of the person being exorcised. Did we think the Holy Spirit less powerful or willing or truthful that we should turn to the Devil for revelation?

Christians have derived this faulty practice from that one instance in which Jesus asked, "What is your name?" And the reply was, "Legion" (Mark 5:9). But let us think about that. Can the reader for a moment suspect that the Lord of all the universe did not know the name?! Of course He knew. He did not ask in order to find out, as many Christians exorcists do today, thinking they follow His precedent. Note the use of singular and plural in the text: "Then Jesus asked *him* 'What is your name?' 'My name is *Legion,*' he replied, 'For *we* are many.' " Jesus addressed the man, himself, not the demons. He asked *"him,"* not *"them."* When a psychiatrist enters the room of a mentally ill patient (remember, this was an insane man living among the tombs), sometimes he asks him, "What is your name?" If the person can answer the question correctly, that tells the psychiatrist the patient is, for the moment, in control of himself. Answering sanely strengthens the resolve of the patient. Jesus, by asking, was giving to the patient the opportunity to stand in faith by trying to state his own true name. But it was the demons who answered ". . . *we* are many." Since they spoke through the patient's vocal cords, the Scripture records that *"he"* replied, but the plural "we" informs us it was the demons who spoke through him. Can anyone in his right mind suppose that our Lord Jesus Christ required information from demons in order to have power over them?! Jesus, as Lord of the universe, needed nothing from the Devil! And neither do we! To ask demons to name themselves gives them permission to use patients' vocal cords, thus increasing rather than decreasing their hold.

In many cases, no name is needed. An exorcist simply commands a demon to leave, and he must. Such attitudes as lust, pride, fear, etc., are not demons who have that name. They are aspects of our flesh. It is actually confession of that sinful attitude which brings release. Since the Devil requires a foothold in us, when that attitude is washed away in the blood of Jesus, Satan's hold in that area is broken, and thus his energy or presence is expelled from that area. We need only, by the guidance of the Holy Spirit, lead people to specific, detailed confession. When enough of Satan's lodging places are destroyed, he must leave. That is why, after people have named a number of such attitudes as though they were demons, a person finally feels released. It was basically the power of confession and forgiveness which caused whatever exorcisms may have happened.

Discernment of the presence of a demon is *not* a mandate to exorcise in *that moment.* The Body of Christ has done much harm by zeal without wisdom. If a person is not prepared to renounce his sinful ways, if he is not struggling to live Christ's way, and is willfully choosing unrighteousness, then "it goes and takes along seven other spirits more evil than itself, and they go in and live there; and the last state of that man becomes worse than the first" (Luke 11:26).

In Elijah House, we seek to uncover root causes for the demonization, thereby to demolish the residence of the demon through forgiveness and the cross. We seek to discover whether there is sufficient resolve by which the counselee will discipline himself to try to walk in a new and holy way. We want also to ascertain whether his family and a church body will be there to support him. We want to see indications of repentance and of real hatred for the sins the demon has been perpetrating through the person. Only if such attitudes are present will we choose to exorcise, unless the Holy Spirit, for His own reasons, sovereignly initiates or orders us into the exorcism.

Exorcisms are best done by teams. After the warfare of exorcism, exorcists and their team would be well advised to cleanse themselves by prayer, lest something latch onto them. Paula and I know of several who found themselves inhabited or demonized for quite a long while after becoming involved in exorcisms.

Above all, we plead with the Body not to rush around seeing demons behind every illness and each sinful propensity in people's lives! That is soulish and carnal nonsense. It gives glory to the Devil. It turns eyes from Jesus and celebrates Satan's supposed power. It spreads fear and confusion. It edifies no one. It releases few, especially in any permanent way. Paula and I, in our twenty-five years of Spirit-filled counseling, have most likely done more valid exorcisms than almost any other servants alive and ministering in the Body today! We do not speak from disbelief or unthinking disregard, but from years of learning by experience in our Lord Jesus Christ; ". . . solid food is for the mature, who *because of practice have their senses trained to discern good and evil*" (Heb. 5:14).

Attitudes such as hate and fear may become infested with demonic power, but they are themselves characteristics of our flesh. To try to cast them out is to attempt psychological surgery and to invalidate our Lord's work of transformation whereby He uses those very structures in the heart, crucified and born anew, as power for ministry.

It is, however, not mainly for correction that we write about demons and exorcism. It is for teaching concerning healing. Demonic presences sully and ravage the personal spirits of those they beleaguer. Exorcisms therefore should also contain prayers for cleansing and healing. Affection and much warm human contact should follow exorcism. Newly delivered people ought not to be left alone too soon afterwards. Devils want to return, however wise and timely the exorcism. The protective presence of friends is needed. Wholesome earthy involvements will help, such as eating a good balanced meal, or visiting about nonspiritual matters with family and friends, or working together with others doing simple chores that require some manual labor.

Most importantly, mates need to be quietly held for relatively long periods of time in warm embrace. There is nothing wrong with a newly delivered wife's curling up on her husband's lap and drinking from his presence. His balance and wholeness, his saneness and calmness settle and heal her spirit. Contrariwise, a husband may lie quietly chest to chest with his wife, enjoying her presence and her sweet nurture singing gently into his cells the song of wholesome earthy life.

Freshly delivered people may find it jangling to be plunged immediately into tension-filled situations or family hassles. An exorcism is somewhat like an engine overhaul. We do not want to run such a motor at full power until piston rings have had time to settle and seat themselves. Just so, we need time to accustom ourselves to the new us. Wise counselors will so advise.

Sleep is important. Many people succumb to demonic presences in the first place because they have neglected good sleeping habits. Fatigue and nervous stress serve to weaken immunity not only to physical disease but also to demonic inroads. After exorcism, nothing so invites re-entrance of demons as a return to the same sins, but a close second is lack of sufficient sleep. Relatives and friends should not be reticent in insisting upon rest.

Simple cleanliness heals the person and wards off the return of demons. Soaking in the tub is good for those newly reclaimed from Satan's empire. Being well groomed helps to restore a sense of well-being. Note that the Word of God records that after Jesus exorcised the Gadarene demonic, the people "found the man . . . *clothed* and in his right mind" (Luke 8:35).

Relatives and friends would do well to protect newly exorcised people from the prying of nosey "well-meaning" friends and neighbors who ask questions like, "What's it like to have a demon?" and "How do you know they're all gone?" Sometimes Jesus told people, "Tell no one" (Luke 5:14; 8:56; 9:21); other times, "Return to your house and describe what great things God has done for you" (Luke 8:39a). Exorcised people can profit by the wise counsel of mature Christians whether and when to share, how much and how often.

Some have said that women ought not to attempt to do exorcisms. We have not found that to be either scriptural advice or wise counsel. Women ought to follow the same counsel as any man, to do exorcisms only under proper authority, within the enfolding protection of a team whenever possible, and only when group wisdom says it is time. ". . . make war by wise guidance" (Prov. 20:18b). But we see nothing in Scripture forbidding women to be exorcists. Agnes Sanford was an effective exorcist, and it was Alice Fogg, the rector's wife, who took the lead in exorcising me when I needed it. Many pompous people make pronouncements when God has not told them to speak, and I greatly doubt any man's warranty in the Lord who protests that women are unfit for this ministry. Men more easily wield authority, but nothing prevents the Holy Spirit from expressing copious authority through a woman. I have seen strong men properly daunted when Agnes Sanford, under His annointing beetled her brows and spoke with sternness as His messenger.

Finally, relatives and friends should persist in watching over an exorcised person for several weeks following the exorcism. Relapses are common. Secondary exorcisms are often forthcoming, like aftershocks following upon a major earthquake, as other things may shake loose in the personality.

A blessedly healing conclusion to all exorcisms, for the liturgically minded, is frequent visits to the Lord's table in communion or daily Mass.

> I am the bread of life. Your fathers ate the manna in the wilderness, and they died. This is the bread which comes down out of heaven, so that one may eat of it and not die. I am the living bread that came down out of heaven; if anyone eats of this bread, he shall live forever; and the bread also which I shall give for the life of the world is My flesh. . . . He who eats My flesh and drinks My blood has eternal life, and I will raise him up on the last day. For My flesh is true food, and My blood is true drink. He who eats My flesh and drinks My blood abides in Me, and I in him. As the living Father sent Me, and I live because of the Father; so he who eats Me, he also shall live because of Me. This is the bread which came down out of heaven; not as the fathers ate, and died; he who eats this bread shall live forever (John 6:48-51, 54-58).

Chapter Twelve

Spiritual Adultery and Idolatry

You shall not make for yourself an idol in the form of anything in heaven above or on the earth beneath or in the waters below. You shall not bow down to them or worship them; for I, the Lord your God, am a jealous God, punishing the children for the sin of the fathers to the third and fourth generation of those who hate me, but showing love to thousands who love me and keep my commandments (Deut. 5:8-9 NIV).

How can you say, "I am not defiled; I have not run after the Baals?" See how you behaved in the valley; consider what you have done. You are a swift she-camel running here and there, a wild donkey accustomed to the desert, sniffing the wind in her craving—in her heat who can restrain her? (Jer. 2:23, 24a NIV).

Our purpose in this chapter is to reveal how to heal the results of idolatry. However, since today nobody makes figurines and sets them in niches to worship, we need to see idolatry in a different sense. We cannot state it any better than we did in Chapter Seventeen of *Restoring the Christian Family*. Therefore we begin this chapter by quoting ourselves.

There is no sin which does not involve idolatry. If we steal, we have valued whatever we took more than we valued God. If we commit adultery, we have elevated that woman or that man as more important to us than God. If we choose not to be in church on Sunday, we have made an idol of whatever we wanted more than obedience—pleasure, business, repairing the house, laziness, etc. If we do not tithe, mammon is our god, no matter what we say. We may protest with our lips that we love God, that we are born anew, that we have all manner of wondrous experiences with God, but if we have not put our money where our mouth is, all our belief and experiences testify only to God's grace, not our faith. Apart from works, faith lies dead (James 2:17). Proof is written unequivocally in the history of our giving. "No man can serve two masters; for either he will hate the one and love the other; or else he will hold to the one, and despise the other. Ye cannot serve God and mammon" (Matt. 6:24). We are all inveterate idol-makers. We do it by nature. For example, all we need is an anointed worship service, and the next time we get together we will try to copy what we did last time. We are no longer seeking the Lord himself. We want that experience of power, and the goose bumps. These things have for the moment become our God, the idol we worship.

We often idolize pastors and other spiritual leaders. That is why we hate them so when they fall. They shattered our god.

If we check the many hundreds of little unconscious, unnoticed ways we break God's laws, we will see that even if we have tried, attended church and prayer meetings, and paid our tithes, we are still habitual idol-makers. How about when the wife is angry, so we don't tell her the whole truth, "just to keep the peace." Peace is now the idol we have served which justified lying. God said through St. Paul, "Do not provoke your children to anger" (Eph. 6:4 RSV). When we keep pushing the children away because they interrupt the ball game on TV, we have worshiped TV more than God. When the boss not only fails to compliment, but criticizes, and we blow up, it's a sure tip-off that we serve the idol of self. And so it goes, through every aspect of life. Idolatry is the first and greatest sin, behind all we do.

The most common form of idolatry with which we have to do as counselors is in relation to marriage. The command is "Be subject to one another out of reverence for Christ" (Eph. 5:21 RSV). We have found that that command contains an unrelenting principle: in whatever degree we are not subject to Christ, we cannot be subject to one another! But more to the point, in whatever degree we are not in reverence for Christ, we idolize one another. There is a God-sized hole in us. Nature abhors a vacuum. If we do not fill it with Jesus, we *will* fill it with something—commerce, friends, sports, hobbies, etc. Most often we ask more from our mates than they were intended to give.

Idolatrous requests wound the spirit because the mate feels the weight of demand. People placed in that position *know* they cannot supply what is wanted. No one can fulfill our need for God. Since both the asking and the attempt to respond are unconscious, that fills both partners with anxiety and frustration and puts strain on the marriage.

Many husbands have spoken to us of their wounding and confusion. They say they love their wives. They always desired to be wanted. They can't understand why they cannot simply rejoice and give the love they want to. "I just feel 'checked,' like something's wrong, and I don't know what." The great relief they express when we explain how idolatry blocks tells us how much being put in that position wounds and confuses their spirit. The confusion and inability to express love for their wives had greatly undermined their confidence and their identity as husbands. Their spirits sensed and properly refused idolatry, but their minds had not understood.

When either spouse in childhood has been neglected, rejected or abused so as to evidence insecurity, counselors should look immediately for signs of wounding from idolatry towards their mate. Frequently, husbands whose mothers failed to affirm and give affection not only idolize their relation to their wives, they relate to them as mothers, which wounds even more. Rejected and neglected girls also

345

tend to relate to husbands as fathers. In these instances, teaching alone is healing.

Marital counselors should instruct couples how to recognize when they are being projected wrongly into a parental position or being asked to fill God's shoes. The counsel of transactional analysis is quite correct, to teach them to say "I am not your mother" or "I am not your father." The same can be said in relation to God. "You're asking me to give you what only God can." This kind of counsel is predicated upon instruction and trust that the couple can hear one another and discuss their problems, rather than blow up!

In the meantime, the counselor should be exploring roots of insecurity in each, applying healing, and attempting to evangelize the heart so as to fill that gap with God. Until that interior vacuum is filled, understanding the problem cannot be sufficient. No matter what our mind knows, our spirit searches for fulfillment. Not finding it, it nurses resentments. Unhealed roots send repeated shoots of trouble to the surface. It will not be enough to forgive resentments and bring self-defensive and aggressive practices to death on the cross. Only a full infilling of the love of Father God can take care of that vacuum and heal a wounded child's spirit. "For my father and my mother have forsaken me, But the Lord will take me up" (Ps. 27:10) is true here for healing also. We must invite Father God to fill their hearts and then incubate them in His love, somewhat in and through us as counselors, until they can believe and sense His fullness within their own hearts, apart from us.

The second kind of spiritual fornication commonly observed by counselors is in relation to authority figures. We make gods of pastors, presidents, teachers, political leaders, parents, husbands and wives and our counselors. The tragedy is that we crucify our gods! We make scapegoats of authority figures, projecting our sins and all blame onto whoever is handy. Unconsciously we hate our sin in the other and crucify it. Any pastor worth his salt has suffered from being idolized and consequently persecuted. If he has not, I suggest he most likely was not preaching God's Word!

The man who was most formative in my (John's) schooling was Dr. Ernst Jacob, a rabbi who had fled from persecution in Nazi Germany. At Drury College, Springfield, Missiouri, he taught me European History, Old Testament History, Prophets, and German. I shall never forget how one day, when he had taught us about all the miracles God wrought for Israel in the Exodus and during the forty years in the wilderness, we asked him, "Rabbi, when the Jews had seen God work all those miracles for all those years, and they knew God was real, how come they so quickly turned to worshiping idols? Why did they turn from the God they *knew* was absolutely real, to worship idols they made with their own hands?"

Rabbi Jacob leaned back, grinned a great, wide smile, and said, "Ven Gott ist Gott, Gott ist Gott. Gott insists on being Gott. Gott ist in control. But, ven mann hast ein idol, mann ist Gott. Mann ist in control!"

That lesson burned all the way through my heart and mind, and I thought of the Scripture, "But these enemies of mine, *who did not want me to reign over them . . .*" (Luke 19:27a). The issue is always, "Who is in control?"

Whenever a pastor truly preaches God's Word, that Word is sweet to the taste but bitter as gall in the stomach (Rev. 10:9). It enters the heart and disturbs. Its truth exposes sin and forces decision. People whose lips honor Him but whose hearts are far from Him (Matt. 15:8, Mark 7:6) find themselves idolizing their pastor for the greatness of his ministry, but then so often choosing to persecute him rather than face sin and die on the cross! "He who is estranged seeks pretexts to break out against all sound judgment"! (Prov. 18:1 RSV). Any pretext will do.

Earle Tyson was persecuted because he set up his tent in the backyard for his children to play in—he was building additions without a permit! I was criticized because I went to weed my garden barefoot—disgraceful! I was also criticized because I wore colored socks in the pulpit rather than black—of all things for a pastor to do! The Word forces decisions; we must either change or find something wrong with the messenger—anything—to justify our not being willing to face sin.

There is that in us which hungers for the King of kings and Lord of lords. That is why teenagers who do not truly worship God fasten such devotion upon rock stars. We *must* worship something. Worship is built into us as fundamentally as breathing. We can't live without it. That hunger rushes to locate somewhere, fasten onto something, and express itself. There is a cult whose members worship the memory of Elvis Presley! One young man came to our door for counsel, convinced that Elvis was the reappearance of Christ! And a more recent cult is sure that Michael Jackson is the Messiah!

Look what has happened in the charismatic movement. Every teacher God has raised up, we have idolized! What a dangerous pedestal we have placed these men upon! God, who is rightly jealous because He loves us, had to move to deliver both the teacher and His Church. He warned and remonstrated, but if the teacher did not hear, or if he heard but his constituency did not, God had to bring him down! God raised up the five great teachers, Bob Mumford, Charles Simpson, Derek Prince, Don Basham and Ern Baxter. Who among us did not gratefully sit at their feet! But who heeded the warnings? Shepherding and discipling went off balance and brought them crashing down! They still teach, but their ministry to the whole Body is shattered and gone.

I cut my eyeteeth on the teachings of Ken Hagin and quoted from him in *The Elijah Task*. He and Ken Copeland led into faith teaching, which went off balance (no blame intended to them), and now their ministry to the Body as a whole is ended. God raised up our friend, Father Francis MacNutt, to minister across the world to Roman Catholics and Protestants alike. We were called to speak together in a Camp Farthest Out in Hawaii, he on healing, I as a proph ʻ

I warned all there that whenever anything or anyone is elevated too far, God himself must smash that idolatry. I received a tremendous outcry of angry protest. Within a few months, Francis married Judith and was excommunicated, his books banned in many Catholic places! I grieved for my friend, that none could hear the warning. In the very moment of rejoicing for Francis and Judith in the happiness of their marriage, Paula and I grieved for the loss of his ministry to his own church.

I love and honor all these men. They are still, one and all, great teachers. We especially love Francis. The point is that by God's mercy, one way or another, He has smashed the pedestals on which all of them stood, and graciously saved them for further service in the Kingdom! God will not suffer idolatry to continue.

Nevertheless, healing is needed. Many throw away faith altogether when their idols fall. Disillusionment breaks the heart of many. Confusion and lack of understanding provide fertile ground for seeds of division in the Body. There is no need to argue whether shepherding and discipling was all wrong, or had valid points we all should hear, or whether the faith teachings were right or wrong, or whether Roman priests should be allowed to marry. All that is beside the point. Once we established those men on pedestals, God was forced to do something about it. Had it not been the way history's leaves fell, some other thing— maybe less gracious—surely would have happened. The result is the same in every case. The idol worship is gone, forever smashed. Let the Body draw a breath of thanks and repent, for we did it *to* them.

I have little hope we shall have learned our lesson. We'll do it again. But let every counselor and prophet become a watchman who warns as in Ezekiel 33. There are those on our Elijah House board who announce themselves regularly as faithful watchdogs to keep us humble. Most of the time, however, our clay feet leave such muddy tracks that we bring ourselves down all by ourselves with little need for help from anyone else!

Counselors should look for other than those internationally known instances of idolatry. It happens all around us. Some sure indications are as follows (concerning the way we relate to our church, or pastor, or teacher, or political hero, whomever):

Inordinate defensiveness. "Don't you dare criticize that man!" Scripture tells us to be prepared always to make a defense for our faith (1 Pet. 3:15) and that there is a friend who sticks closer than a brother (Prov. 18:24), but idolatry is indicated when defense, usually with rancor, continually blocks out what should be heard and heeded.

Bias which blinds. True relationship is not naive. It sees both the blessings and sins of friends, and loves anyway. But those in idolatry gloss over faults. Their eyes are full of stars of fancy. They make excuses for faults rather than confront in love.

Persecution complexes. This involves seeing reactions of people to our idols not as possible warnings of error but as persecution for righteousness. Since sometimes persecution is indeed because of righteousness, the distinctive factor is unwillingness to see both possibilities. It *has* to be persecution. That conclusion is seized without waiting for all the facts or for clarification or verification from the Holy Spirit. Error is ruled out, and with it repentance.

Martyrdom. True martyrdom ordinarily is not sought. It happens *to* the saint despite his attempts to live quietly (1 Thess. 4:11). True martyrdom gives glory to God. Somehow those who idolize only sniff the winds of possible martyrdom and trumpet the cause so that the hero receives the glory. "You're making a martyr of him!"

Sexual confusions and attachments. Both women and men are tempted to throw themselves at figures they idolize. How many hundreds of times have we heard of some saint whose ministry was ascending to the heights who came crashing down by falling into adultery?! Sexual trouble is the natural end of idolatry, as surely as water flowing downhill must eventually find a body to rest in. Conversely, true servants seldom find people attaching to them sexually or trying to seduce them. What emanates does not send such signals. Flesh attracts flesh. Spirit attracts spirit. "For the one who sows to his own flesh shall from the flesh reap corruption, but the one who sows to the Spirit shall from the Spirit reap eternal life" (Gal. 6:8).

Twisted teachings. Too much emphasis begins to be placed on a few Scriptures, more and more understood out of context. This is so whether the teacher himself is out of balance, puffed up in his own arrogance, or defiled by the idolatry of others. What started out as truth goes too far, and the weak and immature suffer.

Anger. Somehow, everybody seems to become over-invested in the project and becomes quickly or inordinately angered. Just as fury overtook Nebuchadnezzar (in Dan. 3:19), anger, sometimes followed by violence, is a sure sign of the presence of idolatry.

Each man to his own tent. Armed camps. Division in the Body. Isolation. When idolatry is *not* present, participants can hear the sound advice of Gamaliel to wait and see whether this thing is of God. If not, it will die of its own accord. If we oppose it right away, we may find ourselves opposing God (Acts 5:34-39). But, when idolatry *is* present, there is no waiting. Participants must choose sides, right away.

Satan's work has always been to cut up and divide. Look at the residue from shepherding and discipling and the faith teachings. There are still far too many sitting in pockets of loneliness saying, "We were right after all, and why don't you see it and receive us?" Understand, we do not blame the teachers who began the movements. It was idolatry, far beyond their ken and control, that carried things to their natural end.

Paula and I, and every other teacher in the Body, should pray fervently and regularly that we and our teachings may be delivered from the defilements of idolatry in the Body, and that these movements of which we have spoken may yet be recovered from whatever effects still bedevil and sour what would otherwise produce good and wholesome fruits. Each leader must bear his own load, but the sin has been that of the entire Body. Therefore, *the repentance and the cry for mercy should come from the Body, too.*

Individuals who have been involved at either end of idolatry, as leaders or as those who have idolized them, need to find healing in the church or in a counselor's office. Law has been transgressed. Iniquity *will* be visited with judgment. The Lord will visit "the iniquity of the fathers on the children, and on the third and the fourth generations of those who hate Me" (Deut. 5:9). How often we have seen the children and grandchildren of spiritual leaders suffer all manner of tragedies! As counselors used to hearing stories of tragedy, even we are amazed how often, when investigating family histories (as discussed in Chapter Thirteen, "Generational Sin"), we discover behind a singularly tragic family record an ancestor who was a pastor or spiritual leader of some sort. It seems their descendants ought to be most blessed, and indeed we are sure most often they are. "A good man leaves an inheritance to his children's children . . ." (Prov. 13:22a). Without statistics, could we guess that ninety percent of the time such descendants are most blessed? But there is a risk in serving God. Servants can fall into snares and traps. "Let not many of you become teachers, my brethren, knowing that *as such we shall incur a stricter judgment"* (James 3:1). In Deuteronomy 5:9 we learn that it is primarily the sin of idolatry which causes judgment to be visited upon the descendants of the sinner, and idolatry is the most common error to which teachers and leaders fall prey!

When counselors discover idolatry, they should pray as described in Chapter Thirteen, to stop the descent of harm to *future* generations, by the blood and cross of Jesus. It would be well to check the history of the ancestry as well, to determine whether patterns of idolatry have descended through *past* generations. Those who may think it harsh of God to visit the iniquity of parents through several generations would do well to read no further until having read Chapters Eight, Nine, and Ten of *The Elijah Task* and Chapters Four, Five, Six and Fourteen of *The Transformation of the Inner Man*. God is neither unjust nor unkind, as those chapters explain.

The individual himself should be led through prayers of repentance and forgiveness. If he is one who has idolized a leader, it may be wise to counsel him to go to that leader and confess, asking forgiveness, if he had close enough contact to warrant such an approach. If he is the leader who in one way or another sought others to put himself on a pedestal, or even if it only happened to him, the counselor should pronounce forgiveness for the sin of playing God. The counselor should lead him through the Abraham-Isaac prayer, in which his ministry is treated as his Isaac, and left as dead in Christ at the altar. God will restore his ministry, but no longer as his to be possessed and defended. It will belong to God alone.

It is "grass-eating time." When Nebuchadnezzar failed to heed the warnings of the Holy Spirit through his dreams and through Daniel's interpretations (see Dan. 1-4 and Chapter Seventeen, "Nebuchadnezzar's Image," in *Restoring the Christian Family*), the watchers proclaimed that he would be driven from his kingdom to eat grass until his mind should some day (after seven periods, 4:32) be restored to him (4:34). If repentance and self-humbling do not soon enough allow the grace of God, the servant must learn the hard way. He goes off balance. He makes a fool of himself. He may even lose his sanity in megalomania. He must eat grass for a while. The simple meaning of this in our modern vernacular is that he is "grounded." God will allow him no more flights of fancy and imagination, no more mystical heights. God humbles, even humiliates His servant again and again until even onlookers want to cry out, "Enough is enough!" But enough isn't enough until the servant is so crushed he never again wants the taste of being idolized, nor of idolizing another. It must be written in indelible ink on his heart and in his mind.

The counselor's part in all this is to be a friend. Counselors must not try to ameliorate the situation. We must only stand by. Our compassion and understanding will help the afflicted one comprehend what and why he is suffering, but no more than that. We must not blunt the sword of God's judgment. There will come a time when the servant ceases to cry Job's cry, and like him cries out, ". . . I have declared that which I did not understand, Things too wonderful for me, which I did not know. I have heard of Thee by the hearing of the ear; But now my eye sees Thee; therefore I retract, And I repent in dust and ashes" (Job 42:3, 5, 6). Until that time, what the one in God's grinding machine needs is a friend who has faith in God to know he will come all the way through, when it seems to him he'll never make it. Love *"believes* all things" (1 Cor. 13:7b); love believes for us when we can't anymore.

There may be others involved. A man may have dragged his family, against their better judgment, into following some would-be Christ. ". . . many false prophets will arise, and will mislead many" (Matt. 24:11). "For false Christs and false prophets will arise and will show great signs and wonders, so as to mislead, if possible, even the elect" (Matt. 24:24). ". . . do not go after them" (Luke 21:8). That form of spiritual adultery requires several prayers. One, that all the words and thoughts implanted during that sojourn be brought to nothing by the fire of the Holy Spirit, that every false teaching be rooted out, leaving only the deposit of wisdom and wariness. Two, that the servant's family be likewise delivered and cleansed. Three, that he be helped to eat humble pie by talking it out with whatever participating family members will sit down with him. Four, that forgiveness and reconciliation be voiced and acted out in and beyond the family. Five, that somehow the counselor work to restore respect of the person in the family. If the man is a husband and father, then headship and trust in his leadership need to be restored. This latter may require teaching the rest of the family how what we go through can make us wiser and prepare us rather than disqualify us to lead.

Good-natured joshing and teasing is a grand re-entry tool. Not ridicule, which demeans, but rather banter which asserts and teases in an attitude of respect. Those who have been "on a trip" into idolatry have taken themselves too seriously. They need to be helped to laugh heartily at their mistakes.

Experiences in the out-of-doors should be prescribed for those who have been delivered from idolatry. It was not by accident that the prescription for Nebuchadnezzar's healing was that he should eat grass! We need to soak up good old earth for a while. Earth is not the world. Earth has been cleansed by the blood of the Lamb (Acts 11:9). The great poet, Wordsworth, used to become so caught up in mysticality that he would grab hold of a tree until balance returned. Lots of work in the yard and garden are a grand tonic for the self-important.

The purpose of this chapter is also to teach how to heal spiritual adultery. We have spoken so far of the many ways we can idolize and worship what we ought not to. But there are many ways to commit spiritual adultery without idolizing. Whenever we give to someone else what belongs only to our mate, that is *spiritual* adultery. Physical adultery occurs when we proceed beyond that to give our *body* to another. The Lord spoke of spiritual adultery when He said,

> You have heard that it was said, "You shall not commit adultery"; but I say to you, that every one who looks on a woman to lust for her has committed adultery with her already in his heart" (Matt. 5:27, 28).

Many Christians circumspectly keep their hearts from thinking lustfully and so congratulate themselves that they have never been involved in spiritual adultery. But the ways of our heart are more elusive than that.

By the grace of God, I have never been to bed with anyone other than my wife. And I have been careful never to allow myself to dwell on sexual thoughts concerning any other woman. I have been well aware of the Scripture which says,

"Do not desire her beauty *in your heart"* (Prov. 6:25) and of the wise old proverb which says, "Look not long upon beauty belonging to another." But that did not keep me from spiritual adultery.

In the early years of our marriage, Paula and I had not yet crossed the bridges of communication by the spans of wisdom and the cross. We were often at odds. Paula did not know how to reach past my bristles to comfort me, nor did I know even what I wanted, which was really only her whole being to hold and nurture mine as God intended.

That left a vacuum. I was vulnerable. I gravitated to whatever men or women in less-threatening secondary relationships could comfort, affirm or flatter me. I could open up and share easily with them what should have been discussed only, or at least first, with Paula. Many times Paula was grievously wounded when at a social function she would overhear me easily telling someone else something I had not yet shared with her. That was spiritual adultery. I had given that communion of heart, that deep fellowship which belongs between a man and his wife, to someone else.

When Paula remonstrated with me, I would try to remember, attempting to decipher by logic what was hers alone and what could be shared with others. It was sweaty work, and unsuccessful, because the problem was in my heart. My heart had not yet learned to find its only source of manhood in relation to Paula. I was still set to find self-fulfillment and self-definition elsewhere. That is spiritual adultery at root level, looking for somewhere to happen. Naturally, it happened again and again.

When Paula would fuss and storm about it, my mind easily saw—at that moment—that she was right. But since my heart was still not right, my mind would lose it again and again. Remorse did not become repentance. But her fuming convinced my frightened heart not to open to her, the very one whom God had designed for its refreshment! That increased the vulnerability, for nature abhors a vacuum.

Even while becoming aware of the problem and determining to be faithful, I became worse. Men, but especially women who seemed to be wise and understanding, gentle and comforting, became so tonic to my lonely soul that I unconsciously sought more and more excuses to spend time with them. I was not aware that undealt-with areas in my heart dulled and warped my judgment so that I often accepted as wise counsel and comfort only that which did not challenge or threaten as Paula's counsel seemed to do. I was also naive concerning the hidden needs and motives of others and unprepared to recognize the difference between clean affirmation and manipulative ego building. Some, equally lonely and spiritually adulterous, latched on to me in return. At last, though I never ever hugged another woman wrongly, or kissed anyone, or even let myself think a sexual thought, Paula cried out, "We aren't even alone in bed anymore!" She could feel the presence of those other women's spirits who had latched onto me.

Fortunately, the Lord's grace had built me so morally, mainly through the strong morality of my ancestry, that the Lord could catch me before I went any farther. At last He revealed to my *heart* what Paula was talking about and I could come to repentance rather than to mere remorse. Together, we prayed through everything we could think of, among them unfulfilled needs for mothering, desires to turn women on for ego's sake, fear of true vulnerability which left me vulnerable at lesser levels, unconscious hatred of women which wanted to draw women to me and then punish them by turning them away unfulfilled, ways of taking vengeance on Paula by giving what was hers to someone else, etc. ad nauseam. One large blockage which had to come to the cross was that I had, because of the tension in my childhood, learned to *dissociate* comfort, ease, refreshment and gentle nurture from anything having to do with "home." I had to bring many judgments and fears to death in order to discover the truth which Paula had (not always graciously in her frustration) tried to communicate, "Someday you will learn that I'm the best friend you have, and that your children can be refreshment, not always just a heavy responsibility!"

Most importantly, Paula and I learned not to identify one another as antagonists. We *joined together* to fight hand-in-hand against the blockages in each other's flesh which kept us apart. Even so, long after beautiful bridges had been built and we had crossed many times to find glorious picnics in each other's parks, I still had to fight tendencies to flee. I found I desperately feared total vulnerability. I could even warp Scripture to justify my flights, "Do not give your strength to women . . ." (Prov. 31:3). I told myself I could be swallowed up, or become a "woman's man," or lose my headship—anything would do to justify fleeing from vulnerability and commitment. I found it necessary to pray again and again, especially when the sweetness of marital sex had threatened to open all my gates, "Oh, Lord, I *choose* to be vulnerable. Open me to Paula. Don't let me flee out!" I could tell when my heart was beginning to close. God gave me a barometer—my tongue. When it wanted not to perform with Paula and found itself easily waggling with other people, I knew I had to battle again with my nature!

The Lord has won the battle with us. We may slip occasionally, but He has us, and we are "locked on target." Our oneness is now what validates our message to many. But our story is not unique. We have counseled more thousands like us in the matter of spiritual adultery than concerning any other problem in human nature.

Though women also have ways of fleeing from full partnership, we find that men much more often than women resist true union. Most likely the greatest root derives from men having fought off, as boys, mother's tentacles of control. Few mothers have known how to give their boys nurture without smothering. We have learned early on not to tell women our secrets: they have elephantine memories and are determined to use them on us! Many women unconsciously castrate their husbands and sons.

Little sisters find power over stronger brothers by tattling. Countless hurtful ways may have to be tracked down to set a man free to relate to his wife. Deeper than all these is the racial memory of every man all the way back to Adam. It is no joke that we remember what Eve got Adam into! The cross of Christ must find the reasons for the problems in all our relationships before we are fully free.

God said to Eve, ". . . your desire shall be for your husband" (Gen. 3:16c). Women tend to press in, seeking to find their place with their man. At the deepest racial level, sin has forfeited woman's place as the full and equal partner of her husband. In Christ, woman's place is restored, but that, like other things, must also be worked out. Therefore, something in her deep mind remembers and presses to recover that position. That, so long as flesh governs it, comes across as demand to husbands, from which they flee. Osage Indians used to say, "When you see a white man coming to you with a gleam in his eye to help you, run like the wind the other way!" So do men from women, like Li'l Abner from Daisy Mae on Sadie Hawkins' Day!

Though sometimes women find shelter and strength in some other man and so commit spiritual adultery, the most common thing we deal with in Christian counseling is that kind of confusion which happens when wives unconsciously transfer to the Lord what belongs only to the husband. The fact that Christ is the groom to all the Church (the bride) becomes a temptation rather than a blessing when a woman's heart is not right. Her husband senses the adultery and may react violently. How can he compete against such a rival? In retaliation some men have left the church in anger. We have encountered a number of women so vulnerable by not having "made it" with their husbands that seducing spirits have actually convinced them that the Lord is so much their husband they are entitled to enter into sexual union with Him. Spirits have so seduced some women that they have experienced the feelings of intercourse, including orgasm. That kind of spirit is called an "incubus." (The same kind of seduction can happen with men, in which the spirit is called a "succubus.")

Women may find in prayer groups the security they should have found in their husband's headship. Leaders who rightly attempt to be father figures for all in their group may find confusing kinds of relationships and feelings developing in the group, as women unconsciously —or consciously and sinfully—attach themselves. Because of so many unhealed wounds in so many hearts in so many prayer groups, spiritual adultery is perhaps the most common sin in the charismatic movement.

Many fathers have horribly wounded not only their daughters or stepdaughters but themselves by falling into incestuous molestation. The most common cause is spiritual adultery. They really loved and wanted their own wife. But the relationship faltered, bridges fell and isolation took over. Neither partner was aware of the depth or power of loneliness. A daughter often resembles the way her mother looked at an earlier age. Her virgin beauty triggers into his memory and desire for his own younger wife. Before he knows it, his needs to defile a woman because inner angers at both mother and wife have combined with present frustrations and sexual appetite to plunge him into activities he never thought himself capable of.

Affairs usually do not commence as affairs, at least among Christians who intend to walk in His way. It is unconscious spiritual adultery which hooks both participants. When true union fails, particularly in the areas of communication and heartfelt sharing, husbands and wives are left open to another who may *seem* to be able to fill that gap. Many who have fallen to physical adultery have said to us in counseling, "I don't understand it. I had good sex at home. My wife is great sexually—this other woman can't even hold a candle to her—so what am I doing wanting her? I don't get it!" Or women have ranted and raved and cried out, "He had all he wanted! Whatever can he see in her?!" However, it was not sex which was wanted.

It was that union of hearts and spirits of which sex is only the climax. Because sex is the climax, other kinds of adulterous union naturally gravitate there.

There are no heroes in this kind of warfare. There are only holy cowards. Counselees must be taught to avoid encounters once entered. They cannot remain in relationships which have become spiritually adulterous and remain pure and safe. Sooner or later they will plunge over the lover's leap unless grace intervenes to heal in full each heart and each marriage.

Sometimes continuing relationships cannot be avoided. A brother-in-law or sister-in-law is likely to remain in the family. We may not be able to withdraw graciously from a prayer group and join another. Besides, if the heart's condition is not healed at root level, we will find the same problem with someone in the next group, and sooner or later we are going to run out of groups! Certainly we don't want to be transferring from church to church, or firing secretaries regularly, or dropping out of club after club.

The rule is that when relationships have been so deeply engaged that tracks of familiarity have been built and danger of further fulfillment lurks, whatever price must be paid must be paid, even if we have to indeed change churches or jobs or towns altogether. But if dabblings have been caught in time, we can remain where we are while counsel discovers and heals roots. The second rule is, however, that participants in spiritual adultery, at whatever stage, must not be allowed to be the ones to decide how safe or not safe they are. That decision must be entrusted to the wisdom of friends and counselors. Fools think that they are still safe, and that they can stop any time they want to. Discerning friends are protection from folly.

Spiritual adultery requires healing on two levels. The presence of tendencies to spiritual adultery ought to be taken as a sure indication to counselors that root troubles exist in relation to mothers and fathers. Deep inner healing should be engaged, particularly in search of areas such as lack of fulfillment, deprivation of affection, criticalness and wounding, inability of parents to appreciate and foster talents, and most specifically in relation to possible hearts of stone and inner vows not to be vulnerable. Once the inner one is healed of resentments, that vacuum must be filled with love. Then the counselor can deal with present frustrations and blockages and instruct the couple in the art of true sharing and meeting.

One thing about spiritual adultery is more insidious than most other sins: it may not seem like sin at all. It appears to be good to be able to enter into seemingly deep relationships with people, especially if we are strongly moral people; we know we will never let things get out of hand. The fellowship appears to be tonic to our soul. The esteem of others inflates our ego. It may nag at the back of the mind as a curiosity, or even be a painful awareness, that we can share so easily with someone else but not with our own mate. But if we have some training in psychology or sociology we can easily chalk that off to the common knowledge that one can almost always be nicer to secondary people than to primary. It may be difficult to hate it enough to stop. Our advice: look at it from another angle. Stop justifying it out there. Start seeing it as harm to your mate. Put yourself in your mate's shoes and feel the loneliness, the desolation and betrayal. Learn to hate it for what it does to loved ones rather than measuring it by your own feelings.

Perhaps we should not leave the subject without mentioning that spiritual adultery is not confined to marital relationships. When we wander from pastor to pastor and church to church, that is spiritual adultery. If Paula and I serve under the anointing of an inviting pastor to teach, and leave, that's fine. But if we pull his people after us, that's adultery. If in a church we counsel people the pastor appoints, that is good. If we let too many find help from us who should be obtaining it from their own group or from his counsel, that becomes adulterous. We could list a thousand ways, all assumable under the simple definition that whenever we drink from some other cistern than God has appointed, we engage in adultery.

Occasional listening to another teacher is not adultery (lest we lock ourselves into cultish rigidity through the above definition). "One sows, and another reaps" (John 4:37). No one husband, wife, pastor, teacher, or friend can be *all* to anyone. Trying to be everything to another can itself become adulterous. The mark of distinction is in the heart. If our heart is attached where it belongs, whatever other source of refreshment becomes ours will only heighten our basic attachment. But if we begin to disrespect where we belong and hunger for something else and more, then we are in danger, and any other source will become an adultery. We need to be watchdogs of our hearts (Prov. 4:23). So long as we seek first and fully our own mate and church and friends, we are on track. But when hungers and lusts arise, we must take these as signals and flee to our own mate and whatever friend or counselor can help us to discover what is the matter.

We can also be adulterous toward things. Many wives have had good cause to hate their husband's job, or the car, because he caresses it and not her. T.V., *football!*, golf, chores, hobbies—anything can become the object of our adultery. Women are not so likely to be adulterous in those areas, but how many mothers have given to their children what belonged to their husbands and then justified it because he "left them" first? We fall into adultery toward things for the same reasons as with people, and healing is accomplished in the same way. Adultery with things, however, may be more insidious since it is generally less recognizable as such, and ways to deal with it are more difficult to live through. A man cannot quit his job, and a woman may feel as though her husband is asking her to worship him more than God when he fusses about her giving so much attention to the church rather than to him. Nevertheless, the price must be paid. Half of the game is won when we truly see it, the other half when we determine to pray it all the way through .

Spiritual adultery and idolatry are similar. There is only one difference. In idolatry we put someone or something in

God's place and worship it. In adultery we put God or some other person or thing in our mate's place and love it. Spiritual adultery and idolatry merge when we also idolize the person or thing we present ourselves to. It usually is not long before adultery also becomes idolatry. In one sense it is idolatry at inception, for whatever is more important than what God has given us is already our idol. Idolatry is unavoidable; we idolize because that is the basic sin of our nature.

Behind every other idolatry is one worse than all. It lies at the core of all of us. It is the kingdom of self, where self rules all our hidden motives. The throne may be given to Jesus, but self still fancies itself the power behind His throne.

At the core of us is something so evil it cannot be healed, only slain. There is a spirit which is us, determined to be like God. There is a ruling center so devious as to allow us to role-play all the actions of surrender to God, or service and love to others, without ever allowing itself to be detected, much less brought to death. Counseling, and our progess in the Lord, can be described as a gradual peeling of an onion, skin by skin, not to uncover the sweet heart but to find rottenness, roaring defiance, within, unbowed and unsurrendered.

Countless times Paula and I have watched the "pilgrim's progress" of a brother as he became what seemed to him saintlier and saintlier. We knew, as we observed, that there would come a time, when he was ready, that Christ would uncover the last shrouds of deceit to discover sheer sin, untouched by goodness! There is great risk at that time. Even the Lord cannot force us to choose rightly. The way of life and death lies starkly before us at that moment. A choice must be made. It is predicated on bare and simple *trust.* At that moment the sinner must be willing to say, "Yes, Lord, I *will* see it. I *will* own it. I *am* totally depraved and helpless." It does little good to confess total depravity theologically before that moment. We have seen many fundamentally sound brothers who have come to that moment of full experiential acknowledgment, and have fled from it in sheer terror! It is amazing how, after years of being in Christ, we still want to hang on to some tiniest shred of righteousness or some merest inch of control, as though our salvation depended on that!

The brother pastor of whom we spoke in the chapter on defilement (Chapter Eight) was a member, with his wife, Paula and me, and an elder and his wife in a small support group. One day we were all sitting in the warm sunlight on the elder's balcony. The Lord had been working in the pastor's heart for weeks, revealing, step by step, further and further interior caverns filled with filth and webs of deceit. Now, our gentle Lord was opening more to this pastor He loved. The brother's words still ring in my ears. "I don't believe I'm going to like what I see when I get in here." Sure enough, it was too much for him. He fled out— and shortly thereafter the defilement of delusion caught him. He has never returned to full and joyous faith.

On the other hand, we have seen many come to that point, and laughingly enter rest. "Well, what do you know. I don't have anything to defend anymore. I'm sin, and I'm loved anyway. Jesus has me. His righteousness will be mine. I don't have any. Hallelujah!" St. Paul came to that point and chose the righteousness of Jesus. "For I *know* that *nothing good* dwells in me, that is, in my flesh" (Rom. 7:18). For "He is the source of your life in Christ Jesus, whom God made our wisdom, *our righteousness* and sanctification and redemption" (1 Cor. 1:30 RSV). At the depths of all of us is a spirit which masks its basic idolatry all our life until that moment of revelation in Jesus. *We want to be God! We are jealous of Jesus who was elevated to be Lord of all. We are full of striving, therefore, to establish the kingdom of self, none more so than those who have learned the secret of service to others. How better to play God?* The sin of self-idolatry causes all our works for the Lord to be shot through with self-aggrandizement and self-glorification no matter how many times we say we will give Him all the glory. The truth is, we have to say we will give Him the glory precisely because we are inclined not to. That self-idolizing means that while we smile and rejoice in our brother's success, inwardly we grind our teeth in jealousy and surreptitiously "rejoice in unrighteousness" (1 Cor. 13:6) when our brother stumbles. We are compelled to put everyone else down and elevate self without ever realizing we do it!

We are all shrikes at heart, for self-vaunting is the ruling attitude in every person's hidden heart. The moment we see our basic sin of idolatry and how it is the spider at the center of all our webs of deceit, we enter rest—if we choose to let go and let Jesus.

But not all choose rightly. "And this is the judgment, that the light is come into the world, and men loved the darkness rather than the light; for their deeds were evil" (John 3:19). What deeds? Listen to it the other way around. " 'What shall we do, that we may work the works [deeds] of God?' Jesus answered and said to them, *This is the work of God, that you believe in Him* whom He has sent' " (John 6:28, 29). *The evil deed at the core is unbelief, distrust that Jesus actually is the Risen and Present Lord who can and will hold my life if I let go of it!* How many times we have counseled brothers who lived in and for the Lord in the church, who celebrated the Risen Lord every Sunday, who at this crucial depth did not know and could not believe that He is the Risen Lord! The evil deed is to walk in oneself, to hang onto the center of control, to walk in one's flesh by unbelief, which is idolatry, the worship of self.

The choice is upon us. "No one can serve two masters; for either he will hate the one and love the other, or he will hold to one and despise the other. You cannot serve God and mammon" (Matt. 6:24). Mammon is the god of this world's wealth, which is the meaning of this word in the context of Matthew 6. But that verse may as accurately be applied to pose the question, "Who is master of our spirit, self or Jesus Christ?" I know by our years of counseling that most who read this chapter will nod their heads knowingly, thinking they have been through this death and rebirth. But few have. There are many levels—practice runs, as it were—before the final revelation and death. It must be lived, all the way through.

One lady who counseled with me over fifteen years ago has again been in with one of our Elijah House staff. Having been through the process a few years ago himself, he knew the path. He watched as week by week she came closer and closer. She made a covenant with him. "This time I will not flee out!" At last there came a day when the presence of the Lord came upon her and she broke through in a moment of full revelation to exclaim, "Oh, Fletch, I see it! I have been like a black widow spider sucking the righteousness out of everyone around me—my husband, my children, everyone!" Fletch leaned forward and gently said, "Dolores [the name is changed], at last you've become real!" She had indeed been a full-fledged shrike (see Chapter Nine); her diagnosis was true. God had shown her the core of self which ruled all her doing.

Fletch left the counseling session rejoicing in the Lord. "At last she has seen herself and faced her sin. She's come home, Lord. Thank you, Lord." He expected to see her at the next session at rest and radiant. But the kingdom of self was not that easily dethroned. She lit all over him with vituperation, and accused him of calling her a black widow spider! She was there to tell him she would have no more of that! It mattered not at all that Betty (who was working those days with Fletch as a team counselor) pointed out to her, "Dolores, Fletch didn't say that to you. You said it to him!" She could not hear. The heart's doors were closed. She *had* to have *some* righteousness. When her time came, she simply could not believe the grace of God. She has fled now to another counselor who will speak to her the easy things that her kingdom of self wants to hear.

We write for warning, friends, "Humble yourselves, therefore, under the mighty hand of God, that He may exalt you at the proper time" (1 Pet. 5:6). Again, I say, *humble yourselves.* Don't flee out. Be determined to face it all the way through. You have nothing to lose but your wickedness. This is the core, the deepest thing, the center of all that keeps us from the fullness of the Kingdom of God—self! Idol worship! Our spirit on God's throne in us—years and years after our conversion experience! Let us press on for the prize of the upward call of God in Christ Jesus (Phil. 3:14).

Since we cannot die that death in reality until He brings us to it, ". . . choose you *this day* whom ye will serve; . . . but as for me and my house, we will serve the Lord" (Josh. 24:15 KJV).

SECTION IV
Things Which Impinge Upon
and
Wound Our Spirit From Outside

Chapter Thirteen

Generational Sin

> You shall not worship them or serve them; for I, the
> Lord your God, am a jealous God, visiting the iniquity
> of the fathers on the children, and on the third and the
> fourth generations of those who hate Me, but showing
> lovingkindness to thousands, to those who love Me and
> keep My commandments (Deut. 5:9, 10).

Sometimes counselors can exhaust every track of
personal sin in a counselee, only to find great trouble still
besetting the person's life and family. It does not seem
possible that the tragedies which continue could have had
their origin in personal sin yet undiscovered. The answer is
this: sometimes troubles originate from causes outside a
person's own guilt or sin nature. Sin and its effects may
descend through family lines. We call that "generational
sin."

Generational sin and its effects come to us in three ways.
First, we may inherit our propensities to sin through our
genes. Far more descends through our physical inheritance
than we may suspect. One Italian counselee informed me
that her doctor advised her never to allow her daughter to

date another Italian because through her bloodline ran a tendency to a particularly tenacious variety of depression. Black people have long suffered from sickle-cell anemia. Physicians routinely question diabetic patients concerning history of diabetic or blood disorders in their families. Heart diseases, back disorders, tendencies to lung conditions, allergies, etc., are known to descend as physical weaknesses or tendencies. Job 17:5 says, "He who informs against friends for a share of the spoil, The eyes of his children also shall languish." We need to be careful not to assume that *every* person who wears glasses had some ancestor who told lies against friends for false gain! But this Scripture does give us a clear instance of descent of a particular physical condition as a direct result of the sin of an ancestor; ergo, *some* people who have eye trouble *may* have had ancestors who were dishonest. These things are clues for counselors who seek to lay the axe to the root.

Not only do physical conditions descend; personality and behavioral tendencies do so as well. As a child, I (John) was such an absentminded dreamer that when my folks would send me upstairs to procure something, I not only often forgot what I was to get, I forgot I had been sent to get it! Pretty soon they would have to send someone else after it—and me. By the time I was eighteen I had largely outgrown that. But our son Mark followed exactly in my pattern. He would fall into a daydream on the way to school, kicking cans and leaves along the berm. At noon the school office would call to ask, "Where is Mark today? Is he sick?" Paula would find him somewhere halfway to school, totally oblivious to reality. In the morning one of us might walk by Mark's door and happen to observe him pulling on a sock. Half an hour later, there he would be—in exactly the same pose—catatonic, lost in a dream world! He had never seen my example. We had not discussed it. Where did it come from? Genes, of course.

About age twelve, I had a penchant for brushing my teeth. After every meal, or any snack between meals, I would rush to the bathroom to brush my teeth. The entire family would be sitting in the car, motor running, and someone would say, "Where's Jackie (my nickname)?" And the exasperated reply invariably was, "In the bathroom brushing his teeth!" Long before my marriage at twenty-one, that habit was totally forgotten and never mentioned. Precisely at twelve, Mark not only took up the exact same habit, he carried toothpaste and his toothbrush in his pocket, in case he ate something somewhere!

Johnny caught Paula's stubbornness, Ami my mystic nature. What family has not marveled at the way peculiar characteristics have traveled seemingly by no other possible route than through the genes?

Brothers and sisters separated at birth and raised in different families in altogether different cultures have discovered, when reunited, similar likes, dislikes, talents, weaknesses, mannerisms and habits which could have come from no other source than physical inheritance.

There is a mystery connected with the loins which far surpasses our understanding. "And, so to speak, through Abraham even Levi, who received tithes, paid tithes, for *he was still in the loins of his father* when Melchizedek met him" (Heb. 7:9, 10). It may be startling enough to realize that the Holy Spirit through Paul is indicating that Levi *actively* participated through Abraham, i.e., Levi "paid tithes." It is more startling that the Holy Spirit says that Levi was *"in* the loins of his father." But it boggles the mind when we realize that Levi's father was not Abraham but Jacob. Jacob's father was Isaac. Isaac's father was Abraham. Therefore, St. Paul was poetically using the word "father" while actually saying that Levi actively participated in paying tithes while *in* the loins of his *great grandfather!* Who can understand such a mystery?

Let me share from my family history. I was raised in Missouri and Kansas, where there was a great deal of racial prejudice. "Nigger jokes" were standard fare at most gatherings. Blacks served as housemaids and janitors—and nowhere else! Being a normal kid, I wanted to be like everyone else, and, being as sinful as any other, I tried to hold the same prejudices. But I couldn't. For some unknown reason I found I loved black people. To me they were unaccountably beautiful, and I liked to be around them. I still do. I couldn't understand why it hurt me so deeply when people told "nigger jokes."

While Paula and I were working our way through seminary in Chicago, I drove a taxi at night and went to school during the day. Just prior to my starting on this job, some white drivers had been held up in black neighborhoods and one had lost his life. The air was full of fear. The law required that a cabbie take a fare wherever the passenger desired; whenever a driver was requested to take a passenger into one of the black sections, he would lock his doors, roll up his windows and deadhead (i.e., travel without a passenger) out of there, sometimes not even stopping for stop signs. That meant by the law of supply and demand that much business was available in black neighborhoods. Consequently, I drove there most of the time. Drivers all around me told stories of being harrassed by black customers. That was never my experience! We visited and chatted merrily. Other hackies told of being "stiffed" constantly (that means not to be given a tip— cabbies depend on tips for their livelihood). Black people tipped me as generously as anyone else.

Fellow drivers in my garage were held up. One brother was taken into the sticks (far out in the suburbs, away from any cab stand), whereupon a gun was placed against his neck, followed by a harsh, "Gimme your dough! Nice shirt, buddy. Hand it over. Nice pants—" My buddy wound up standing barefoot in his shorts in sub-zero weather at 2:00 A.M. watching the thief drive off with his cab!

In those days I was a foolhardy, adventurous nut who wanted to be held up just once, for the experience of it! I couldn't even accomplish that! My black passengers were thoughtful and courteous and protective of me. One had a fresh bullet hole through his shoulder next to the clavicle, but all he wanted was a doctor, quick! One night police pulled me over and hustled my burly black passenger against the cab and frisked him, finding a big black pistol! But he turned out to be a night watchman on his way to work.

I seemed to lead a charmed life. I never was hassled by anybody. I knew next to nothing about faith in those days, but enough to know that God was protecting me through my black passengers. We had a grand time together. I couldn't understand what made me so different from all my buddies in the garage.

After being born anew and filled with the Holy Spirit, I was drawn particularly to minister to black people. Rev. Ev Carter-Spencer became a spiritual daughter to Paula and me.

Then my father came to live with us. He had so hated his tenure as a Marine in the First World War that he would never talk about his war experiences. But one night he opened up and began to share. As an eighteen-year-old immature lad off the streets of Joplin, he had been placed as a guard over hardened criminals on their way to the Front for their last chance to serve honorably. Upon arrival in France, his captain ordered the entire company to step forward as he called their names. Dad's name was the only one not called. Apparently his guard duty had set him apart and caused the roll call officers to forget him. He inquired of the captain, who responded, "I have no orders for you, son. Just wait here until orders come." Whereupon the captain marched the company away and left dad standing alone and frightened on the docks in a foreign country at war!

Dad looked around and found two companies serving as stevedores. One was a white company made up of men who were mostly from the streets of New York. Many had been gang toughs and still tended to get into knife fights with little provocation. The other was a black company, who chanted as they worked. Those black men took him in, fed him, gave him a place to sleep and protected him until the roll officer remembered him and sent him off to the Front.

As my father told the story, my spirit was leaping! I knew why I had always felt gratitude in my heart for black people and why I had loved to listen to black people sing! Here is the mystery: Was I, like Levi, *in* the loins of my father? Was there some way in which I, too, participated? I have no answers. Only what I feel in my heart. Could my spirit have known that had it not been for black people, I might not be here?! Could their protecting my father have built something within me so that I unconsciously *expected* to be protected among black people? Surely more descends than we know, and mysteries abound.

I also was raised in a strongly Protestant region, in which much anti-Roman Catholic sentiment prevailed. Catholics were going to take over the world! Catholic churches had guns in their basements and the Pope would persecute Protestants wherever he could get the power! Never mind that historically my own denomination (Congregational) did not allow anyone not a member of the Congregational Church to vote in Massachusetts until after 1834, while Maryland (named for Mary), a Roman Catholic state, gave freedom of religion and power to vote to all! Prejudice says, "My mind is made up; don't confuse me with facts." I am as sinful as anyone and wanted to share in anti-Roman Catholic stories. But again, I couldn't. I hated to hear stories of hate and prejudice. I found great respect for the Roman Catholic Church welling up in me, and wondered, "Why?"

After the baptism of the Holy Spirit, I found myself ministering often among Roman Catholics and loving it. In my youth I had attended only one Mass, on a Christmas Eve. The sanctuary was so crowded that I had to stand in the narthex, peering down a long nave at a man mumbling something unintelligible in Latin. The man behind me was so drunk, I was high on the fumes! Wonder of wonders, whenever I subsequently attended a Catholic Mass, my spirit soared in worship and sang within itself, "I'm home. I'm home. I love it." That totally blew my mind. I could not understand why I felt so much sense of belonging. I still love a Catholic charismatic Mass far above all other forms of worship. Why?! This Protestant never expected anything like that!

Then the elders of the church I was serving said, "John, you are getting too tired. Don't go on any more teaching-healing missions unless you take a team along to protect and support you." I was to go to Tiffin, Ohio, to a Christian camp, but couldn't find anyone free to go. At last, only our daughter Ami and one Catholic laywoman could go. This was to be that lady's first occasion to act in a ministering capacity in a Protestant gathering, for she would help me with the counseling. She was none other than Barbara Shlemon, now one of the leaders of the Catholic charismatic movement, and author of *Healing Prayer*.

We arrived in Tiffin a half day before camp was to start, and, having seen an interesting church as we drove in, decided to walk across town to find it. Ami and Hal Spence, Jr., son of the chairman of the camp, went with us. As we entered the sanctuary of St. Mary's Catholic Church an anointing came upon me the like of which I had never, or ever since, experienced! It was so full and powerful I thought I might translate—and wondered if hitting the ceiling on the way up would hurt! Ami took one look at me and said, "Dad, what's happening to you?" I said, "I don't know."

We sat down to pray. The Lord then revealed that He had brought Barbara and me together, along with Ami and Hal for support, in order that we as a Catholic laywoman and a Protestant minister might pray for the healing of memories and reconciliation of the Roman Catholic and Protestant churches. We were to pray through the entire history, from 1515 to the present, in mutual repentance, asking for forgiveness and praying for healing for all the hatred, wars, prejudices, confusions, broken and divided households, suspicions, disrespects, etc. All week, we spent hours in prayer together, proceeding through all the history we could remember, applying the blood and the cross of Christ.

On July 23rd we prayed for the healing of every occasion in which Catholics and Protestants had married, only to be cast out of one or both churches. We prayed for families to be healed, divisions overcome and unity restored. That day being my birthday, my mother called to wish me a happy birthday. I told her, "Mom, I'm doing part of what God commissioned me to do," and told her what Barbara and I and Ami and Hal were doing and how we had prayed that day for intermarriages to be healed.

She said, "Oh Jack, you never knew. I never told you. All the Osages of your family line were devout Roman Catholics. They attended Mass every morning. Your grandmother, my mother, was a strong Catholic during her youth. When she married Frank Potter, your grandfather, she was 'churched' [a colloquialism which meant to be excommunicated or put out of the church]. That's why you have always known her as a Methodist. She became a Methodist shortly after they were married." By one of God's coincidences, I had prayed for the healing of my own beloved grandmother that birthday, and on the same day discovered my own unsuspected heritage in the Catholic Church!

Now then the mystery: Was I also in some sense in my maternal grandparents' loins? My spirit leaped in understanding as my mother related those facts to me. Did I only inherit love and respect through the genes, or was I also *in* my maternal grandparents' loins? How could anyone be in both at once?! Or do we only inhabit a father's loins? If we somehow inhabit both, what if my father and mother had never found each other?! What mysteries await revelation when at last we can sit down with our beloved Lord and say, "What about that?" and "How about this?" Surely there are mysteries of inheritance far beyond us all.

At last, whether by being in the loins, or by inheritance, I understood why I loved black people and the Roman Catholic Chruch. I share these stories in hopes that many may find revelation, or at least mysteries to ponder, in thinking about our heritages. Surely we should give thanks and praise for all the blessings which have come down to us through our family heritages.

Unfortunately, however, it is not solely blessing which has come down to us from our ancestors. As we shall see, we need to bring all of our past to the cross, even the blessings, that the good may be filtered and the detrimental stopped altogether.

The second way sin descends is by example. We have taught this in every book and tape we have produced, that children learn to become what parents are, rather than what they teach. We need not expand again here. But let the reader not think brevity signifies lesser importance. How could anyone not see that our formation with our parents perpetuates sin in our lives and in our children's and grandchildren's? Example writes what we become, unless grace intervenes, all the way back to Eden and forward to our Lord's return. It is the primary reason why fathers' hearts must be turned to children and children to fathers, lest the earth be smitten with a curse.

The third way sin and its effects descends is perhaps the most cogent, if not in the long run the most influential—the law of sowing and reaping. Reaping for sin is seldom immediate. It is also never without increase, since all seeds of sin ripen to produce thirty, sixty or a hundredfold (Mark 4:8 and 20). Time, though not the only factor, remains a major reason why children reap what fathers and grandparents and great-grandparents have sown.

When David sinned, his child died (2 Sam. 12:1-24). When Josiah humbled himself before the Lord, the prophetess Huldah told him, "you shall be gathered to your grave in peace, neither shall your eyes see all the evil which I will bring on this place" (2 Kings 22:20)—which meant, of course, that he would not reap, but his children would! A rather dubious blessing!

It may seem unfair that unborn children, years later, are required to suffer the effects of the law for sins committed by ancestors who may even be unknown to them. Of course it is not fair. God is fair, but since sin entered God's world, life is not fair. God has worked from the beginning to re-establish His justice through the cross of Christ. He suffers far more for our injustices than we who cry out the age-old cry, "It's not fair!"

God established the law of sowing and reaping before sin entered the world. The law was designed to increase blessing. As men labored and sowed to the spirit (Gal. 6:8b), they were to reap blessing. Thus the universe would upbuild itself in love (Eph. 4:16). But when sin entered, those same impartial laws of sowing and reaping and of increase worked as dispassionately and inexorably to bring destruction. Now, when men sow to the flesh, they reap corruption (Gal. 6:8a) from the very laws which were designed to bring them blessing!

So it is that, despite God's first will, which is always love and blessing, the good will of God, which is impartial law, also binds God to abide its actions. Wherever men will let Jesus Christ reap the dire effects of law through forgiveness and atonement on the cross, God can prevent tragedy. But even He has set himself to obey His own laws. So whenever men will not repent, and by that fail to give Him access, men must reap, generation to generation whatever is sown, however unfair that may be to the unborn.

Furthermore, every material blessing we enjoy has come down to us from the labors of our ancestors. We reap every blessing fully unmerited. Did any of us invent the cotton gin or the looms which have spun our comfortable clothing? Did we produce central heating or air conditioning? Did we discover the medical advances which have saved our lives and wiped many diseases from the face of the earth? Who among us invented his own combustion engine or fashioned his own automobile? How about dishwashers, clothes washers and dryers, toasters, microwave ovens, to say nothing of gas and electric ranges? Apart from material things, what have we reaped without effort from education, the glory of music, the beauty of art, the fun of wholesome comedies, novels, theatre in general? Every good thing we enjoy has come to us as unearned increment—even the printing press, the paper, the easy chair, the light and the ability to read which enables us all to gain whatever knowledge this book offers at this moment!

Shall we say then that it is fair of God that we should reap every good blessing we have in life from the labors of our ancestors, but unfair if we also reap from their sins?! Is it somehow God's fault, or is life to blame, if human sin abrogates the will of God and generations to come suffer its sad effects? Sin is to blame. And sin before that. And before that. All the way back to poor old Adam—and Satan at last! In this we see the contest of the ages, wherein God would make amends for the sin of one of His creation! He himself suffers our death due to our sin, and brings to naught the work of Satan in bringing death. In Jesus, the Man of Nazareth, the God of life restores blessing where sin has reaped death. God is more than fair; He is unfathomable love and healing to a world which deserves nothing but destruction and death. Puerile children cry out that life must be made fair. Those who are wise praise God from a full and willing heart of thanksgiving, in the midst of an unjust and crooked world.

What we and many other counselors in Christ have discovered is that destruction often rains upon people when nothing inside them any longer attracts it. Then it is that we see that generational sin may be the cause.

We discovered generational sin when a lady came to us in depression and fear. She was one of thirteen children; nine boys, four girls. Not finding full explanation of the source of her problems in her own life, I felt led by the Holy Spirit to ask about her entire family. Every one of her brothers had become alcoholic, and some had died early in tragic circumstances. The last brother was a Satanist. Each of the women was mentally ill, except my counselee, and she herself was dangerously close to it.

We saw patterns of rejection and divorce throughout the family. All the men in the family were either being destroyed or were already dead. Whenever such a pattern emerges, indicating destruction upon the males of a family, we call that an "ahaseuritic." In the story of Tobit, in the Apocrypha, any man who married Sarah, daughter of Raguel, wife of King Ahaseurus, would be torn apart that night by the demon Asmodeus (Tobit 3:7). (Since we use this as as example, not the scriptural base of the teaching, we feel free to refer to the Apocrypha, which are regarded by Protestants as inspired but not as equal to canonical Scripture.)

I prayed with the lady about her family, as we will share later. About two years afterwards, Bishop Bill Frey of the Episcopal Church of Colorado asked us to speak to a charismatic gathering in his diocese. We taught about generational sin, testifying in disguised form about that lady's family and how we had prayed for her. After the talk, a woman approached us and said, "You don't recognize me, do you?"

I said, "No."

She said, "I'm the one whose story you just told!" I couldn't believe it. That woman had been skinny and haggard, ashen, with stringy hair. Here was a beautiful woman, ruddy of complexion, well-built, healthy and vital! She went on to report that after our prayer she had gone through a time of trial in which she had to walk in a discipline of affirming God's presence and power in her life. Since then she had been watching her brothers and sisters leave alcohol and come to the Lord, one by one. She exclaimed, "It's been like watching popcorn!"

Since that first eye-opener, Paula and I have regularly checked the family background of counselees. We may say, "Did your father have brothers and sisters? How many? Start with the eldest and tell me the salient facts—health, marriage, children, longevity, tragedies, divorces, etc. Now the next uncle or aunt, and the next." Finally, "How about your grandparents?" That done and duly noted, we ask the same questions concerning the maternal side. And then concerning their own brothers and sisters. We look for recurrent patterns, both of blessing and of harm.

Sometimes divorce runs rampant. One man came who was the result of his mother's third of five marriages. His mother was one of twelve children. His father was one of twelve. Among all those relatives, not one had been married only once; most of them had been married several times! He was himself failing in his third marriage. Sometimes there are patterns of diseases, or miscarriages, or early deaths. Sometimes there are closed wombs, or only male or only female children born in a family. Abraham opened the wombs of Abimelech's people; for the sin of Abimelech had closed all their wombs (Gen. 20:18). Sometimes drugs or alcohol beleaguer generation after generation. One man came whose great-grandfather had tragically died at thirty-nine or so, whose grandfather had tragically died at the same age, whose father had died in the same way at the same age. He was then thirty-eight, and counting down.

In my (John's) family, on my father's side, my grandfather had been a wealthy lumberman and bank president. During the Depression, he tried to carry his friends, and lost everything. My father was indicted for a crime a man in his employ had committed, and though he was acquitted, court costs and fees cost him all he had and bankrupted his business. My brother Hal entered a business which folded and plunged him into debt. Coincidence? Not likely. We prayed for that pattern to end on the cross.

On my mother's side, the Osage Indian tribe was moved in 1869 and 1870 from eastern Kansas to northern Oklahoma. The white soldiers who were conducting them, knowing how fiercely Osage braves defend their squaws, raped some of the women, seeking to provoke the men to battle, as a pretext to destroy the tribe. The Osages could do nothing but seethe in bitterness. Thus took root a bitter judgment that worthless white men would take advantage of Osage women.

The tribe was governed at the time by councils of wise and prayerful men. They settled in Osage County, and made it law that any Osage allottee could sell his 770 acres, but that whatever was in the air above, or the ground below, would belong to the entire tribe, no matter who privately owned the land. When oil was discovered in Osage County, the entire tribe became wealthy, all at once! Worthless white men then wooed and married young Osage women in order to live in luxury from their oil payments. Many were alcoholic, beat on their wives, and were selfish and lazy; it is suspected that some killed their wives in order to inherit their allotment. Thus the bitter-root judgment and expectancy became ingrained that men who married into the family would be alcoholic, lazy, unable or unwilling to support their wives, violent and generally worthless men.

I do not know whether, or to what extent, any other families among the Osage were affected, but in our family that pattern was an unmitigated curse. My father was a good man but succumbed to the pattern. By the time I was ten he had lost it to alcohol, and was unable to support the family. My aunt married a man who became a medical specialist. His $30,000-a-year income would have been tantamount to about $100,000 today. But he refused to support the family and was alcoholic and violent. My aunt finally divorced him. My parents had one daughter. She married a man who was gentle with her, but hopelessly alcoholic. He failed to support her. She went to work and supported the family. He sat at home and drank himself to death. They had three daughters. Each one of my nieces married the same kind of man and divorced him. Now that prayers have been said, two have remarried fine Christian men. My aunt's daughter married the same kind of man her father was, and divorced him. Our daughter Ami almost lost her marriage until counsel and prayer restored her husband. Except by grace, not one woman in our entire family has escaped the pattern! Now those effects of generational sin have been shattered on the cross and succeeding generations will be free from them.

Occult sins create the most destructive patterns we have seen. In checking family histories in order to stop generation sin, Paula and I routinely ask whether anyone in the family has been involved in the occult. The law requires, "I will also set My face against that person and will cut him off from among his people" (Lev. 20:6). Immediately the law begins to operate, so that the blessing of God is withdrawn, and succeeding generations reap multitudinous ways of being cut off. In some, the male line, which of course carries the name, ceases—no male children are born, or tragic deaths or divorces prevent succession. In some, financial tragedy occurs in generation after generation. The telling mark of descent of harm from occult sin is that it seems there is a curse upon the family. Whatever shape it takes, whether deaths, divorces, finances, illnesses, accidents, etc., such coincidences happen that one can hardly miss seeing design behind it all. Happenstance plagues all of us occasionally, but in these families so much happens so interconnectedly that even impartial observers are forced to admit, "This is too much—it can't all be coincidence!" Truly there is a curse that is irrevocably prescribed by law! "I will cut that man off."

Descent of that kind of harm by sin is not at all affected by whether we believe in God or His laws. Laws of the universe operate whether we know about them or not, believe or don't believe in them, want them or reject them. We will not affect the law; it will affect us! Abimelech was neither a Hebrew nor a believer in the God of Abraham. But he had sense enough to know there are laws which affect us and cried out when Isaac had said that Rebekah was his sister, "What is this you have done to us? One of the people might easily have lain with your wife, and *you would have brought guilt upon us*" (Gen. 26:10). Abimelech knew firsthand what ravages come when law is transgressed, for Isaac's father Abraham had done the same thing to him, and Abimelech had taken Sarah, unaware she was Abraham's wife. God had come to him in the night then and said, "Behold, *you are a dead man because of the woman whom you have taken*, for she is married" (Gen. 20:3). Abimelech protested that he did not know. But then mark how even this heathen king knew how sin affects all under a man's charge. He exclaimed, "Lord, wilt Thou *slay a nation*, even though blameless?" (v. 4). God replied that He knew Abimelech was innocent and therefore He had kept him from touching Sarah, and that he should have Abraham pray for him and he would live and not die (vv. 6, 7). Abimelech did so, "And Abraham prayed to God; and God healed Abimelech and his wife and his maids, so that they bore children. *For the Lord had closed fast all the wombs of the household of Abimelech because of Sarah*, Abraham's wife" (vv. 17, 18). Judgment had descended immediately! Law is absolute, upon Jew or non-Jew, believer or non-believer.

One might ask, "Why did not all harm stop when we died and were born anew in Christ? Why did not our conversion end it?" Perhaps it should have. In many their belief structure at conversion gave our Lord ample room to act to end at least some of the effects of generational sin. Nevertheless, we have ministered to hundreds upon hundreds of Christians who have been many years in the Lord who still suffered great harm from patterns of generational sin. These were stopped and reversed to blessing when we discerned their source in their ancestry and brought an end to them through specific application of the blood and the cross of Christ.

Ezekiel 18:2 and Jeremiah 31:29 both say the same thing. "In those days they will not say again, 'The fathers have eaten sour grapes, And the children's teeth are set on edge' " (quoted from Jeremiah). Ezekiel went on to say, "Behold, all souls are Mine; the soul of the father as well as the soul of the son is Mine. The soul who sins will die. But if a man is righteous . . ." (vv. 4, 5a). "The person who sins will die. The son will not bear the punishment for the father's iniquity, nor will the father bear the punishment for the son's iniquity; the righteousness of the righteous will be upon himself, and the wickedness of the wicked upon himself" (v. 20).

However, both Psalm 14 and Romans 3 tell us:

There is none righteous, not even one;
There is none who understands,
There is none who seeks for God;
All have turned aside, together they have become useless;
There is none who does good,
There is not even one.

—Rom. 3:10-12

The only righteous one is our Lord Jesus Christ. In His righteousness, and only there, do we have any righteousness. That righteousness becomes ours only through our death with Him, on the cross. It is only the cross which stops generational sin so that a son does not die for his father's sin. God cannot, and does not, contradict himself. Ezekiel, or even the Holy Spirit himself through Ezekiel, could not set aside the old law, expressed in the Ten Commandments. Only the cross of Christ fulfills the demands of the law and so sets men free from its effects. Therefore, that promise in Jeremiah and Ezekiel waits upon one thing for its fulfillment—faith in the cross of Christ.

For some reason, explicable perhaps only to God, He has left it so that we must claim this prayer also. Though we are positionally totally dead in Christ when we first receive Him, He has left it so that step by step we must reckon our sin nature as dead on His cross (Rom. 6:4). In like manner, apparently we must see and stop generational patterns of sin by direct action in prayer. I personally cannot understand this, unless God knows we shall only be built up to stand as warriors in Him if we have to exercise discipline to claim our freedom. Perhaps it would be too much a matter of cheap grace, or too sudden a change, if everything were done all at once. Suffice it to say that the evidence for us is undeniable; we have seen countless long-time Christians suffer from generational patterns until someone by God's grace prayed effectively to stop that destruction.

In sharing our way of praying about generational sin, we do not mean to offer a magic ritual or incantation.

Let the reader spring from our insights and our ways to find his own effective way to pray. Here are the steps we follow:

First, we spend considerable time asking the counselee to relate as much as he can recall of the family history. As our questioning prompts counselees, often their eyes widen and they exclaim, "I never saw that. I never put two and two together until now. Look at that. Every one of my uncles suffered tragedies, and so have my brothers. What did you call that?"

"An ahaseuritic—that's when all or most of the men are afflicted, one way or another."

"Well, let's pray, before it gets me too!"

In prayer, we place the cross between the person and his mother and father, their mothers and fathers, and theirs. We do that simply by stating it by authority in Jesus.

Usually, we begin the prayer by thanking and praising God for all that has come to us through our forefathers. We thank God for all the good we inherit daily. But then we pray that even the good be filtered through the cross.

We call for the blood of Jesus to flow back through the family bloodlines throughout their history, by forgiveness washing away the ground of Satan's attack. We ask in repentance for forgiveness for all sins, wherever possible (some things must wait for conscious repentance and confession).

Whatever patterns we have seen and discussed, we ask Jesus to destroy and transform on His cross. "The Son of God appeared for this purpose, that He might destroy the works of the devil" (1 John 3:8b). We believe this to be the most important part of the prayer. *It is through unforgiven sin and consequent descending patterns that Satan perpetuates his destructions on families.* Wherever sin has allowed access, Satan enters to prey upon physical weaknesses, to exploit sinful tendencies, to cause proclivities to become addictions, proneness to accidents to become tragedies, bad examples to become traps, necessities to reap to escalate to whirlwinds of destruction.

"The thief comes only to steal, and kill, and destroy; . . ." (John 10:10a). Family patterns are the handles by which Satan pumps the bellows of the fires of hell in any family. The greatest necessity in praying for the cessation of ruination in families is to stop generational patterns on the cross, calling for their death and transformation to blessing.

We name each pattern, describing it, and calling specifically for our Lord to destroy it. In this prayer, we are not merely praying for the counselee, but for him in proxy for his entire family. The counselee is the beachhead of heaven's attack upon the powers of darkness and the land to be occupied is the counselee's entire family. We pray that whatever pattern we describe may be destroyed from the life of every brother and sister, uncle and aunt and cousin, grandparent and great-grandparent, and each adopted or in-law person connected to the family.

We do not have to know who among the family is living or has already died. The Lord can take the prayer and apply it wherever appropriate. About half of the church believes it is forbidden to pray for the departed, and half believes we are commanded to pray for the deceased. There need be no quarrel. Let each brother pray "according to the proportion of his faith" (Rom. 12:6c). The Lord will answer according to His will and knowledge of what is right.

Many people have little or no knowledge of their family history. Adopted people especially may have no awareness. In such cases, we pray generally, and if the Holy Spirit gives a word of knowledge, we pray about that. A word of caution: some pray arrogantly about what they think they see, forgetting that St. Paul said, "We know in part, and we prophesy in part" (1 Cor. 13:9). The Revised Standard Version reads, "For our knowledge is imperfect, and our prophecy is imperfect." We do not always hear accurately. It does not hurt to say, "Lord, I think I hear you saying, this and therefore I pray that that pattern be stopped. If I don't hear rightly, Lord, I trust you to apply the prayer to what does need to be dealt with, or to reveal it later on more accurately so that we can pray again and so have the complete victory you intend." Humility is not lack of power but gain.

Having prayed for destructive patterns to be destroyed, we are sometimes led to rebuke the powers of darkness and to command them to leave. Often I am caused by the Holy Spirit to bring forth this command in a loud voice. Sometimes, for reasons known only to himself, the Holy Spirit, who is the general on the field, knows that *loud* authority is what is required. "In the day of His flesh, when He offered up both prayers and supplications with loud crying and tears to Him . . ." (Heb. 5:7). On many occasions, having prayed so for large groups, we have received testimony that at that shouted word of command hearers have felt powers of darkness leap away from them. People have testified then to feeling "breakthroughs," lightness and joy, freedom and certainty.

We ask Father God to send His angels to encamp about every member of the family (Ps. 34:7), to protect each one (Ps. 91:11, 12), and to bring each one out of darkness into light (Heb. 2:14). We call for the Lord to send forth His warrior angels to do battle for the family.

Some time ago a heresy was taught that men should command the angels specifically, telling them what to do. Only God orders His angels. But we can pray to the Lord, asking Him to send His angels to minister to our families, to save them from harm and to bring them messages of salvation. And we can believe that with or without the help of His angels, if we have faith, God will save us and all our household (Acts 16:31).

We believe that this key of overcoming generational sin is one of the most important the Lord has revealed to us and to other servants like us. Families languish in fear and harm who ought to walk free and easy in God's kingdom. We *can* set families free. Paula and I have received countless testimonies from people who have seen all the members of their families delivered and set free one by one after such prayers.

Prayers for the cessation of generational sin, like prayers for conversion, are normally one-time prayers. However, as bits and pieces of history are newly revealed, specific prayers about those revelations are not redundant. They are a continual working out and development after the first general prayer.

Whoever voices this prayer must know his authority in Christ as a child of the King. Powers of darkness do not yield territory to halfhearted mumblers.

God wants us to advance, occupy and hold territory for Him. This prayer to stop generational sin is not merely for healing. Nor is it only defensive, as though stopping the encroachments of darkness were enough. It is aggressive warfare on the march to recover lost souls from the grip of darkness. It is a delight to all who enter the lists and challenge the champions of darkness.

> Let the godly ones exult in glory;
> Let them sing for joy on their beds.
> Let the high praises of God be in their mouth,
> And a two-edged sword in their hand,
> To execute vengeance on the nations,
> And punishment on the peoples;
> To bind their kings with chains,
> And their nobles with fetters of iron;
> To execute on them the judgment written;
> This is an honor for *all* His godly ones.
> Praise the Lord!
>
> —Ps. 149:5-9

Chapter Fourteen

Burden Bearing—and Leeches

Bear one another's burdens, and thus fulfil the law of Christ (Gal. 6:2).

[We are] always carrying about in the body the dying of Jesus, that the life of Jesus also may be manifested in our body. For we who live are constantly being delivered over to death for Jesus' sake, that the life of Jesus also may be manifested in our mortal flesh. So death works in us, but life in you (2 Cor. 4:10-12).

For each one shall bear his own load (Gal. 6:5).

We have written much about burden bearing (Chapter Twenty-One in *The Transformation of the Inner Man* and Chapter Nine in *the Elijah Task*) and produced a two-tape series, "Burden Bearing" and "Intercessory Prayer." But the subject deserves fuller treatment on two counts. First, because it is so important and needful for the Body to understand; second, because burden bearing touches on healing the wounded spirit. It does so in two areas. First, burden bearing is one of the primary ways by which our Lord heals wounded spirits. Second, burden bearers may receive wounds while healing others and people suffer hurt when drained by spiritual leeches.

A leech is the opposite of a burden bearer. A leech is a person who does not pay the price of prayer to sustain his own life, and perhaps fails to maintain emotional or mental hygiene and discipline as well, who therefore sustains himself by drawing on the strength of others. "The leech has two daughters, 'Give,' 'Give,' " (Prov. 30:15a). At times, all of us need to lean on our brothers and sisters. God has designed us to give and receive strength and comfort from one another.

> Blessed be the God and Father of our Lord Jesus Christ, the Father of mercies and God of all comfort; who comforts us in all our affliction so that we may be able to comfort those who are in any affliction with the comfort with which we ourselves are comforted by God. For just as the sufferings of Christ are ours in abundance, so also our comfort is abundant through Christ. But if we are afflicted, it is for your comfort and salvation; or if we are comforted, it is for your comfort, which is effective in the patient enduring of the same sufferings which we also suffer (2 Cor. 1:3-7).

It is good to give and receive comfort one to another. By such sharing, our love for one another in Christ grows into the fullness St. Paul spoke of in Ephesians 4:11-16.

But leeches do not give back. They only drain. While true sharing of one another's sufferings is a gift of God by faith among those who have faith, leeching is a dead sucking of life by those who have insufficient faith to stand on their own two feet. Leeching is of the flesh, not of the Holy Spirit; it is a taking which prevents giving. Leeches hear Galatians 6:2 to mean that the Body should bear their burdens, not that they should bear the burdens of others. Leeches fail to heed Galatians 6:5, that each man must bear his own burden. With leeches there is no stopping place; they continually suck the energy of others, like vampires in the night.

Burden bearing is predicated upon the capacity of our spirit to identify with another, to empathize, to share and shoulder emotional loads. In the same way that two physically can carry a log which one alone cannot lift, burden bearing takes one end of a load, and so enables a brother to survive and function. Whereas two must be in proximity to lift something physically, burden bearing requires no spatial nearness. We can feel, identify, share and pray about another's burdens at whatever distance we may happen to be.

When we are apart, or for some other reason cannot communicate, we may shoulder a brother's burden and be unable to identify not only what the burden is, but which brother's burden we are carrying. That hurts, for we hunger for knowledge.

> But we, brethren, having been bereft of you for a short while—*in person, not in spirit*—were all the more eager with great desire to see your face. For we wanted to come to you—I, Paul, more than once—and yet Satan thwarted us. For who is our hope or joy or crown of exultation? Is it not even you, in the presence of our Lord Jesus at His coming? For you are our glory and joy. Therefore *when we could endure it no longer*, we thought it best to be left behind at Athens alone; and we sent Timothy, our brother and God's fellow-worker in the gospel of Christ, to strengthen and encourage you as to your faith (1 Thess. 2:17-3:2).

Any burden bearer who has carried another in his heart knows by experience the weight of Paul's words, "when we could endure it no longer." We *can* endure mere curiosity about our brother's welfare, but love and concern for the other nearly overwhelms us when we are bearing burdens and can obtain no news. We hunger desperately to hear how that one is. Knowledge enables us to pray specifically and to release burdens to the Lord. Lacking that, we continue to labor.

Throughout the New Testament we are commanded to love one another. We all know that. But what does that mean? What do we do which is uniquely, peculiarly love for our brother? James gave us part of the answer. "If a brother or sister is without clothing and in need of daily food, and one of you says to them, 'Go in peace, be warmed and be filled,' and yet you do not give them what is necessary for their body, what use is that?" John echoed that in 1 John 3:16-18, "We know love by this, that He laid down His life for us; and we ought to lay down our lives for the brethren. But whoever has the world's goods, and beholds his brother in need and closes his heart against him, how does the love of God abide in Him? Little children, let us not love with word or with tongue, but in deed and truth." Love is therefore not so much a feeling in the heart as it is a matter of specific actions. We learn in other places that such actions are composed of forgiving, preferring others' interests before our own (Phil. 2:4), not insisting on our own way (1 Cor. 13:5) and that "love bears all things, believes all things, hopes all things, endures all things" (1 Cor. 13:7).

One can classify love in two kinds. The first might be called nonaggressive love, and has two parts. It is first of all what one might also call forbearing love, which means the self-discipline not to act in any way which could harm another; and second, spending ourselves in prayer to forgive others when they hurt us. On the other hand, love is composed of activities that are positive aggressive steps taken to benefit others.

Intercessory burden bearing is intentional, aggressive action taken for others. It is in fact cross bearing. We commonly say, "Oh, that brother has a cross to bear," or "What a cross I have to carry!" But let us free our Christian mentality from false usages. Troubles and tragedies which befall us are not crosses to bear. They are simply and only that, troubles and sorrows which test and refine us. Nor is the abuse we take from relatives or friends or someone else. Abusive people are what the Bible calls our "thorns in the flesh" (Num. 33:55, 2 Cor. 12:7). But they are not crosses to bear. *Nothing which involuntarily befalls us is a cross to bear.*

Cross bearing involves at least three aspects peculiar to itself. First, it is volitional. The cross did not happen *to* Jesus. He *accomplished* it. "And behold, two men were talking with Him; and they were Moses and Elijah, who, appearing in glory, were speaking of His departure which He was about to *accomplish* at Jerusalem" (Luke 9:30.31). "Jesus said to them, 'My food is to do the will of Him who sent Me, and to accomplish His work' " (John 4:34). That work was to die on the cross, where He cried out that the work of redemption was accomplished, "It is finished!" (John 19:30). Being volitional, cross bearing is also purposeful. "Now My soul has become troubled; and what shall I say, 'Father, save Me from this hour'? But for this *purpose* I came to this hour" (John 12:27). The cross is love in action in which Christians purposefully, knowingly lay down their lives for others.

The second peculiar aspect of cross bearing is that it is redemptive suffering. Simple reaping of suffering because we deserve it is in no way to be identified as "a cross I have to bear." It is disgraceful to think of our well-merited suffering under judgment as a cross. It is the opposite; we often suffer because we would not repent and let Jesus bear it on the cross for us. We suffer because of our sin, not for righteousness' sake.

Some may question whether, since Jesus has accomplished all on the cross, it is scriptural, or wise, to think of any human being other than Jesus as suffering redemptively for another. But this is another of those areas in our Lord's wisdom in which only "both and" rather than "either or" thinking ought to be applied. He did accomplish all. Redemption is a finished work. We cannot add one iota to His perfected work of salvation. On the other hand, in His wisdom and in the mystery of time, He intends to complete that work of redemptive suffering through the Body of Christ. How else can we comprehend St. Paul's "Now I rejoice in my sufferings *for your sake,* and in my flesh I do my share on behalf of His body (which is the church) in filling up that which is lacking in Christ's afflictions" (Col. 1:24)? We find the same way of thinking in the texts at the head of this chapter. We carry *"in the body the dying of Jesus,"* and "so death works in us but life in you." As we will see more fully later, redemptive suffering for others is not only possible and scriptural, it is commanded by our Lord himself (John 14:21, 23, Gal. 6:2, John 15:13-16).

Cross bearing is redemptive suffering for others, purposefully, willingly undertaken in obedience to our Lord Jesus Christ. It should be understood that redemptive suffering for others cannot be accomplished by our flesh, nor indeed by us at all. Redemption is the providence of Jesus, and Jesus only. It is Jesus who, *in us*, suffers redemptively for others. It is in Him that we bear burdens; if we are not in Him we only worry in the flesh. We bear whatever burden He bears in us so long as He chooses to bear it in us—and not one second longer—else we need the healing of which we will write later in this chapter. St. Paul said we *"share his sufferings,* becoming like him in his death . . ."* (Phil. 3:10 RSV). In His wisdom, our Lord allows us to share in miniscule portions His redemptive suffering for humanity.

To us, that is what is meant by the so often quoted phrase, "to minister to the Lord." We may minister to others in many ways, but it seems to us that only those who have learned to bear His burdens with Him truly minister to the Lord himself. And what a blessing and a joy that is!

The third aspect peculiar to cross bearing is death. Mere personal pain may or may not bring death of self, depending on our faith and comprehension. But that kind of death of self is only our own crucifixion, for our own sin, for our own salvation's sake. *Cross bearing is unique in that death is entered for others' sakes.* Whatever personal death we may come to because of what trials come upon us, let us never seek to ennoble that as cross bearing. Our own death does not participate in such glory. How often St. Paul said that what he did or what he suffered was "for your sakes" (2 Cor. 2:10, Col. 1:24, 2 Cor. 4:15). St. Paul wanted his friends to know that what he suffered was not for himself, but in love for them, or for Jesus' sake, "For we who live are constantly being delivered over to death *for Jesus'* sake . . ." (2 Cor. 4:11). "For to you it has been granted *for Christ's sake,* not only to believe in Him, *but also to suffer for His sake,* experiencing the same conflict which you saw in me, and now hear to be *in* me" (Phil. 1:29, 30).

Hear again 2 Corinthians 4:12: "So death works *in* us, but life *in* you." Note, not death working *upon* us, but *in* us. In burden bearing, we take another's death *into* ourselves. More accurately, our Lord reaches from His cross through our heart and spirit to draw our brother's death to himself on the cross. Suffering which does not involve this altruistic sharing of another's death for his sake is neither intercessory burden bearing nor cross bearing.

At one time in my meditations, I was wrestling with these matters when the Lord said to me, *Look up Romans 8:1-4.* So I did. This is one of those familiar passages we have all read so many times that we are sure we understand, and therefore don't at all! The Lord proceeded to reveal this to me. I thought, "Oh, yes, Lord. That means that because I have accepted you as my Lord and Savior, I am free from sin and death."

He said, *Yes, Paul did say that, in many places, but that is not what he was saying here.* So I looked again, and saw "Spirit" in verse two.

"Oh yes, Lord, since I have the baptism of the Holy Spirit, I am free from sin and death." And now I had scriptural warrant. I quoted, ". . . and where the Spirit of the Lord is, there is freedom" (2 Cor. 3:17b RSV).

Yes, John, He responded. *The Holy Spirit does bring freedom, and St. Paul did say that, in many ways. But that is not what he was saying here. Look again.*

So I looked again, and this time He caused passages to leap off the pages into my eyes. "For the *law of the Spirit of Life* in Christ Jesus has set you free from the *law of sin* and of death." Oh! He wasn't speaking here of His blood and His cross, nor of the Holy Spirit primarily, but about the *law* of the Spirit of life, and the *law* of sin and death!

"Well then, what is the law of sin and of death?" So He directed me to Romans 7, reminding me that when Paul wrote, there were no chapters or verse numbers; it all ran together as one message. Again, He caused the word "law" to leap off the page.

> For I joyfully concur with the *law* of God in the inner man, but I see a different *law* in the members of my body, waging war against the *law* of my mind, making me a prisoner of the *law* of sin which is in my members. Wretched man that I am! Who will set me free from the body of this death? Thanks be to God through Jesus Christ our Lord! So then, on the one hand I myself with my mind am serving the *law* of God, but on the other, with my flesh the *law* of sin (Rom. 7:22-25).

At last the Lord revealed to me what St. Paul was talking about. When we receive Jesus Christ as Lord and Savior, our sins are washed away and our sin nature is dealt a death blow. Then begins the process of santification by which He daily brings us more and more to crucifixion of the practices of our old nature (Col. 3:9, Gal. 2:20 and 5:24). Much of that death is accomplished by prayer for inner healing. But I had been agonizing over why so many receive much inner healing but never go on to become whole. He was answering to say that there remains another crucial step which some take, and thereby become whole, and others do not. That is, to learn to live the *"law of the Spirit* of life in Christ Jesus." It was not enough merely to bring to death the old man. A new law, a new *way* of living had to be built in!

St. Paul, who as a scholar under Gamaliel, knew how to employ the word "law" in its strictly legal usages, was applying the word "law" in a most poetic, non-legal way. That "different law in the members of my body, waging war against the *law* of my mind" the Lord revealed to me was another way of speaking of the old nature. The "body" St. Paul wanted to be set free from is not the physical body.

He was using the word "body" in the same way we speak of a group of things as "the main body of the army" or a "body of people." "Who will set me free from this *body* of this *death*" therefore means "Who will set me free from this body of many warring things in my old nature which continually re-entraps me in its old ways? How do I finally get free from the body of the world's ways in me to walk in the body of Christ's ways? How do I finally get free from the 'law' of the old way?" How? By learning and living a new "law," which replaces it!

First we receive Jesus and are free from guilt. Then we crucify the old man daily on the cross. But then we learn to live the "law of the Spirit of life in Christ Jesus," and that law finally overcomes the old practices by building in the new *way* of Christ.

What, then, is "the law of the Spirit of life in Christ Jesus"? Jesus answered, "For whoever wishes to save his life shall lose it, but whoever loses his life for My sake, he is the one who will save it" (Luke 9:24). And in John 15:13, "Greater love has no one than this, that one *lay down his life* for his friends." And in Luke 14:27, "Whoever does not carry *his own cross* and come after Me cannot be My disciple." St. Paul said, "Bear one another's burdens, and thus fulfill *the law of Christ.*" What is Christ's commandment? What is the *law* of Christ? "This is My commandment, that you love one another, just *as I have loved you*" (John 15:12). How did He love us? By laying down His life for us. St. Paul was saying in Romans 8 that we break free from our captivity to our old habits when we learn at last the law of Christ, to lay down our lives for others! It is not enough to take away sin and its practices. The new way of sacrificial love must be learned and lived.

But then the Lord told me, *You didn't understand what it is to lay down your life either, John!*

I thought, "Well, if I just lay down my selfish interests and my sins and spend some time helping others, that's laying down my life."

But the Lord said, *John, your selfishness and your sins*

are death, not life. I didn't say to lay down your death for others. I said to lay down your life.

So I thought, "If I lay down my time and energy for others, and spend my life serving other people, surely that's what it is to lay down my life."

The Lord said, *No, your time and energy are not yet your life. I said to lay down your life.*

"Well, what is my life?"

He said, *John, what was My life?* And then He opened the Scriptures to me, as He had done for Cleopas and the other disciple on the road to Emmaus (Luke 24:27).

> I and the father are one (John 10:30).
>
> The words that I say to you I do not speak on My own initiative, but the Father abiding in Me does His works (John 14:10b).
>
> He who has seen Me has seen the Father (John 14:9b).
>
> And He who sent Me is with Me; He has not left Me alone, for I always do the things that are pleasing to Him (John 8:29).

The life of Jesus was His relation to His Father. He had left Heaven to come to earth, but He had never yet left His Father. "Wist ye not that I must be about my Father's business" (Luke 2:49 KJV). When He was tired, He went to the mountains to be with His Father. That relationship with His Father, which was life itself to Him, was the very thing He was called upon to lay down!

"And if a man has commited a sin worthy of death, and he is put to death, and you hang him on a tree, his corpse shall not hang all night on the tree, but you shall surely bury him the same day *(for he who is hanged is accursed of God)* . . ." (Deut. 21:22, 23a). In planning His own death on the cross, Jesus knew that the price to Him was to be far more than physical pain, which could only last a few hours at most. The inestimable cost to Him was to become accursed of God!

"Thine eyes are too pure to approve evil, And Thou canst

not look on wickedness with favor" (Hab. 1:13). Never had the Lord Jesus been outside of His Father's favor, nor for a moment out of His sight. The face of the Father was always toward His Son. Now, He who knew no sin was to become sin: "He made Him who knew no sin to be sin on our behalf, that we might become the righteousness of God in Him" (2 Cor. 5:21). Note carefully, Jesus was to become *sin*, *not sinful*. His own heart toward God remained pure. He remained the sinless, pure sacrificial Lamb of the Passover, while filled with the sin of the world. When He obediently took into himself our sin, He became for the first time unacceptable to the Father's sight.

It should be said again that the word was *not* that He was "to become *sinful*." He became able to bear our chastisement (Isa. 53:5) because He had become as us; He had become our *sin*. That is, He bore our sin much as a washcloth has taken into itself the filth it wipes up. But He did not sin. "For we do not have a high priest who is unable to sympathize with our weaknesses, but we have one who has been tempted in every way, just as we are—*yet was without sin*" (Heb. 4:15 NIV).

A recent heresy took this teaching out of balance to the point of saying that He himself became sinful, *had* to fall into Hell and himself needed redemption. A thousand times no! He was the spotless Lamb. In himself He remained pure. It was our sin He carried to the cross. But when He became our sin, the Father could no longer behold Him. For the first time He knew in full our estrangement. He had to become like us in being "tempted in that which He has suffered" (Heb. 2:18), which included knowing separation from His Father, until He cried out from the cross, "My God, My God, why hast Thou forsaken Me" (Matt. 27:46).

It could have meant little to Jesus to die physically. St. Paul said, "To die is gain" (Phil. 1:21). For Jesus, apart from our sin, to die would have been only to return His spirit to Him who gave it (Eccles. 12:7). That would have been joyful beyond measure to our Lord, the Son of God.

The greater death, even for a short span, was to die to His Father's favor and presence! That was a far more important way to lay down His life, and the greatest cost to Jesus. It was for this reason, not for fear of physical suffering and death, He cried out whether this cup could be taken from Him (Matt. 26:39). Even that loss and separation, the greatest death for Him, Jesus suffered for us.

What then is our life? What is it we are called to lay down for others? When we receive Jesus and are filled with the Holy Spirit, for the first time we have full access to the Father. We feel clean and good. "Who may ascend into the hill of the Lord? And who may stand in His holy place? He who has clean hands and a pure heart . . ." (Ps. 24:3, 4a). Our heart is sprinkled by the blood of Jesus (Heb. 10:22). We delight to come into His presence in corporate worship and private devotions. Our heart is more free and open to share with brothers and sisters. That communion in him and fellowship with our brothers and sisters has become our life, our joy, "For who is our hope or joy or crown of exultation? Is it not even you, in the presence of our Lord Jesus at His coming? For you are our glory and joy" (1 Thess. 2:19, 20).

During the week we may become overburdened and borne down, but worship lifts us. His Word cleanses, and we are again free to reach out and touch the Lord and others. That is our life. That cleanliness, that capacity to hold the heart clean and open for the Lord and others, that life-giving ability to relate vulnerably and refreshingly with Him and others is the very thing He calls us to lay down in death for others!

We may leave an anointed service refreshed and clean, like a radio freshly cleared of static to receive our wonderful Lord's broadcasts, only to run into a brother or sister at coffee hour who just has to tell us the latest juicy bit of gossip! In that moment we have to make a decision. The temptation is to hug our newly regained righteousness to ourselves, saying, "God, I thank Thee that I am not like other people, swindlers, unjust, adulterers, or even like this tax-gatherer" [how about inserting "slanderer" right there?]. "I fast twice a week; I pay tithes of all that I get" (Luke 18:11b, 12). "You've just washed me clean, Lord, I want to stay that way." So we turn off. We reject that person. We give him or her the cold shoulder. That way we have not been like the Galilean Sea which receives refreshment from the mountains and pours it out to all the valley below. We have become like the Dead Sea, which takes in all the Jordan can give, and gives nothing out. We stagnate. We have not learned the lesson that he who would keep his life will lose it and he who would lose it will keep it.

The better decision would have been, "Lord, this child is hurting, or he wouldn't need to hurt others. I will open my heart and spirit to become one with him. I will let you, Lord, go through Gethsemane in me to absorb his hurt to yourself, and so set him free." In Gethsemane, Jesus entered into prayer, and as the God-man (not half-God, half-man, but fully God and fully man) He reached across time and space to become our rottenness, our doubt, our fear, our jealousy, our hate. He became everything which is sin in every person who then lived, had lived before, or would ever come to live on earth. That work was so exhausting that it broke His capillaries and He sweat blood (Luke 22:44), which means medically that He nearly died! The Father sent an angel to strengthen Him (Luke 22:43). Peter, James and John were so overcome by the burden of it they could not stay awake (Matt. 26:40-45).

Consider this: When Jesus left heaven to come to earth, He became *a* man. But He yet remained *one* individual, by himself. In the Garden of Gethsemane He became *mankind*. Until the agony He endured in the garden, His death on the cross might possibly have meant little, for He would only have died alone, as himself only, affecting little, other than by example. But when He became *as us*, then He was for the first time in position to reap on the cross as us for us. He had to become our sin in order to take on himself all that we were due to reap.

Forgiveness is not God overlooking sin. Jesus came to

fulfill the law, not to abolish it (Matt. 5:17). On the cross, because He had become as us in the garden of prayer, He fulfilled all the demands of the law for reaping. He could not have reaped our sin apart from us. The law does not work that way. He had to be *as us to reap for us.* Gethesemane was not a lapse into fear which Jesus overcame by prayer long enough to endure. Gethsemane was integrally necessary to the accomplishment of redemption by His death on the cross! Gethsemane was that requisite action of our Lord which purchased for Him the ability to pay the price for us. He had to become no longer one solitary saint but *as all of us for all of us,* or the cross could have had little more effect than that of the thousands who had already suffered similar deaths. Though He was God himself, only *as us* could He ransom us. Only *as all of us* could He bear *all of our chastisement.* In Gethsemane He accomplished the work of empathetic identification, the work of burden bearing which made the cross effective.

We do not belabor this point for theological correction only. It is essential that those called to burden bearing comprehend His work in Gethsemane, for that is their primary calling and work. We are to prepare the way of the Lord (Isa. 40:3, Matt. 3:3).

How? What is it to prepare the way of the Lord? Many things, of course, like preaching, teaching, repenting, etc. But the primary, prerequisite *preparation* is in the heart, by burden bearing. Hear the word "preparation." Eventually, every person must make his own confession. But when their hearts are not free to do that, then only as Jesus reaches through willing hearts, who will let Him identify with the sin of a brother or sister, in them, can He effectively take enough of their imprisonment in their sin to His cross to set them sufficiently free to make their own confessions. *Burden bearing is that specific portion of intercessory prayer which locks the cross to the heart long enough to slay and set free from sin.*

When we do that, when we invite the Lord to draw another's death through our own body to His cross, that is what it is for a man to "carry His own cross" and so become "My disciple" (Luke 14:27).

When we offer ourselves for burden bearing, we may not feel as good as before. We hurt with our brother's hurt. We tremble with our sister's fear. We wrestle with our friend's anger. We struggle to overcome the jealousy that our neighbor suffers. We agonize with doubts we ourselves thought we had long overcome. Our confidence muddies into confusion. We may temporarily lose our glibness before the Lord. We stammer and stutter and are weighted down with feelings of guilt and unworthiness. Our brother's death is truly in us in fact and in effect upon our heart and mind. Thus we have in reality laid down that life which was our ease of access and communion with God and others. Our heart is too loaded to be as clean and free with God and others as we were.

But that increases faith. We learn by practice to believe He is there, still blessing us fully, when we can no longer appropriate and feel His Presence. By losing our life again and again, day in and day out, and regaining it just as often, we shatter dependence on feelings. We know by more than belief. We *know* our life in Him.

Burden bearers become obedient to the command of Romans 12:1, "I urge you therefore, brethren, by the mercies of God, to present your *bodies* a living and holy sacrifice, acceptable to God, which is your spiritual service of worship." Moreover, they come to understand it from within. The command was not to present the mind or heart or spirit as a living sacrifice, but the body, because it is our body which contains our mind, heart and spirit, and it is in the body that one bears "the burden and the scorching heat of the day" (Matt. 20:12).

Burden bearers realize by continual experience what those blessed words mean: "your spiritual service of worship." Note how worship is connected to service. Often, the Church, like a spoiled child, wants to sit on Daddy's lap and call that pleasing to Daddy's heart. But the Father would have been far better pleased by those children who hoed His garden and swept His house and then came for refreshment on His lap. The labor of burden bearing is itself our spiritual *service* of *worship!*

Paula and I said the same prayer every night for three years, not so much so that God who heard it the first time would heed but so that every cell of our bodies would hear and receive: "Lord, we give you our heart, mind, body, soul and spirit, our past, our present, our future, our ambition and our destiny; we are yours. Use us in any way you desire. You may lay any burden on us any time of the day or night, forever." Our ears are pierced through; we are His (Exod. 21:5, 6).

Therefore the Lord has permission, and avails himself of it, to involve us in sharing His burdens at any time, night or day. Paula may say to me, "Have you been feeling weighted down and fearful the last hour or so?" I say, "Yes, I have," and we enter prayer together to discover whose burden we are carrying or what to do about it. Or I may say, "Have you found yourself becoming angrier and angrier, and there's nothing to be angry about?" When she concurs (we almost always feel the same burdens at the same time), we proceed to prayer. Sometimes the burden of grief is so heavy in our chests we can hardly breathe. It is our Lord's grieving for the Body. He stands in front of some other Lazarus' tomb, who is more than four days dead in some stinking way, and weeps before He calls to life (John 11). We are given the joy of participating with Him in His redemptive work, and there is also an undergirding sense of His peace and well-being which lies beneath the burden we carry for another.

What exactly does our bearing our brother's death in us accomplish, other than making us feel miserable? It is one door, from heart to heart, by which Jesus can enter and save. Since we live on earth, and we are one with our brother, our prayer gives our courteous Lord permission and access to act.

One could ask, "Why did Jesus come to earth at all? Why didn't He wipe out sin and Satan from Heaven once for all?" The answer is, among other things, free will. He had to come and be one of us in order to gain access and permission. My brother's free will still means that our Lord's access to his life is limited, though the Lord possesses all the power of the universe. The Lord has returned to Heaven; His Body remains here. To the degree then that my heart, as a fellow human being, becomes as my brother's heart, to that degree our Lord can begin to save him from whatever his problem is.

The Holy Spirit knows the stopping places. He knows Galatians 6:5 as well as He knows 6:2, and stops the burden bearing at that point at which our brother must make his own invitation and bear his own load. But my heart prepares the way of the Lord to my brother's heart. I carry that which would crush and defeat without redemptive effect. I lighten my brother's load until he can stand free in Jesus.

There is no poesy involved in "And if one member suffers, all the members suffer with it; if one member is honored, all the members rejoice with it" (1 Cor. 12:26). St. Paul was describing the fact of our mutual existence. We *are* that corporate. We think nothing of the well-known fact that radio and T.V. waves permeate the air around us, requiring only proper receiving to produce sight and sound. Why then should it seem strange to realize that every person on earth is a broadcaster whose waves permeate the air about us, requiring only eyes that see and ears that hear? Burden bearers are radios who have been tuned by the Holy Spirit to bear and sometimes identify the signals every person on earth both sends and receives. We all rejoice and grieve unceasingly as we live among our neighbors. "(For by what he saw and heard that righteous man, *while living among them, felt his righteous soul tormented day after day* with their lawless deeds)" (2 Pet. 2:8). Burden bearers are not merely subject by virtue of existence to the hurts of others, they consciously invite more than they would have received incidentally by "living among them." They seek out the hurt in order to transmit it to the Lord.

Burden bearers receive several rewards distinctive to

their labor. We all want to be where Jesus is. Our hymns celebrate an eternity of being with Him. But until eternity, how shall we abide in Him, and so bear much fruit (John 15:4)? We must go where Jesus goes. Jesus is the water of life. Water flows downhill. If we would be where Jesus is, then we must seek Him where He is always going—to the lowest point—of suffering, hurt, fear, death and shame! By suffering *with* Him in others, burden bearers learn what it is to truly abide in Him. Jesus ceases to be their Santa Claus, a means merely to procure good gifts for their own selfish lives. He becomes their life, poured out for others. Burden bearers are privileged to be with Jesus *in reality*, because Christ is allowed to continue His work of redemption in and through them. They know no separation from Him because He always lives to work the Father's good pleasure in them (Phil. 2:13). They do not measure His Presence or proximity by ephemeral feelings. They *know* whom they have believed because they work with Him every day.

Burden bearers progress more quickly in their own sanctification by crucifixion. If the Lord has dealt with an area of my heart and I identify with the hurt and sin of a brother in some similar or identical area, I am transparent. The yoke is easy and the burden is light, as it ought to be (Matt. 11:30). It passes through me to the cross without interference. But if I identify with some sinful characteristic in a brother and my own heart yet retains the same or similar undealt-with sin in my carnal nature, then the "gunk" gets stuck in me! My brother's hurt and sin does not pass easily and lightly through me to the cross. His sin now sits heavily on my heart, and I am forced to see my own sin. That, happening so often as it does, drives me to my own death on the cross. I cannot fool myself and congratulate myself that I am acquitted of sin in an area in which my brother's sin lingers and will not depart to the cross. Thus the labor of laying down my life to bear death for others also brings me to my own confession and death.

410

Burden bearers come to know Jesus better than all others who have not yet responded to that call. The more we bear the burdens of others, the more we feel the weight and horror of sin. Therefore the more we begin to sense the price our Lord pays for our very continued existence! We see in real terms the love of Jesus each moment of time in action to save. We see how if Jesus stopped interceding before the Father, the weight of mankind's sin would destroy the earth in thirty seconds! Our heart becomes enraptured in love and awe for Him. Until we begin, in whatever tiniest modicum He allows, to experience His suffering for others, we have no way to truly appreciate His continual gift of redemptive suffering for all mankind every moment of life!

Listen to how beautifully St. Paul said it:

> More than that, I count all things to be loss in view of *the surpassing value of knowing Christ Jesus my Lord,* for whom I have suffered the loss of all things, and count them but rubbish in order that I may gain Christ, and may be found in Him, not having a righteousness of my own derived from the Law, but that which is through faith in Christ, the righteousness which comes from God on the basis of faith, *that I may know Him,* and the power of His resurrection *and the fellowship of His sufferings, being conformed to His death;* in order that I may attain to the resurrection from the dead (Phil. 3:8-11).

If anyone already knew Jesus, St. Paul did. But there is more to know. St. Paul was the very one who preached most about the *free gift* of eternal life, but here he said, "I may *attain* to the resurrection from the dead." We submit that in this instance St. Paul was not speaking at all about going to Heaven. We have nothing to do to "attain" Heaven other than to receive Jesus. He is our simple ticket home to eternity. We need do nothing else. St. Paul was speaking about attaining to the fullness of Resurrection Life here and now! He went on to say he was forgetting everything else in order to "press on toward the goal for the prize of the upward call of God in Christ Jesus" (v. 14). Many, many Christians have striven with utmost zeal for the same goal, only never to escape self-centered striving for personal perfection, a striving which can end only in Phariseeism and misery! Burden bearers learn the secret of life, which is to lose life in order to find it. They swim in the fullness of the stream which refreshes the city of God (Ps. 46:4). Others try to find their own life and so lose it. Burden bearers forget about themselves by becoming so engrossed in the burdens of others that the Life of Jesus fills and refreshes faster than they can pour it out. Their cruse of oil, poured out in the Elijah task, can never be emptied, for they walk in the life style of Jesus. They begin to enter into the sweetness of Resurrection Life here and now.

Burden bearers come eventually to an even sweeter reward. They come to know the Father God as Jesus knows Him, and Father God abides in their heart. (I repeat here a testimony given in *The Elijah Task*, Chapter Nine, pp. 133-134, and in several tapes, for the reason that it is the summum bonum of a burden bearer's life and so not only appropriate but the climax of any text on burden bearing.)

One night as I (John) was driving home alone on the freeway from Spokane, there came a tap on my shoulder, a very real physical tap. The Lord said, *John?*

I said, "Yes, Lord."

He said, *I have someone I want you to meet.*

I said, "Yes, Lord."

I want you to meet My Father.

"Yes, Lord."

The next second, pouring over me was the most wonderful, gracious, tender, safe and secure Presence I had ever experienced. As one can know a multitude of things in a split second, I knew that this was not a passing experience. Father God had come to stay. In that same instant I knew Father God was not at all like my childish reading of the Old Testament had said He was when I read how God was angry when Saul failed to kill all those Amalekites (1 Sam. 15). Father God was perfectly tender lovingkindness.

I knew in that moment that the battle and the search was over; from that moment on Father God *had* me, and nothing could be more wonderful. I felt safe, at rest and secure. I could do nothing but hang onto the wheel, grateful that in His wisdom He had come when the freeway was empty, and cry out, over and over, "Oh Father." I *knew* why St. Paul had written ". . . you have received a spirit of adoption as sons by which we cry out, 'Abba! Father!' " (Rom. 8:15b). "Abba! Father!" means the very thing I found myself involuntarily whispering—"Oh, Father! Oh, Father!" For two weeks I staggered around overwhelmed by the Father's loving presence and knew firsthand what the Scripture means when it says, "God *is love*" (1 John 4:8) and "God is light, and in Him *there is no darkness at all*"(1 John 1:5) and "Every good thing bestowed and every perfect gift is from above, coming down from the *Father* of lights, with whom *there is no variation or shifting shadow*" (James 1:17).

By then, however, I had been down so many seemingly good blind alleys, and suffered so many misleading mystical experiences, that though I was certain this was what it seemed to be, I wasn't going to have even this wonderful gift unless the Lord could show it to me in Scripture, and said so. He replied, *John, look up John 14:21.* He simply quoted it for me (isn't it great that the Lord knows the Scripture)! "He who has My commandments and keeps them, he it is who loves Me; and he who loves Me shall be loved by My Father, and I will love him and will disclose Myself to him." The very things we have been teaching, that His commandments are to lay down our life for our friends, to love as He has loved! Here he was adding that such burden bearing is the very prerequisite to arrival in a special relationship with the Father. Jesus was saying that one really does come to know him—He is disclosed—when one shares His suffering for others, keeping the commandment of Galatians 6:2!

Stubbornly, I said, "That's not enough, Lord."

He said, *Look up John 14:23.* Again He quoted it, "If anyone loves Me, he will keep My word; and My Father will love him, and *We* will come to him, and *make Our abode* with him," the very thing which was just happening to me! My heart swelled and my mind fairly burst with light. My thoughts were saying, "Oh, yes, I see, I see. Why did I never see it before!?" while to the Lord I said, more humbly but just as determinedly, "That's still not enough, Lord." So He quoted to me all of Ephesians 3:14-19.

> For this reason, I bow my knees before the Father, from whom every family in heaven and on earth derives its name, that He would grant you, according to the riches of His glory, to be strengthened with power through His Spirit in the inner man; so that Christ may dwell in your hearts through faith; and that you, being rooted and grounded in love, *may be able to comprehend* with all the saints what is the breadth and length and height and depth, and *to know the love of Christ* which surpasses knowledge, *that you may be filled up to all the fulness of God.*

Then, while I basked in the Father's presence, and drove slowly on, Jesus taught me. He said, *John, when you received Me as Lord and Savior, I entered with My Father and with the Holy Spirit. Implicitly, you possessed all three of us then. You soon learned you needed to experience the Holy Spirit explicitly. But I came with the Holy Spirit precisely in order to restore you to My Father! That's My purpose. You needed to experience the Father explicitly too. This is the way you or anyone comes into "the fullness of God."*

I remembered then that "No one can come to Me, unless the Father who sent Me draws him" (John 6:44) and more to the point, "no one comes to the Father, but through Me" (John 14:6b). Jesus the Son had just drawn me to the Father. In the process He had taught me that burden bearing is not merely the work of a few adepts who happen to have that strange and different gift. It is the province and calling of every Christian; the very prerequisite to coming into fullness of life with God the Father for every Christian!

Since that time I have been far more at peace and rest. I *know* Father God has me. The search is over. I know if I fall, Father God will pick me up. I know the source of power. Jesus said, "The words that I say to you I do not speak on My own initiative, but the Father abiding in Me does His works." It is the Father who sent Jesus who sends us all. It is the Father who works in Him who works in me. I do not have to strive to make anything happen. It is the Father's work and His responsibility. I only have the joy of serving the most compassionate, tender, safe and loving Father who ever was.

Burden bearing is the key to fullness of life. We cannot arrive merely by coming into the Father's house and celebrating how good it is to be saved. Worship without service eventually hears again the prophet's cry:

> When you come to appear before me, Who requires of you this trampling of my courts? Bring no more vain offerings; incense is an abomination to me. New moon and sabbath and the calling of assemblies—I cannot endure iniquity and solemn assembly. Your new moons and your appointed feasts my soul hates; they have become a burden to me, I am weary of bearing them. When you spread forth your hands, I will hide my eyes from you; even though you make many prayers, I will not listen; your hands are full of blood. Wash yourselves; make yourselves clean; remove the evil of your doings from before my eyes; cease to do evil, *learn to do good; seek justice, correct oppression; defend the fatherless, plead for the widow* (Isa. 1:12-17 RSV).

Paula and I can confidently say, after serving as counselors for more than twenty-five years, that the central sin behind all sin-caused suffering in human life is one simple thing—self-centered selfishness! By that we do not mean stinginess. Generous, ever-giving people may yet remain self-centered, so long as those services originate in their definition of themselves as loving people rather than in the Holy Spirit's outpouring of Jesus' life. Among those who remain self-centered, their good deeds arise from their need to fulfill their picture of themselves rather than from the Lord's calling. Such good deeds often bother people more than they help.

Self-centered selfishness continues as the center of our being long after our sins are washed away, long after the sin nature receives its initial deathblow, and even long after we begin to learn to lay down our life in burden bearing! Salvation is a process, positionally begun and ended at conversion, but worked out in fear and trembling (Phil. 2:12).

> So then, my beloved, just as you have always obeyed, not as in my presence only, but now much more in my absence, *work out your salvation with fear and trembling* (Phil. 2:12).

> In this you greatly rejoice, even though now for a little while, if necessary, you have been distressed by various trials, that the proof of your faith, being more precious than gold which is perishable, even though tested by fire, may be found to result in praise and glory and honor at the revelation of Jesus Christ; and though you have not seen Him, you love Him, and though you do not see Him now, but believe in Him, you greatly rejoice with joy inexpressible and full of glory, *obtaining as the outcome of your faith the salvation of your souls* (1 Pet. 1:6-9).

We must persevere in burden bearing until it becomes more than an occasional thing we just happen to remember to do. Burden bearing must become an automatic unconscious built-in life style. Only so does the work of it become enough, and so engrossing as to overcome the core of our self-centered nature and so set us free. St. Paul wrote, "We have come to share in Christ *if* we hold firmly till the end the confidence we had at first" (Heb. 3:14 NIV). The Body has come to understand that to mean that we must grit our teeth and hang onto our belief until the end. St. Paul meant much more. He wrote that in the context of Hebrews 4, which is the chapter about entering into *His rest.* "There remains, then, a Sabbath-rest for the people of God; for anyone who enters God's rest also *rests from his own work,* just as God did from his" (v. 9). The principal work which our self-centered nature must lay down and cease doing is our perpetual striving to build, defend and live for our own self-image. *Whoever holds his confidence in Christ long enough to persevere in burden bearing until fatigue crushes him discovers he can no longer bear burdens as a part of fulfilling his own self-image.* Love for, and desire to, bear burdens must come to death by the continual weight of it, until one only does it by obedience, letting Him do it in us, as us, for us. That death brings us into both freedom and rest. Romans 7 and 8 and Hebrews 3 and 4 become one message, written on our hearts, when burden bearing, by obedience alone, finally slays self-centeredness at its core. We enter the freedom of Romans 8. We abide in the restfulness of Hebrews 4.

Even so, all I need to do is to become tired of burden bearing, refuse a few callings of the Lord, and my self-centered selfish nature reasserts itself. I must either walk in Jesus' continual self-giving, or my self-taking reassumes command of me and I fall from rest to self-centered striving all over again. Burden bearing, laying down life for others, is thus not a nice option. It is the quintessential sacrificial life which alone ensures death, and thus life, for every Christian.

Oh that this immature, selfishly-celebrating-its-own-salvation Body of Christ would hear the call of the Lord to service, let alone the service of burden bearing! How I hate our continual celebrating that we are going to Heaven, as though that were the be-all and end-all of salvation! It's great to celebrate going to Heaven as an occasional reminder and feast of joy. But if that is all we know and do, it stinks! Body of Christ, the fields are white unto harvest, and salvation is only begun, not ended. Let's learn that which truly brings us into the fullness. Burden bearing is not, as we have thought, the province of those few unfortunate weirdos who happen to be sensitive to what others feel. It is the *first calling* and *primary labor* of *every* Christian, the very *life/breath* of the *normal Christian life,* the key by which we come into the fullness of relationship with the Father and into sufficient death of self to enter freedom and rest. It is simple—respond and serve—or fail to enter the fullness.

Having said all those good things about burden bearing, we must now look at the other side, for there are pitfalls. Burden bearing is not always safe, either from what may be encountered, or from one's own sin nature. Temptations are always present, temptations to do too much, to take oneself too seriously, to judge and blame, to become overburdened and confused, to think of one's own problems as someone else's, or vice versa.

Often, in counseling, Paula and I discover natural burden bearers who have never understood what their spirits have leaped to do, uninformed and unaided. These people enter a room and almost instantly sense and take on nearly everyone's burden. Their hearts reach out instinctively to enfold and comfort. For many such people, life becomes too heavy a burden.

I speak from painful experience. I cannot remember when I was not like that. When the fullness of the Holy Spirit came, the burden of it became much too much. I couldn't control it, much less stop it. In worship services and prayer meetings, others would be rejoicing, smiling and laughing, while I sank in sorrow as I sopped up the hurts they were not letting themselves feel. I would try to be happy, but my smile would freeze and fade. I could not be happy. Eventually, the Lord gloriously healed that, as we will share presently.

Natural burden bearers become wounded spirits unless fortunate enough to find instruction and the protection of wiser friends. Their lack of understanding throws them into hurtful strivings of the flesh. What should be easy, light and joyous (Matt. 11:30) becomes heavy and oppressive. If they happen also to be performance-oriented persons, as I was, they try too hard and take to heart each failure to help others and so become loaded with false guilt. If they happen to be parentally inverted like me, they can't let go and rest. The whole world seems to rest on their shoulders.

Burden bearers often pick up on sorrow and hurt in their friends when their friends are laughing and totally convinced that they are happy.

A wise proverb says, "knowledge increases sorrow." Burden bearers live with the loneliness of knowing things others do not know and may not want or be able to bear. If a burden bearer lacks ego strength (courage of spirit), he may become confused and uncertain about his own perceptions. If he is arrogant and insensitive to how others may receive what he says, he may confuse, anger or wound others by blurting out his perceptions without wisdom.

People may become afraid of such a person. So often I asked people why they felt like they did when they thought they had their feelings well hidden, and so frequently added a bit of perception or the gift of knowledge, that many in our town became afraid of me! "He knows too much." "He's got x-ray eyes." "I feel like he's looking right through me." That wounds the spirit of both the friends and the burden bearer. On the other hand, if sensitivity to the fears of others caused me not to ask questions, that stuck me with too many heavy and unidentifiable burdens. I felt like Jeremiah, "But if I say, 'I will not remember Him Or speak anymore in His name,' Then in my heart it becomes like a burning fire Shut up in my bones; And I am weary of holding it in, And I cannot endure it" (Jer. 20:9).

Most often we have found such natural burden bearers driven into silence and loneliness. They have learned in pain not to share. Others didn't understand, or denied their perceptions, or were affronted as though they had been some kind of spiritual voyeurs, peeping behind curtains which ought to have remained drawn. Of course, sometimes this accusation was hurtfully true, for the Holy Spirit is a perfect gentleman; He respects privacy, but our flesh does not.

Some burden bearers are immature, or acting in the flesh, or even unconverted, or become enamored of their

419

gift, or love the feeling of power and so unwittingly enlist the aid of demons. In the end, their gift turns from burden bearing to suspicion and gossip. In short, burden bearing without instruction and propriety in the Holy Spirit wounds the personal spirits both of the burden bearer and his "victim." Both need healing, which is done by simple investigative inquiry and prayer asking Jesus to heal and restore.

I leaped characteristically whole-hog into burden bearing, long before I had gained any tact or wisdom in the Holy Spirit or had learned about proper separation of soul and spirit. It became utterly oppressive. I did not suffer the kind of true fatigue spoken of earlier which would have brought true death and rest. I experienced flesh fatigue which produced only pride in my own false martyrdom. The Holy Spirit in me would only have taken on those burdens in people which Jesus was at that moment enduring. But the flesh leaped grandly to do everything all at once and congratulated itself that the fatigue was for Him and the adverse reactions of some people were noble persecutions to be reveled in. In time, however, the game became too crushing, and I had to look honestly at myself. The Lord send brother Winston Nunes, who explained separation of soul and spirit to me and prayed me through.

Soul and spirit cannot be separated in terms of space, but in terms of function. "For the word of God is living and active and sharper than any two-edged sword, and piercing as far as *the division of soul and spirit,* of both joints and marrow, and able to judge the thoughts and intentions of the heart" (Heb. 4:12). Brother Winston explained that the Lord has built us like an automobile engine, which has separate places for oil and water and gasoline. If water enters where gasoline or oil should be, trouble ensues, or gasoline where oil and water, or oil where water and gasoline operate. Just so, God designed the mind to do certain tasks, the heart others and the spirit others still. But the Fall so scrambled us that emotions flood beyond their bounds and adversely affect or sometimes fully overcome the mind and spirit. Similarly the mind can stifle emotions or block the spirit and the spirit can run amok beyond the controls of the mind, causing us to sail into far-out mystical experiences. He explained that after conversion, we need prayer to unscramble our inner being and settle our parts, each into its own sphere. If soul and spirit are properly settled into separate functions, then our Lord can lay a burden into our spirit and we are not torn up everywhere all at once. Our own emotions and thoughts remain undisturbed, though participating. We maintain sufficient detachment to identify and pray and remain in balance. If our heart and mind become engaged in a problem, our spirit remains at peace. Each part properly supplies its contribution without overriding the functions of other parts. We enter another dimension of the rest spoken of in Hebrews 4 because our emotions no longer run amok, our mind no longer overcontrols, and our spirit does not splay itself out, unguarded by the mind and the heart.

When Winston Nunes prayed over me that the Lord separate the functions of my soul and spirit and bring to death the overstirrings of my flesh, it was as though he had lifted a thousand-pound weight from my shoulders! I came home light and free as a bird! No longer did I *have* to bear burdens Jesus did not require of me. No more did my own emotions and mentality become garbled. Each part of me could work in cooperation with each other part. Even my health and physical coordination as an athlete dramatically improved.

There are countless natural burden bearers staggering around without an informed Christian to teach them and set them free. Paula and I have discovered hundreds since then (circa 1970-72) and have had the joy in the Lord of setting them free as our Lord did through Winston for me.

Then our delightfully humorous Lord set about through His own ways to "restore to me the joy of Thy salvation" (Ps. 51:12). Pat Brooks wrote a book entitled *Out In Jesus' Name.* I took exception to some things in her book, and for the first time in my life I wrote a critique, and sent it to her.

I wrote in longhand, and, not having her address, sent it to her publisher to be forwarded. Not being able to decipher my chicken scratchings, the publisher thought it was addressed to Pat Boone, and sent it on to him! Pat found himself bemused, unable to apply the contents to his book, but intrigued by the comments. He took the letter to his pastor, Jack Hayford, and the two of them discerned that I lacked the gift of joy! Whereupon they prayed for me to have that gift!

One morning subsequently, the Lord held His usual discussion with me: *You didn't understand that Scripture.* This time it was to say that I missed the point of the verse we sing, "The joy of the Lord is my strength" (from Neh. 8:10). He said, *John, you thought that meant you had to have some joy in order to be strong. So you tried to stir some up. And every time you failed to feel joy because you were over-burdened with My sorrows, you felt you had failed, and put yourself under condemnation. But you didn't really see what it said.* He went on to tell me, *It says, "the joy of the* Lord.*" It is My joy which is your strength, not yours. You tried to be joyful, and couldn't. But you didn't understand. Where do I live, John?*

"In me."

John, I always have joy, whether you do or not. Therefore, My joy is always in you, whether you feel it or not. It is My joy which is your strength!"

The next morning Paula and I had one of those rare moments for us when everything we said and did went at cross-purposes. I had just told the Lord I wasn't too happy with His gift to me and I wasn't too happy with Him either, when the first carload of counselees appeared in the driveway. I walked out to greet them still murmuring under my breath. The first one stepped out of the car and exclaimed, "Oh, John, the joy of the Lord is just pouring out of you this morning!"

I thought, "That's just the trouble, it's pouring out!"

But the Lord said, *Do you see, John, my joy is always there, and when you least feel it, others can still see it pouring* out! At last I believed, and came to rest. I didn't have to experience it all the time to believe that His joy was still my joy and my strength.

The Lord then opened Ecclesiastes 7:2-4 to me.

> It is better to go to a house of mourning Than to go to a house of feasting, Because that is the end of every man, And the living takes it to heart. *Sorrow is better than laughter, For when a face is sad a heart may be happy.* The mind of the wise is in the house of mourning, While the mind of fools is in the house of pleasure.

The Lord applied that to entering into the chore of burden bearing as contrasted to remaining in the house of self-centered celebrating. He explained it to me like Walt Whitman, "Do I contradict myself? Very well then I contradict myself, (I am large, I contain multitudes)." Since my soul and spirit contain separate functions, I could enter sorrow in burden bearing, and rejoice with Him in the labor of it on a deeper level in my spirit, all the while doing something on the surface as different as enjoying a child's birthday party. I did not have to be consistent in the sense of having the same emotion throughout. Each part of me could entertain a separate experience all at once! Thus I could giggle in "joy inexpressible and full of glory" (1 Pet. 1:8) in one level of my spirit while fully borne down and sobbing with Jesus over recalcitrant Jerusalem in another, while playing a game with my children.

I know from counseling experiences how desperately many Christians, both burden bearers and others, need to learn this lesson. Countless Christians suffer personal condemnation because they think something must be wrong with them when they want to laugh and cry at the same moment! In John 11, Jesus entered Bethany *knowing* He would raise Lazarus. He had already told the disciples His intention, two days beforehand (vv. 1-5). His Spirit must have been rejoicing in anticipation of the great miracle He was to accomplish, for Lazarus' sake if for nothing else. But in front of the tomb, identifying in empathetic burden bearing with Martha and all the people, He wept (v. 35). We do not have to be consistent, only Christian! We are able to feel many things in many levels of our being, all at once.

Burden bearers need friends who watch over them to see when they are falling into the flesh, taking on too much too long, or too little too briefly. We need to help one another, to encourage one another (Phil. 2:1, 3), to look out "for the interests of others" (Phil. 2:4), to lift one another up (Eccles. 4:9-12), to supply to one another (Eph. 4:16). In short, no burden bearer (thus no Christian) should ever serve alone.

Mainly, we need the hugs of Christian friends and relatives. Physical touch resonates. As one tuning fork can be struck and another chimes, so Christians restore one another to right keys and tones by touch. Paula restores me to who I am when the burdens of eighty people fill my heart and threaten to overwhelm and confuse my identity. A friend's pat on the shoulder may be sufficient, or a knowing look of empathy. We need to drink balance and give refreshment among friends.

In that lies access to leeches, however. Leeches are like vampires. They are already virtually dead. They sustain themselves by drinking the blood (energy) of others. They operate in the night (in the darknesses of misunderstandings and hatreds of self). They cannot stand the light of day (revelations of their own sins). They cannot stand mirrors (reflections of their own self and their sin).

Leeches attach themselves to people who have life in Jesus but who have not yet learned to die to the need to be needed. Leeches fasten onto people who *need* to have a ministry, who have not yet reckoned their gifting as their Isaac and sacrificed it on the altar. People who are more mature, who have died to self-importance and sacrificed their Isaacs, quickly discern and avoid the tentacles of leeches. They do not continue to give where the Lord does not.

In the early years of our ministry, Paula and I became surrounded and nearly borne down by spiritual leeches. These were weak people who liked to be dependent. They always had another emotional problem to be dealt with, another runny nose to wipe. They could latch onto us because we had not yet learned to say no. We were still pleased in our flesh that someone needed us. It made us feel important and successful to have people around us who hung on our words and asked us questions which made us feel wise and competent.

Hugs usually make one feel comforted, or refreshed, or fulfilled. Hugging a leech leaves one feeling drained. These people are like vacuum cleaners, only they suck out the cleanness rather than the dirt! It seems as though burden bearers become filled with leeches' dirt to no avail. It would be okay, indeed our purpose, if, like St. Paul, death could be at work in us but life in them. With leeches, it doesn't seem to do any good. Leeches feel better, but only momentarily. No life seems to be working in them. They fail to take hold and run on their own batteries.

Again it was Winston Nunes who set me free. We had been reading many works by Watchman Nee, especially *The Latent Power of the Soul*, and had come to see that much of our ministry was only soulish striving, and that truly "the flesh profits nothing" (John 6:63). But we didn't know how to get out of it. It was Winston who said,"John, your ministry is your Isaac. God wants you to sacrifice it."

Having accepted Winston as a man of God, I obeyed, little comprehending what I was doing. Afterwards I saw that so long as a man holds any gift or talent, he and his soulish flesh, rather than God, manipulate it. It possesses and drives him, rather than God possessing both it and him. Winston led me through the prayer of renunciation as an Abraham surrendering his Isaac. And he explained to me the meaning of Luke 14:26, that every skill in us is as our child, which is still flesh, coated in the old wineskin. We must turn to hate even the garment spotted by the flesh (Jude 23) and bring to death on the cross everything in us, or it, rather than Jesus, will possess and control us.

The moment Winston led me through that prayer and I shared it with Paula, our need to be needed died. Our ministry had died. Therefore, we did not need hangers-on to convince us of the supposed worth of our ministry. It took discipline to learn to activate discernment. It took a while to learn to say no. In the process we learned that unwittingly we had not been living for Jesus only, but for the ministry, using Jesus to further our ministry. When that died, our security was again in Jesus, not in how well the ministry seemed to be going.

That meant that we were no longer blind to the leeches. We didn't have to do anything. Their blood supply dried up because we no longer poured out our own being to them, thinking it was Jesus. They just naturally wandered off to find some other "suckers." A few, finding the false supply shut down, turned and found their death and rebirth in Christ.

Counselors need to comprehend this aspect, actually the limit to burden bearing, as in Galatians 6:5, "For each one shall bear his own load." Understanding it, they can lead others through the Abraham-Isaac prayer, as in Luke 14:26. Sometimes I have felt led to add, "Now Lord, we close all those inner doors which have been too open," or, "We loose this person from the spirits of all those who have latched onto him. Lord, seal up his inner being so that none may find wrong access to him again."

Unless one has become as crushed and overburdened as have some of us unwise uncrucified natural burden bearers, he cannot fully appreciate the blessed relief and release such understanding and prayer affords! Let pastors examine their most faithfully serving sheep. So many servants have tragically burned out who need not have been lost had we understood the lessons of Isaac and Luke 14:26!

We need not only to teach and pray release, we need to heal. We ought in each case to pour the balm of the Lord into all those overtired, overtaxed areas of the inner being of our well-meaning friends who have rushed to serve, unprotected by enough wisdom and self-death.

It is not necessary to mount our charger to chase all the leeches out of the flock. God may use leeches to bring His servants to sufficient disgust to quit the self-filled game of ministry. And some of the leeches may find true faith. Let us only watch to minister to the Lord's servants such relief as we ourselves have found when we died to the need to be needed.

We close this chapter on burden bearing here, for only those who have learned the secret that *God needs no one* are safe to continue the hazards of burden-bearing ministry. We are not going to be allowed to retain a handle on God. He loves us all. And in the sense that every father needs every one of his children, God needs us. But in no other sense does He need us. He could replace us by another in a moment. He alone is God. He will not share His glory with another—for our sakes. It is not good to be needed. All need relationships are unstable. The world wants handles. It wants to be needed. Christians are free. They are not needed, but oh, so loved and wanted. They are free to give and receive love without making anyone dependent. Whoever thinks his church—or anyone, for that matter—cannot get along without him is in for a rude surprise. Let's teach every Christian to "resign the general managership of the universe"! It's quite a shock—and then fun—to discover how well family and friends, and the whole world, can get along without us! If we discover that, God is free to let the world need us because we don't need it and neither we nor they will fall to idolatry. Here, as everywhere, death is the key to life.

Burden bearers only find it hard to die because they think they already have.

Chapter Fifteen

Grief, Frustration, and Loss

A tranquil mind gives *life to the flesh*, but passion makes the bones rot (Prov. 14:30 RSV).

A joyful heart makes a cheerful face, But when the heart is sad, the spirit is broken (Prov. 15:13 NAS).

A cheerful heart is a good medicine, but a downcast spirit dries up the bones (Prov. 17:22 RSV).

Grief, frustration and loss come in two kinds. There is that which befalls us from loss of aspirations, frustrations in vocation or job, or loss of income or cherished objects. These are all hurts in relation to things, a dream or a hope being as much a thing to our heart as a cherished teapot handed down from grandmother. And there is that kind of grief, frustration and loss which happens in relationships to God, others or oneself. Of the two, the second is far more formidable. Lost things become only a memory. God and people continue to live, and their life calls to our life. Their continued existence alone summons redress and restoration.

We have written somewhat of grief in Chapter Seven on "Depression," and in some aspects about frustration and loss in *The Transformation of the Inner Man* in the chapter on "Destiny Malaise." There are many excellent books on the subject, one of the best being *Healing Life's Hurts* by the Linn brothers. This chapter is not to repeat what has already been covered, but to address the subject from the more specific aspect of how grief, frustration and loss affect our personal spirit and thus our bodies, and how such effects can be healed.

When we come into the world, our spirit is not something apart from our body and our heritage. It is integrally involved with both. This means that our spirit instinctively looks to no one as primarily as to our own father and mother for definition and fulfillment. To lose a parent, especially in the formative years, is not like the loss of a limb. One can lose an arm and still adjust because the central core of the person remains intact, along with supportive systems of friends and relatives. But a parent has a far more foundational function in our life than even our own legs.

A child's spirit drinks definition and fulfillment daily from his parents. Being with them sings to the very DNA cells of his being how to sing the zipper songs of the RNA. Presence and association resonate through a child's spirit into the very bones of his being.

There is a direct relation of our spirit's health to physical health, especially regarding primary people. "A good wife is the crown of her husband, but she who brings shame is like *rottenness in his bones*" (Prov. 12:4 RSV). Grief from loss of loved ones affects the physical health of our very bones:

> For my life is spent with sorrow, and my years with sighing; my strength fails because of my misery, and my *bones waste away* (Ps. 31:10 RSV).

> Is it nothing to you, all who pass by? Look and see if there is any sorrow like my sorrow which was brought upon me, which the Lord inflicted on the day of his fierce anger. From on high he sent fire; *into my bones*

> he made it descend; he spread a net for my feet; he
> turned me back; he has left me stunned, faint all the
> day long (Lam. 1:12, 13 RSV).

Stress affects our spirit and thus our health, specifically
our bones:

> A tranquil mind gives life to the flesh, but passion
> makes the *bones rot* (Prov. 14:30 RSV).

It should be mentioned that the word "passion" here
does not mean proper healthy sexual passion but fleshly
aggravations.

> A cheerful heart is a good medicine, but a *downcast*
> *spirit dries up the bones* (Prov. 17:22 RSV).

Anticipation of stress likewise affects our spirit, thus our
health, most specifically our bones. Habakkuk prophesied
of approaching judgment for sin,

> I hear, and my body trembles, my lips quiver at the
> sound; *rottenness* enters *into my bones*, my steps totter
> beneath me. I will wait quietly for the day of trouble to
> come upon people who invade us (Hab. 3:16 RSV).

Job, under the stress of loss and sorrow, suffered in his
spirit and in his bones, and his friends spoke of sin affecting
the spirit and bones (as described in the Revised Standard
Version): trembling so that all his bones shake (Job 4:14);
his bones cleave to his skin (19:20); the night racks his bones
(30:17); there is "continual strife in his bones" (33:19). On
the other hand, Job described those who are blessed by God,
who enjoy health, by speaking of their bones full of youthful
vigor (20:11); "wholly at ease and secure, his body full of fat
and the marrow of his bones moist" (21:24).

Sin immediately affects the spirit and thus the bones.

> There is no soundness in my flesh because of thy
> indignation; there is *no health in my bones because of*
> *my sin* (Ps. 38:3 RSV).

> For my days pass away like smoke, and my *bones*
> *burn* like a furnace. My heart is smitten like grass, and
> withered; I forget to eat my bread. Because of my loud
> groaning *my bones cleave* to my flesh (Ps. 102:3-5 RSV).

When I declared not my sin, my *body* wasted away through my groaning all day long. For day and night thy hand was heavy upon me; my strength was dried up as by the heat of summer (Ps. 32:3, 4 RSV).

He loved to curse; let curses come on him! He did not like blessing; may it be far from him! He clothed himself with cursing as his coat, may it *soak into his body* like water, like oil *into his bones!* (Ps. 109:17, 18 RSV).

The discipline of the Lord directly affects our bones.

There they are, in great terror, in terror such as has not been! For God will *scatter the bones of the ungodly;* they will be put to shame, for God has rejected them (Ps. 53:5 RSV).

Fill me with joy and gladness; let the *bones which thou hast broken* rejoice (Ps. 51:8 RSV).

Let a good man strike or rebuke me in kindness, but let the oil of the wicked never anoint my head; for my prayer is continually against their wicked deeds. When they are given over to those who shall condemn them, then they shall learn that the word of the Lord is true. As a rock which one cleaves and shatters on the land, *so shall their bones be strewn at the mouth of Sheol* (Ps. 141:5-7 RSV).

Why are bones so important? How does what happens to our spirit so quickly and directly affect our bones? Listen to these simple facts (from the *Reader's Digest Medical Encyclopedia,* pp. 527-8):

Bones are the *source* of vital constituents of blood. They are the *storehouse* from which the calcium in blood plasma is obtained. The pores and cavities . . . are filled with red marrow. Red marrow consists largely of *blood corpuscles in all stages of development. About 5 million mature red blood cells . . . are produced and released every second.* The blood, platelets, which are *essential* for blood clot formation, and the *white cells which protect the body against infection are also formed in the red marrow* . . . [italics mine].

Now let us hold in mind that startling fact that *every second five million new red blood cells* are released into our body, and that the red marrow produces white cells which protect us from disease, while we consider the following Scriptures:

> Trust in the Lord with all your heart, and do not rely on your own insight. In all your ways acknowledge him, and he will make straight your paths. Do not be wise in your own eyes; fear the Lord, and turn away from evil. It will be *healing to your flesh and refreshment to your bones* (Prov. 3:5-8 RSV).

> Pleasant words are a honeycomb, Sweet to the soul and *healing to the bones* (Prov. 16:24 NAS).

> The light of the eyes rejoices the heart, and *good news refreshes the bones* (Prov. 15:30 RSV).

> You shall see, and your heart shall rejoice; your *bones shall flourish like grass;* and it shall be known that the hand of the Lord is with his servants, and his indignation is against his enemies (Isa. 66:14 RSV).

In Isaiah 58 the Lord calls for men to serve Him as they ought, and says,

> Then shall your light break forth like the dawn, and your healing shall spring up speedily; your right-esousness shall go before you, the glory of the Lord shall be your rear guard. Then you shall call, and the Lord will answer; you shall cry, and he will say, Here I am. If you take away from the midst of you the yoke, the pointing of the finger, and speaking wickedness, if you pour yourself out for the hungry and satisfy the desire of the afflicted, then shall your light rise in the darkness, and your gloom be as the noonday. And the Lord will guide you continually, and satisfy your desire with good things, and *make your bones strong* (Isa. 58:8-11a RSV).

The Psalmist spoke of his bones rejoicing in the Lord,

> Then my soul shall rejoice in the Lord, exulting in his deliverance. *All my bones* shall say, "O Lord, who is like

433

thee, thou who deliverest the weak from him who is too strong for him, the weak and the needy from him who despoils him?" (Ps. 35:9 RSV).

One of the promises of God concerning righteousness and bones was fulfilled by the fact that the soldiers did not break the legs of Jesus, as the custom was, but only pierced His side: "Many are the afflictions of the righteous; But the Lord delivers him out of them all. *He keeps all his bones; Not one of them is broken*" (Ps. 34:19, 20).

So we see that (1) bones and the spirits of men and God have a special direct relation; (2) there is something precious and important spiritually and physically about bones, more so perhaps than other parts of the body; (3) bones immediately and directly register sin and righteousness in terms of sickness and wholeness, "dryness" and "moistness"; (4) sin sometimes results in broken bones; (5) confessions, repentance and the favor of the Lord result in refreshment to the bones, and thus in health to the whole body.

Amazingly, we see in 2 Kings 13:20, 21 that bones become such a repository of spirit and light that even long after death they contain healing power!

> And Elisha died, and they buried him. Now the bands of the Moabites would invade the land in the spring of the year. And as they were burying a man, behold, they saw a marauding band; and they cast the man into the grave of Elisha. And when the man touched the bones of Elisha he revived and stood up on his feet!

What can all this say about arthritis? Bursitis? Leukemia? Tendonitis? Ability to rebuild body strength through the blood? What can it reveal to us about all the blood and bone diseases to which we sometimes succumb? What may it say about the effect of rejection in utero? About attempts at abortion? Quarrels between parents while a fetus is in utero? Violence to pregnant mothers? And so on?

On the other side, what does it say about the power of prayers which apply the blood of Christ? About the value of the sacrament of communion? About the salutory effect of the indwelling of the Holy Spirit? No wonder the Word promises, "Yet those who wait for the Lord will gain new strength; They will mount up with wings like eagles, They will run and not get tired, They will walk and not become weary" (Isa. 40:31).

It has long been noted that those who receive our Lord and walk in Him look years younger. Their vitality mounts. I (John) can testify not only for myself but for many acquaintances that athletic coordination increased dramatically. Let us cease to think of the spirit like water and of our bodies like glasses. That is Docetic heresy. The Holy Spirit inhabits all of our spirit, like pouring red dye into blue, resulting in purple. Something new and tremendous results. The Holy Spirit and our spirit infuse, flow through, live in, breathe through, saturate, activate, revive, refresh, and empower every cell of our bodies! The Holy Spirit works to make us new in every way.

The entire import of this chapter so far is to make us aware that when we speak of the baptism of the Holy Spirit, of prayer, of sin and stress, of redemption and the blood of Christ, we are addressing down-to-earth, tremendously practical realities. Let us banish from our minds that falsity of thought which long compartmentalized life as though what we did on Sunday took care of God, and the rest of the week we could spend on the real and the practical, and of course only the foolish would think that the Sermon on the Mount was ever intended to be lived by anyone but naive idealists and cloistered saints! Faith, living with God, and communing with His Spirit are practical and life-giving. The Sermon on the Mount was not only intended for practical living, anything less is less than practical! God's Word is eminently practical. Man's ideas and customs produce death. God's Word is life:

The law of the Lord is perfect, *restoring the soul;*
The testimony of the Lord is sure, making wise the simple.
The precepts of the Lord are right, *rejoicing the heart;*
The commandment of the Lord is pure, *enlightening the eyes.*
The fear of the Lord is clean, enduring forever;
The judgments of the Lord are true;
   they are righteous altogether.
They are more desirable than gold, yes, than much fine gold;
Sweeter also than honey and the drippings of the honeycomb.
Moreover, by them Thy servant is warned;
In keeping them there is great reward.

                         —Ps. 19:7-12

St. Paul commanded his followers:

> Finally, brethren, whatever is true, whatever is honorable, whatever is right, whatever is pure, whatever is lovely, whatever is of good repute, if there is any excellence and if anything worthy of praise, *let your mind dwell on these things* (Phil. 4:8).

Too many of us have thought, "That's nice," while also thinking, "But of course it's not really relevant. We have to live in the real world." Thus we fail to receive the benefit of the next verse. "The things you have learned and received and heard and seen in me, *practice* these things; *and the God of peace shall be with you"* (v. 9). St. Paul went on to say in the next verses that he had learned the secret of facing everything and that he can do all things through Him who strengthens him. Science now tells us one in four Americans (not living in His Word) suffer some degree of mental illness—and we think God's Word is impractical! "Thou wilt keep him in perfect peace, whose mind is stayed on thee" (Isa. 26:3 KJV).

Secular science has been learning—unaided by the safeguards of God's Word—to apply positive words to illness, often with spectacular success.

An excellent study of cancer development, its relation to stress, and description of an effective program of treatment can be found in the book *Getting Well Again* by Carl Simonton, M.D., Stephanie Matthews-Simonton and

James Creighton. Dr. Simonton is medical director of the Cancer Counseling and Research Center in Forth Worth, Texas. The Center's research shows the following to be the typical components of cancer patients' histories: The patient's youth was marked by feelings of isolation, neglect, and despair, with intense interpersonal relationships appearing difficult. In early adulthood, the patient was able to establish a strong meaningful relationship, or found great satisfaction in his or her vocation. Tremendous energy was poured into the relationship or role. The relationship or role was then removed. The "bruise" left over from the childhood despair was painfully struck again. The result was despair "bottled up." These individuals were unable to let other people know when they felt hurt, angry or hostile. They tended to be the kind of people who were tremendously concerned to minister to the needs of others, but could not feel free to share their own feelings or burden others with their problems. In their innermost thoughts they saw the end as a disaster they had always half expected. Superficially they continued to function, but the zest went out of their lives. Seventy-six percent of five hundred patients interviewed shared this kind of history. (The Simontons drew this information from studies by Dr. Lawrence LeShan, *You Can Fight for Your Life: Emotional Factors in the Causation of Cancer.*) The Simontons also reported, from a study by Dr. D.M. Kissen, that the major differences between heavy smokers who get lung cancer and heavy smokers who do not is "poorly developed outlets for emotional discharge" in the former. From studies by D. E.M. Blumberg and Dr. B. Klopfer they reported that fast-growing tumors are often related to extreme desire to make a good impression, and to ego-defensiveness and loyalty to one's own version of reality.

Our own teachings on performance orientation, bitter roots, and inner vows certainly confirm this information.

The Simontons explained in simple layman's terms the effect of psychological stress on the physical body, which results in an imbalance of adrenal hormones which in turn creates greater susceptibility to carcinogenic substances, and finally results in suppression of immune activity, increase of abnormal cells, and cancerous growth. In their treatment program the Simontons attempted to introduce elements of hope and anticipation in a discipline to create changes in perceptions of self and problems. They insisted that it is not stress itself, but the way of reacting to stress, that makes a difference in susceptibility to disease. By psychological intervention to change the patient's ways of reacting to stress, the destructive process in the body can be reversed to result in cancer regression.

The following describes in brief form the basic steps of the Simonton plan to anticipating return to health. We place those steps in a parallel column with our references to what the Bible says on the same subjects. The question we offer to our Christian readers is this: If cancer regression can be successfully achieved as it has in this program *without* specific reference to God (though we believe that no real healing happens outside of Him), how much *more* could be accomplished with a combination of common sense, medical knowledge, and *prayer*, especially for inner healing which reaches all the way back to those feelings of isolation, neglect and despair the patient experienced in his youth?!

> Now may the God of peace Himself sanctify you entirely; and may your spirit and soul and *body* be preserved complete, without blame at the coming of our Lord Jesus Christ (1 Thess. 5:23).

Basics of Simonton's Plan for Anticipating Return to Health to Support Medical Treatment:

FIRST WEEK:	**WHAT THE BIBLE SAYS ABOUT THE SAME . . .**

FIRST WEEK:

Reading: *Getting Well Again,* Simonton; *The Will to Live,* Dr. A. Hutschecker; *Seeing With the Mind's Eyes,* Samuels; *Mind as Healer, Mind as Slayer,* Dr. K. Peletier

Relaxation and Imagery— cancer cells weak, confused, healthy cells have no difficulty repairing damage; army of white cells is vast and overcomes cancer cells; white cells are aggressive, eager for battle, quick to seek out cancer cells to destroy them; dead cancer cells flush naturally; by end of imagery you are healthy; you see yourself reaching goals, fulfilling your life's purpose.

SECOND WEEK:

Continue relaxation and imagery. *Identify major stresses* occuring eighteen months prior to diagnosis. *Relate those to earlier similar stresses. Identify the "benefits" of illness.* Emotion is now expected and accepted, you have permission to ask for help, love, attention, express unhappiness. You have an acceptable reason for not performing stress-related tasks, etc.

WHAT THE BIBLE SAYS ABOUT THE SAME . . .

PEACE, REST, FORGIVENESS

Gal. 5:22—fruit of the Spirit is peace . . .

Eph. 2:14—He is our peace

1 Thess. 5:23—may the God of peace sanctify you entirely

Luke 6:45—(we express out of treasure that fills our hearts)

Luke 6:46-49—(after we come to Jesus we are willing to let Him examine and re-lay our foundations)

Jer. 6:16—rest for your souls

Matt. 11:28—I will give you rest

Matt. 11:29—for your souls

Heb. 12:10-15—(discipline, forgiveness, healing) . . . see to it that no root of bitterness springs up to cause trouble.

Mark 9:50—Be at peace with one another

1 Thess. 5:13—live in peace with one another

Heb. 5:10—the one who has entered His rest has himself also rested from his works, as God did from His . . .

THE WAY WE SEE IT: OUR VULNERABILITY

Matt. 6:22, 23—The lamp of the body is the eye . . .

THIRD WEEK:
Relaxation and imagery, *Physical exercise*, one hour, three times a week. *Counseling:* minister, counselor, psychotherapist, one who really *cares*.

THE NEED FOR
A COUNSELOR
Prov. 25:1-4—glory of kings to search out a matter . . .
James 5:16—Confess your sins to one another, and pray for one another, that you may be healed.
Prov. 20:5—A plan in the heart of a man is like deep water, but a man of understanding draws it out.

FOURTH WEEK:
Continue all of the above. *Face fears* concerning death. *Overcome resentment. Forgive. Bless* the one you forgive.

CONDITIONS OF
FORGIVENESS
Matt. 6:14, 15; Prov. 3:6-8—(healing to body)
Ps. 32—(sin-sickness); Ps. 38:8-11—(crushed, agitated, heart throbs, fails in strength)

FIFTH WEEK:
Continue all the above. *Set goals* for three months, six months, one year. *Incorporate these into the imagery* process. See yourself reaching goals.

GOALS, FULFILLMENT
Eph. 2:10—For we are His workmanship, created in Christ Jesus for good works which God prepared beforehand, that we should walk in them.

SIXTH WEEK:
All of the above. Get in touch with your *"inner guide,"* (a wise old person within, or even someone you call Freddy Frog).

INNER GUIDE—
HOLY SPIRIT
Ps. 139:23, 24—Search me and know my heart . . .
John 14:26—Holy Spirit will teach you all things . . .

We have taught all this because we know that such knowledge is itself the beginning of our healing. However, Christian counselors must come to see that truly the gospel "is the power of God for salvation" (Rom. 1:16). As Christians we should appropriate what is valuable from secular research and techniques of healing which produce positive results. But we are not limited to those. God's Word *is* power. Our Lord *himself* is healing. We have often grieved to find counselors who call themselves Christian and yet are apparently "ashamed of the gospel" in that they are afraid to incorporate prayer in their ministry; they rely altogether on secular techniques. We believe that secular modes of the healing art can be vehicles or packages for healing. But God himself is the content of the package, the power which makes the vehicle move. Only prayer fully applies that power.

> I pray that the eyes of your heart may be enlightened, so that you may know what is the hope of His calling, what are the riches of the glory of His inheritance in the saints, and *what is the surpassing greatness of His power toward us who believe* (Eph. 1:18, 19).

All of this means that when we hear of a great loss, we have power to heal.

> He was despised and forsaken of men, A man of sorrows, and acquainted with grief; And like one from whom men hide their face, He was despised, and we did not esteem Him. Surely our griefs He Himself bore, And our sorrows He carried; Yet we ourselves esteemed Him stricken, Smitten of God, and afflicted. But He was pierced through for our transgressions, He was crushed for our iniquities; The chastening for our well-being fell upon Him, And by His scourging we are healed (Isa. 53:3-5).

By faith we are healed and we heal others when we ask Jesus to identify with hurt and grief and take it to himself. We do not need regressions to primal screams to heal the wounds from infancy! We need only prayer and the burden bearing of our Lord Jesus Christ.

Whatever the hurt, whatever the loss, however great the tragedy, every Christian counselor needs to hold in mind Romans 8:28, "And we know that God causes *all things* to work together for good to those who love God, to those who are called according to His purpose." If we only comfort and heal, our patient may find himself also confirmed in his self-pity. He may remain unwilling to let go of his dour feelings because that stance of self-pity seems to purchase rewards from important people around him. Prayers for healing should contain assurances that God will make that pile of bitter ashes into a fountain of glory for ministry to others. Subsequent counsel needs to call for a discipline of prayer and faith which looks *through* problems and determines not to hug pain to oneself, for whatever reason.

It may be well to repeat (from the chapter on depression) that grief may be quickly healed and banished by faith, whereas sorrow may return many times. Sorrow and tears are not marks of lack of faith. Sorrow is a healthy release of loss and hurt. For many months after grief is assuaged, tears may well up, especially at holidays or when some incident triggers a cherished memory. *Such sorrow is not something to be done away with, nor banished as one would cast away a demon, nor healed too quickly.* It is not something bad or evil. It is something to be endured and sweetened by. It is a mark of love's knowing the pain of loss. It will pass away naturally in time, when its work is done in the heart.

Sorrow does evil work only when we fear it or otherwise handle it badly. Repressed sorrow eats into the marrow of the bones and destroys vitality. It can result in many psychosomatically caused diseases. Sorrow "used" can become a tool wielded to control others. Sorrow feared can increase to emotional tantrums.

The trouble with many is that we may have pockets of sorrow never yet released to tears. We would not let ourselves grieve at the proper time and have persistently repressed the sorrow, which then becomes something else, more akin to anxiety. It rumbles around like a freighter in a fog-bound ocean looking for somewhere to head in. If no lighthouse of revelation pierces the darkness to let it unload its frieght wholesomely in a proper dock of awareness and expression, it may founder and strew its contents in many inappropriate places. The hurt of loss is often behind psychosomatic illnesses or depressions or mental conditions.

One teenager in a congregation I served had had many conflicts with his father. He never felt he had come into easy acceptance and approval. Before he had an opportunity to talk things out so they could work through their problems, his father suddenly tragically died. Now everyone eulogized the father. It seemed the height of disloyalty to say or even let himself think anything negative of this man whom the community honored as a servant to all. That locked up this son's sorrow and all his other undealt-with emotions. He reached out to the Lord in an increasingly frantic attempt to find someone big enough to lift the weight off of him and hold his world together. One day he invited us to his home to see a picture of Christ that he had purchased for the dining room. It covered an entire wall! For him the largeness of the painting was an expression of his wanting Jesus to take over his entire life; he needed to rest in the enveloping presence of the Lord. But the exaggerated size of the painting was also to him a symbol of the enormity of the Father image, impossible to live up to, and beyond his reach.

At this point the young man's prayers and Bible reading, and the attempts of his pastor and friends to counsel him in order to bring him relief and rest, were interpreted by him to be more that he had to live up to. The result was depression which became so unremitting and severe that a period of committal to a mental hospital became the only recourse. Not sorrow but inability to express it became his dungeon until the Lord finally reached his heart. Many people in the community did not understand what he was going through at all, and blamed his breakdown on "religious fanaticism." When he had fully recovered, his psychiatrist said that the very fact that he had reached out to God was his way back to sanity and health.

> Make friends quickly with your opponent at law *while you are with him on the way,* in order that your opponent may not deliver you to the judge, and the judge to the officer, and you be thrown into prison. Truly I say to you, *you shall not come out of there, until you have paid up the last cent* (Matt. 5:25, 26).

In our modern court system, lawyers often attempt to bargain before an issue comes before a judge, sometimes settling out of court, usually at lower cost than had the case proceeded to trial. In biblical days much the same happened. Both the plaintiff and defendant and their counselors were forced to travel together, sometimes long distances, to wherever a judge resided who could settle the issue. It was common practice to hash things out on the way, and everyone knew that it always cost far more if the judge did have to make a judgment. The point Jesus was making could not be missed in its time. Hardening the heart rather than forgiving was likely to result in painful cost.

The same is true concerning grief. When we will not deal with it on the way, i.e., in the right time and way, it becomes repressed but in no way silenced. At some time it *will* have its day in court. We are thrown into painful mental and psychosomatic "prisons," and we do not get out until we have paid the last emotional penny! The principle of the parable is, face griefs (or anger, hatred, fear, whatever) while it is rising to consciousness ("on the way with you"). The penalty is fullness of pain, as our young friend suffered when pressures blocked the handling of grief.

So simple a thing as having to move away from friends, or the loss of a beloved piano teacher, or the death of a pet, may lie behind a closed heart. Whether loss was early or late, mild or severe, a person may unconsciously or consciously decide that love costs too much. He may shut up his heart, making an inner vow never again to love or to be vulnerable. Hardened hearts are the most common result of undealt-with buried sorrow. As we have seen earlier, such withdrawal often results in disease, most commonly cancer.

Unfortunately, Christians sometimes mistake the effects of shock for faith. When loss traumatizes the inner being, the homeostatic or balance principle within us may shut off all feeling for a while, as protection from what threatens to become too much emotional stress. The resultant false peace may be taken by the Christian as victory due to faith. I think of one friend whose husband died. She sailed smilingly through the funeral and its aftermath, certain that her faith had given her victory over sorrow and tears. She was fond of quoting, "and He shall wipe away every tear from their eyes; and there shall no longer be any death; there shall no longer be any mourning, or crying, or pain; the first things have passed away" (Rev. 21:4). But we could sense in our spirits the gusher of grief she was suppressing. Fear of letting down, of displaying emotions in public, of not demonstrating what she thought was faith, caused her to disregard the simple fact that those first things have not yet all passed away, and the time for that prophecy to be fulfilled in toto has not yet come. About three years later, physical problems signalled inner trouble, and after much counsel she broke down and cried the tears she should have allowed to flow much earlier.

Loss often results in anger. Inevitably the heart's cry is, "Where were you, Lord? Why did you let this happen?" It is not lack of faith to think such thoughts. It is not sin to be angry at God (see Chapter Eight for a fuller discussion about anger at God). Many Christians have been burdened with guilt because they thought anger itself a sin. Jesus never sinned, yet Mark 3:5 says, "And after looking around at them with anger, grieved at their hardness of heart, He said to the man, 'Stretch out your hand.' " St. Paul commanded, "Be angry, and yet do not sin; do not let the sun go down on your anger" (Eph. 4:26). What we do with anger makes it either righteousness or sin. Even those who know that with the mind seem not to know it in the heart, for all too many suppress anger, failing to locate it properly and deal with it specifically through forgiveness. Even though we may know it's okay to become angry, nevertheless it does not seem right to be angry at God. The mind says He is perfect, and how could He be at fault? But the heart could not care one whit for such logic. "The foolishness of man subverts his way, And his *heart rages against the Lord*" (Prov. 19:3). Such raging is healthy—initially. It says we believe in God and therefore expect that He ought to be there for us. Later we will come to some wisdom about how our sin or circumstances blocked Him from acting. For the moment our anger says we love. St. Paul knew this, and so wrote to the Corinthians,

> Now all these things are from God, who reconciled us to Himself through Christ, and gave us the ministry of reconciliation, namely, that God was in Christ reconciling the world to Himself, not counting their trespasses against them, and He has commited to us the word of reconciliation. Therefore we are ambassadors for Christ, as though God were entreating through us; we beg you on behalf of Christ, *be reconciled to God* (2 Cor. 5:18-21).

We have grieved to hear counselees report that they finally worked up enough courage to admit to someone their anger at God, only to hear, "Oh now, let's not be foolish. You have no right to be angry at God. Let's come off that." Worse yet someone might have said, "That's blasphemy. You know better than that." Please hear this, counselors—God can take it. He doesn't need you to defend Him! Let people express their angers. What such people may be doing is cathartic. Catharsis is outpouring of pent-up emotions. Never interrupt a catharsis. Let people spend themselves. There will be time enough later to talk rationally. Further talk may not even be needed, for in the outpouring of emotion a counselee may see and repent. When counselors jump in to shut off catharsis, the truth is they are afraid of such emotional outbursts, most likely because they are afraid of their own pent-up feelings. God is not an immature earthly parent who cannot allow his child to express anger at Him.

446

> The Lord is compassionate and gracious, Slow to anger and abounding in lovingkindness. He will not always strive with us; Nor will He keep His anger forever. He has not dealt with us according to our . . . iniquities. For high as the heavens are above the earth, So great is His lovingkindness toward those who fear Him. As far as the east is from the west, So far has He removed our transgressions from us. Just as a father has compassion on his children, So the Lord has compassion on those who fear Him. For He Himself knows our frame; He is mindful that we are but dust (Ps. 103:8-14).

Some people express anger at God and actually mean it. They do really blame God for their troubles. It is not that they, like all of us, have normal present angers at parents, or at the Parent. Unconsciously, they project their unrecognized (or unknown) stored-up angers and judgments at their parents onto God. They feel that God (actually their parents) has let them down. They want to know why a good God can allow such things as tragedies to happen. "Either He doesn't care or He is impotent" is their cry of rage. They may launch into complicated philosophical delvings into the entire question of the existence of good and evil, trying actually to justify God to themselves because they lack sufficient blind trust to rest in Him.

We have taught much about this biblically and theologically in Chapters Eight and Nine of *The Elijah Task*. It is not our purpose here to explain the workings of God relative to His dealings with evil. Rather, our purpose here is healing. Therefore our counsel is not to defend God at all. He is not the problem. We simply say, "What was your father like?" We want to know whether the father gave affection, whether he was present to the children. Was he violent? Could he understand with a sympathetic compassionate ear? Or did he leap to conclusions and judge unfairly? Were the children afraid of him? And what was the mother like? This also is devloped further in Chapter Two of *The Transformation of the Inner*

Man, "How We See God." What is important here is to realize that expressions of hurt and anger are not so important in themselves as they are clues to areas needing healing in the early life.

Having healed the inner man of ancient hurts, and transformed resultant structures, we may not yet have sufficiently dealt with the hurt itself. Our personal spirit is different than our memory stream and our soul's structure. Our personal spirit may yet need to be comforted and soothed. We accomplish that by continuing to pray, after we have prayed for transformation of memories and structures, that the personal spirit be comforted by God. We may quote Psalm 27:10, "For my father and my mother have forsaken me, But the Lord will take up me," and ask God to ". . . make up to you for the years That the swarming locust has eaten, The creeping locust, the stripping locust, and the gnawing locust, My great army which I sent among you. And you shall have plenty to eat and be satisfied, And praise the name of the Lord your God" (Joel 2:25, 26). We ask God the Father to gather the person into His arms again and again, until the little one *knows* in every particle of his being that he is loved and chosen, that he belongs and is cherished.

It is not enough merely to take the negative to the cross. The child within needs to feed on that time of cherishing until he is whole and free. That means he needs to be encouraged to participate in small-group and church worship, in small fellowships and primary relationships until his inner spirit no longer is starved but entirely fed and made whole. Hugs and laughter, friendship and fun are in order, to put into the person the wholesomeness of childhood he never before possessed.

There are those who overexpress sorrow and anger, for many psychological reasons. Most commonly, however, what we as counselors must do is to release to the surface what has long been suppressed or forgotten. Sometimes people are wounded without knowing it. "Even in laughter the heart may be in pain, And the end of joy may be grief" (Prov. 14:13). I (John) am one of those who may be terribly hurt without realizing it at the moment. As a child in a sometimes tempestuous home, I built in a capacity to shut off present feelings so that their only function would be to inform my mind, which became steeled to analyze and handle calmly whatever threatened to become chaotic. That discipline has served me well through the years. But along with that has come a tendency to become lost from my own true feelings, years later to suffer through in increased pain what could have been lightly experienced nearer to the moment.

Many men have built in such disciplines. I have had to learn to say to the Lord as did St. Paul, "I am conscious of nothing against myself, yet I am not by this acquitted; but the one who examines me is the Lord" (1 Cor. 4:4). "Against myself" can be changed to, "I am conscious of no feelings of sorrow or anger or resentment, Lord, but they may be there. You search me out, Lord, and either cause me to feel them or deal with them by faith." "Create in me a *clean heart*, O God, And *renew a steadfast spirit* within me" (Ps. 51:10).

People who have learned to wall off feelings in order to remain calm and efficient under stress should be counseled not always to handle things alone, in private prayers. Just as a man who is his own lawyer may have a fool for a client, so whoever always counsels and heals himself has a fool, and someday a collapsing Christian, for a counselee. As we learned earlier, seventy-six percent of those who contract cancer are those who would not let others minister to them. Friends see our hurt when we don't. Friends feel our sorrow when we have covered it even from ourselves.

> The way of a fool is right in his own eyes, But a wise man is he who listens to counsel (Prov. 12:15).
>
> . . . the tongue of the wise brings healing (Prov. 12:18b).
>
> He who neglects discipline despises himself, But he who listens to reproof acquires understanding (Prov. 15:32).

Anxiety in the heart of a man weighs it down, But a good word makes it glad (Prov. 12:25).

The teaching of the wise is a fountain of life, To turn aside from the snares of death (Prov. 13:14).

Often, in counsel or prayer, both counselor and counselee may inadvertently tap into an underground river of tears. Many times in discussion or prayer, or by a single question, counselees have suddenly broken into crying so heavily it seemed they could barely catch their next breath. Neither the counselor nor counselee should fear such occasions, nor try to top off the geyser. Such crying releases pent-up energy. Tears are a gift of Heaven. Such sudden uprushes of tears are nearly incontrovertible evidence that the quest has neared the mark of truth. Counselors have only to wait out the sobs, perhaps kneeling beside the person and placing an arm of comfort over the shoulders, as though to say, "Have at it; I'm here to stand beside you. It's okay." Usually the aftermath of such outbursts is a time of quiet revelation. The force of the crying tells the counselee beyond argument how great his hurt was. The emotional release usually opens doors to insight. The counselee may then begin to remember long-forgotten or repressed details. Precious ground may be covered in the afterglow of tears.

Counselors win trust by letting counselees sob it out, without scolding or trying to shut it down. Once the counselee has shared his greatest depths of sorrow and let go his self-control in emotional outbursts, and his counselor has not said as perhaps his parents did, "Oh, dry up!", or "Crybaby! Get yourself under control!", or "Shut up that bawling or I'll give you something worth crying about!" his heart knows it can take refuge in his counselor. He knows then that he will not be rejected. That acceptance grants his spirit courage to face truth and share it. The counselor need only be patient and quietly insistent, encouraging the counselee to continue to share. Several times in one session a person may suddenly be overcome, once the flood gates have been opened. That itself may frighten him. The counselor should assure him that he is quite normal and that such feelings and expressions are okay and healthy. By his quiet strength and calmness the counselor says, "It's all right. Continue. Live it all the way through." It is a matter of rejoicing when people break through into great gushers of sobbing and tears. Let us never be afraid of it. There are some people, of course, who fake tearful uprisings and outbursts. The Lord can provide the counselor with discernment to know the difference. I have never known real tears to be anything other than a sign of deep healing.

Often, if a person has been starved for affection or for understanding, when someone bids to supply that long-pent-up need, great tears are the result. By that fruit, we may discern the depth of deprivation.

It may not seem to many counselees very real or important nor necessary to embarrass oneself by talking about old things. Counselees may want to escape, to seek some pretext to avoid more pain. But I have never known anyone who has experienced a sobbing catharsis of sorrow who has not immediately seen its reality and value.

Counselees know they cannot have faked that kind of outburst. They feel peace following the release. They know what it means then to cleanse their inner house. We insist to counselors that they never say, "Oh there now, don't cry." So many times we have heard of counselors becoming Job's comforters, missing the entire import of what was happening! "Rejoice in the Lord always; again I will say, rejoice!" (Phil. 4:4), your counselee is becoming real. He is getting at where it really is. "Let your forbearing spirit be known to all men" (to your counselee, v. 5). "The Lord is near to the brokenhearted and . . . crushed in spirit" (Ps. 34:18). "Be anxious for nothing, but in everything by prayer and supplication with thanksgiving let your requests be made known to God. And the peace of God, which surpasses all comprehension, shall guard your hearts and your minds in Christ Jesus" (Phil. 4:6, 7).

Counselors, knowing the value of cathartic release, may be tempted to try to cause it to happen. Please don't! The Holy Spirit is the great physician. He knows when boils are ready to be lanced. He knows when wells of stored sorrow are ready to be drained. He knows when the grapes of the heart are ready to be squeezed for the best wine for the feast. Be at rest. Our Lord will minister. Sometimes I have thought, "Surely now that this person sees it, he will feel something. Surely he will express it." Nothing seemed to happen. Six months later, even three years, counselees have suddenly (it seems) broken into tears or anger, fear or hate. It took that long for the heart and mind to ripen to the moment of expression. Counselors should not be dismayed nor frustrated with counselees who can't seem to feel anything. Feelings may be unnecessary altogether, or perhaps the Lord will release a geyser later.

Some people feel that what is bottled in their heart can never be dealt with because, "After all, he's dead and gone; I can't go back and ask his forgiveness, or tell him how he hurt me." Many times they don't really believe that. They know in part of their mind that such thoughts are only a dodge. They know they can settle it by confession. They only want a convenient excuse not to have to go through the process. We seldom tackle that delusion head on. Earlier we said that anger is inevitable. All of us have anger at God and anger at parents whether we were ever aware of it or not. We normally want to congratulate ourselves we don't have resentment and bitterness. We want to assure ourselves that we are in control of our life. To be made aware that we have hidden emotions and drives is therefore to be told that we are not as much in control of ourselves as we had thought. That may be more threatening than the possible existence of anger.

Many people labor under the delusion that if we love someone, we of course can have no negative feelings toward them. It seems disloyal to admit resentment for lack of affection from a father who knocked himself out in every other way to provide for us. Loyalty locks frustration and sorrow into silence. We don't want to admit we were hurt and cherished resentment at the critical tongue of a mother when our mind tells us she was overworked and under great stress. Counselees need to be told that thoughts like these are only the admirable way the mind tried to handle our hurt, but that it did not suffice to clear the heart of wounding. There is no shame in admitting the other side of our feelings. No dishonor is intended toward a parent we mean to honor when we cry out the hurts we have long repressed. It is as simple as when our child comes running to leap into our lap and we can readily see that he is hurting and angry at us. We say, "Come on, honey, tell me. What is it?" Our child's blurting out what he is hurting about, even if it involves talking about things we did wrong, does not dishonor us. It tells us our child loves us enough to suffer real hurts. It honors us that his trust of us is strong enough that he can be honest with us and know we will accept and love him anyway. Just so, sharing with a counselor does not dishonor our parents. It heals. If the parents, or whoever else was involved, have gone on beyond the portal of death, wounds can still be healed merely by the prayers of the counselor. And who is to say that our loved ones are not aware and blessed on the other side as they dwell with the Lord? Jesus' story of Lazarus and the rich man seems to indicate that the departed do see what happens here (Luke 16:19-31). Whether they see or not is inconsequential to the counselee's healing. Prayer reaches beyond inner portals of the heart to heal. We must never allow fear of embarrassment, or hesitancy to dishonor, or any other thing block us from becoming whole.

To accomplish healing in all aspects of sorrow, frustration and loss, it is not enough to discuss hurtful incidents. It is not enough also to haul to the cross resultant structures such as hearts of stone and inner vows we have made not to be vulnerable. To pray about those things is necessary and good, but incomplete. Our personal spirit still hungers for supply of what was lost. When loved ones are gone, only our Lord can fully meet that need Spirit to spirit. We are called to be present, as His instruments for touch, assurance, acceptance and affection. But only His fullness of spirit can bathe that wounded spirit and breathe vitality into him again. We pray simply for the Lord to accomplish that, loving the person into wholeness and fullness.

For all, but especially for widows and divorcees, we may quote for our counselees:

"Fear not, for you will not be put to shame;
Neither feel humiliated, for you will not be disgraced;
But you will forget the shame of your youth,
And the reproach of your widowhood you will
    remember no more.
For your husband is your Maker,
Whose name is the Lord of hosts;
And your Redeemer is the Holy One of Israel,
Who is called the God of all the earth.
For the Lord has called you,
Like a wife forsaken and grieved in spirit,
Even like a wife of one's youth when she is rejected,"
Says your God.
For a brief moment I forsook you,
But with great compassion I will gather you.
. . . with everlasting lovingkindness
    I will have compassion on you,
Says the Lord your Redeemer.

—Isa. 54:4-8

Chapter Sixteen

Dwelling Within a Sinful Group

Then I said, "Woe is me, for I am ruined!
Because I am a man of unclean lips,
And I live among a people of unclean lips;
For my eyes have seen the King, the Lord of hosts.
(Isa. 6:5)

. . . (for by what he saw and heard that righteous man, while living among them, felt his righteous soul tormented day after day with their lawless deeds) (2 Pet. 2:8).

See to it that no one takes you captive through philosophy and empty deception, according to the tradition of men, according to the elementary principles of the world, rather than according to Christ (Col. 2:8).

Several years ago Paula and I were invited to teach in San Francisco. The other couple on the podium were cult deprogrammers who had made it their life's work to deliver men and women, young people especially, from the grasp of cults. They informed us that at that time they had been able to identify more than one hundred cults operating in the Bay Area alone! What has given rise to such a drastic increase in cult activity? Or have we only become aware of what has been happening all along?

It is hunger for authority, according to these deprogrammers, which serves as the lure for young people. In short, the absence of fathers. If we will remember, or take a few moments to review, what was said in Chapter Five concerning "The Slumbering Spirit," we will see that multitudes of young people have slumbering spirits, which means that their spirits cannot discern the true from the false, at the same moment that great gaping wounds cry for love, strength and security from a father figure. Deprogrammers inform us that it is hunger for a father figure to tell them what to do which locks young people into being controlled by authoritarian cult leaders. Young people, despite their protests for independence, look for the security of being told what to do. If one unites such awareness with understanding of performance orientation (see Chapter Three in *The Transformation of the Inner Man*), one can readily see the inner dynamics by which young people's lives are taken captive.

It is fear which rules and fear which chains. Fear of rejection. Fear of not belonging. Fear of punishment. Fear of "missing the Lord." Fear of "missing the kingdom." Fear of not living up to the Lord's demands (actually the warped regimen of the cult leader). Fear of reprisal if caught. Fear of being trapped again in the prison world of the parents and society. (Cult leaders portray everyone else as the prison and their way as the only freedom.) Fear of hell, pictured as waiting just outside the pale of the group. Expectation to be persecuted, so that the remonstrations of parents, pastors and friends are taken as persecution, confirming their leader's "righteous" stance. Fear not to be "in," not to suffer the outrages which confirm everyone else in the group as true suffering servants standing against this crooked and perverse generation. All such groups participate in and feed upon a paranoid messianic complex which identifies them as the good guys, the elect, the elite remnant who alone have the truth and must suffer for it. Part of the tragic confusion is that there are today many real martyrs, for instance the suffering church behind the Iron Curtain, whom such people can falsely adopt as role models.

It is not, however, merely psychological forces which captivate cult members. It is the power of archetypes. It is thought-control by powerful devices in our flesh. (Archetypes can be seen more fully by reviewing Chapter Eight, "Defilements, Devils and Death Wishes" or by re-reading Chapter Sixteen of *The Transformation of the Inner Man.*) It is enough here to say that archetypes are practiced ways of thinking which inhabit the sea of thought we all share. They are not inert, like books on a shelf, ineffective till opened and read, but active monsters of energy, which can clamp about the mind of a person until he can think no thought outside the parameter of the archetype. Archetypes serve like cowboys, to run down any straying thought and turn it back into the herd. Their specific purpose is to prevent free thinking, to "take captive through philosophy and empty deception." It is the hold of archetypes, aided in their heinous task by the fears listed above, which must be broken be deprogrammers.

Our purpose here, however, is not to write a manual for deprogrammers. That is a separate field altogether, in which Paula and I confess little expertise. It is rather to teach that form of healing which should follow after the work of deprogrammers, lest the child remain vulnerable to those who would lure him into repeated delusion.

Those who have been delivered from cults rightly fear being caught again. But that fear can turn into hyper-caution which may in turn prevent whatever wholesome associations would serve to provide needed nurture.

In the early days of Elijah House, one of our members had been a cult member. His fear of domination and control so controlled him that he continually caused trouble in the group by falsely imputing to me and other leaders in authority motives and actions to control and imprison.

457

We failed to learn soon enough the lessons we now share so that this man, still hungering for the very authority he feared, left us and was again caught up in a rigid authoritarian cult.

A couple came out of a cult which insisted on intense shepherding and discipling. The leaders of this cult went so far as to insist on choosing who would be their friends and who would not. This couple entered Cornerstone Christian Fellowship, in which our son Loren is the pastor. Many small groups are the very life stream of Cornerstone. This couple desperately needed fellowship and support but feared to enter any small group, unable by the numbing power of unhealed memory to discern that Cornerstone's small groups bear no resemblance whatsoever to the cult groups which formally controlled them.

It takes patient fellowship and soaking healing prayer to overcome the deposits of cult membership. Erstwhile cult members remind us of crayfish, backing away with eyes bugging out and claws extended in defense. It may take many experiences of love and acceptance, despite cult members' tendencies to alternately attack and flee away, to reestablish the kind of trust which is the basis of all free friendship and fellowship. The key to the healing of former cult participants is long-suffering love. Former cult members are acutely sensitive to anything which remotely appears to manipulate and control them, while unconsciously, by bitter-root expectancy and judgment, they set up friends and acquaintances to do just that to them.

When long-suffering, forbearing love has laid the groundwork for receiving ministry, many simple acts of healing can follow. First, bitter-root judgment and the anticipation of being dominated and controlled should be brought to the cross, not only from the recent cult experience but from early childhood parental frictions. Most importantly, such people need fathers and mothers in Christ. It was the very hunger for such relationships which trapped them under a despot. But since they now fear and flee from the very thing they most need, wise counselors can simply fulfill the function without putting a name on it. Holding in the heart, loving unconditionally, being available, interceding continually, giving counsel without ever impinging upon free will, supplying as much affection as the other will receive, all these and more can be done without ever labeling such acts as father and mother tasks.

Deep basic trust needs to be restored. These people must come to realize that it is again safe to unfold and bloom and that no one will curb, crush, or rip the tender petals. They must learn that it is okay to be vulnerable again, but not safe. We are never safe. Life always contains risk. They need to regain enough confidence and freedom in God to risk, to know He will restore his people if they fail and they do in fact get hurt again.

Ex-members of cults are uptight. They must have enough penetrative healing to their spirits so that they can relax from deep within and open to the winds and cross-currents of life again. That is perhaps the most basic and needful healing of all, to restore the ability of the personal spirit to unfold, expand, meet others and interrelate without excessive fear and guard-all walls. It is accomplished by praying aloud with the person for the Lord to comfort, to heal and restore trust as a sovereign gift, an act of His grace, a miracle of resurrection in the heart.

Their healing does require a miracle of resurrection. Like the man lame from birth whose muscles had so withered and atrophied that they had to be recreated and regenerated with power to run and leap (Acts 3:1-10), so the spirit's abilities have been so trampled and withered that one must call for a miracle of recreation and rejuvenation. Like the man with the withered hand (Luke 6:6-11), former cult members have faculties which no longer can operate. Their inner being no longer can reach out and take hold, unless the power of the Lord's command enables the spirit to stretch out and venture again. Akin to the paralyzed man who was let down in front of Jesus (Mark 2:1-12), they possess many talents of the spirit paralyzed by fear.

"And Jesus seeing *their faith* said to the paralytic, 'My son, your sins are forgiven' " (v. 5). Those who pray must have faith *for* such people. Their ability to trust has been paralyzed. God will answer the faith of those who pray, only secondarily the weak faith of the recipient.

There is a particular sin which needs to be recognized and forgiven. That is the sin of burying one's talents. Cult membership is actually a cop-out from life. The proselyte who enters a cult thinks he is boldly stepping forward to commit himself wholly for the Lord's cause. In actual fact, he has unconsciously chosen a way to flee from having to make decisions, to have to stand to the consequences of free choices. He has in effect said to Moses, "Take me back to slavery. I can't stand freedom out here in the deserts of life. At least I knew how to behave there because everyone told us what to do. I didn't have to think. I only had to behave." What has happened to him is the legal result of flight and burial—even what he thinks he has, has been taken from him (Luke 19:11-26). His freedom is forfeited. Most cults isolate their members from parents, relatives and friends. The cult member's confidence in Christ in himself is destroyed. His ability to stand alone has been lost. His freedom from fear has vanished. His freedom to come and go as he wills, to meet friends, attend parties, and enjoy life is either radically curbed or gone altogether. In short, all the gifts of Jesus which mean abundant life have been taken from him.

What did those have to whom more is given, and what did a cult proselyte lack that so much was taken? Trust! Those who trusted freely ventured their talents and doubled their value (vv. 16 and 18). The one who lacked trust buried it for fear of loss and gave it back unchanged and consequently undeveloped and unused. That sin needs to be forgiven. Counselors should make the person cognizant of the sins behind his choices and pronounce forgiveness for them.

Those delivered from cults also need healing from shame. So many we have talked with feel devastated by shame. They figure they have so blown it they could never be used again or that God would or should never again trust them with a task. They are apt to view their entire cult experience as valueless, a prodigal journey which wasted all their Father's sustenance. They should be helped to see again that indeed all things do work together for good, that all is not lost, that they have learned valuable lessons which can be ministered as blessing to others.

Behind all other wounds is destruction of confidence. Praise God that all their confidence in men and in themselves in the flesh has been shattered. That lesson alone pays for the whole trip! To know never again to put confidence in princes is a value all the rest of the Church which idolizes pastors, leaders and television idols could well learn from people who have freed themselves from cults. But confidence in the Lord in themselves, like trust, must be restored as a miracle gift from the Lord by prayer. Let us praise God with them for valuable lessons learned, and then help them to learn to cherish that healthy disrespect of their own fleshly perceptions they have gained the hard way. How valuable it is to have learned so unmistakably that "There is a way which seems right to a man, But its end is the way of death" (Prov. 14:12). To have seen that one can be completely convinced of the rightness of one's own insights and yet be totally deluded is a precious safeguard for any Christian. If former cult members can be helped to see and cherish not only healthy skepticism but all the other things they have learned in the wilderness, that will itself become part of their restoration of confidence. "Hey, I *have* gained something. I *am* more mature and aware by what I have been through. It wasn't all loss." But since the other side of such wilderness learning is fear and reticence, healing of the spirit is necessary to set one free.

Part of what locked cult people in was fear of failure. Being performance-oriented, they were not free to make mistakes. The essence of Christian freedom is liberty to err. Not to use that freedom as a pretext for foolishness or purposeful sin, but freedom to try things and fail. We must have confidence that our gracious and compassionate Lord has made life fun, a place in which we can try for Him. If we fail, He will turn it to glory. That aspect of confidence and trust needs to be regained. Most likely former cult members never had it in the first place. It needs to be revived from early childhood loss. Healing ought to be two-dimensional, in the present from recent devastations, and in healing of the inner man for reconstruction of trusts and freedoms which parents, by trying too hard, unwittingly demolished.

Former cult members have learned not to trust the heart of another. They have learned that even if he meant well, their leader was deluded and controlled. If he was evil, he had learned how to prey upon the naive good intentions of others. On one side, that also is a valuable lesson.

> Many a man proclaims his own loyalty, But who can find a trustworthy man? (Prov. 20:6).

> Do not trust in princes, In mortal man, in whom there is no salvation (Ps. 146:3).

> It is better to take refuge in the Lord Than to trust in princes (Ps. 118: 9).

Those delivered from cults have learned caution the hard way. "A prudent man sees evil and hides himself, The naive proceed and pay the penalty" (Prov. 27:12). But the casualty in this case is inability to abide in friendship. They fear to risk involvement again. They need now to be taught that their experiences have so conditioned them that healed bitternesses will serve to better equip them to enter true friendship by keeping them from ever again idolizing another and consequently abdicating responsibility for their own lives. They must now learn that since no Christian should naively trust any other, it is only safe to trust a brother by trusting Jesus in him. Their experience has prepared them to learn true trust and friendship, to trust our Lord in another while protecting him from sinning against us by being aware and prepared to handle his propensity to sin. Our naivete invites the worst in any brother, until maturity protects him by giving sin in him no opportunity. It is good to suspect the worst and draw forth the best by Christ Jesus.

Cult escapees usually have lost the gift of joy. Life has become too deadly serious for them. The childlike, which needs to live in all of us, has not only been slain, it is feared, because it is now identified and confused with unwanted naivete.

But the childlike are not naive. Childlikeness is the gift of being a child of God. I no longer have to settle problems which only He can handle. I no longer have to try to be God by solving dilemmas which are only His to solve. I can play, enjoy life, laugh at life and myself, and know that my Lord is so much Lord of life He laughs at problems, and at persecuting people. "The kings of the earth take their stand, And the rulers counsel together Against the Lord and against His Anointed . . . He who sits in the heavens laughs, the Lord scoffs at them" (Ps. 2:2 and 4). He will warn me of danger, and both counsel and empower my choices. He is my defense. He is responsible for me. Christians' joy is predicated upon the incontrovertible fact that the Lord *has already won the victory.* What matter any temporary setback? He will turn it to glory.

Again, however, it is not simply that these people have lost their joy. They most likely also never had it. The joy of a child is free to flourish only if parents provide security. Father and mother provide love, assurance, comfort and safety, which in turn grants freedom to romp and play. When parents fail to provide that ambiance, joy is frustrated; life becomes too serious, too soon.

Joy is native to the heart. God has created it as the natural ground of all creation. The offspring of every species in nature instinctively play, with joy! One does not have to inspire it or make it happen. One has only not to frustrate and prevent it. Therefore counselors should aim to heal until that wellspring flows unhindered again.

The key is restoration of trust. When trust in His Lordship installs assurance, comfort and safety, joy will flow naturally. We need only heal the earliest and latest memories and set joy free to flow.

Many people who have come out of the occult fear anything supernatural. They want to immerse themselves in the good earth and forget all that spiritual stuff and junk. Who could blame them? Praise God they have learned that fools rush in where angels fear to tread. Even holy visitations of the presence of the Lord in worship services and prayer meetings may spook them. We have seen them terrorized and ready to flee out when everyone else was joyfully receiving quiet anointing and blessing from the Lord. They could no longer trust their discernment, so that any visitation of God frightened them. Anything beyond what the five senses could handle was too much for them. They have known goose bumps galore—and deception with it! So they fear even His presence, having lost the trust required to rest.

> Now suppose one of you fathers is asked by his son for a fish; he will not give him a snake instead of a fish, will he? Or if he is asked for an egg, he will not give him a scorpion, will he? If you then, being evil, know how to give good gifts to your children, how much more shall your Heavenly Father give the Holy Spirit to those who ask Him? (Luke 11:11-13).

These Scriptures lock out fear for the normal, but not yet for former cult members, until healing proceeds apace. It may therefore not be wisdom to subject those newly delivered from cults to high-powered services or prayer meetings. Much good human fellowship, laughter and joy, light tasks and rest should be prescribed at first. If these people always insist on sitting near an exit, let them. If they resist touch, leave them alone. If they don't want to share vocally in a prayer meeting, don't insist that they do. The Body should offer consistent warm invitation with no pressure to accept.

Many intercessory burden-bearing healing prayers, *apart from* the person, are in order. Walks in nature, good, sweaty earthy labor, athletic exercise, good balanced meals, abstinence from sweets and good sleep all are healthy antidotes to the tensions in which they have lived. These people will not lose spirituality by being immersed in the good earth. They will gain it. In J.R.R. Tolkien's trilogy, *The Lord of the Rings*, it is the hobbits, a diminutive, hardy, non-mystical, down-to-earth people, who resist the wiles of Sauron (the devil of that series) and maintain the stamina to keep going when others would drop. Tolkien makes it plain they obtain their strength from their simple earthiness, enjoying good food and fun and get-togethers as often as they can. Having been a super-spook myself, I can testify that Tolkien's grasp of reality is accurate. It is the earthy who can be safely spiritual. Time enough after rest and earthiness for the newly delivered to return to high spiritual labors.

Some escapees fear demons everywhere. Some were taught to look for them in everyone—and of course saw what they looked for, whether they were there or not. Dr. Bill Johnson, head of psychology at Whitworth College, is a Spirit-filled believer who simply says, "All that psychology can do is to chronicle the deceits of the flesh." When the leader of a cult movement took over the headship in his church, the congregation was told from the pulpit that anyone who had anything to do with psychology was filled with demons! Those false teachers saw demons in everything and everyone. Of course they were the only ones not possessed and therefore proximity to them became the only safe place to dwell! Fear of demons thus slammed the prison doors shut for all who believed the false perceptions of the cult leaders. Many Christians, lacking the wisdom of the deprogrammers of whom we spoke, have sought to shout demons out of cult people, trying to set them free. That memory may also be part of what makes them continue to remain skittish and fearful. Such people need time and earthines in order to appreciate again that "this is simply this" and "that is only that," and not everything is fraught with demons.

We caution counselors to avoid doing exorcisms either on or in the presence of ex-cult members. If demons do indeed bother them, let us bind them silently, and wait awhile. There is no hurry. Time is on our side. The person is moving into more and more light; he is becoming stronger day by day. If a counselor leads into healing inner wounds and so sets the person free, demons lose power to entrap their intended victims in trouble again. The possible presence of a demon does not dictate exorcism. Our Lord does, in His own time and wisdom.

Reconciliation to family and friends eventually is in order. Sometimes that should be postponed, when one sees that the overbearing or angry or critical nature of family members would harm more than help. Usually, however, the sooner the better. Family and friends can be prepared for reunion by being advised not to scold or to ask too many questions too soon. Family members should be instructed to express affection and gratitude to have the cult member home again, and to be as natural and open as the heightened emotions of the moment will allow. Family should not overdo and make him feel like a pampered guest. That says, "You're not home yet, and we know it." Old routines and chores have a tonic effect when we come out of the bizarre to the home again.

Whisperings behind the back will most likely be noticed. Awkwardness is to be expected. It would be the same were he only coming home from war or a long stay in college. Just weather it. He wants to be treated like anyone else, not as special or different.

Former cult members may want to talk. Family members should let them, but be instructed to view most of it as cathartic, a mere need to get things off the chest. The former cult member should not be taught, scolded or counseled by his family, or anything else than merely heard and understood. Most returnees lapse into silence rather than talk too much. It helps to allow some withdrawal but to prevent too much by drawing the person into family events, like picnics, ball games, fun around the table, etc.

Most of all, the family should not be isolated. Continued contact with and advice from counselors or deprogrammers is nearly a must. Situations will arise in which parents and relatives have no idea which is the wise way to act, nor how the ex-cult son or daughter most likely will be affected. That is why we are a Church rather than solitary pilgrims. Wise parents and friends will avail themselves of counsel.

Heart-to-heart talks with father and mother are extremely desirable. Most parents would be well advised to undergo some counseling themselves before that opportunity presents itself. Even if a father thinks he has no problems and doesn't require counseling for himself, going through it will build into him awarenesses which will stand him in good stead when his son or daughter comes to talk. Self-awareness normally grows by leaps and bounds under counseling, whereas most parents without undergoing counseling usually shoot down their position with their children by remaining too unaware how what they say or do affects them. Especially, a father or mother needs to be helped to see how the family members' life styles affected or afflicted the son or daughter and caused or helped to create the weaknesses by which the child became enmeshed in the cult. Counsel will also help the parents to confess their own faults to the child and to ask forgiveness rather than self-righteously blame their son or daughter for falling.

Finally, former cult members need somewhere to lay the shoulder to the wheel, somewhere to contribute in a worthwhile way to find wholeness. Perhaps after a time of rest a good job can be found, or some form of ministry. Nazi scientists who were so under the spell of Nazism that they brutally used slave labor and caused horrible deaths to thousands were so shocked and overwhelmed with guilt when the evil cloud lifted that many of them poured themselves unremittingly into efforts to contribute their knowledge to good causes. All redeemed persons want to serve somewhere to make amends. It is especially tonic to cult escapees, for it also helps to restore confidence in themselves as once again being part of an ongoing society. Cults catch hold of the immature at the point of rebellion. All of society is to them "establishment" and evil, and they think they must go to opposite extremes to stand over against it. Cults seem to offer a "holy" corrective like the only ten righteous who could save the city of Sodom. Once delivered, the former cult member says, "I now want to contribute to the society I once despised. Let me work. By doing so, I enter the stream of life and learn at last to accept the unworkable and the imperfect within it."

The end result of freedom from cults should be maturity. If the person remains naive and frightened, something hasn't happened. More counsel is needed. Persons free from cult experience should be given when ready the robe of ruling, the ring of authority and the fatted calf of celebration. Who knows better than these returned prodigals the pitfalls of faith? Who has learned more intensely than they to abide in Jesus and put no trust in men? As men continue to wander into humanism, as homes continue to fracture more and more, religious cults and political demagoguery will increase. We shall need the experience and consequent wisdom of those who have been there and back again. In the meantime, let us not treat them as second-class Christians. They will have become wise and chastened, when counsel has winnowed the wheat, kept the kernels and blown away the chaff.

The second portion of this chapter has to do with the wounds we all receive by living in this sin-sickened culture of ours today. Since we have already spoken much of defilement from persons and healing from it in Chapter Eight, we deal here only with that aspect of defilement which comes into our minds, and so into our spirits, from our culture, through all the various media—education, news, television, movies, novels, etc.

There is little need to document the miasma of false example and teaching which flows through every form of the media. "And the serpent poured water like a river *out of his mouth* after the woman, so that he might cause her to be swept away with the flood" (Rev. 12:15). Whatever else that may mean, it certainly is a vivid description of the spate of movies, rock stars, drugs, false teachings of novels, magazines and T.V. dramas, etc., ad nauseam, which have flooded like an unceasing Niagara onto our heads. Surely its aim is to sweep away the Church who is the woman! Regrettably, we have heard of hundreds of cases of Christians who are living together in sin, outside the sanctity of marriage, who have bought the lie that love makes it all right—"and anyway, everybody's doing it these days." Christian singles groups are all too frequently full of those who praise God on Sundays and fornicate all week! What would have been rated "X" a generation ago is now unthinkingly accepted as "PG." Almost every hero figure in movies, T.V. and novels is portrayed as thinking nothing of hopping into bed with anyone anytime. When 007 has intercourse with every heroine and villainness, that's bad enough, but now hospital head surgeons, police chiefs, and every other kind of hero are explicitly pictured as having the same kind of illicit love affairs! Movies make champions of thieves, and induce vast audiences to hope they escape scot free. And there is no end in sight.

The battle is on for the control of men's minds. In this warfare, counselors should pray for each counselee's spirit to be cleansed and awakened. In the end, however, each man will have to fight his own mind's battle. The antidote is simple. There is no other nor better solution than settling it once for all in the mind, in the will and in the heart that God's laws, expressed in His Word, are absolute!

Today there is little or no proper fear of God. "The fear of the Lord is the beginning of wisdom, And the knowledge of the Holy One is understanding" (Prov. 9:10). But how shall we regain true fear of God, for ourselves and our people? The crux of this portion of this chapter depends on the reader's comprehending what makes the difference between those who determine to believe the laws of God but who, when the pressures are on, cannot remember or persist, and those who make the same determination and truly can live by it. The telling factor is one thing only. Some have a root, and some do not. "And those on the rocky soil are those who, when they hear, receive the word with joy; *and these have no firm root;* they believe for a while, and in time of temptation fall away" (Luke 8:13).

What is it to have a root? How do we get one? Roots reach into the soil and drink nurture. Roots must have good soil or their plants starve. Roots must reach to water or their plants wither. Parental affection, love, acceptance, security and discipline are the ground from which children's roots drink nurture. Their roots are their family and heritage, but it is their spirits which reach beyond their bodies into the fertile soil of affection and acceptance to drink strength in the spirit, first from their parents, and then, by that enabling, from God. As children drink nurture through their roots by their spirits, they learn respect, admiration and trust. When awareness of God comes, those qualities become awe and reverence, which become true fear of God. True fear of God is birthed and housed in the life of our personal spirits, or not at all. We learned in Chapter Five that children who do not receive sufficient nurture have slumbering spirits. Their hearts are rocky soil, and they have no awakened spirit to push through its crags and fractures to find footing and nurture in love and affection in God or in mankind. Thus they have no root. Mental determination and willpower are not enough. As we saw in Chapter Five, their conscience does not work because their spirit fails to function. Therefore they fall in time of temptation.

Preachers may blast away at the onrushing flood of our culture and exhort manfully—and fail miserably—until they realize that unless their people have viable roots, they cannot stand! How then shall we settle it once for all that God's law is absolute? Not by fleshly willpower. That won't work. Not by screwing up our determination to believe. We hear much about "faith" today, but often it seems merely a catch word with little or no real content. Faith is relationship. It is real, undeniable constantly experienced

470

relationship with God. The only way we can travel those eight inches from head knowledge to true faith *"rooted* and grounded in love" (Eph. 3:17) is to obtain a functioning root system by reviving and awakening the personal spirit of each person!

In the beginning of our ministry, I tried to do something about the flood of pornography which was even then beginning to sweep across the land. Learning of the organization, "Citizens for Decent Literature," I stumped through every civic body where I could wangle an invitation to speak in Streator, Illinois, warning of danger, calling for belief, and enlisting citizens in CDL. In the end we had over fifty clubs and societies involved, and hundreds of alerted citizens. The only fruit I could see which resulted from all that effort was that more people bought smutty magazines and streamed to risque movies! They wanted to know what they were against! It was as though like the Roman Catholic Church I had banned books only to make sure everyone ran right out to buy one! Prohibition of alcohol made millionaires of black marketeers and entrenched the Mafia in America. I learned the hard way that preaching and teaching against evil will only publicize and spread it. Not that we should not do so occasionally. Once in a while alerts our people to danger. But constant trumpeting produces drastically reversed returns. *It is the preaching of good news which has power!* Only as true faith is birthed, and spirits awaken, do men truly stand!

Not knowing or understanding this, too many pastors weary themselves trying to stamp out brush fires of sin until the Lord returns, and have as little lasting effect as tumbleweeds blown across the land! Please hear it again. *Only* as men gain true rootage in Him do they have power to stand. Much of our effort today reminds me of those new-fangled birthday candles, designed to re-ignite after being blown out. We huff and puff at sin, only to see it flame up again as soon as we turn to the next subject.

471

Hear again the prophecy of Malachi 4:5 and 6:

> Behold, I am going to send you Elijah the prophet before the coming of the great and terrible day of the Lord. And he will restore the hearts of the fathers to their children, and the hearts of the children to their fathers, lest I come and smite the land with a curse.

Only as fathers' hearts are turned to their children will children's hearts be rooted and grounded in love. Only then will spirits truly be rooted in the fear of God. Only then will lives have strength of spirit to "put on the full armor of God, that you may be able to stand firm against the schemes of the devil . . . and having done everything, to stand firm" (Eph. 6:11 and 13). Do pastors want to give their congregations ability to stand, holy and strong? Let them work to restore their families! Let them heal the hearts of the wounded and revive and awaken the slumbering. Just so, and only so, will men truly believe and stand to His Word.

Truly each man must make his own decision, and determine to stand. But hollow men cannot stand. We must give them the equipment. We must set their spirits free from stupor. Once men's spirits are awakened, righteousness will roll down like a mighty river, and men's outraged spirits will no longer tolerate the evils we now only mildly deplore. Healing of wounded and slumbering spirits is the only viable key to rearming a moral society. Let's get at it!

Bibliography

The Amplified Bible (Grand Rapids, MI: Zondervan, 1965.)

M.A. Atwood, *Hermetic Philosophy and Alchemy* (New York: Julian Press, 1960).

R. Gladstone, Jr., *Mind Over Matter,* American Child Psychology, 1974), quoted by Kenneth McAll, *Journal of Christian Healing,* Vol. 5, No. 1

Marshall Hamilton, *Father's Influence on Children* (Chicago:Nelson-Hamilton, 1977).

Jeff Lane Hensley, Ed., *The Zero People* (Ann Arbor, MI: Servant, 1983).

The Holy Bible—Revised Standard Version (New York: Collins, 1952).

The Holy Bible—New International Version (Grand Rapids, MI: Zondervan, 1978).

King James Version of the Bible

New American Standard Bible (Carol Stream, IL: Creation House, 1973).

Oxford Universal Dictionary (London: Clarendon Press, 1933).

Leanne Payne, *Crisis in Masculinity* (Westchester, IL: Crossway, 1985).

John and Paula Sandford, *The Elijah Task* (Tulsa, OK: Victory House, 1977).

John and Paula Sandford, *Restoring the Christian Family* (Tulsa, OK: Victory House, 1979).

John and Paula Sandford, *The Transformation of the Inner Man* (Tulsa, OK: Victory House, 1982).

William Shakespeare, *Hamlet*

William Shakespeare, *Macbeth*

O.Carl Simonton & Stephanie Simonton, *Getting Well Again* (Los Angeles: Cancer Control Society, 1978).

J.R.R. Tolkien, *The Lord of the Rings* trilogy: *The Fellowship of the Ring, The Two Towers, The Return of the King* (Boston: Houghton-Mifflin, 1974).

Thomas Verny & John Kelly, *The Secret Life of the Unborn Child* (New York: Summit Books, 1981).

ELIJAH HOUSE MINISTRY CATALOG

A catalog is available from Elijah House that lists products and resources in the following categories:

I. **COUNSELOR RESOURCES** — *Unique tools of reference for any counseling office.* Audio tapes: Theology of Healing; The Healing Process; Healing Early Experiences; Burnout; Responses and Behaviors; Healing Spiritual Wounds; Healing Sexual Abuse; Chemical Dependency.

II. **MINISTRY TRAINING TOOLS** — *Practical teaching for pastors and church leaders.* Audio tapes and manuals: Divine Doctoring of Small Groups; Prayer Ministry Teams; New Testament Church; Prayer Ministry Teams.

III. **ADULT EDUCATION** — *Terrific curriculum for adult study.* Audio tapes: Life in Christ; Healing the Wounded Spirit; Renewal of the Mind; Twelve Functions of the Prophetic Office; Nurturing the Prophetic; What God Is Saying to the Church.

IV. **PERSONAL STUDY LIBRARY** — *Anyone can benefit from these teachings about marriage, children, and understanding ourselves.* Audio and video tapes: Before You Say 'I Do'; Married Forever; For Men Only; Functions of a Father's Love; Ministering to Youth and Children; Parental Love; Keeping Your Healing; Living a Full Live!' Comfortably Corporate; Garlands for Ashes; How Could It Happen?; Life's Common Sexual Experiences; Homosexuality.

V. **BOOKS** — *Ground-breaking books about inner healing and issues facing the Church today.* The Transformation of the Inner Man, Restoring the Christian Family; Healing the Wounded Spirit; The Elijah Task; Why Some Christians Commit Adultery; Healing Victims of Sexual Abuse; The Renewal of the Mind; Wounded Warriors; Healing Womens' Emotions.

Write to:
Elijah House
1000 S. Richards Road
Post Falls, ID 83854

RESTORATION FOR THE ABUSED

With profound empathy and clear understanding, Paula Sandford ministers healing to all who have been victimized by sexual abuse — the abused child, parents, relatives and friends, as well as the abuser. She has dealt with this problem through many years of counseling and teaching, and this book shows how the victims of sexual abuse can find new life and freedom.

HEALING FOR THE WOUNDS OF STRESS

The author of *Wounded Warriors*, Pastor R. Loren Sandford, knows what it's like to be in a stressed out and wounded condition, as he came near to a total breakdown while ministering to others.

His book provides believers with an honest look at stress — its symptoms, causes and effects — and it shows how to deal with this all-too-common problem in effective, lasting ways. For the person who lives with or counsels a wounded warrior, this book imparts empathy and wisdom. For the wounded warrior himself, this book imparts hope, peace and healing.

TRANSFORMED BY THE RENEWING OF YOUR MIND!

THE RENEWAL OF THE MIND glows with fresh insights and anointing. Its revolutionary approach will still the battleground where carnal thoughts and feelings rage. There is a solution — a process of spiritual transformation by the renewing of your mind. As you read, new peace and life will fill your innermost being.

WHY ADULTERY?

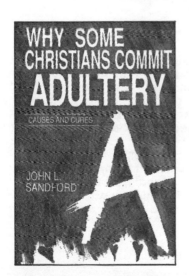

John L. Sandford founder of Elijah House, and author of several books on inner healing, provides answers for all who are concerned about this issue. He explores the personal causes that may lead a Christian into adultery and reveals biblical cures.

The book's main purpose, the author states, "is to provide informed bases for compassion and healing, and keys of knowledge for protection from falling."

AVAILABLE AT CHRISTIAN BOOKSTORES EVERYWHERE.

PROPHETIC INSIGHT

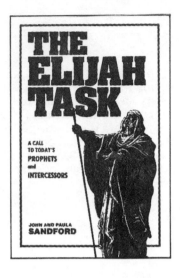

In the **Elijah Task**, John and Paula Sandford give a clear message, a balanced and practical in-depth study of the office of a prophet in the church and world today, the power and ways of intercession, and prophetic listening to God.

A HANDBOOK FOR FAMILIES

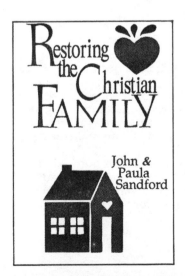

"And He shall turn the heart of the fathers to the children, and the heart of the children to their fathers" (Mal. 4:6). God is restoring families to His original purpose — to be the foundation of society, the seedbed for Christian values. Those who have discovered this treasure chest of teaching report that it has transformed their families. Fresh insights from the Sandfords' teaching and counseling ministry will enable your family to grow and develop according to God's plan.

AVAILABLE AT CHRISTIAN BOOKSTORES EVERYWHERE.

BOOK ORDER FORM

To order additional books by John and Paula Sandford or Loren Sandford direct from the publisher, please use this order form. Also note that your local bookstore can order titles for you.

Book Title	Price	Quantity	Amount
Healing Womens' Emotions	$ 9.95	_____	$ _____
The Renewal of the Mind	$ 9.95	_____	$ _____
Why Some Christians Commit Adultery	$ 9.95	_____	$ _____
Healing Victims of Sexual Abuse	$ 8.95	_____	$ _____
The Transformation of the Inner Man	$10.95	_____	$ _____
Healing the Wounded Spirit	$11.95	_____	$ _____
Restoring the Christian Family	$10.95	_____	$ _____
The Elijah Task	$ 9.95	_____	$ _____
Wounded Warriors (by L. Sandford)	$ 7.95	_____	$ _____
Total Book Amount			$ _____
Shipping & Handling — Add $2.00 for the **first** book, **plus** $0.50 for **each** additional book			$ _____
TOTAL ORDER AMOUNT — Enclose check or money order (No cash or C.O.D.'s)			$ _____

Make check or money order payable to: **VICTORY HOUSE, INC.**
Mail order to: **VICTORY HOUSE, INC.**
P.O. Box 700238
Tulsa, OK 74170

Please print your name and address clearly:

Name _____

Address _____

City _____

State or Province _____

Zip or Postal Code _____

Telephone Number (_____) _____

Foreign orders must be submitted in U.S. dollars. Foreign orders are shipped by uninsured surface mail. We ship all orders within 48 hours of receipt of order.

MasterCard or VISA — For orders totaling **over $20.00** you may use your MasterCard or VISA by completing the following information or for **faster service** call toll-free **1-800-262-2631.**

Card Name_____

Card Number _____

Expiration Date _____

Signature_____
(authorized signature)